TRUMP VS. CHINA

TRUMP VS. CHINA

FACING AMERICA'S GREATEST THREAT

NEWT GINGRICH

WITH CLAIRE CHRISTENSEN

NEW YORK NASHVILLE

Center Street
Hachette Book Group
1290 Avenue of the Americas, New York, NY 10104
centerstreet.com
twitter.com/centerstreet

First Edition: October 2019

Center Street is a division of Hachette Book Group, Inc. The Center Street name and logo are trademarks of Hachette Book Group, Inc.

The publisher is not responsible for websites (or their content) that are not owned by the publisher.

Library of Congress Cataloging-in-Publication Data has been applied for.

ISBNs: 978-1-5460-8507-2 (hardcover), 978-1-5460-8534-8 (B&N.com signed edition), 978-1-5460-8535-5 (signed edition), 978-1-5460-9988-8 (international edition), 978-1-5460-8511-9 (ebook)

Printed in the United States of America

LSC-C

10 9 8 7 6 5 4 3 2 1

To my grandchildren, Maggie and Robert, who will have a dangerous future if we don't face the realities of the modern Chinese Communist Party's tyrannical rule.

CONTENTS

SECTION ONE

TRUMP VS. CHINA

After decades of misunderstanding China and its ruling Communist Party, I've come to realize that China is a much more formidable competitor than our politicians, academics, and news media have realized. We had accepted a fantasy version of China. The truth is, the real modern China is a totalitarian communist dictatorship that wants to be the world's dominant superpower—and the United States is in the way.

CHAPTER ONE

AMERICA'S GREATEST CHALLENGE

This book is a report on two strong leaders, two strong countries, two strong visions—and the competition that will decide which vision succeeds and which vision fails.

As president of the United States, Donald Trump is the leader of the free world. It is his duty and responsibility to uphold our nation's values, protect our democracy, defend the rule of law, and preserve the individual rights endowed to each of us by our creator. As our commander in chief, President Trump is sworn to protect our American national identity, our way of life, and our sovereignty. The ideas of freedom and sovereignty are so important to who we are as Americans that President Trump used the word "sovereign" or "sovereignty" 21 times in his September 2017 speech to the United Nations and "free" or "freedom" 13 times.[1]

But today, the interests, security, and values that our country cherishes, and the free world in which we are accustomed to living, is being challenged by General Secretary Xi Jinping and the Chinese Communist Party.

As general secretary of the Chinese Communist Party, Xi Jinping presides over the communist totalitarian dictatorship that has been in power since the founding of the People's Republic of China in October 1949. Using surveillance, control, deception, and cheating as methods for preserving the power of the Chinese Communist Party—examples of which are provided throughout this book—General Secretary Xi Jinping and the Chinese Communist Party are constructing a different kind of world that threatens the survival of our free and sovereign nation.

To illustrate this competition, consider the words of these two leaders. Let's start with the differences put forth in the two leaders' visions for the future: President Donald Trump's Make America Great Again initiative and General Secretary Xi Jinping's China Dream proposal.

President Trump at his inauguration on January 20, 2017, said:

> "So to all Americans, in every city near and far, small and large, from mountain to mountain, and from ocean to ocean, hear these words: You will never be ignored again. Your voice, your hopes, and your dreams, will define our American destiny. And your courage and goodness and love will forever guide us along the way. Together, We Will Make America Strong Again. We Will Make America Wealthy Again. We Will Make America Proud Again. We Will Make America Safe Again. And, Yes, Together, We Will Make America Great Again. Thank you, God Bless You, And God Bless America."[2]

That is a patriotic vision of national success that looks to its people for leadership. American voices, hopes, and dreams will bring our nation to a better future. It is ultimately because of the ingenuity and effort of the American people that our nation is the world power that it is today. Putting America first and Making America Great Again starts *with Americans.* That is the way our country's system was built more than two centuries ago, it is the way the US continues to prosper today, and it is how we will continue to grow stronger in the future.

Six months later, General Secretary Xi gave a speech about realizing the China Dream in July 2017, which gave his vision for China's future:

> "The whole Party must uphold socialism with Chinese characteristics and remain confident in the path, theories, system and culture of Chinese socialism, ensuring that the development of the Party and the country proceeds in the right direction. On the basis of a thorough understanding of the phases of China's development and the people's aspirations for a better life, we should adopt new ideas, strategies and measures to advance the overall plan of seeking economic, political, cultural, social, and ecological progress.... In our final spring towards a moderately prosperous society, we will strive for the [China] Dream of national rejuvenation through successes in Chinese socialism."[3]

Xi's vision places the socialist system above the Chinese people—and calls on them to follow and depend on it to improve their lives. It represents a vastly different pattern of thought from President Trump's words.

Now, consider President Trump's remarks at a rally in Phoenix, Arizona, in August 2017:

> "We can do anything, we can build anything, and we can dream anything. It's time to remember what our brave soldiers never forgot. Americans share one flag, one home, and one glorious destiny. We live according to the same law, raise our children by the same values, and we are all made by the same Almighty God.
>
> "As long as we remember these truths, as long as we have enough strength and courage in ourselves, then

> there is no challenge too great, no task too large, no dream beyond our reach. We are Americans, and the future belongs to us. The future belongs to all of you."[4]

Here again, the ownership of America's future success "belongs to all of you." By contrast, during a speech on May 22, 2019, Xi described each generation of Chinese people as being on their own Long March. The Long March refers to the Chinese communists' more than 4,000-mile-long retreat from their Nationalist opponents during China's civil war. The Long March is historically referred to with a sense of pride by the Chinese Communist Party, as this yearlong determined effort led to the rise of Mao Zedong as the central communist leader. Mao eventually established the People's Republic of China that today is ruled by the Chinese Communist Party.

According to Xi, each generation engages in its own long march to slowly move the country. It is arduous, difficult, and requires great sacrifices from the Chinese people. Xi said there was "no easy path to realizing a great ideal" and that "[t]here can be no room for any desire for ease and comfort, any desire to avoid the fight, any arrogance and complacency, or any lack of drive to carry on forging ahead." He had specific instructions for the Chinese people for succeeding in their current long march to achieve two Chinese Communist Party–determined centenary goals:

> "To carry forward the spirit of the Long March and succeed in our present long march, we must remain committed to the great ideal of communism and the common ideal of Chinese socialism and engage in a tireless struggle to realize our ideals and beliefs.... On our new long march, we must firmly believe that the path of Chinese socialism is the only path that can lead us to socialist modernization, and the only path that can create better lives for the people.... As we advance on this

> path, we must vigorously promote the spirit of the Long March, and draw on this spirit to inspire and encourage the whole of the Party, all our military, and every Chinese person, especially the young, to devote themselves to making the country strong; to continue the great cause our predecessors started; and to write a new, glorious chapter in our new long march to attain the Two Centenary Goals and realize the [China] Dream of national rejuvenation."[5]

President Trump and General Secretary Xi both have a deep sense of national pride and have presented clear visions for the future direction of their countries. But the distance between their ideal worlds is vastly greater than most Americans think. Importantly, they are mutually exclusive. If one vision succeeds, the other will fail.

There is also a real chance that Xi's vision (which is the Chinese Communist Party's vision) will prevail. This would be a disaster for everything that we hold dear as Americans.

In America, the news media, businesses, much of academia, and many of our political leaders (down to the state, county, and city levels) have fallen for a "nice, new China" model and have ignored the fact that the country is ruled by a communist totalitarian dictatorship. The Chinese Communist Party has intelligently mounted a 40-year-long propaganda campaign (going back to Deng Xiaoping's first visit to the United States) to create an aura of normalcy and acceptability. This is a false front for the real China. It has led to an acceptance of a wave of victories by the ruling Chinese Communist Party with limited American reactions.

For the first time in a generation, we have a president who realizes that China and its communist leadership pose a challenge. President Trump has begun to take on this communist dictatorship in a variety of ways. The Trump administration is the most methodically critical of China—and the most committed to developing serious strategies to counter the communist dictatorship—that we have seen in at least a half-century. The contest between President Trump and General Secretary Xi may decide the future of freedom for the foreseeable future.

This book is going to introduce you to the greatest threat to a free America that we have faced in our lifetime. It is also going to suggest some urgent steps that we need to take if America is going to survive. This may sound extreme to some. However, after a lifetime of studying world conflicts—and recently more than a year focused on studying the current situation in China—I'm confident in saying that China is the greatest competitor the United States has had to deal with in its 243 yearlong history. China's totalitarian system, extraordinary organization, and immense population make this communist nation incredibly formidable.

Before outlining the challenges that communist-run China poses for the United States, I would like to emphasize that this is *not* a competition between Americans and Chinese people at an ethnic level. When I describe ways in which China is trying to subvert or defeat our country, I *do not* mean that every Chinese person you meet is a sincere supporter of the Chinese Communist Party who is seeking to undermine our freedom and way of life. This is a competition between two different systems—not civilizations. America could collaborate with a noncommunist China with entirely different expectations and concerns. It is the ambitions of the leadership—not the characteristics of the people—that make a totalitarian communist-ruled China dangerous.

India is projected to soon have more people than China, yet the very nature of Indian democracy, and the general process of the rule of law and free speech, make India a potential ally rather than a threat. Indonesia also has a large population, but it is a regional power with a broadly democratic system. Brazil is a massive country, but its robust system of law and free speech with free elections makes it a positive neighbor and an occasional ally rather than a threat.

What makes China different is the combination of a Leninist totalitarian system with a historic belief that China should naturally be the Middle Kingdom at the center of all things. Combine this notion with a long tradition of methodical, disciplined learning and work going back to the civil service examination system—China's main method for choosing officials, which dates back to at least the seventh century and has its roots in the Han Dynasty (more than 2,000 years ago).[6] It is this Leninist totalitarianism with Chinese characteristics that is a mortal threat to the future of freedom and the rule of law in which Americans believe.

We would be incredibly uncomfortable living in a world defined by the Chinese Communist Party's censorship, surveillance systems, and pattern of jailing anyone who disagrees with the government. Yet, we have opened up world trade to China, invested heavily in the country, and allowed many of our supply chains to become dependent upon it. So, we now find ourselves in a long-term competition with a system that is antithetical to our own. If we lose this competition, America as we have known it could be submerged by a foreign totalitarian system of dictatorial control. President Trump's concept of Making America Great Again (and now Keeping America Great) is simply incompatible with General Secretary Xi's China Dream. One or the other will ultimately define the future of the human race. Some Americans will reject this stark analysis or reply that the threat isn't this dire. This book will answer these objections and outline some stark and sobering truths.

Let's begin with the structure of power in China—and how we have profoundly misunderstood it to our detriment. Xi Jinping is general secretary of the Chinese Communist Party, chairman of the Central Military Commission, and president of the People's Republic of China—*in that order.*

Xi's true power base is the Chinese Communist Party. He reinforces this power by controlling and politicizing the military. In China, the People's Liberation Army is loyal to the Communist Party and is an instrument of its power—not the instrument of government power. On the 90th anniversary of the founding of the People's Liberation Army in 2017, Xi commanded the military to "carry forward and implement the Party's absolute leadership." He said, "As comrade Mao Zedong once pointed out, our principle is to have the Party command the military, not the military command the Party."[7]

The number one job for General Secretary Xi is to secure the future for the Chinese Communist Party. Every trade negotiation, policy, and investment is made with the intent to ensure the power, and increase the strength, of the Chinese Communist Party. Within this context, today's China is a starkly different country than the one our analysts and policy experts have explained for the last half-century.

Not only do we use the wrong model to understand the Chinese communist dictatorship but we also use the wrong time horizon. The American news media has evolved into a remarkably shallow, short time horizon, gossip system. The news channels essentially play bunch ball with a compulsive, overwhelming focus on whatever trivia defines the day's "big story." These channels have become political in the narrowest sense. Some are pro-Trump, most are anti-Trump, but all are focused overwhelmingly on the partisanship headline of the day. This distorted sense of *only-right-now-matters* makes it much harder for the country at large to understand what the Chinese communist system has been doing. Chinese strategies are based on studying, thinking, and planning. The Chinese leadership is dominated by pragmatism—not theory. Its leaders think methodically, and they execute over time with intentional purpose.

Americans are profoundly weakened in our effort to analyze the communist dictatorship by our sense of immediacy. The US watches the Chinese Communist Party implement the same patterns—in area after area—while we sit passively without understanding.

For instance: China has been stealing American intellectual property for decades. One recent estimate suggests that China's cyber hacking cost the US $360 billion in one year (more than all American exports to China that year).[8] Presidents Clinton, Bush, and Obama worked out agreements with China to stop the stealing of our technology—or signed legislation into law to protect American intellectual property. In every case, China continued stealing, and America did not impose (or even create) a meaningful plan of deterrence.

China bases its claims to the South China Sea on historical records from the Xia and Han dynasties that are thousands of years old.[9] Based on a map from the 1930s, China has laid claim to the area within an arbitrary "nine-dash line" and has been occupying both natural and artificial islands in the South China Sea. First, they promised "to exercise self-restraint in the conduct of activities that would complicate or escalate disputes and affect peace and stability." They later promised not to militarize these islands.[10,11] Then, they built airfields and fortified ports on the islands. China dramatically increased the number of fishing trawlers in the area and formed them into a maritime militia. Now, China is further strengthening its military capabilities and has effective control of the region. Meanwhile, China is pursuing a similar incremental project with steps toward controlling key strategic points on the Moon.

When China wants to dominate a particular industry, it relies on government financing and subsidies for Chinese companies, so their products and services can be radically less expensive than their foreign competitors. This approach destroyed the American solar power industry, greatly harmed our steel and aluminum manufacturers, and decimated key parts of our technology hardware industries. The Chinese Communist Party simply drove American companies out of business when American companies couldn't match the impossibly low subsidized prices of their Chinese competitors. Past American leaders have raised objections and signed hollow agreements, but China continued doing what was best for China despite the agreements.

The same cheap financing model is beginning to be used to destroy the entrepreneurial American space launch companies. Innovation is an inadequate basis for success if the competitor is so heavily subsidized that their prices are too low to match. China is using the same financing strategy for the Chinese telecommunications giant, Huawei. There is a serious possibility that Huawei will dominate the 5G rollout on a worldwide scale and create a next-generation internet that is defined—and controlled—by China. When the prices are low enough, many countries will ignore potential security problems just to get the latest technology.

The list of China's strategic initiatives is lengthy. Our news media, academic scholars, and government analysts generally do not connect the dots and come to grips with the underlying Chinese Communist Party strategies and the momentum behind them.

I have been studying China and its communist leadership since 1958.

About 17 years ago, after I left Congress, I began to sense just how big China was becoming and that its reach was beginning to span worldwide. I tried and failed to put a system in place whereby every military attaché in the world would provide a weekly report on China's state or Communist Party activities using only open-source material—so that it could be distributed widely throughout the American system. Unfortunately, that project was never developed. We would have a far better understanding of the Chinese communist totalitarian challenge today if we had written and circulated routine reports for the last few decades.

However, some in the public and private sectors are beginning to see how dramatically the Chinese communist system is growing in power—and influencing our everyday lives. It is not too late to respond to this challenge, but it will require a major American effort and require significant changes in our thinking and actions.

The national effort to solve the challenge to American

survival posed by the rise of the totalitarian Chinese Communist Party-ruled system will take at least a decade. It is useful to compare our current reality to the other great challenges of survival that America has previously faced to understand just how big this effort will be, how much learning and change it will require, and how persistent we will have to be to succeed.

There have been four great challenges to American survival during our 243 yearlong history. In each case, we had to confront the high cost of losing and the threat of surrendering our God-given rights and freedoms. The rise of China as a totalitarian global competitor is the fifth of these challenges to American survival. Communist-controlled China poses a challenge of survival to the US because if America falls behind a totalitarian communist Chinese system, the ensuing erosion of our values, democratic system, and law-based order will be enormous and possibly decisive.

In the first four great challenges to the survival of the idea of America (individual rights coming from our Creator and implemented within the rule of law), our opponents could have won. If America had lost any of these challenges, life as we know it today would cease to exist. We would live in a different world.

The first challenge was the question of whether we could win our freedom from the British empire and become an independent country based on a new principle of individual rights endowed by our Creator. The entire project could have collapsed since Britain was the wealthiest and most powerful empire in the world. Moreover, at least one-fifth of the American colonists wanted to remain British subjects and rejected the very concept of independence. A militarily coerced America would have been a different place and the history of freedom on the planet would have been much more subdued.

The second challenge was the question of whether the US could survive and win a brutal Civil War to preserve the Union and end the system of slavery. A Union victory was not inevitable. The war went so badly that as late as August 1864, President

Abraham Lincoln thought that he could lose the election and the Peace Party would seek an armistice with the South. Imagine a world with the United States torn in two, the cause of freedom diminished, and slavery continuing for another generation or more.

The third challenge was the difficulty of recognizing the threat from the Axis powers (Nazi Germany, Imperial Japan, and Fascist Italy) during World War II and organizing an extraordinary national mobilization to win a global war with total victory. Victory was likely once the United States joined Great Britain and the Soviet Union because the Allies had an enormous long-term advantage in resources. However, it is easy to forget how close the Japanese came to winning at Midway in June 1942. It is also easy to forget how close the Germans came to capturing Cairo and the Suez Canal in the summer of 1942. We also cannot forget how close the Soviets came to collapse under the first year of German onslaught and the enormous casualties and loss of equipment the Soviets endured. Additionally, if Normandy had failed, the Americans and British might not have had the nerve to launch a second invasion on that scale. If a decisive Allied victory did not happen, the world today would be vastly different.

The fourth challenge was the sudden shift from the Soviet Union's role as a wartime ally of the United States to a serious global threat. This led to a diplomatic, economic, psychological, technological, and military effort lasting until the collapse of the Soviet Union 45 years later. In the late 1940s, both France and Italy seemed to be on the verge of electing communist governments that would have allied with Joseph Stalin. Moreover, Greece was in a civil war that the communists had a real chance to win. In Asia, the communists were on offense in China and Vietnam. Consequently, President Harry Truman took a series of strong steps, including a number of secret actions in Greece, France, and Italy. The potential for a Soviet-dominated world was much greater in the late 1940s than we can imagine 70 years later. There was no "inevitable" victory for freedom in the Cold War. Similarly, victory over China's communist system is not guaranteed. We must begin to adapt and develop new ways of meeting and exceeding this challenge.

THE FIRST STEPS

We are well behind in this competition, but America is still the most powerful, wealthy, and innovative country in the world. If we take the challenge with China seriously, we will prevail and survive. However, there are a few key things the Trump administration must do now to lay a foundation for success.

First, we must educate the American public by establishing an unclassified website that regularly details China's activities around the world. Every embassy and every federal agency should be tasked with filing open-source reports on China's state and Communist Party activities. The website's archive must be available, accessible, and understandable for citizens and the news media to use as an easy entry point. It should be organized by country, industry, and activity. This information provided by agencies and embassies around the world should be included in monthly and annual summary documents. This recommendation comes first because educating the American people, the news media, and the Congress about the scale and momentum of China's efforts is the precondition to sustaining a long-term survival strategy.

Separately, our intelligence, military, and law enforcement agencies should generate secret monthly reports for the president, members of the executive branch (including political appointees and senior civil servants), and every member of the Congress. A monthly 30-minute briefing on what we are seeing around the world will rapidly lead members of the Congress and leaders of the various federal bureaucracies to construct and implement a much more assertive response.

To act on these briefings, Congress should create a Joint Committee on China's Activities in Congress. If a new joint committee is established, this committee would need to have recommendation authority that would allow it to look at every aspect of the legislative process. The top leaders in both the House and Senate should be ex officio members—so that bipartisan groups in both the House and Senate are committed to undertaking the reforms needed to succeed in surviving the China challenge. There are too many institutional reforms across the federal government—and too many regulatory changes—needed to develop a successful high tempo, high tech, all-of-society system that can outperform the Chinese dictatorship. The failure to effectively compete with Huawei for worldwide 5G implementation is a symptom of the deeper challenge that is occurring in zone after zone of activity or industry. Ultimately, the legislative branch has a big role to play in creating a more dynamic, faster-moving, and more decisively assertive America.

At the societal level, we must dramatically expand Chinese study programs for graduate degrees and continuing education. In the early years of the Cold War, the government made a major investment in getting people to study the Soviet Union. It also developed a lot of learning material to help people understand our adversary. The China challenge will be so large—and will evolve so rapidly—that we can't rely entirely on the intelligence or the diplomatic community to solve every problem that arises. Every government department will be affected by China. Every aspect of the American economy will be affected by China. There will be continuing efforts to shape our culture, communications, and news media. Combating this effort is going to require a system for helping educate many Americans at many different levels (including public education programs aimed at the general public).

In this vein, we must reverse the decline in American students in STEM (science, technology, engineering, and math) programs by dramatically expanding the scholarships and fellowships to help everyone who enters these fields. Since the basic knowledge in these fields has to start in middle and high school, we should consider providing extra pay for STEM teachers. We should also invest in many more seventh–twelfth grade scholarships to go to specialty STEM high schools—and more programs of recognizing achievements in STEM. We were innovative and aggressive after the launch of Sputnik in October 1957. We have now become timid, bureaucratic, and lethargic. We have talked about the crisis in education since *A Nation at Risk* was published under President Reagan in 1983. Yet, we have consistently failed to develop adequate breakthrough programs to deepen and broaden our STEM capabilities. After Sputnik frightened us, with the danger of falling behind the Soviets in science and engineering, we passed the National Defense Education Act in 1958. I know how important this program was. I got my PhD with a National Defense fellowship. Instead of complaining about how few American students now occupy our STEM classes, we need aggressive programs of incentives to attract young, capable Americans into these fields.

Finally, we must take into account the growing Chinese-Russian alliance when constructing an American strategy. When General Secretary Xi says he has met with Russian President Vladimir Putin nearly 30 times in the last six years, and that "President Putin is my best friend and colleague," we have to take him seriously. American planners must take into account the potential that there will not be a conflict in isolation with either Russia or China. Instead, we must build capabilities that could cope with a joint effort by the two countries.

These are just a few of the critical actions we must take now to cope with the Chinese Communist Party's strategies—and win. I hope this book will help launch a national debate about the Communist China challenge and the necessary American response. If America is to survive and continue to lead in the future, we must come to grips with how great the challenge is and what must be done for freedom to endure and prevail.

CHAPTER TWO

THE REAL MODERN CHINA

Our citizens did not win freedom together, did not survive horrors together, did not face down evil together, only to lose our freedom to a lack of pride and confidence in our values. We did not and we will not. We will never back down.

—President Donald Trump, July 2017[1]

In recent years, some public opinions at home and abroad have raised the question of whether what China is doing is still socialism.... We say that socialism with Chinese characteristics is socialism, that is, no matter how we reform and open up, we must always adhere to the road of socialism with Chinese characteristics...

The belief in Marxism, socialism and communism is the political soul of the communists and the spiritual prop of the communists to withstand any test. The party constitution clearly stipulates that the highest ideal and ultimate goal of the party is to realize communism.

—General Secretary Xi Jinping, January 2013[2]

Since President Nixon visited China, the West has consistently underestimated and misdiagnosed China's activities. Clearly, the hopes for China's development and transformation into a nation that would mirror the United States, or our Western allies, proved to be just plain wrong. Many perceptions that were held in Washington, DC, at the turn of the century (which have been perpetuated today) contributed to our flawed assessments.

Hubris infected a great deal of analysis. After victories in both world wars and the collapse of the Soviet Union, hubristic confidence spread and grew. Americans cherish and take pride in our system's heritage of adherence to the rule of law, protection of individual freedom, and promotion of moral values. The collapse of the USSR reinforced the notion that alternative systems that didn't uphold our values were likely to result in failure. The demise of the Soviet Union also ended the bipolar world and briefly led to a monopolar world dominated by the United States. Since the early 1990s, when the US started promoting the idea of creating a "New World Order," we have assumed that our American system is universal and would continue to spread, even if gradually. By accepting this sense of global power and prestige, we assumed others would study us—and that we did not have to study them. Given the American aversion to learning history or studying other cultures, this led to a natural belief that China would grow into being more like us. This was incredibly naive and indeed ignorant on our part.

Moreover, our memories of China led us to accept our own projected image of the country's weakness, poverty, and backwardness. From the novels written by Pearl S. Buck to the images contained in *The Sand Pebbles* or *55 Days at Peking*, we consistently accepted depictions of China as an impoverished country mired in old customs and failed, obsolete institutions. With this imagery in mind, we approached and perceived Chinese economic development as a charitable way to help millions rise from poverty—with no notion that a renewed China could eventually threaten our position in the world.

Our happiness at improved economic conditions for the Chinese people was multiplied by the flood of inexpensive Chinese goods that flowed into the US. These goods lowered the cost of living across the country and increased consumers' range of product choices. This "Walmart Effect" increased the purchasing power of millions of Americans.

Corporate investment into China quickly increased as the business community sensed that China was the next great profit opportunity. No one wanted to look too closely at the communist control of the country or the national security implications. China became the goose that laid golden eggs—and even communist eggs increased profits for American businesses.

Meanwhile, the same pattern of emphasizing the positive and minimizing the negative about China was occurring in other American institutions. A strong self-serving desire to see, hear, and report no evil in China afflicted the news media and academic communities—and it still does today. Reporters or academics who do report negatively find themselves being pressured by their peers in a self-reinforcing system that rejects talk that could be construed as aggressive or overly hawkish. Meanwhile, some reporters and academics are pressured by the Communist Party and its agents directly. News services who are too negative can find their access more heavily restricted. Academics who are too critical find it harder to get visas and permission to study in China. This pressure serves to accentuate the positive and minimize or eliminate the negative.

So, Western analysts have been misled by false images of China and have dramatically failed to see the deeper picture. Simply put: We have seen what we wanted to see and have ignored what we didn't. We have brushed aside China's 5,000-year history, refused to admit that the Communist Party isn't interested in adopting American values, and largely ignored China's efforts to control its image. Consequently, up until now, we have been ill-equipped to correctly analyze China's goals, intentions, and methods and what they mean for the United States.

Americans must adjust their thinking, recognize certain realities, understand why China is the way that it is, and be aware of what modern China under the control of the Communist Party aims to accomplish. These steps are essential for the United States to continue to have a relationship with China that protects American interests, security, and values worldwide.

VLADIMIR LENIN, NOT JAMES MADISON

This should be profoundly clear: The Chinese Communist Party is deeply Chinese. The party is also fundamentally Leninist. Yet, the West often forgets this. Chinese communism is both Chinese *and* Leninist. Recognizing the role both factors play in the Chinese government's policies and directives is critically important.

With the fall of the Soviet Union, Western interest in studying Leninism and Stalinism faded. Yet the core of the Chinese communist experience was built around constant study of Lenin and guidance from Stalin. Any analysis of China that does not account for the Communist Party and its history of Leninism is simply wrong.

The Communist Party in China originated from a study group that researched Marxism. The founding generation of party members were so deeply Stalinist—and believed so much in Joseph Stalin's ideology—that when Nikita Khrushchev denounced Stalin in his 1956 Secret Speech, the Chinese communist leadership sided with Stalin's memory and attacked Khrushchev as a heretic.

The first leader of the communist People's Republic of China, Mao Zedong's, radical policies during his Great Leap Forward and Cultural Revolution periods were instituted in a fundamentally Leninist fashion. The estimated tens of millions of deaths and catastrophic devastation that resulted from these projects reinforce this assertion.

In the late 1950s, following years of conflict in China, Mao instituted a campaign that would strengthen China's economy by modernizing industry and agriculture—the two key sectors of a communist command economy as represented on the Soviet flag by an industrial hammer and agricultural sickle. This effort was known as the Great Leap Forward. The campaign was a complete failure and tragically led to the devastation and death of millions in China, largely from starvation.

After the failure of the Great Leap Forward, Mao's power was significantly weakened, and he believed that the Communist Party leadership in China was pushing the country toward revisionist policies. In 1966, he announced the Cultural Revolution, which created an environment where he could lead China back in the direction he wanted and purge all officials and citizens that did not fall in line—effectively reconsolidating his power through fear. The Cultural Revolution aimed to rid China of the "representatives of the bourgeoisie who have sneaked into the Party, the government, the army and various spheres of culture" as well as the old ideas, customs, culture, and habits, known as the "Four Olds."[3,4]

Mao's adherence to Leninism was obvious, but when Deng Xiaoping came to power in the late 1970s following Mao's death, doubts that China would continue to believe in this sort of radical ideology set in. With Deng's policies during the reform and the opening-up period that followed—reinforced by Jiang Zemin's furthering of these policies—how could China possibly still be Leninist?

Especially after Deng's Southern Tour in 1992—which, in effect, ensured the continuation of his legacy after leaving power—many people thought that his messages outlining his commitment to free markets would naturally lead to a free political system in China. However, Deng's biography makes apparent that he had been a committed Communist since his time in France as a young man. While there, he was mentored by Zhou Enlai—who was a central figure in the founding generation of the Chinese Communist Party and later became China's first foreign minister. Deng later fondly called Zhou, "my elder brother."[5] By 1922, as a young man, Deng had joined the Communist Party of Chinese Youth in Europe. In 1926, he even went to Moscow for revolutionary training as a hard-liner Leninist. Evidently, from the start, he fully believed in a centrally controlled party dictatorship.

Moreover, decades later, the result of Deng's reformist policies didn't match up with American expectations. China didn't evolve in accordance with the free markets and inevitably establish a free political system. Instead, the US has supported prosperity for China's people while its Leninist leaders have systematically crushed dissent and reinforced the Communist Party's total control of the country.

Consider the tragedy of Tiananmen Square. The massacre at Tiananmen in 1989 was not an aberration. It was the only possible response from the Leninists who controlled China through their totalitarian instrument—the Chinese Communist Party. Virtually no one in the US who protested the massacre understood it was the signal of who the Chinese communist leaders really were—and the lengths they were willing to go to in order to maintain control and stability. Today, we see this same pattern of extremism being taken to ensure the party's control with the atrocities being committed against the Muslim Uyghurs, Catholic bishops and priests, and the Falun Gong.

Still, it is almost impossible to get Western elites to understand how deeply communist, Leninist, and totalitarian modern China is.

As I mentioned in the first chapter, the highest ranking title that Xi Jinping holds is general secretary of the Chinese Communist Party. Western and English translated media often refer to President Xi Jinping, but this state title is a misnomer that simply makes Xi seem more relatable. The actual state title that Xi holds is *guojia zhuxi*, which directly translates to "state chairman." In fact, decades ago, the People's Republic of China switched to translating this state title to "president." According to *The New York Times*, this move is speculated to have been done so that China more closely resembled other modern countries.[6] If the American news media and the American government consistently referred to the Chinese leader as general secretary rather than president, Americans would rapidly learn how different China's system is. Referring to Xi as president distorts the truth and leaves the impression that China's system is structured like ours. It is not.

The base of power in China is in the party. There are almost 50 percent more Chinese Communist Party members (close to 90 million) than Americans who voted for President Trump (almost 63 million) in the 2016 election. Moreover, the number of Communist Party members is larger than the combined populations of America's three most populous states—California, Florida, and Texas. Despite all of the evidence of the pervasiveness and centrality of the Chinese Communist Party, Western governments and their bureaucracies continue to focus on China's subordinate government and private sector entities—even though both are under party control.

In the Leninist tradition, Xi is deeply committed to the continued pursuit of communism and fundamentally rejects capitalism. In a 2013 speech to members and alternate members of China's Central Committee, he said:

> "[O]ur party has always adhered to the lofty ideals of communism. Communists, especially leading cadres, should be staunch believers and faithful practitioners of the lofty ideals of communism and the common ideals of socialism with Chinese characteristics. The belief in Marxism, socialism and communism is the political soul of the communists and the spiritual prop of the communists to withstand any test. The party constitution clearly stipulates that the highest ideal and ultimate goal of the party is to realize communism....
>
> "Facts have repeatedly told us that Marx and Engels' analysis of the basic contradictions in capitalist

> society is not out of date, nor is their historical materialism view that capitalism must die out and socialism must win. This is an irreversible general trend in social and historical development, but the road is tortuous. The final demise of capitalism and the final victory of socialism must be a long historical process."[7]

General Secretary Xi sees the ideologies of the Communist Party and the West in direct, stark competition with one another. He believes that communism will prevail, while capitalism will dramatically fail. There is no doubt that his goal is to continue the legacy of his Leninist predecessors—the legacy that we completely misunderstood for decades. Xi concluded:

> "We must have strong strategic determination, resolutely resist all kinds of erroneous ideas of abandoning socialism, and consciously correct erroneous ideas beyond the stage. The most important thing is to concentrate on running our own affairs well, continuously strengthen our comprehensive national strength, continuously improve the life of our people, continuously build socialism with superiority over capitalism, and continuously lay a more solid foundation for us to win initiative, advantage and future."

In his own words, Xi completely rejects the naive Western belief that China will eventually democratize.

THE CHINA DREAM

There is a common saying in China: "Under Mao the Chinese people stood up; under Deng, the Chinese people got rich; and under Xi, the Chinese people are becoming stronger." Beginning with Mao, China's communist leaders have been focused on growing, strengthening, and returning China to its former glory while following Leninist ideology. Under Xi, the vision for China's reemergence as an influential power is branded as the "China Dream." In some ways it is their version of "Make America Great Again."

Speaking to the 19th National Congress of the Communist Party of China in October 2017, General Secretary Xi said, "The Chinese Dream is a dream about history, the present, and the future." The central elements of Xi's China Dream involve reaching two centennial goals. The first 100-year goal entails turning China into "a moderately prosperous society" by 2021 (the 100th anniversary of the founding of the Communist Party).[8] In this case, "moderately prosperous" means that citizens in China, both rural and urban, will have attained (what is for China) a high standard of living. The second centenary goal involves transforming China into a "modern socialist country that is prosperous, strong, democratic, culturally advanced and harmonious" and transforming China into a fully developed nation by 2049 (100th anniversary of the founding of the People's Republic of China).[9] According to Robert Lawrence Kuhn, author of *How China's Leaders Think: The Inside Story of China's Past, Current and Future Leaders*, in an article for *The New York Times*, "'Modernization' means China regaining its position as a world leader in science and technology as well as in economics and business; the resurgence of Chinese civilization, culture and military might; and China participating actively in all areas of human endeavor."[10]

There are four primary elements that make up the China Dream according to Kuhn. These four parts include advancing goals for a "Strong China (economically, politically, diplomatically, scientifically, militarily); Civilized China (equity and fairness, rich culture, high morals); Harmonious China (amity among social classes); [and] Beautiful China (healthy environment, low pollution)."

You may have noticed that I have been calling this idea the "China Dream," while the English translation of Xi's speech refers to it as the "Chinese Dream." Oftentimes, throughout

China's state-translated media, this concept is written as the "Chinese Dream" in English—not the "China Dream." This is a subtle but important difference. In Chinese, this phrase is written as: 中國梦. 梦 is the character for "dream," while 中國 is translated as "China" and 中國人 is translated as "the Chinese." It is impossible to translate "China" into "the Chinese" without adding that extra character. So why the difference? This was a deliberate decision by the Communist Party. Using "Chinese" instead of "China" gives English speakers the impression that the dream originates with the Chinese people, when in fact, it is an idea orchestrated by the party.

As Elizabeth Economy noted in her book *The Third Revolution*, Xi's China Dream is centered around collective values, while the American dream is focused on individualism. Referencing Xi's speeches, Economy described that for Xi, the China Dream is the dream of both the nation and every individual in China. If the country and the nation succeed, only then can the people succeed.[11] This is the reverse of the American Dream, which emphasizes that if the people succeed, only then the nation can succeed. In America, national success begins with the greatness of the American people.

In October 2017, General Secretary Xi described China's focus on turning the China Dream into a reality and the Chinese Communist Party's and the people's role in pursuing it:

> "It will be an era for all of us, the sons and daughters of the Chinese nation, to strive with one heart to realize the [China] Dream of national rejuvenation. It will be an era that sees China moving closer to center stage and making greater contributions to mankind....
>
> "Our mission is a call to action; our mission steers the course to the future. We must live up to the trust the people have placed in us and prove ourselves worthy of history's choice. In the great endeavors of building socialism with Chinese characteristics in the new era,

> let us get behind the strong leadership of the Party and engage in a tenacious struggle. Let all of us, the sons and daughters of the Chinese nation, come together, keep going, and create a mighty force that enables us to realize the [China] Dream."[12]

Despite past difficulties and failures, the China Dream is supposed to instill hope in the Chinese people for a better future under the Chinese Communist Party. This can be compared to President Trump's Make America Great Again movement, which provides hope for the American people following years of frustration. After enduring years of failed policies, corrupt politicians, and economic hardship under the Obama administration, Americans voted for candidate Trump to bring back American values and restore the country to its former greatness. The Make America Great Again movement has reinvigorated the values that Americans have learned from history and passed down through generations. It is a reminder that America has always been a free, strong, courageous, innovative, and faith-centered country, which is why the movement is not called "Make America Great" but instead "Make America Great *Again*."

In this way, we can draw comparisons between the American Dream and the China Dream, but more closely find parallels between the China Dream and the Make America Great Again movement. Both seek to reinvigorate a nation of people after enduring difficulties and hardship.

Knowing the goals and intentions of your competitor is crucial. However, understanding the methods and strategy your competitor will likely use to reach these goals is equally important. Sun Tzu, the legendary Chinese military thinker and attributed author of *The Art of War* (one of the most famous classics on military doctrine) wrote, "Hence the saying: If you know the enemy and know yourself, you need not fear the result of a hundred battles. If you know yourself but not the enemy, for every victory gained you will also suffer a defeat. If you know neither the enemy nor yourself, you will succumb in every battle." In the case of China, the US needs to fully understand our serious and capable competitor. The ruling Communist Party is challenging our way of life, national security, interests, and values as it works to achieve its goal of fulfilling the China Dream.

We must recognize, however, that the realization of the China Dream in and of itself is not a bad thing. A strong, civilized, harmonious, and beautiful China sounds as though it would be beneficial for the Chinese people and for the world. The problem is the way by which the Communist Party's Leninist leaders are working to achieve these goals. Everything from intellectual property theft, widespread human rights abuses, illegally claiming territory in the South China Sea, conducting foreign surveillance and espionage, and using aggressive and restrictive business practices contribute to the goals set out in Xi's China Dream—but they all directly threaten US interests and security. This poses some serious immediate and long-term problems for America. We must get a better sense of how the Chinese Communist Party plans to reach the China Dream—remember this is a dream orchestrated by the party, not originating with the people. In order to successfully counter China's worldwide aggression, we must learn how they strategically operate and think.

CHAPTER THREE

TRADE & THEFT

To build on our incredible economic success, one priority is paramount—reversing decades of calamitous trade policies.

We are now making it clear to China that after years of targeting our industries, and stealing our intellectual property, the theft of American jobs and wealth has come to an end.

—President Donald Trump, February 2019[1]

We will work to ensure that capable people are spotted and their talent is valued, respected and put to use, and create a stimulating environment for their development. We will discover, nurture and retain capable people throughout the whole process of innovation. We will appeal for talent around the world and let more of them display their potential to the full.

. . . We will increase protection of intellectual property rights, and introduce policies oriented to rewarding knowledge, including raising the share of benefits to researchers from commercialized research results, and giving them the incentives they deserve, such as stock shares, options and dividends.

—General Secretary Xi Jinping, May 2016[2]

As I'm writing this, President Donald Trump and General Secretary Xi Jinping are locking horns over trade tariffs. President Trump rightly has been leveraging the power of the US economy to convince Xi to stop unfairly subsidizing Chinese goods and dumping them into US and other international markets. The president has received a great deal of criticism for this trade war. No doubt, small and medium-sized American businesses that have built their models around exporting and importing goods to and from China are feeling some pain. Larger businesses have felt some too, but they are in better positions to adjust their supply chains.

Indeed, many Americans are puzzled over President Trump's trade fight—largely because the American news media is wholly uninterested in any kind of deep reporting on the matter. They are happy to parrot large industries that care more about their bottom lines than the future of our country. They are also happy to use the trade fight as an excuse to criticize the Trump administration. However, every American must understand that the Chinese Communist Party's commitment to intellectual property theft is at the heart of this trade fight.

Again and again, we have seen leaders from both countries say they are close to a deal. The Trump administration receives assurances that intellectual property protections will be included in the final trade agreement. Then, when it has been time to sign on the dotted line, we have seen the Chinese negotiators attempt to strip these protections at the last minute—presumably hoping President Trump and his team don't notice or are too exhausted to push back.

This tactic has worked for the Chinese Communist Party with past administrations—but it has not worked with this one. President Trump has continued to stand his ground. This is exactly what happened on May 5, 2019, when President Trump decided to increase tariffs from 10 to 25 percent on $200 billion in Chinese goods.[3] The Chinese negotiators had backed out on verbal agreements to include strict intellectual property protections in a trade deal. To make his position clearer to Xi, President Trump then said that he would expand tariffs on more Chinese goods.

This toughness on intellectual property theft has long been a cornerstone of the Trump administration's policies. In June 2018, the White House Office of Trade and Manufacturing Policy published a report titled *How China's Economic Aggression Threatens the Technologies and Intellectual Property of the United States and the World*. The report details the various tactics and strategies China uses in order to dominate various industries. The report concluded that "Given the size of China's economy, the demonstrable extent of its market-distorting policies, and China's stated intent to dominate the industries of the future, China's acts, policies, and practices of economic aggression now targeting the technologies and IP of the world threaten not only the U.S. economy but also the global innovation system as a whole."[4]

Engaging in intellectual property theft is one of the key components of China's strategy to control future industries. Dr. Peter Navarro, director of the Office of Trade and Manufacturing Policy, said in a December 2018 interview with Nikkei that "China is basically trying to steal the future of Japan, the US and Europe, by going after our technology."[5] This specific problem is so big and pervasive—and so many previous administrations have tried and failed to solve it—it warrants its own chapter.

Virtually every American industry is becoming more and more reliant on proprietary trade secrets and technologies. In fact, some of the most valuable assets that companies have are their ideas—algorithms, new chemical processes, more efficient battery designs, or better ways to build tractors. The companies that innovate the most and develop the most good ideas will lead the future of business, and the country that fosters the most innovation will lead the future of the world—unless of course these ideas get stolen.

On November 3, 2015, then–presidential candidate Donald Trump declared to an incredulous interviewer on ABC's *Good Morning America* that "[China is] an economic enemy, because they've taken advantage of us like nobody in history. They have; it's the greatest theft in the history of the world what they've done to the United States. They've taken our jobs."[6]

Two weeks later, William "Bill" Evanina, the director of the National Counterintelligence and Security Center, confirmed Trump's claim and put a figure on it. Chinese-led industrial espionage costs American companies $360 billion a year through hacking alone with China accounting for 90 percent of total corporate theft via hacking. If other types of intellectual property (IP) theft are factored in, the annual figure is much higher.

According to the US IP Commission's 2017 report on China's practices:

> "The annual cost to the U.S. economy continues to exceed **$225 billion** in counterfeit goods, pirated software, and theft of trade secrets and could be as high as **$600 billion.** It is important to note that both the low- and high-end figures do not incorporate the full cost of patent infringement—an area sorely in need of greater research. We have found no evidence that casts doubt on the estimate provided by the Office of the Director of National Intelligence in November 2015 that economic espionage through hacking costs $400 billion per year. At this rate, the United States has suffered over $1.2 trillion in economic damage since the publication of the original *IP Commission Report* more than three years ago." [bold theirs][7]

To put this in perspective, the theft is the equivalent of China stealing the entire economic output of Alabama (approximately $225 billion) on the low end or Georgia (approximately $600 billion) on the high end every year.[8] The scale is mind boggling, and Chinese IP theft does more than deprive Americans, their companies, and communities of the fruits of their labor and resulting prosperity. It enriches China's Communist Party while imperiling our national security and economic competitiveness for generations to come.

The Trump administration's 2017 National Security Strategy outlined why our private sector innovations matter to national defense:

> "The landscape of innovation does not divide neatly into sectors. Technologies that are part of most weapon systems often originate in diverse businesses as well as in universities and colleges. Losing our innovation and technological edge would have far-reaching negative implications for American prosperity and power."[9]

China's espionage does not need to target defense applications' research and technology (although they frequently do) to be an effective form of asymmetrical warfare. The concepts and prototypes developed in both academic and corporate settings are often applicable to national security purposes.

Today, American businesses and innovators are more vulnerable to such threats than ever before as the economy has evolved. According to the Harvard Business Review, in 1975, more than 80 percent of the S&P 500's listed companies' market value was tied up in tangible assets (plants, machinery, and property). By 2015, the equation had flipped with more than 80 percent of market value linked to intangible assets including intellectual property.[10] This shift means hostile state actors or state-owned enterprises can weaken or wipe out American companies by stealing cutting-edge American innovations.

In early 2019, CNBC polled North America-based companies on the CNBC Global CFO Council regarding Chinese IP theft. More than 20 percent said Chinese companies had stolen their intellectual property in the past year—another 10 percent acknowledged such theft over the previous decade.[11] Moreover, approximately 20 percent of the American Chamber of Commerce in Shanghai members have incurred pressure to transfer technology to Chinese companies, while 41 percent of chamber members in chemicals and 44 percent in aerospace industries have received "notable pressure" to do so.[12]

In addition to penetrating computer systems from afar through hacking—and producing fake goods like DVDs, clothing, and watches—China is engaged in a systematic campaign to pilfer valuable trade secrets for countless industrial and consumer goods. This effort aims to reverse engineer non-Chinese goods and then flood foreign markets with stolen and knockoff products and technologies. The theft is myriad and distressing. A few examples illustrate the depth and breadth of the theft.

State-of-the-Art Microchips: In 2018, a federal grand jury indictment was filed against a Chinese state-owned enterprise, a company in Taiwan, and three individuals who worked to steal the technology behind "dynamic random access memory" or DRAM microchips from Micron, a semiconductor company based in Idaho. China did not possess this technology but had made acquiring it a national security priority. Micron's market share was worth 20–25 percent of the $50 billion DRAM market.[13]

Textile Fibers and the Color White: In December 2017, almost two dozen Chinese bureaucrats raided the Shanghai offices of American chemical producer, DuPont. They demanded "passwords to the company's world-wide research network," printed internal company documents, took off with computers, and harassed employees.[14] The reason was simple: DuPont had the audacity to complain that its partner in China had been stealing the company's proprietary technology for a $400 million-a-year corn-based fiber.[15] Cowed into silence, DuPont instructed US officials to not lodge a complaint in the trade talks. Only a few years earlier, a Malaysian-born US national of Chinese heritage was convicted of an espionage campaign against the firm that lasted for more than a decade. After recruiting embittered former DuPont employees, the agent of Beijing and a state-owned Chinese competitor of DuPont's stole plant designs and formulas for a brilliant white-colored paint technology that adheres to everything from refrigerators to cars. He was convicted and sentenced to serve 15 years in prison in the US.[16]

Stealing Steel and Aluminum: In 2014, the Department of Justice indicted five of China's People's Liberation Army hackers for a breach that targeted six American victims including aluminum maker Alcoa, US Steel, industrial components maker Westinghouse, and the steelworkers union from 2006 to 2014.[17] Notably, American crude steel production remains flat while China has doubled its output since 2006.[18]

Nuclear, Wind, and Battery Power: Another Chinese state-owned enterprise enlisted an engineer to acquire components for its reactors. The agent then recruited employees to steal technical reports on nuclear reactors from the Tennessee Valley Authority and a Florida utility. The engineer later pled guilty to conspiracy.[19] A Chinese company also stole wind turbine software from an American firm, which valued its loss at more than $1 billion in addition to almost 700 lost jobs resulting from the theft.[20] Recently, at Phillips 66, an American energy firm, an employee took files on the company's protected technologies for batteries worth more than $1 billion to provide to a Chinese company.[21]

These examples are just the tip of the iceberg of intellectual property theft coming from China. The real scale and nature of the theft are obscured by coercion and shame.

In the first instance, Chinese law expressly requires foreign companies to operate in joint ventures with a Chinese partner across 35 business sectors. *The Wall Street Journal* described the prescribed arrangement as "Foreigners bring cash, technology, management know-how and other intellectual property while the Chinese partner usually contributes some land-use rights, financing, political connections and market know-how."[22] But this practice makes American company's intangible assets vulnerable to being stolen and transferred by the partner, resulting in the cannibalization of the US company.[23]

The Chinese Communist Party feels entitled to Western ingenuity as well. As one Chinese government official told *The Wall Street Journal* in 2018: "China's offer to the world has been straightforward.... Foreign companies are allowed to access China's markets but they would need to contribute something in return: their technology."[24]

According to the 2018 Office of Trade and Manufacturing Policy report:

> "Chinese industrial policy features a wide range of coercive and intrusive regulatory gambits to force the transfer of foreign technologies and IP to Chinese competitors, often in exchange for access to the vast Chinese market.... China's instruments of coercion to force the transfer of foreign technologies and IP to Chinese competitors include: (1) foreign ownership restrictions such as forced joint ventures and partnerships that explicitly or tacitly require or facilitate technology transfers; (2) adverse administrative approvals and licensing processes; (3) discriminatory patent and other IP rights restrictions; (4) security reviews; (5) secure and controllable technology standards; (6) data localization; (7) burdensome and intrusive testing; (8) discriminatory catalogues and lists; (9) government procurement restrictions; (10) imposition of indigenous technology standards that deviate significantly from international norms and that may provide backdoor Chinese access to source codes; (11) forced research and development (R&D localization); (12) antimonopoly laws; (13) Expert Review Panels; (14) Chinese Communist Party Committees that influence corporate governance; and

> (15) placement of Chinese employees at foreign joint ventures."[25]

The second and most difficult phenomenon that facilitates, and hides the true cost of, further IP theft is the unwillingness of American and other foreign companies to reveal to Western authorities or the public that they have been victimized. DuPont, which has been a repeat victim of Chinese espionage, did not want its case profiled. Similarly, many companies fear repercussions from Chinese authorities if they cry foul.[26] Furthermore, going public for company executives is risky business. Publicly acknowledging IP theft puts executives in the hot seat in front of their boards and shareholders, scares their vendors and clients, and rattles markets. Such news can make it seem that growth projections and company health are not as rosy as they have been portrayed. Corporations going to law enforcement to reveal an employee breach or computer hack shakes confidence and through discovery could entail further exposure of trade secrets in public filings. Worse yet, the authorities can rarely do anything about the theft.

"GREATEST THEFT IN THE HISTORY OF THE WORLD"

In 1992, the George H. W. Bush administration boastfully announced that it had wrung major concessions out of Beijing regarding intellectual property theft. China promised to pass a stringent new law protecting IP. Victimized American industries crowed that China was finally going to stop stealing. Then, the Chinese Communist Party made no effort to enforce the agreement, and the rampant theft accelerated. The Clinton administration redoubled American efforts to force a crackdown and received another agreement in 1995 that Clinton's lead negotiator said was "the single most comprehensive and detailed [IP rights] enforcement agreement the US has ever concluded."[27] Like many of my colleagues in Congress, I was hopeful. Beijing then flouted its own pledge and Clinton threatened tariffs, but he relented under pressure from industry groups who wanted access to the growing Chinese market and cheap imports. Instead, Chinese leaders signed yet another deal (the third in a four-year time span) they had no intention of honoring. Clinton, in his second term, pushed through Permanent Normalized Trade Relations, which was approved by Congress in 2000 and helped secure China's admission to the World Trade Organization (WTO) in 2001.[28] The Chinese Communist Party once more agreed to play by the rules, including IP treaties. Beijing then defied the world yet again.[29]

President George W. Bush kept up the public and diplomatic charade that China was a rule-follower and deserved a place among free and fair trading partners. Despite assigning IP attachés to China postings, raising the issue at international summits and bilateral talks, and issuing annual reports on economic espionage and intellectual property theft, the second Bush administration turned a blind eye to China's large-scale and strategically directed theft of American ingenuity.[30]

Similarly, President Barack Obama talked tough on China while campaigning and backed off when it came time for action. Despite repeatedly raising the issue of Chinese IP theft at high-level meetings, Obama did little aside from prosecuting identifiable perpetrators residing within the US of corporate espionage through the Department of Justice.[31] Obama even refused to be effectively stern with General Secretary Xi Jinping, whose government the Justice Department directly implicated in massive hacking and espionage cases.[32] In 2015, after a rash of high-level prosecutions of Chinese government agents and the discovery of the hack of the Office of Personnel Management (OPM) files, Obama obtained another promise from Xi. This time, China and the US jointly pledged to not conduct government-sponsored cyber espionage. Obama denied the US engaged in "cyber economic espionage for commercial gain" at all, and Xi's words were vague. According to translated remarks by Xi given alongside Obama in the Rose Garden:

> "[C]ompetent authorities of both countries have reached important consensus on joint fight against cyber-crimes. Both sides agree to step up crime cases, investigation assistance and information-sharing. And both government will not be engaged in or knowingly support online theft of intellectual properties. And we will explore the formulation of appropriate state, behavior and norms of the cyberspace. And we will establish a high-level joint dialogue mechanism on the fight against cyber-crimes and related issues, and to establish hotline links."[33]

As expected, Xi's statements were lip service, and the American response to continued intransigence was tepid at best.[34] Just six months following China's promises regarding intellectual property theft, Obama's own National Security Agency (NSA) director and US Cyber Command Admiral Michael Rogers told Congress: "China's leaders pledged in September 2015 to refrain from sponsoring cyber-enabled theft of trade secrets for commercial gain. Nonetheless, cyber operations from China are still targeting and exploiting U.S. government, defense industry, academic, and private computer networks."[35]

Although detectable Chinese hacks did decline briefly following the Obama-Xi summit in 2015, the reduction may have been a result of strategic realignment rather than a willingness to comply. Instead of using the Chinese army's hacking assets, Beijing shifted toward its intelligence service, which possesses much more sophisticated tools and greater stealth. Infiltration may have continued without our knowing it.[36]

ALL OUT OF CARROTS, A LOT OF STICKS LEFT

Having tried for three decades to cajole the Chinese Communist Party into line, US officials have exhausted most incentives for China to play by the rules. However, short of war, America still has a number of tools to curtail Chinese aggression and theft.

From China's accession to the WTO in 2001 until President Trump took office in 2017, the US pursued close to two dozen complaints against China for unfair trade practices and violations.[37] Only one of these cases that was brought to the WTO concerned intellectual property. In that 2007 case—and the lion's share of US complaints—the US won a costly victory, and China agreed to change its laws on some issues. But in the end, WTO rulings are only as good as the word of the adversarial parties' willingness to accept an outcome and institute an earnest remedy.[38,39] Making things worse, China has already proven that it will not play by the WTO's rules. Among a laundry list of grievances, the United States Trade Representative's *2018 Report to Congress on China's WTO Compliance* noted that China has an "extremely poor record" of abiding by the WTO's transparency obligations and "has failed to fully address U.S. concerns in areas that have been the subject of WTO dispute settlement."[40]

Another recourse for American officials seeking to combat China's intellectual property theft, hacking, and espionage is the *Special 301 Report*—an annual report that specifically outlines the economic cost of other nations' trade malfeasance to the United States regarding intellectual property. It also classifies countries that "present the most significant concerns regarding IP rights" by placing them on a "Priority Watch List" or "Watch List." In the 2019 report, China remained on the Priority Watch List. The report concluded that "Necessary progress will not be achieved unless China can demonstrate its resolve to protect and enforce IP rights" and stressed that "China remains a precarious and uncertain environment for U.S. right holders."[41]

But the *Special 301 Report* is no more than a name and shame tactic. These reports are largely informed by voluntary submissions by American corporations and businesses impacted by IP violations. Although valuable as plain-language indictments of international trade cheating, these reports only lay the groundwork for substantial and tangible consequences.

In addition to gaining positive verdicts at the WTO, the US government must establish swift, direct, and firm consequences for IP theft by China. President Trump has laudably begun this process. Broad and highly targeted tariffs against the People's Republic of China for its theft may well be a necessary cudgel to compel the Chinese Communist Party to get serious about IP theft and hacking. However, the US needs more precise solutions as well.

One powerful idea already floated by the Trump administration is sanctions.[42] There will be consequences for any entity, state-owned or otherwise, that steals from or cheats American companies. The US Treasury Department and the Department of Commerce should sanction any entity that procures and/or receives stolen intellectual property—banning business with American entities around the world. This should include a ban on imports from the guilty party into the United States.[43]

The individual and targeted sanction against Russian officials during the Ukraine crisis established a clear precedent that this could be achieved quickly.[44] Congress should be consulted on these actions, but there's no need to pass new legislation since the Defend Trade Secrets Act of 2016 was enacted. It demonstrated the will of the Congress that the American government will not accept continued and flagrant cheating and theft by China.[45]

Furthermore, scholars at the American Enterprise Institute outlined potential retaliation against Chinese concerns by "hacking back" to degrade their capabilities to mount cyberattacks.[46] The strategy also recommends prohibiting Chinese companies who blackmail US companies into "voluntarily" turning over IP from doing business in the United States.

Similarly, we might develop a system to force price honesty—or match China's subsidies—with counter subsidies to enable American companies to buy back the customers China is acquiring through government-supported losses (including loans that don't have to be repaid). Predatory financing by the Chinese communist system is a major problem. It does not matter how innovative you are if your competitor can underprice you at a level that will forcibly drive you out of business. We cannot talk seriously about matching China in the world market unless we solve this financing problem. The rise of the Chinese telecommunications company Huawei and its ability to undercut every non-Chinese competitor is a sober warning of what is to come in every industry the Chinese Communist Party wants to dominate. This process was used to dominate the solar power industry, and experts believe it is about to be used to try to drive the American commercial space companies into bankruptcy.

Protecting the forced transfer of critical US technology and encouraging domestic investment in American companies will also help. A second and even more serious form of predatory financing is the strategy of finding small companies with great potential, buying them, and then absorbing their technology into the Chinese Communist Party's system. Many smaller American companies can find angel investors, but when they get to the next size of funding requirements, they find it much harder to attract American investors. At this point, China steps in with large and almost irresistible offers. The result is Chinese acquisition of many of the best American innovators and entrepreneurs. As I've previously mentioned, in some cases China forces data to be localized in China, or for foreign research and development to be localized in China as a condition for access to the large market. In other cases, China leverages its vast China leverages its vast market size to force US companies to enter into joint ventures or partnerships with Chinese companies (sometimes requiring a majority stake) for market access.[47] Additionally, the United States must protect developments obviously related to national security, but it also must protect dual-use technology and foundational technology that can lead to entire new fields of capability.

These concrete steps will demonstrate to Beijing that

Washington will not put up with further intellectual property aggression without serious consequences. And the consequences have to be serious enough and painful enough to get China to close down its government-run theft systems.

Intellectual property theft by China robs American inventors and companies of the incentive to innovate in the first place. According to the Global Innovation Policy Center, more than 45 million Americans work in IP-intensive industries. Intellectual property is worth $6.6 trillion to our economy, and the economic impact from innovation accounts for upward of 40 percent of our economic growth and employment.[48] Make no mistake: When we talk about the theft of intellectual property, we mean the theft of American jobs. These are not just high-skilled jobs, like those that design the iPhone or develop solar technology. There are many lower-skilled jobs that intellectual property supports. Indeed, IP theft deprives lower-skilled workers of some of their best employment opportunities. According to one study of employment data, low-skilled workers in IP-intensive industries made an average salary that was 40 percent more than workers in non-IP heavy industries. In general, industries that relied on IP paid workers an average of 60 percent more than industries not reliant on IP—and created jobs even during economic downturns.[49]

Those in business, politics, and economics who are wary of tackling the China threat should take their heads out of the sand. Inaction is no better than surrender. President Trump's promise and efforts to stop the theft better reflect a commitment to free trade and free markets than the do-nothing skeptics. There's nothing virtuous about the American government being passive when sovereign states steal from private American businesses and undermine our competitiveness and national security in the process.

I have no way to predict where the US-China trade fight will be by the time this book is published. However, President Trump should stick to his guns on this. Yes, the trade tariffs are hurting business in America, but the overall economy is strong. Now is the moment when we can wage this fight. We would never be able to extract meaningful concessions from China if we didn't have the economy to weather the storm. Furthermore, American businesses will be much better off if and when the world's second largest economy is forced to start playing by the rules.

This is a fight we must have—and it is one we must win.

CHAPTER FOUR

BIG DATA, AI, & E-TYRANNY

> To truly make America safe, we truly have to make cybersecurity a major priority....
>
> The scope of our cybersecurity problem is enormous. Our government, our businesses, our trade secrets and our citizens' most sensitive information are all facing constant cyberattacks and review by the enemy.
>
> —Presidential Candidate Donald Trump, October 2016[1]

> Development is one overriding principle; stability is another. We should attach equal importance to both. We should firmly adhere to the path of social governance under socialism with Chinese characteristics. We will leverage the Party's leadership and China's socialist system, which are our advantage, in strengthening social governance.
>
> —General Secretary Xi Jinping, September 2017[2]

There was a moment at the start of the millennium when it appeared China's totalitarian system would start to develop openings for democracy. As Christina Larson wrote for the *MIT Technology Review* on August 20, 2018, Hu Jintao, the general secretary of the Chinese Communist Party who preceded Xi Jinping, had begun permitting average Chinese citizens to petition the party about grievances. This all ended with Xi. According to Larson, "[Xi's] strategy for understanding and responding to what is going on in a nation of 1.4 billion relies on a combination of surveillance, AI, and big data to monitor people's lives and behavior in minute detail."[3]

Monitoring its citizens is an important priority for the Chinese Communist Party. In November 2018, the government started requiring alternative fuel vehicle manufacturers in China to send the real-time location and operational data of the vehicles directly to the Chinese government. According to the Associated Press (AP), "More than 200 manufacturers, including Tesla, Volkswagen, BMW, Daimler, Ford, General Motors, Nissan, Mitsubishi and U.S.-listed electric vehicle start-up NIO, transmit position information and dozens of other data points to government-backed monitoring centers."[4] Most often, the car owners have no idea this is happening. The AP reported more than 1.1 million cars in China were being tracked under this system. As electric and other alternative fuel vehicles become more efficient and popular, this number will soar. In a matter of decades, it could represent the majority of vehicles in China. (The Chinese government also put in place production minimums for alternative fuel vehicles that kicked in this year, according to the AP.)

The Chinese government claims it uses the data to improve infrastructure, public safety, and industrial planning and to curb abuses to a clean fuel subsidy. However, no other country that gives subsidies for alternative fuel vehicles (or deals with public safety or infrastructure woes) is requiring that said vehicles be tracked around the clock. Critics of China's law told the AP, "It could be used not only to undermine foreign carmakers' competitive position, but also for surveillance—particularly in China, where there are few protections on personal privacy."

With this data, the Chinese Communist Party could know—at any given moment—the location and routine driving habits of anyone with an alternative fuel car. It could immediately know if a large group of these drivers were converging on one location—perhaps to protest against the government. Furthermore, if the Chinese Communist Party was interested in tracking a particular activist, journalist, or political dissident who happened to own an alternative fuel vehicle, it has the ability to know exactly where that person is likely to be at any given moment.

Aside from personal surveillance concerns, the AP reported some manufacturers were worried that China would use the data to ascertain proprietary information from their vehicles and create Chinese versions of their designs that would crowd them out of the market. This is also entirely within the realm of possibility—and mirrors other economic espionage and IP theft practices by China.

This is just one example of what Canada's CBC News described as "an entire network" inside China that is focused on gathering, categorizing, and compiling information. CBC reported that a group of researchers at the University of Toronto's Munk School of Global Affairs has begun looking into the vast array of data that Chinese companies and government agencies are collecting. By reverse engineering popular Chinese mobile applications such as WeChat (a Chinese multipurpose app owned by Tencent with features that can be used for messaging, social media, sending payments, and more), the group "found it contains various hidden means of censorship and surveillance." Ronald Deibert, the director of the group of researchers (which is known as The Citizen Lab) told the Canadian news outlet China's leaders "have a wealth of data at their disposal about what individuals are doing at a micro level in ways that they never had before."[5]

Following the electric car tracking model, many of China's

industries are doing all the data collection on the government's (or more accurately, the party's) behalf. CBC News reported that industries are also putting the information up for sale. Citing a report by the *Guangzhou Southern Metropolis Daily,* a major Chinese newspaper, a great deal of this compiled information can be bought by anyone. According to CBC:

> "Using just the personal ID number of a colleague, reporters bought detailed data about hotels stayed at, flights and trains taken, border entry and exit records, real estate transactions and bank records. All of them with dates, times and scans of documents (for an extra fee, the seller could provide the names of who the colleague stayed with at hotels and rented apartments).
>
> "All confirmed by the colleague. And all for the low price of 700 yuan, or about $140 Cdn."[6]

Unsurprisingly, an enormous amount of this data is being mined by Chinese mobile phone apps. Abacus (a news website owned by the *South China Morning Post*—which is owned by Chinese tech behemoth Alibaba) reported in January 2019 that 13 Chinese apps had been called out for collecting too much user data. Abacus reported that the Internet Society of China, a nongovernment regulator, said that the apps were "collecting excessive amounts of potentially sensitive personal data including SMS messages, address book, location, and recordings. Among them are Taobao's spin-off Tmall, popular travel app Ctrip (which owns Skyscanner), and short video app Kuaishou."[7] In a previous study, Abacus reported a Chinese selfie app called Meitu was accused of "snatching our faces" by "excessively collecting recognizable biodata and financial information from its users."

The degree to which the Chinese government is gathering precise personal data through Chinese industries is breathtaking.

But the Chinese Communist Party surveillance effort is not limited only to China. On May 20, 2019, CNN reported that Chinese-made commercial drones in the United States could be gathering and sending critical data to their manufacturers in China (and potentially the Chinese government).[8] The Department of Homeland Security's (DHS) Cybersecurity and Infrastructure Security Agency sent out a warning to Americans using these drones, saying that the machines "contain components that can compromise your data and share your information on a server accessed beyond the company itself," according to CNN.

Under Chinese law, Chinese companies are legally compelled to cooperate with the Communist Party's intelligence operations. Because of this, the DHS alert said the US had "strong concern" that China's government could use data collected by the drones to gather "potentially revealing data about their operations and the individuals and entities operating them." According to CNN, 79 percent of all the commercial drones in the United States and Canada come from one Chinese company called DJI. In 2017, the US Army banned DJI-made drones from service saying that the company had passed important data to the Chinese government. Both CNN and the *Financial Times* also reported that Immigrations and Customs Enforcement agents in Los Angeles had found the company was seeking to gather data on US law enforcement and critical infrastructure.

This is a fairly ingenious plan for international data collection, and it shows how seriously the Chinese Communist Party is taking it—along with high-tech surveillance. Most of these drones have high-speed, high-definition cameras. They have software to determine their positions and locations at any given time—and virtually all of them can connect to wireless networks. The *Financial Times* reported that many also use "sophisticated facial-recognition and object-detection software to aid piloting and image capture."[9]

These drones are used by police and firefighters to surveil

dangerous situations. They are used by government inspectors to survey hard-to-reach or remote infrastructure. Private companies use them to easily get top-down views of large installations and facilities. And they are used by hobbyists who just like to fly them around and take interesting pictures of their neighborhoods or surroundings. From a data collection standpoint, the amount of information and surveillance a single drone can capture is breathtaking. Consider what an entire fleet could do.

ARTIFICIAL INTELLIGENCE

Now, heaps of data are largely useless if you don't have a focused method of sorting the datasets and finding key information. China is collecting it on a massive scale because data is the fuel for perfecting artificial intelligence systems.

The Chinese-made social media app TikTok is a good example of how Chinese technocrats may plan to use facial recognition and large-scale data mining to build and develop artificial intelligence capabilities. TikTok was created after the Chinese company Bytedance purchased Musical.ly in November 2017, according to an April 17, 2019, *Bloomberg Businessweek* article by David Ramli and Shelly Banjo.[10]

At first glance, TikTok appears to be a normal social media platform. Users can watch and upload an untold number of short videos in which people (most of them teenagers) sing songs or do ridiculous things on video to share with the world. However, the algorithms that run TikTok work differently than those that underpin Facebook, Twitter, and other American social media platforms.

Instead of curating content from your connections, TikTok probes specific information about you—and what you are watching. According to Ramli and Banjo:

> "TikTok decides what videos to show by tapping into data, starting with your location. Then, as you start watching, it analyzes the faces, voices, music, or objects

> in videos you watch the longest. Liking, sharing, or commenting improves TikTok's algorithm further. Within a day, the app can get to know you so well it feels like it's reading your mind."

A significant portion of TikTok's users are minors. Because of this, the company has worked to curb vulgar and lewd content, identify and block potential predators, and block some features of the app for users who are younger than 13. One of the company's tactics for achieving these goals has been to beef up its data collection. According to Ramli and Banjo, "[TikTok] started using facial-recognition software to identify youthful faces, expelling underage creators, and preventing younger viewers from seeing mature content." It has also initiated a Chinese-style censorship program for content on its app. According to the *Bloomberg Businessweek* article, "the company's long-term goal is to eliminate objectionable content entirely, to be 'controversy free.'"

Naturally, many parent and child safety groups are glad that TikTok is taking broad steps to clean up its content (although the company did pay a $5.7 million settlement to the Federal Trade Commission on allegations that Musical.ly illegally collected data on minors before Bytedance transformed it into TikTok). However, there are some deeper implications here. First, a Chinese company (which is legally obligated to share its information with Chinese government intelligence services) has enough data about millions of young Americans that its app can identify these youths by photo—and appear to read their minds. *Bloomberg Businessweek* reported that the company claims its servers are kept outside of China and therefore are not subject to Chinese laws. This is baloney. If the Chinese Communist Party wants something from Bytedance, the party will get it. However, even if the Chinese government never confiscates TikTok's user data, it could still confiscate its algorithms and use them as a basis to create its own systems for identifying people, tracking their locations, and predicting what they think.

And China is pouring a significant amount of resources into perfecting artifical intelligence (AI).

The Verge reported in March 2019 that China is very close to overtaking the US in AI research. In fact, citing General Secretary Xi's intention to become the world leader in AI by 2030, the outlet reported, "by some measures China has already succeeded in this goal—a decade ahead of schedule."[11] Not only have the Chinese been producing more research papers on AI than the United States (which has been true since 2006) but Chinese papers are increasingly being cited in the AI research community.

According to the Verge: "These findings should make for interesting reading for the US government. Although analyzing research is only a single metric when it comes to measuring the overall AI output of any country, academics and industry experts have warned for years that America needs to do more to maintain its lead."

Additionally, the Chinese company Megvii Technologies is reputed as one of the world's leading companies in facial recognition AI. According to *Forbes* contributor Bernard Marr, its technology, known as Face++, has become a world leader largely due to the company's access to the mountains of Chinese data to which it had access. Facial data from a host of Chinese companies and government agencies were used to train the AI software, Marr wrote in May 2019. The software scans 106 data points on the human face which help it "confirm a person's identity with a high degree of accuracy," according to Marr.[12]

The success of facial recognition systems using AI in China is largely why the technology has been harnessed by law enforcement worldwide. Marr wrote, "China already has a vast surveillance network with 170 million security cameras in use for its Skynet system and 400 million more on the way."

Set aside that China's world-record-sized police surveillance system is called Skynet (the name of the nefarious robot overlord system of *Terminator* fame), but it has served as a model for facial recognition policing worldwide. Chinese facial recognition technology is presently used by police forces across the globe—including the New York Police Department.

To really make the highest use of its data and AI systems, China will need to excel in quantum computing and achieve so-called quantum advantage. In plain terms, quantum advantage refers to the time at which a next-generation computer will perform at speeds significantly faster than the personal computer you may have at home. By significantly, I mean thousands of times faster. Quantum supremacy is a step beyond this in which the machines of the future will be able to handle and process data that current computers simply cannot.

As Sarah Feldman explained in an article for Statista on May 6, 2019, traditional computers process information in binary code (as 1's and 0's). A classical microchip is simply a complex board of relays that flip in the 1 position or the 0 position. Electricity flows through the board based on the position of these switches to complete the computer's operation. A single data point on the board is a bit. Feldman wrote that quantum computing breaks the binary bonds and allows the computer to process bits in two dimensions (becoming qubits) such that each "qubit can hold a zero, a one, or any combination of both zero and one at the same time."[13] This will allow quantum computers to process data at an exponentially faster rate.

Now, this is complicated. And my description is a profound oversimplification of quantum computing. That is OK, this isn't a book about the future of computing. The important thing to understand is that true quantum computing will totally change the world as we know it. Consider how significantly our society and culture has changed since the late 1960s, when the miniaturization of electronics started to proliferate. This is what made personal computers, mobile phones, video game consoles, modems, and digital televisions possible. Consider that your current mobile phone has considerably more computing power than the world's most powerful supercomputer available in 1982. If the Chinese are going to successfully create data and AI systems that can police and control its 1.4 billion people—along with other populations in which the Chinese Communist Party becomes interested—quantum computing will be absolutely necessary.

E-TYRANNY

Starting in 2020, the world will be able to get a first full look at China's brand of e-tyranny, when the country's social credit score system is fully implemented. First announced in 2014 as a pilot program, the social credit scoring system is something straight out of the pages of George Orwell's *1984*.

According to NPR, under the system, each one of China's 1.4 billion people will be initially assigned a social credit score of 1,000. From there, the Chinese Communist Party will use its vast surveillance systems (and data mined from Chinese tech and financial companies) to monitor virtually every action taken by every Chinese citizen. Those who buy the right products, say the right things on social media, walk their pets the right way, and conduct themselves properly (all according to the Communist Party, of course), will earn points and enjoy perks. They will be able to waive deposits on big purchases, they will get preferential treatment at hotels, they will get in shorter lines at bureaucratic offices, and they will be deemed "trustworthy" by the Chinese government.[14]

Those who do not meet the Communist Party's standards will be punished. According to Business Insider, citizens who spread fake news online (remember, this is fake according to the Chinese Communist Party) will get points deducted. Smoking in a no-smoking zone will also dock points—as will poor driving, spending too much money on recreational activities, loitering, and failing to walk your dog on a leash.[15]

The consequences range from inconvenient to debilitating.

Those with low scores can be barred from riding the train or buying plane tickets. Business Insider reported that 9 million people in the pilot program have already been kept from some domestic air travel. Three million have been denied business class tickets on Chinese trains. Those who engage in online conversations deemed inappropriate could have their internet connections interrupted or slowed. Companies in China are also urged to use the social credit score system in making hiring decisions, and parents who are labeled untrustworthy—or blacklisted altogether—can have their children blocked from attending certain schools. Finally, for dog owners who don't use a leash—the Chinese government will simply take away their dogs.

Of course, there is no true independent court system in China. If citizens dispute an allegation about their behavior or think some demerit they earned was unfair, there is no clear recourse or system of appeal. Furthermore, many of the Chinese citizens that have been unwillingly caught up in the pilot program for the social credit system are not even made aware when they are placed on blacklists or labeled untrustworthy.

This may all seem far-fetched. It isn't.

If you are having trouble imagining how this type of technological totalitarianism could work, simply look at China's western Xinjiang Uyghur Autonomous Region. Let me be clear: the region is autonomous in name only. *The New York Times* went there—to a town called Kashgar. What reporters found was a system of surveillance that they described as automated authoritarianism.[16] There is a brilliant photo article of their trip documenting the massive surveillance state the Chinese Communist Party has developed in the region. There, the Chinese Communist Party has imprisoned and suppressed millions of Uyghurs and other Muslim and ethnic groups in various towns throughout the region. Kashgar is one town in which hundreds of thousands of members of these Muslim minorities are constantly surveilled and controlled by the Chinese government. It is a modern-day computerized concentration camp operating in the second largest economy in the world. It is also reminiscent of some of the West's starkest dystopian fiction.

The New York Times reporters were unable to speak with any of the Uyghur residents because the journalists were constantly followed by Chinese police dressed in plain clothes. But they didn't need to interview anyone to recognize the electronic tyranny China has inflicted on Kashgar's inhabitants. The people forced to live under these conditions pass through militarized checkpoints every 100 yards to get around. Cameras using facial recognition software check them to make sure they are authorized to pass the checkpoints. Armed police (some of whom were conscripted Uyghurs themselves) sometimes check the residents' phones to make sure they have the required surveillance software installed. The same types of surveillance measures are employed if any of the Muslim inhabitants dare to go to one of the few remaining mosques for worship.

These checkpoints are punctuated by thousands of surveillance cameras spread throughout the town. The reporters counted 20 on one side of a short stretch of street. While *The New York Times* couldn't confirm it, it's entirely likely these cameras are absorbing mountains of data and using facial recognition to track every person in the town. We already know that Chinese companies are increasingly active in developing sophisticated surveillance software that is used by the government. *Forbes* reported in February 2019 that the personal information of 2.5 million people was leaked after the Chinese software company SenseNet left its database unprotected.

According to a Dutch cybersecurity firm cited by *Forbes*, SenseNet "make[s] artificial intelligence-based security software systems for face recognition, crowd analysis, and personal verification. And their business IP and millions of records of people tracking data is fully accessible to anyone."[17] This leaked data included recent location tracking, nationality, sex, home addresses, photographs, birthdays, and many other key pieces of personal information. There is no reason to believe the Chinese authorities in

Kashgar—and throughout the rest of Xinjiang—are not making use of software that yields the same mass data collection results.

Also, recall the alternative fuel vehicle monitoring system I mentioned earlier. A sort of pilot program for this effort was initially tested in Xinjiang. The AP reported that residents in Xinjiang were required to install GPS tracking devices in their cars—as well as radio transmitters in their windshields that send information to roadway checkpoints as they pass.

The reporters in Kashgar described the surveillance state as being "as much about intimidation as monitoring." Even when the Uyghurs are not trying to move around the city, they are subject to constant, unexplained searches. *The New York Times* reported that Uyghurs are given "reliability scores" that the authorities use to determine whether they are trustworthy. Those who have low scores can be further detained in indoctrination camps that have been built on the far side of the town—isolated from visitors and tourists. (Does this sound familiar?) According to the photo article, even children are interrogated about whether their parents teach them the Quran. Sometimes, according to *The New York Times*, these children become orphans if they answer "yes."

The New York Times reporters themselves were also regularly searched, and their "police minders" would delete photographs they deemed sensitive. After one deleted an interesting-yet-benign picture of a camel, the journalist questioned the decision. According to the report, the policeman said, "In China, there are no whys."

If you are wondering how China selected who would be sent to these camps, the answer is more of the same. According to Reuters, in 2016, China had begun using "predictive software that combines data on everything from security camera footage to health and banking records" to first identify the Uyghurs and minority groups who are now detained in the Xinjiang concentration camps.[18] Maya Wong, a researcher for Human Rights Watch in Hong Kong, told the news wire service that "[f]or the first time, we are able to demonstrate that the Chinese government's use of big data and predictive policing not only blatantly violates privacy rights but also enables officials to arbitrarily detain people."

The Chinese government, of course, denied the allegations by Human Rights Watch that it was specifically targeting Uyghurs, and police didn't respond to requests for comment from Reuters. However, the wire service reported that "[o]fficial reports about the programme say it has helped police catch criminals guilty of petty theft and illegal financial dealings, as well as to find Uyghur officials who are disloyal to the ruling Communist Party."

Larson with the *MIT Technology Review* wrote that the Chinese government does not disclose what behaviors cause the algorithms to flag someone as dangerous; however, "it's believed that it may highlight behaviors such as visiting a particular mosque, owning a lot of books, buying a large quantity of gasoline, or receiving phone calls or email from contacts abroad."[19]

Because the system is so opaque, there is no way for us to know whether the people being detained really represent public safety threats or if they are just a marginalized group the Chinese Communist Party seeks to control. However, we do know that the system is being fully implemented. As Larson wrote, "in the western region of Xinjiang, the available information shows only that the number of people taken into police custody has shot up dramatically, rising 731 percent from 2016 to 2017." In fact, Larson reported that one in ten Uyghur or Kazakh adults have been sent to the "reeducation" facilities.

I have been personally told by high-ranking Chinese officials in America that these camps resemble boarding schools and are simply job-training sites in which native minorities can learn Chinese languages, gain modern job skills, and better integrate to society. If this were true, then the Uyghurs would not be experiencing serious human rights abuses in these facilities. In fact, what we are seeing in Xinjiang is more likely a rough draft of the system of electronic tyranny the Chinese Communist Party is working to perfect.

As China is engaging in mass data collection domestically, developing cutting-edge technology to make use of the information, and is exporting these systems and technologies abroad, the US needs to recognize that the deployment and use of this new technology make a new kind of global warfare increasingly likely. Cyber war is inherently global. AI and quantum computing both have the potential to be global players. The initial steps that have already been taken toward a global command post must be dramatically intensified and resourced. A high-technology global conflict will occur at speeds that we can't imagine and will totally overshadow the capabilities of combatant commands to deploy assets. Realistic war games must be initiated to look at how global systems might be engaged in real time using the technology that is being developed.

CHAPTER FIVE

CRUSHING DISSENT

> We put faith and family, not government and bureaucracy, at the center of our lives. And we debate everything. We challenge everything. We seek to know everything so that we can better know ourselves.
>
> And above all, we value the dignity of every human life, protect the rights of every person, and share the hope of every soul to live in freedom. That is who we are. Those are the priceless ties that bind us together as nations, as allies, and as a civilization.
>
> —President Donald Trump, July 2017[1]

> We should take a clear-cut stand against any problem that is detrimental to CPC [Chinese Communist Party] leadership, socialist political power, and national systems and the rule of law, and harmful to the fundamental interests of all the people, never letting it prevail in the name of diversity. This is our political red line, and it must not be crossed.
>
> —General Secretary Xi Jinping, May 2015[2]

When people discuss human rights in China, they are often referring to the treatment of Uyghurs and Tibetans. This is understandable because of the extremes the Communist government has gone to crush the spirit and undermine the culture and beliefs of these two non-Han groups of people. Yet in a more profound way, it is fundamentally misleading to focus a discussion of human rights in China on these two minorities alone. There are an estimated 6 million Tibetans in China and more than 11 million Uyghurs in China's western Xinjiang region.[3,4] Together, they represent about 1.2 percent of the total population in China. Yet, the other 98.8 percent of people in China also endure serious human rights abuses. In fact, the total number of persecuted Chinese people dwarfs the total population of Tibet and Xinjiang.

For example, the totalitarian regime persecutes practitioners of the spiritual discipline Falun Gong (which in 1999, reached at least 70 million members) and, according to reports, has abducted, interrogated, and killed believers.[5] Rumors suggest that Falun Gong practitioners have been killed so their organs could be used for transplant operations. To take another example, there are as many as 130 million Christians in China.[6] Yet, in China, every Christian church faces the threat of extinction and every Christian worshipper faces the prospect of persecution—in some cases imprisonment.

Then, of course, there is a largely invisible but persistent movement for more freedom for the people and more government accountability. This pro-democracy movement on mainland China remains largely out of sight because it is seen by party leaders as a direct—indeed mortal—threat to the Chinese Communist Party. On a regular basis, democracy advocates are imprisoned and sometimes killed by the government. Many become exiles spending their lives overseas.

The simple fact is: There are no human rights in China. The so-called rights granted by the Chinese Communist Party and the totalitarian state are poor facsimiles of what we consider inalienable human rights. This is a system with a much bigger internal police force than its military. It seeks to track and keep score of every citizen. True human rights come from God and belong to the individual—not the state. This is, by definition, not possible in a totalitarian system in which the state has a total interest in you, your beliefs, and your actions.

General Secretary Xi's anti-corruption campaign is a clear example of this lack of objective rights. Expert analysts with deep experience in China are not sure how much of Xi's anti-corruption campaign is aimed at rooting out corrupt officials and how much is aimed at eliminating political opponents. The question is not about fighting crime and finding culprits. Instead, it is a matter of who gets charged and for which crime. It is a political process, not a criminal justice process.

The great test of the current dictatorial system's stability came in June 1989 at Tiananmen Square in Beijing. Pressures had been building for reforms. There were hundreds of cities across China in which people were protesting China's government and demanding change. The center of the places where demonstrations were taking place was in the heart of Beijing, at Tiananmen Square. Among other grievances, these protestors were calling for further political liberalization—a direct threat to the Communist Party's totalitarian power.

The Chinese communist leadership was concerned with this call for reform, as they had seen what happened when efforts were made to reform the Soviet Union. They remembered that in 1956, when Nikita Khrushchev had criticized Joseph Stalin and called for more humane policies, the Hungarians had rebelled and been repressed in a bloody fight and the Poles had come close to waging war against the Soviets. Then, they had watched Mikhail Gorbachev try to reform the system. His policies led to economic stagnation and enormous dissatisfaction in the Eastern European satellites, and were clearly threatening the stability of the Soviet Union (which disappeared in December 1991).

The Chinese leadership remembered all too vividly the pain and disruption of both the Great Leap Forward and the Cultural Revolution. They had all lived through or been persecuted by Mao Zedong during the Cultural Revolution. They had seen how dangerous a student-led rebellion could become. They were not about to appease the demonstrators and run the risk of the spirit of rebellion and reform growing out of control. To stomp out the opposition, the Communist Party leadership cracked down and sent troops to brutally massacre students and demonstrators on June 4, 1989, in Tiananmen Square. The pictures of the unarmed demonstrator standing in front of a tank went around the world and became a symbol of the inhumanity and brutality of the Chinese communist dictatorship.

For a few years, there were calls for reprisals from foreign governments. Strong words followed but no strong actions. The dictatorship purged those leaders who had favored reform and hardened its position against tolerating dissent and rejecting any opening-up process that would increase popular participation in a reform movement. The Chinese dictatorship gambled that the short memories of the Western system combined with the economic interests of much of the business community would erode anger over repression.

In 1994, despite a lack of significant improvements being made by China's government to protect the human rights of the Chinese people, President Clinton renewed China's most-favored-nation trade status—which treats countries as normal trading partners. What was notable about President Clinton's decision to renew this status for China was the fact that he did so by separating human rights from other issues relating to trade and engagement with China. Of the decision, President Clinton stated, "This decision offers us the best opportunity to lay the basis for long-term sustainable progress on human rights and for the advancement of our other interests with China."[7] Clinton noted, "I think we have to see our relations with China within a broader context" rather than only tied to the issue of human rights. He added that there was no longer a reasonable link between rights and trade. He said, "We have reached the end of the usefulness of that policy."[8]

And while President Clinton was correct in distinguishing

between human rights and different foreign policy issues arising between the US and China, the brutality against the Chinese people instigated by the Communist Party—and the purposes they serve the regime—cannot be forgotten, ignored, or disregarded. The tragedy at Tiananmen Square was the most publicized act of violence committed by the modern Chinese Communist Party against its own people, but it was sadly far from the last.

Americans must understand how fundamentally different our two systems are. We live in a country where power originates from the people, where the government is held accountable to the people, and where the rights to life, liberty, and the pursuit of happiness are prioritized and protected. Our vast human rights and freedoms are inalienable and nonnegotiable.

In China today, the situation is totally different. Power originates from the top of the Communist Party. The survival of the party is prioritized by those in power, and they are held accountable to the party leadership. The concept of human rights is viewed differently by the leadership as well. Peter Walker, senior partner at McKinsey, noted in a speech that as a result of China's civil war and the Japanese invasion, food, shelter, and safety are prioritized over human rights. Moreover, in a Reuters article provided to me by a top-level party official, the deputy party chief of Kashgar (the surveillance-state city in Xinjiang that I mentioned in the previous chapter) was quoted as saying that "stability is the best human right."[9]

This is revealing. In America, our rights to free speech, to assemble, to vote, and to practice religion create a valued competition between ideas that form the foundation of our democratic society. But from an outsider's perspective, it can seem as though these competing ideas result in instability. So in a society where power originates from the top, where the ruling party's strength is prioritized, and stability is considered to be an important human right by government officials, it seems inevitable that rights and freedoms that take power and control away from the central authority would not be allowed. It is important to understand this alternative viewpoint; however, I am by no means arguing that this is justification for the human rights atrocities the Chinese Communist Party has committed in pursuit of its goals. Americans need to be aware of the realities of the hardships that the Chinese Communist Party imposes on its people to preserve its own power.

The US doesn't seek to forcibly impose its system on China. However, as evidenced by many examples throughout this book, the Chinese Communist Party seeks to export its totalitarian system and its repressive practices to other countries. Furthermore, how the Chinese Communist Party treats its citizens is a good indication of how it will treat others outside of its borders. The Chinese Communist Party suppresses human rights because its first goal is to maintain its supreme authority. The Chinese Communist Party achieves this goal by eliminating dissent, manipulating the justice system, and threatening individual livelihood—in violation of rights that should be protected for *any* human being regardless of a country's structure of power and government.

THE CHINESE COMMUNIST PARTY REIGNS SUPREME

Huang Xiaoning, the pastor at the Guangzhou Bible Reformed Church, said, "The Chinese Communist Party wants to be the God of China and the Chinese people. But according to the Bible only God is God. The government is scared of the churches."[10]

Under General Secretary Xi, the Communist Party has implemented more aggressive control over the five state-recognized religions—Chinese Buddhism, Islam, Catholicism, Protestantism, and Taoism—in China.[11] Pulitzer Prize winner Nicholas Kristof wrote for *The New York Times* that "China's Orwellian War on Religion" is "on a scale almost unparalleled by a major nation in three-quarters of a century."[12] Under the direction of a Chinese, atheist, Communist Party, religious groups are essentially being sinicized. In practice, what this means is that China's state-sanctioned organizations supervise worship and religious activity. Additionally, major religious leaders are chosen by the government. The government also dictates where churches and other places of worship are permitted to be built.[13]

Furthermore, according to the state news agency, Xinhua, a 2018 white paper published by China's State Council Information Office declared "that religions in China must be Chinese in orientation and provide active guidance to religions so that they can adapt themselves to the socialist society."[14] By sinicizing religion, the Communist Party is able to ensure further adherence to the party and ensure that citizens' loyalty and allegiances are in line with communist ideology. This is important to the party's survival due to the number of believers in China. The Council on Foreign Relations estimates that there were as many 130 million Christians living in China in 2018 and there could be as many as 247 million by 2030.[15] There are more than 20 million Muslims, and many members of other faiths—the US State Department estimated the total number of religious believers in China in 2016 to be about 650 million people.[16] By comparison, the party itself has 90 million members.[17] Keeping control of worshippers, with a loyalty to a higher power, is a necessity for the Chinese Communist Party.

Moreover, China recognizes that worshippers have foreign loyalties as well. The 2018 white paper stated that "foreign religions in China," namely Catholicism and Protestantism, "had long been controlled and utilized by colonialists and imperialists."[18] An article in *The New York Times* wrote that some estimates conclude that Christianity is China's fastest-growing religion, which many in the Chinese Communist Party believe "promotes Western values and ideals like human rights that conflict with the aims of China's authoritarian government and Mr. Xi's embrace of traditional Chinese culture and Confucian teachings that emphasize obedience and order."[19] Consequently, CNN also reported that analysts and civil rights advocates have observed that the Chinese Communist Party is stepping up its targeted efforts toward worshippers that they view as ideological threats to the power of the party.[20]

The Chinese Communist Party's religious crackdown is widespread. For example, local governments have been shutting down numerous underground or house churches—churches that are not registered with government bodies.[21] In December 2018, the government shut down one of the most popular underground churches, Early Rain Covenant Church, arrested more than 100 of its members, and detained the church's pastor and his wife.[22]

In the case of the Catholic Church, for decades, Chinese Catholics have been worshipping in underground churches that are run by bishops secretly appointed by the Pope and are loyal to the Vatican. China's government has created a parallel system, and Catholics have been divided between the underground churches and China's state-approved and controlled Catholic church. In an effort to unify the split, the Vatican and China reached a provisional agreement in September 2018 to resolve the issue of who has the right to appoint bishops in China. Though the details of the agreement remain vague at the time of this writing, the Vatican handed over some of its regulatory control to the Chinese Communist Party by recognizing seven state-appointed bishops under the agreement. These bishops had previously been excommunicated from the church since they had not been chosen by the Vatican.[23]

Furthermore, crosses have been removed from buildings, churches have been forced into hanging the Chinese flag, and congregations have had to sing patriotic songs. In Guangzhou, police raided a Sunday school for children. Online purchases of Bibles have been outlawed. In numerous schools and cities, Christmas celebrations were prohibited in December 2018. Lily Kuo in an article for *The Guardian* cites a government work plan aimed at "promoting Chinese Christianity" that "calls for 'retranslating and annotating' the Bible, to find commonalities with socialism and establish a 'correct understanding' of the text."[24]

The reason for the Chinese Communist Party's crackdown

on religion can be best summed up in a statement made by Lian Xi, a professor at Duke University who focuses on Christianity in modern China. Lian emphasized the threat that Christianity in particular poses to the Chinese Communist Party's power. "They have come to see the political potential of Christianity as a force for change," Lian said. "What really makes the government nervous is Christianity's claim to universal rights and values."[25]

But the government is not just singling out Christians. As I discussed earlier in this book, one of the most prevalent abuses of human rights is occurring in Xinjiang.

For a long time, the Muslim Uyghur population in Xinjiang and China's leadership have been at odds. This tension came to a head in 2009 when a group of approximately 1,000 Uyghurs gathered to demand a government investigation into a brawl at a toy factory in Guangdong that resulted in the death of two Uyghurs. The demonstration turned into a riot and the Chinese Communist Party responded by blocking internet access for ten months in the region. Later, in 2014, a group of Uyghur separatists stabbed 33 civilians during an attack at a railway station. Consequently, the Xinjiang regional government started a campaign titled "Strike Hard Against Violent Extremism."[26]

The intensity of the effort increased in 2016 when Chen Quanguo became the Chinese Communist Party chief in Xinjiang.[27] Previously, he presided over the intense crackdowns and suppression in Tibet, while he was stationed there as the party's top official.[28] Moreover, Chen Quanguo was also promoted by Xi to be one of the 25 members of the Politburo, the Chinese Communist Party's high-ranking governing body. As Hilary Hurd pointed out in an article for Lawfare, this promotion is a clear indicator of the importance of the repression in Xinjiang.[29]

Surely, combating terrorism is important. However, what the Communist Party is doing in Xinjiang is not—in reality—a counterterrorism effort. Rather, China's Communist Party has taken this initiative to an extreme level. Writing for Lawfare,

Hurd noted that some observers argue that China's government is attempting to "completely erase" the identity of the Uyghur population in the region and "eliminate any local impulse towards independence."[30] US State Department Ambassador-at-Large for Counterterrorism Nathan Sales and Ambassador-at-Large for International Religious Freedom Sam Brownback wrote in May 2019 that the abuses against Muslims in Xinjiang in fact "undermine the global consensus on counterterrorism. Beijing is painting its human rights violations as a legitimate counterterrorism effort, when they patently are not."[31]

According to Chinese Human Rights Defenders, an advocacy group, arrests in Xinjiang in 2017 amounted to 21 percent of China's total arrests—despite the area having a population that is only about 1.5 percent of the entire country.[32] The government has also reportedly imposed strict rules including bans on beards, long skirts, face veils, and Islamic names.[33] With Beijing's support, authorities in Xinjiang are instituting "reeducation"—or brainwashing—programs as additional methods for preventing and/or stifling religious beliefs, cultural practices, and political opposition. Those living "freely" in Xinjiang—under the watchful eye of the Chinese Communist Party's surveillance state—can be subjected to mandatory "education sessions" or propaganda ceremonies. A 2018 Human Rights Watch report detailing the situation in Xinjiang revealed:

> "Inside political education camps, detainees are forced to learn Mandarin Chinese, sing praises of the Chinese Communist Party, and memorize rules applicable primarily to Turkic Muslims. Those outside the camps are required to attend weekly, or even daily, Chinese flag-raising ceremonies, political indoctrination meetings, and at times Mandarin classes. Detainees are told they may not be allowed to leave the camps unless they have learned over 1,000 Chinese characters or are otherwise deemed to have become loyal Chinese subjects;

> Turkic Muslims living outside are subjected to movement restrictions ranging from house arrest, to being barred from leaving their locales, to being prevented from leaving the country. Inside, people are punished for peacefully practicing religion; outside, the government's religious restrictions are so stringent that it has effectively outlawed Islam. Inside, people are closely watched by guards and are barred from contacting their families and friends. Those living in their homes are watched by their neighbors, officials, and tech-enabled mass surveillance systems, and are not allowed to contact those in foreign countries."[34]

Citing interviews, Human Rights Watch outlined accounts of physical and psychological punishments and suicide attempts described by former detainees. One described being held in solitary confinement and said, "They put me in a small solitary confinement cell...in a space of about 2 x 2 meters. I was not given any food or drink, my hands were handcuffs [sic] in the back, and I had to stand for 24 hours without sleep."[35] According to the Human Rights Watch report, former detainees also witnessed teenagers, pregnant or breastfeeding women, the elderly, and people who were disabled being imprisoned in the camps.[36] The repression of Uyghurs and other Muslim and ethnic minorities in Xinjiang is catastrophic. The number of Xinjiang residents, in particular Uyghurs, forced into mandatory "educational sessions" or into the political reeducation camps may be as high as two to three million in total according to an August 2018 report by Chinese Human Rights Defenders.[37] Deputy Assistant Secretary Scott Busby testified to the Senate Foreign Relations Committee in December 2018 that estimates of just those who had been detained in the camps since April 2017 ranges from 800,000 to possibly more than two million.[38]

In early July 2019, 22 countries issued a letter to the United Nations High Commissioner for Human Rights, urging China to promote freedom of religion and stop its mass incarceration of Ugyhurs and other Muslim and ethnic minorities. The signatories included Australia, Britain, Canada, France, Japan, Germany, and New Zealand, among others. China issued a strong response, in the form of a letter signed by a total of 37 United Nations ambassadors that praised China's "remarkable achievements in the field of human rights." According to Xinhua, the letter—signed by ambassadors from Russia, Pakistan, Cuba, Saudi Arabia, Qatar, Nigeria, Angola, and others—commended China's "de-radicalization" policies in Xinjiang and claimed that as a result, the "people there enjoy a stronger sense of happiness, fulfillment and security."[39]

Later that month, officials in Xinjiang claimed that a majority of those imprisoned in the reeducation camps were released. However, this assertion was met with skepticism from the United States. A statement released by the State Department and the Pentagon concluded they were "unable to verify the vague claims" and that the Chinese Communist Party continued to exhibit "extreme hostility to all religious faiths."[40] Full transparency is needed to confirm that the situation in Xinjiang has improved, but based on the gross lack of evidence that has been revealed at the time of this writing, it is highly unlikely that the abuse has stopped.

I know I spoke at length about Xinjiang in the chapter on big data and surveillance, but the human rights abuses there warrant attention. The atrocities in Xinjiang are instances of the Chinese Communist Party forcibly imposing its Leninist system and wiping out ideologies different that its own. It is a tragedy. Lives are being destroyed and families are being ripped apart through fear as the Chinese Communist Party further extends control over the people.

This widespread suppression and control of religious and cultural practices is staggering. Yet these groups are not the only targets of the Chinese Communist Party's strategy to suppress ideologies that are different and therefore threaten its power.

CONTROLLING THE OPPOSITION

In April 2019, excerpts from a speech General Secretary Xi gave back in 2013 (before becoming president) were made public. Reflecting on the failure and collapse of the Soviet Union, Xi stated:

> "Why did the Soviet Union disintegrate? Why did the Soviet Communist Party fall? An important reason is that the struggle in the ideological field is very fierce. It totally negates the history of the Soviet Union, the history of the Soviet Communist Party, Lenin and Stalin. It engages in historical nihilism and confuses thoughts. Party organizations at all levels have almost no effect and the army is no longer under the leadership of the Party..."[41]

As China expert and author of the *Sinocism* newsletter Bill Bishop noted, the Chinese Communist Party has learned many lessons from the failures of the Soviet Union, which, as a result, drive many of its policies.[42] One of these lessons is how differences in ideology can cause a communist regime to crack and crumble. Bishop further argued that "Xi is proud to call himself a Communist, and he and the Party see themselves in an existential ideological struggle with the West."[43] Controlling religious and cultural practices is an important part of maintaining the Chinese Communist Party's grip on power, but so is silencing the voices of dissidents reporting on or advocating for policies that contradict the party.

One of the best-known academic activists the Chinese Communist Party attempted to subvert was Liu Xiaobo. Liu was a former literature professor at Beijing Normal University. He was a vocal critic of the Chinese government and focused his writings on Chinese culture and society—in particular democracy and human rights. After supporting students during the 1989 Tiananmen Square massacre, he was put in jail for

21 months. From 1996 to 1999, he was imprisoned in a labor camp for reeducation after criticizing the government's policies on Taiwan and the Dalai Lama (the spiritual leader of Tibet). Then, in 2009, after being involved with Charter '08—a political reform manifesto—he was sentenced to 11 years in prison for "inciting subversion." In 2010, Liu was internationally recognized for his dedicated activist work and was awarded the Nobel Peace Prize "for his long and non-violent struggle for fundamental human rights in China." Even with gaining international support for his efforts, Liu still spent almost eight years in prison and was then transferred to a hospital in 2017 where he died from liver cancer complications.[44]

In most societies, it would be puzzling for a Nobel Peace Prize winner to be imprisoned multiple times throughout his lifetime. However, the Chinese Communist Party truly saw him as a serious threat to its authority and influence. Similarly, Liu's wife, Liu Xia, was only allowed to leave China in 2018. This was after spending eight years under house arrest, though she was never charged with a crime and no judicial proceedings were brought against her.[45] The artist and poet was put under house arrest days after her husband received the Nobel Peace Prize. Though China claimed that Liu Xia maintained her freedom and rights, Western diplomats argued that authorities watched her closely after her husband's death and only permitted her to meet with family and friends in prearranged calls and visits.[46]

Liu Xia's brother was forced to stay behind in China as she boarded a plane for Germany. According to the Congressional-Executive Commission on China's 2018 Annual Report, rights advocates "expressed concern that Liu's freedom of speech outside of China might be compromised because the Chinese government did not allow her brother Liu Hui to leave China with her."[47] This is because oftentimes the Chinese Communist Party uses family and friends still living in China as leverage to control the actions of dissidents living abroad. Consequently, living in a foreign country does not guarantee that dissidents can escape the auspices of the Communist Party's censorship, without the threat of serious repercussions for those they love.

The New York Times reported that a man named Zhuang Liehong was a leader in a series of protests against land grabs that padded the pockets of local officials in his home village of Wukan in 2011. After the protests ended, villagers were given the right to hold local elections and Zhuang became one of seven new committee members. But this apparent victory was short-lived, and Zhuang was forced to flee to New York in 2014 where he believed he could speak freely about the atrocities occurring in his home village. He posted photos on Facebook from family and friends depicting a police crackdown sweeping Wukan. Following a protest in the village in 2016, Zhuang received a disturbing phone call from his father, who was being held in a jail. "Son," his father said, "stop doing what you're doing. It will be bad for your family." According to *The New York Times*, Zhuang "felt the phone call suggested a trade—his father's freedom for Mr. Zhuang's silence."[48] Zhuang received more phone calls in the following months. If he stopped answering calls on one of his several phones, they would come through to another. Zhuang's friends' phones were also tracked by security officers, and they were interrogated if they answered his calls. Zhuang's mother shared a home with his handicapped older brother, and a camera with the state broadcaster China Central Television (CCTV) "mysteriously" showed up outside. His father continued to send him warnings and received a three-year prison sentence. Zhuang's mother called him from Wukan and warned that his safety was at risk—even in the United States.

In another case, when a journalist at the Long Island-based Mandarin-language media company Mirror Media Group started interviewing Guo Wengui (an exiled Chinese billionaire), his wife went missing in China for 90 days. Journalist Chen Xiaoping published an open letter on Twitter in early 2018 to ask the Chinese government for his wife's release. Shortly after the letter's issuance, a video of his wife denouncing his work in the US was anonymously put up on YouTube.[49]

In addition to cracking down on dissidents and their families and friends, the Chinese Communist Party has been increasingly detaining the human rights lawyers and activists that defend them since 2015. This so-called war on the law has been termed the "709 crackdown"—which refers to when the first arrests happened (July 9).[50] According to *The Washington Post*, the campaign uses "arrests, detentions and show trials to punish lawyers who have courageously defended human rights victims in recent years."[51] Within the first five days of the initiative, China Human Rights Lawyers Concern Group reported that at least 146 human rights lawyers, activists, and law firm staff were detained, arrested, incommunicado, summoned, or had their freedoms restricted temporarily.[52]

CNN spoke to Sui Muqing and Peter Dahlin, who advocated for human rights and were affected by the 709 crackdowns in different parts of China. The article said that the men described "being forcibly taken from their homes, detained for weeks, sometimes months, in secret prisons, denied communication with family and legal representation, strong-armed into making videotaped confessions, and ultimately released without being convicted of a single crime." Sui was among the first affected by the crackdown and was named on the list of victims provided by the China Human Rights Lawyers Concern Group.[53] One night in July 2015, he received a call from a security guard while he was in his apartment that his car had been in an accident and was scratched. He said he went outside and was abruptly whisked away by a group of police. Sui wasn't seen for almost five months.

Swedish national Dahlin, the cofounder of an NGO (nongovernmental organization) based out of Beijing that supplied training and legal aid for Chinese lawyers, was tipped off in January 2016 that he may be targeted by the authorities. As he was getting ready to leave his apartment for the airport in Beijing, 20 police officers arrived at his apartment. Dahlin told CNN that he was detained, as was his girlfriend, and the authorities ransacked his home and seized documents and computers.

CNN reported that a key tool being used in the crackdown is the introduction of "residential surveillance at a designated location" (RSDL), which was written into the Criminal Procedural Law in 2012. Under this amended law, residential surveillance should not last longer than a period of six months and families of those detained must be told of the arrest within 24 hours (unless contact is not possible). Moreover, the law mandates that all detainees have the right to a lawyer and to a meeting with their lawyer within 48 hours of the time of the request.

However, CNN wrote that the law "appeared to legalize a long-used practice of 'black jails'—a means of temporarily detaining people outside the Chinese legal system who could not be immediately charged with a crime.... Critics of the new system and former detainees say it gives arbitrary detention a legal gloss and normalizes enforced disappearances."[54]

Michael Caster, editor of *The People's Republic of the Disappeared*, explained the realities of RSDL to *The Diplomat*:

> "RSDL is so feared, arguably, because it is so quintessentially totalitarian, right down to the ubiquity of black hoods and midnight raids, evoking scenes from *V for Vendetta*. Little is known, but that is slowly changing, about what it means to disappear in China. Even a few years after it came into effect, in 2016 many people were still misled by the euphemistic title, the residential in RSDL. Torture is common. RSDL is a tool of repression, designed to terrorize and demonstrate power. It is so feared because it was designed to be feared."[55]

Sui and Dahlin said they were held in rooms that were sparsely furnished, had windows donning blackout curtains, and had fluorescent lights that were turned on 24 hours a day. Guards were present in the rooms watching them at every moment. Reading and writing materials were also prohibited.

Sui was accused by interrogators of inciting subversion and he described being detained at a training facility for police in Guangzhou. He was pressured to provide details regarding his job, his clients, his finances, his personal life, and his contacts. After refusing to answer the interrogators' questions, they continued to press him harder. Sui said, "They wouldn't let me sleep for four days and nights. By the fifth day, I felt like I was going to die." His will to resist was broken after enduring sleep deprivation and being threatened by investigators to have a flashlight shone in his eyes while being dangled from the ceiling with shackled hands.

Dahlin told CNN he was so bored that he almost eagerly anticipated the interrogations that were conducted daily. He said the interrogators used methods that were like those he'd seen in "bad American movies." He said, "They would have lots of people rush into your cell at night surrounding your bed just trying to scare you."

The interrogators were clear that they would also hold Dahlin's girlfriend, a Chinese national, until his case was resolved. Dahlin said, "She was taken hostage just to put pressure on me." He was told his girlfriend was being treated quite well because "[t]hey knew she had nothing to give them."

After enduring captivity for almost one month, Dahlin was informed that he would be released after making a confession on camera. He agreed to the demands to try to speed up his and his girlfriend's release from detainment. Dahlin entered a room with a camera from CCTV and was provided with a script. "I have caused harm to the Chinese government," he said in his confession that was broadcast nationwide and publicized on state-run newspapers. "I have hurt the feelings of the Chinese people. I apologize sincerely for this." Activists denounced this as a forced confession. Comparable confessions have been broadcast on CCTV many times since Xi's rise to power. Though Sui, like Dahlin, still maintains his innocence, he was also forced to do what the authorities wanted and make a similar confession.[56]

In a similar case, the US State Department spoke out against the January 2019 sentencing of prominent human rights lawyer Wang Quanzhang. Wang spent his career defending political campaigners, victims of land seizures, and Falun Gong followers—but ultimately fell victim to the 2015 arrests. He disappeared into what the BBC called "a legal black hole" where "his family did not know if he was alive or dead" for most of the three and a half years he was detained. Wang was not allowed to have family visits and was not able to appoint his own lawyer for his case.[57] Reuters reported he even fired his state-appointed lawyer.[58] When his wife began a 62-mile march to demand her husband's release, she was intercepted by police and placed under temporary house arrest with her five-year-old son. After a closed one-day trial, the court in Tianjin said that Wang was "found guilty of subverting state power, sentenced to four years and six months in prison, and deprived of political rights for five years."[59]

According to Michael Caster, many people in the human rights defense and civil society community "rallied around Wang Quanzhang and his wife Li Wenzu as symbolic of both abuse and resistance under Xi Jinping."[60] Wang, his wife, and so many of the other individuals detained or affected by the 709 crackdown are clear threats to the power of the Chinese Communist Party—especially when they gain support from inside and outside of China.

US State Department Deputy Spokesperson Robert Palladino in a press statement expressed concerns over Wang's sentencing and the continuing deprivation of rights and freedoms in China. Palladino said:

> "The United States is deeply concerned by the sentencing of human rights lawyer Wang Quanzhang...
>
> "We are troubled that China has subjected Mr. Wang to a three-and-a-half-year period of pre-trial detention, and has been held incommunicado, has been

deprived of legal counsel of his choosing, and that his chosen lawyer has been subjected to reprisals.

"...We remain concerned by the deteriorating situation for the rule of law, human rights, and fundamental freedoms in China, and continue to urge China to uphold its international human rights commitments and to respect the rule of law."[61]

TAKING ACTION

The Chinese Communist Party is committing extensive violations of human rights against the people of China. However, the United States can do more than simply issue reports and statements of condemnation. Recently, the Trump administration has taken action in some of these cases.

The case of Xie Yang was one such instance prompting US intervention. According to *The Washington Post*, the May 2017 trial of human rights lawyer Xie (who was taken into custody in July 2015) began "in true show-trial fashion." The court released a video of what was likely a forced confession where Xie admitted to subversion, denied any sort of torture, and attempted to persuade other lawyers not to "smear the image of the nation's party organs" during cases. Xie's daughter (who was born in the US) and other relatives fled China for Thailand but were put in jail for illegally entering the country. While they were being held, Chinese agents were posted at the jail aiming to bring them back to China. However, *The Washington Post* reported that in March 2017, US diplomats in Thailand stepped in by "literally sweeping the family out the back door of the jail to safety."[62,63]

At the time of this writing, the Trump administration is also considering putting restrictions on Chinese companies that are engaged in human rights violations. One such company is Hikvision, a Chinese company that is the world's largest maker of video surveillance technology.[64] According to *The Intercept,* the Chinese Communist Party owned 40 percent of the company as of June 2018.[65] The administration is considering adding it to the Commerce Department's Entity List, which requires US government approval before designated foreign companies and American companies can conduct business together.[66] Essentially, this would limit Hikvision's ability to purchase American technology.[67] *Bloomberg* also reported that Dahua, another video surveillance company, is being considered to be added to the trade blacklist.[68]

Hikvision and Dahua provide approximately one-third of the security cameras across the globe.[69] Both companies have received a total of $1 billion worth of government contracts to install the surveillance system monitoring millions of Uyghurs and other Muslim and ethnic minority groups in Xinjiang, which I have described at length. In an article for *Foreign Policy*, Charles Rollet wrote, "The projects include not only security cameras but also video analytics hubs, intelligent monitoring systems, big data centers, police checkpoints, and even drones."[70]

As Executive Director of the Victims of Communism Memorial Foundation Marion Smith wrote for *The Washington Post*, "[T]he surveillance state that Beijing has established in Xinjiang would not be possible without the companies' help."[71]

Even if the Trump administration does blacklist these companies, it won't prevent American investment from freely flowing into their bank accounts. Surely, if Americans knew about the widespread oppression taking place in Xinjiang, they would not support the Chinese Communist Party's actions. However, likely without the knowledge of individual American investors, many investment funds and state pensions have shares in Hikvision and Dahua.

Some funds in the United States purchase shares of the companies. For example, more than 26,000 Hikvision shares were owned by the New York State Teachers' Retirement System as of March 2019.[72] Moreover, with almost one million members and beneficiaries, the California State Teachers' Retirement System owned more than 4.3 million Hikvision shares as of June 2018.[73]

Americans also invest in Hikvision and Dahua through the MSCI Emerging Markets Index. Some funds are invested into the index directly and some funds follow the portfolio. Last year, the index added A-Class shares from Hikvision and Dahua, meaning that whenever a fund invests in the MSCI Emerging Markets Index, it is purchasing positions in these companies.[74]

Even if the Trump administration decides to add these companies to the Entity List, American individual and institutional investors are still allowed to keep their stocks and/or bonds in their investment portfolios. Moreover, neither the MSCI Emerging Markets Index, nor any other index or US fund, is required to divest such stocks. In effect, this keeps companies funded that have been designated as bad actors by the US government. In the case of Hikvision and Dahua, these companies could still get funding from American investors, despite their role in furthering the oppression in Xinjiang. This is wrong and must be corrected.

If every American investor knew where their money is going, I would suspect that many of them would object to such an atrocity. US funds and indexes need to be doing their fair share in ensuring that US capital does not end up in the hands of companies that are affiliated with committing human rights abuses on a mass scale. As president of RWR Advisory Group Roger Robinson told the *Financial Times* in March 2019, "State public pension funds, the MSCI EM index and other funds under management that hold companies like Hikvision have seemingly engaged in little, if any, human rights or national security-related due diligence."[75]

Though seven indexes have closed their positions in Hikvision at the time of this writing, the remaining funds and indexes should do the same.[76] Additionally, US individual and institutional investors should not be allowed to provide funding for foreign companies designated on the Entity List. This is one way that the US can take a stand against human rights abuses in China, but it is only a start.

The US should follow RWR's recommendation: Every

Chinese Company that is on an American financial exchange or is included in American indexed funds should be required to meet the Security and Exchange Commission's requirements for transparency. For some reason, hundreds of Chinese companies have been allowed to raise capital in the United States with little transparency. Some of these companies are known bad actors, jeopardize American national security interests, and are affiliated with facilitating human rights abuses. The simple requirement that Chinese companies meet the same standards as American companies if they are going to raise money in the United States will provide us with vastly more information about the Chinese economy. It will also pose a real dilemma for those companies where the Chinese dictatorship does not want the details revealed. Robinson has done excellent work as president of RWR Advisory Group to highlight and lead the charge on exposing this serious issue.

The United States should also create a continuing information campaign to get news about the world and about human rights to the Chinese people. Just because the totalitarian Chinese communist dictatorship wants to censor information received by the Chinese people, it doesn't mean we have to go along with it.

In the Cold War, we had substantial information operations including the *Voice of America*, *Radio Free Europe*, and a host of other clandestine activities—such as getting printing presses to Solidarity in Poland. We do virtually nothing about the most grotesque human rights violations against the Uyghurs and the Tibetans. We also fail to consistently recognize that all of China is a police state and that, as a consequence, everyone in China suffers from or is affected by government repression.

We must also draw attention to every religious group being persecuted, to civic groups being persecuted, and to all the other ethnic minorities being discriminated against. This human rights information campaign must consist of much more than just occasional speeches. It must be a structure and system of providing accurate news to the Chinese people despite the censorship efforts of the Chinese Communist Party dictatorship.

This must include a significant increase in online communications, such as sophisticated programs to break through the totalitarian Chinese Communist Party censorship of the internet. In the Cold War, the American government communications programs made a significant difference in holding out hope to dissidents and in getting information through the Soviet's totalitarian censorship. We need to reestablish that aggressiveness and intensity.

Google considered—and then was shamed out of—building a censored search engine for the Chinese Communist Party's government. Code-named Project Dragonfly, work on the initiative has officially been terminated.[77] However, if Google had stuck to its founding company motto of "don't be evil," the company never would have considered this totalitarian project in the first place. If Google upheld its current parent company's motto "do the right thing," it would be aggressively trying to (legally) undermine the Chinese Communist Party's censorship laws and bring freedom of speech and information to the Chinese people.

Following on Google's near fall into darkness, American companies that are participating in building capabilities for police state repression should be identified and required to cut off that type of antihuman rights activity. This is an area in which Senator Marco Rubio has exhibited great leadership.

Our goal must be to become the ally of the Chinese people against the totalitarian dictatorship. America is not the enemy of the Chinese people. America is opposed to the totalitarian system currently imposed on the Chinese people. The United States—at every level—should reach out to every human rights activist group in the world and collaborate on a campaign to end totalitarian oppression and liberate the Chinese people.

CHAPTER SIX

THE ART OF PERSUASION

From the Soviet Union to Cuba to Venezuela, wherever true socialism or communism has been adopted, it has delivered anguish and devastation and failure. Those who preach the tenets of these discredited ideologies only contribute to the continued suffering of the people who live under these cruel systems.

—President Donald Trump, September 2017[1]

We must take cultivating and disseminating the core socialist values as a fundamental project for integrating the people's mindset and reinforcing our social foundations. We should inherit and carry forward the fine traditional Chinese culture and virtues, disseminate the core socialist values and educate the people extensively, guide and encourage the people to act according to them, to respect and follow moral standards, to pursue lofty moral ideals, and to reinforce the ideological and moral foundation of socialism with Chinese characteristics.

—General Secretary Xi Jinping, February 2014[2]

The twentieth century saw the art of persuasion, or propaganda, flourish as a weapon of politics and government. Every radical group that wanted to transform society had to win the war of words and images. Radicals understood exactly what Prime Minister Margaret Thatcher meant when she said, "First you win the argument, then you win the vote." From Lenin, Trotsky, and Stalin to Hitler, Mussolini, and Mao, there was a consistent emphasis on the power of words and the central role of propaganda in ensuring public support for the movement and then the government.

It is no coincidence that George Orwell wrote *1984* to describe the power of the totalitarian propaganda system to define and enforce its version of reality. It is also significant that Orwell placed his totalitarian state in Great Britain. He was arguing that all people everywhere are susceptible to a totalitarian system.

The Chinese Communists studied Lenin and Stalin. They knew that they were in a race with the Kuomintang to attract and mobilize the Chinese people. It was Mao's genius as a charismatic propagandist that propelled him to the leadership of the Chinese Communist Party. Throughout the 1920s, 1930s, and 1940s, Mao and his supporters were focused on winning the propaganda war. As Mao said, the troops are like the fish in the sea of people.[3] Therefore, it was vital for the revolutionary to understand, communicate with, convert, and organize the sea of peasants whose sheer numbers dominated China.

Today, the Chinese Communist Party has nearly a century of manipulating information and people to win the contest for public support. As such, propaganda and silencing dissenting speech are critical principles of maintaining the power of the Chinese Communist Party. Chinese leaders have historically seen free speech and opposing political views as direct threats to the totalitarian regime. You are either with the party, or you are an enemy of the state.

Back in 1957, the CIA found in its *The United Front in*

Communist China report (declassified in 1999) that the Chinese Communist Party uses "a vast and complex network of unofficial (non-party, non-government) organs" to control what its citizens can say and do. The CIA reported that in 1949, China formed a bureaucratic association that all Chinese journalists and professional writers had to join. The party corralled journalists and writers this way "because of their potentially dangerous individualism and usefulness in propaganda activities." According to the CIA, the state-run writers' association had two primary functions: to "identify and control actual or potential dissidents" and to "popularize important programs of the party and government."[4] Moreover, Mao Zedong's ruthless Cultural Revolution, beginning in 1966, implemented aggressive propaganda tactics as this movement was directed toward consolidating his political power. In the preliminary stages of this era, the party published and distributed *The Little Red Book, Quotations from Chairman Mao Zedong.* The military printed the pocket-sized book, which contained 267 of Mao's sayings. China's Ministry of Culture endeavored to distribute a copy to every Chinese citizen. During the Cultural Revolution, authorities routinely checked Chinese citizens to see if they were carrying the book—and challenged them to quote from it.[5]

The state-mandated writers association and Mao's *Little Red Book* set the stage for today's brand of twenty-first-century Chinese communist propaganda. In addition to relying on old techniques, General Secretary Xi Jinping has been solidly focused on harnessing technology to control communication—both public and private—and strictly limiting what ideas Chinese citizens encounter and are allowed to disseminate. During the first meeting of the Office of the Central Leading Group for Cyberspace Affairs in 2014, Xi's instructions were clear:

> "Doing a proper job on online public opinion work is a long-term task, and we must innovate and advance

> online propaganda, using the principles of internet communication, upholding the main theme, inciting positive energy, actively cultivating and putting into practice socialist core values, having a good grasp of timeliness, intensity, and effect in online public opinion channeling, ensuring a clear and bright online space."[6]

The practical application of "doing a proper job on online public opinion work" in part means censoring the internet in China. The so-called Great Firewall of China is highly restricted and blocks thousands of websites from appearing on the Chinese internet. There is no access to Google, Facebook, YouTube, *The New York Times*, or many other staples of the World Wide Web, according to HikingGFW.org, a website created by Xiao Qiang, an adjunct professor at the School of Information at the University of California, Berkeley. In addition to blocking sites and search engines, *Bloomberg* reported that the Chinese communist government regularly employs 50,000 people to "enforce censorship, barring websites it disapproves of and forces search engines to filter out content considered harmful."[7] As such, videos, websites, and articles about the Tiananmen Square protest, for example, have little coverage online.

Because internet content providers must register with the government and are held liable for any content on their sites—regardless of who created it—most internet businesses and social media sites employ in-house censors to protect themselves from reprimand or potential punishment. Further, there are many examples of Chinese citizens being arrested and detained for social media posts and private messages alike. In 2010, authorities arrested Cheng Jianping, a human rights activist, for tweeting "Charge, angry youth" to encourage young protestors. Wang Liming, a cartoonist known as Rebel Pepper, was threatened with arrest after sharing an article about Tibet from a non-Chinese newspaper in a messaging group. He later spent a night in jail for the same offense.[8]

On the proactive propaganda front, the Party Central Committee and the Communist Youth League employ Chinese students to post, comment, and repost articles that align with the Communist Party's positions. According to a March 2014 directive, the students are to:

> "[F]ully implement the directives of the Party Central Committee and General Secretary Xi Jinping; to sufficiently display the power of the university and college Communist Youth League cadres, the mobilization of team cadres, and the strength of young students vigorously advocating for socialist values on the internet."[9]

In addition to assigned content and discussions from the official Communist Youth League's social media accounts, the students are instructed to share, repost, and comment on "any and all politically correct content from various media platforms received via personal accounts."[10]

CHINA'S FAKE NEWS

The Chinese Communist Party's internal propaganda program is robust. But its external propaganda is far more expansive, calculated, and insidious. The US-China Economic and Security Review Commission (USCC) was created by Congress in 2000 to study and analyze potential challenges (and threats) that China poses to the United States. In 2009, the commission reported that the Chinese Communist Party "believes that projecting a positive international image for China is necessary to attract foreign investment and to boost China's economic and technological development."[11] The international propaganda effort focuses on promoting China's economic growth, desire for a peaceful global system, and the Chinese Communist Party's stability.[12] As China continues to expand globally under Xi's leadership, with projects such as the Belt and Road initiative international perceptions and opinions of China and its ruling Communist Party are critical.

According to the USCC, Chinese Communist Party leaders claim Western news outlets seek to undermine party goals and express a negative bias toward the country. To combat this, China has created a fleet of "façade independent news outlets" that are directly—but secretly—influenced either by the Chinese Communist Party or Chinese state-owned organizations. In 2009, the Chinese government instituted a code of conduct for all Chinese journalists (both domestic and working abroad). The code demands that they must "spread positive information" about the country and the Communist Party.[13] To really drive this home, in 2013, China ordered all of its journalists to take Marxism classes, according to the *South China Morning Post*. The article reported that "the nation's 307,000 reporters, producers, and editors will... have to sit through at least two days of Marxism classes" ordered by the Communist Party.[14]

In addition to policing individual reporters, the Chinese Communist Party also controls entire news outlets. Some of these distribute news within the United States and are registered as foreign agents under the Foreign Agents Registration Act.

To those who may be skeptical of China's intention to control its media, consider General Secretary Xi's comments during a February 19, 2016, speech at the China Communist Party News and Public Opinion Work Conference. Xi said, "[M]edia run by the Party and government are propaganda positions of the Party and government, and they must reflect the Party."[15] He went on to say that all work of the party's news organizations must "reflect the will of the Party, mirror the views of the Party, protection of the Party and acting for the Party; they must all increase their consciousness of falling in line, maintaining a high level of uniformity with the Party in ideology, politics, and action."[16]

It is important for Americans—especially in media—to understand that there is no difference between Chinese journalism and messaging from the Chinese Communist Party. They are one and the same. Journalists who break from party messaging or criticize Chinese leadership are often either jailed or forced to flee the country. Freedom of the press in China is nonexistent.

POP CULTURE PROPAGANDA

The Chinese Communist Party has a vice grip on Chinese media, but it has also started to wield alarming power over media from other countries—including America. China has a strong hold on Hollywood and has used its market power to cause several films to alter their final product to be able to distribute in China.

China only started allowing foreign films into the country in 1994. As a result, Hollywood films became extremely popular among the Chinese public. *The Epoch Times* reported that the 1998 film *Titanic* kept a box office record in China for several years. Due to efforts from Hollywood lobbying groups, China started allowing the distribution of 34 foreign films a year on a revenue-sharing basis, as long as those films pass through the Chinese film committee first.[17] (Though this limit has been surpassed in recent years for tactical or unofficial reasons.[18]) Of the top 100 highest grossing films worldwide from 1997 to 2013, China only helped finance 12, according to *The New York Times*. However, the Old Gray Lady found that from 2014 to 2018 China cofinanced 41 top grossing Hollywood films. These included *Transformers*, *Kung Fu Panda*, and *Wonder Woman*.[19]

Hollywood regularly caters to China because of its financial draw and the country only allowing a limited number of foreign films per year. Giuseppe Richeri, with Global Media and China, found that between 2010 and 2015, the Chinese film industry increased the number of movie screens in China from 6,253 to 31,627. The Chinese box office grew from $1.5 billion to $6.8 billion in the same period. Meanwhile, Richeri wrote that in 2015, nine out of the top 20 grossing films in China were produced or coproduced by Hollywood—namely Universal, Walt Disney, and Paramount.[20] The Chinese market for film continues to increase. According to a *Variety* article by Patrick Frater in 2017, ticket sales in China "increased by 18 percent from 1.37 billion in 2016 to 1.62 billion in 2017" and the number of screens "increased by 23 percent from 41,179 to 50,776" between 2016 and 2017.[21] Compared to the United States, China's film market is not very far behind. According to Statista, the US and China dominated the leading film markets worldwide in 2018 by gross box office revenue. The US saw $11.08 billion and China brought in $9.15 billion. For comparison, Japan was the third highest-grossing, with only $2.09 billion.[22] Hollywood continues to cater to China, because, as Richeri wrote, "it is the only large market with the sustained growth prospects."

Essentially, China is using its market power as leverage to influence American films without having to use any means of direct influence. At this point, production companies are self-censoring to ensure their films can make it into the country's enormous and profitable market. As an example, Aynee Kokas, the author of *Hollywood in China* and professor at the University of Virginia, told Business Insider in October 2016 that "no Hollywood producer that wants to take advantage of the Chinese market would at this point include a film that includes anything about Taiwan, about Tibet, about Tiananmen."[23]

According to the Business Insider story, in the original version of Marvel's *Doctor Strange*, the producers changed the character named "The Ancient One" from being Tibetan to Celtic to appease the Chinese Communist Party. It turned out to be a good investment for Marvel. *Doctor Strange* was incredibly successful in China with a $44 million opening weekend, the third highest Marvel opening after *Avengers: Age of Ultron* and *Captain America: Civil War.* [24] C. Robert Cargill, screenwriter for the film, explained:

> "The Ancient One was a racial stereotype who comes from a region of the world that is in a very weird political place. He originates from Tibet. So if you

> acknowledge that Tibet is a place and that he's Tibetan, you risk alienating one billion people who think that that's bullshit and risk the Chinese government going 'Hey you know one of the biggest film-watching countries in the world? We're not going to show your movie because you decided to get political.' "[25]

Similarly, *World War Z* was a 2013 apocalyptic film based on the 2006 novel of the same name. The film depicts an outbreak of a zombie virus that is going to destroy the world. Initially, the script put the virus's origin in China. This small plot point almost got the film barred from China. After watching the final cut, the studio advised the producers to cite a different country as the origin of the outbreak.[26]

In another case, *The Epoch Times* cited the 2012 remake of *Red Dawn*, which was originally a 1984 film about a fictional Soviet invasion of the United States. Originally, the remake script named China as the invading country, but this was met with protests from the Communist country. Eventually, the invaders were edited to be North Koreans so the film could be shown in China.[27] The studio did this out of fear of losing out on a huge box office in China. According to *The Los Angeles Times*, MGM spent nearly one million dollars changing an opening scene showing the backdrop of the film, reediting two scenes, and digitally altering Chinese symbols that were already filmed and replacing them with North Korean symbols.[28]

However, China's influence on American film doesn't stop there. In addition to influencing plot points, China's market power has affected casting as well. Many Hollywood stars have been banned from entering China because they have been critical of the Chinese Communist Party. Brad Pitt was blacklisted just for starring in the 1997 film *Seven Years in Tibet*. This was an additional obstacle for *World War Z* to be shown in China, but it was apparently helped by the studio changing the origin of the zombie virus.

But this sort of intimidation is not just limited to companies in the film industry. In fact, the Chinese Communist Party intimidates a wide variety of American companies when they do not abide by party lines and counter its politically charged messaging.

For instance, several companies were forced to apologize for acknowledging Hong Kong and Taiwan as countries, according to Tara Francis Chan of Business Insider. Marriott was contacted by the Cyberspace Administration of China about a mail questionnaire, which included Tibet, Hong Kong, Macao, and Taiwan under the question: "Which country are you from?"[29] State-run news agency, Xinhua, reported the bureau then conducted interviews with Marriott representatives and ordered the hotel chain to shut down its Chinese website for a week while the site was reviewed by investigators. Wu Hai, a lawyer in Shanghai, told Xinhua that including Tibet, Hong Kong, Macau, and Taiwan as countries "directly violated China's cybersecurity and advertising laws" and, Wu said, "may face a maximum fine of 1 million yuan (153,822 U.S. dollars) or have its business license revoked."[30]

This may seem like a nuanced technicality, but in reality, it is an example of the Chinese Communist Party intimidating private companies into taking political stances on sovereignty issues. Since China has a larger market, the party has more power to force compliance. In a similar case, the Civil Aviation Administration of China demanded that Delta Air Lines offer an apology for listing Taiwan and Tibet as countries on its website, according to Business Insider. The airline quickly responded, stating that it had made a "grave mistake." The Chinese airline regulator said it would "require all foreign airlines operating routes to China to conduct comprehensive investigations of their website" in order to "comply with China's laws and regulations to prevent a similar thing from happening," according to Brenda Goh and Josh Ruwitch of Reuters.[31]

BORROWING ANOTHER PAGE FROM LENIN'S PLAYBOOK

An important concept to keep in mind when looking at the Chinese Communist Party's widespread propaganda efforts is the "united front." United front work is critical for the survival of the Communist Party. It is the strategic concept describing political influence activities used to keep control of the party message by co-opting and suppressing opposition to its ideology and interests. "United front" is a term used to describe a strategy borrowed from the Soviet Union and is in fact a Leninist tactic.[32] In *"Left-Wing" Communism, an Infantile Disorder*, Lenin wrote:

> "The more powerful enemy can be vanquished only by exerting the utmost effort...and also by taking advantage of every, even the smallest, opportunity of gaining a mass ally....Those who fail to understand this, fail to understand even a particle of Marxism, or of scientific, modern Socialism *in general*."[33]

In a 2014 speech, Xi underscored the importance of united front work by describing it as one of China's "magic weapons."[34] In China, united front work is coordinated by the United Front Work Department. Dr. Gerald Groot, senior lecturer in Chinese Studies at the School of Social Sciences, Facility of Arts at the University of Adelaide in Australia, called it "the organization through which the Party reaches out to many key non-party groups within and outside China to achieve important political goals."[35]

Professor Anne-Marie Brady, global fellow at the Kissinger Institute on China and the United States, in a 2017 report titled *Magic Weapons: China's Political Influence Activities under Xi Jinping*, wrote that united front work is essentially a partnership between party and state organizations. Brady noted that it is useful in both domestic and foreign policy. She argued that "united front activities incorporate working with groups and prominent individuals in society; information management and propaganda; and it has also frequently been a means of facilitating espionage."[36]

United front officials do this by trying to "develop relationships with foreign and overseas Chinese personages (the more influential, the better) to influence, subvert, and if necessary, bypass the policies of their governments and promote the interests of the party globally."[37] In the 19th National Congress of the Communist Party of China, Xi announced that the Chinese Communist Party will, "maintain extensive contacts with overseas Chinese nationals, returned Chinese and their relatives and unite them so that they can join our endeavors to revitalize the Chinese nation."[38]

Xi called the united front "an important way to ensure the success of the Party's cause" and called on those present at the 19th party congress to "maintain commitment to it long term" and "uphold the banner of patriotism and socialism, strive to achieve great unity and solidarity, balance commonality and diversity, and expand common ground and the convergence of interests."[39] Moreover, according to a USCC staff research report in August 2018, the goal for overseas Chinese work is to "use ethnic, cultural, economic or political ties to mobilize sympathetic overseas Chinese communities—ideally of their own accord—to advocate for the interests of the [Chinese Communist Party] and marginalize its opponents."[40] One of the party's most important initiatives as a part of China's united front work is the Confucius Institutes that have been established worldwide.

INFLUENCING YOUNG AMERICANS

Perhaps the most insidious effort of the Chinese communist propaganda machine is its infiltration of the American education system. National Association of Scholars Director of Research Projects Rachelle Peterson wrote in *Outsourced to*

China: Confucius Institutes and Soft Power in American Higher Education that there are Confucius Institutes located in more than 100 universities and colleges throughout the United States. (In June 2019, the National Association of Scholars updated this figure to 90 Confucius Institutes in the US.[41]) These are not typical academic programs. The Office of Chinese Languages Council International (commonly known as the Hanban), an agency of the Ministry of Education of the People's Republic of China, oversees and staffs these institutes. Peterson wrote that the Hanban in China also funds and organizes smaller Confucius Classrooms at "501 primary and secondary schools throughout the United States."[42]

According to the Hanban, the goal of these institutes is "to provide Chinese language and cultural teaching resources and services worldwide" and to "contribute to the development of multiculturalism and global understanding by supporting Chinese language programs at educational institutes of various types and levels in other countries."[43] The Hanban provides resources for "Chinese language, culture, humanities, and social sciences to teachers and students of Confucius Institutes (Classrooms), sinologists, scholars in China study and people, especially young people who would like to know about Chinese language and culture." Two examples of courses listed at the Confucius Institute of Rutgers University in New Jersey are:

- Contemporary China: Social Economic and Cultural Perspectives that looks at the "contemporary social, economic and cultural transformations of China in domestic, regional and global context; challenges and prospects of Chinese society in the 21st century."
- Confucianism, Neo-Confucianism, and New Confucianism that covers "the continuity and innovations of the ideas within Confucian traditions and throughout the development of Chinese culture."[44]

On the surface, these institutes seem innocuous; however Confucius Institutes have deep ties to the Chinese Communist Party. In 2009, Li Changchun, a member of the Politburo Standing Committee and Chairman of the 17th Central Leading Group for Propaganda and Ideology, called Confucius Institutes "an important part of China's overseas propaganda set-up."[45] The governing council for the Hanban includes the heads of 12 Chinese government ministries including the State Press and Publications Administration and the Ministry of Foreign Affairs.[46]

First, these institutes pose a potential security risk. FBI Director Christopher Wray testified on February 13, 2018, that the institutes were "something that we're watching warily and in certain instances have developed...appropriate investigative steps." However, on a purely academic level, the professors hired by China are required to adhere to Chinese laws including pledging to "not damage the national interests of China."[47] According to Peterson's report, when Chinese teachers were asked about the importance of Tiananmen Square, they responded by talking about the architecture—rather than the 1989 massacre. This is because professors could be terminated if they violate Chinese law or engage in activities the party deems unfit.[48] Aside from possibly showing American students how totalitarian regimes operate, what possible academic benefit could these institutes provide?

Moreover, the US Government Accountability Office (GAO), in February 2019 reviewed 90 of the contracts between US universities and the Hanban to create Confucius Institutes.[49] The office discovered that in three of the universities the Hanban "agreed to provide funds ranging from $900,000 to $1.7 million to construct new facilities." In 85 of the universities, the Hanban would be responsible for providing teaching materials for the institute. In 86, the Hanban would be responsible for providing at least one teacher and pay his or her salary. In 61, the

Hanban would provide start-up funds ranging from $50,000 to $150,000. Only three stated that Confucius Institute teachers would be subject to the universities' policies.[50]

A US Senate Permanent Subcommittee on Investigations staff report titled *China's Impact on the U.S. Education System* found that "China directly provided over $158 million in funding to U.S. schools for Confucius Institutes." Also, at the onset the "Hanban typically provides a U.S. school between $100,000 and $200,000 in start-up costs."[51]

Notably, the National Defense Authorization Act (NDAA) for Fiscal Year 2019 prohibits funds appropriated for the Department of Defense to be used for Chinese language instruction provided by a Confucius Institute. Furthermore, the NDAA also does not permit funds to be used for a Chinese language program at an institution of higher education that has a Confucius Institute (unless a waiver is granted).[52] This decisive congressional action helped to reaffirm many concerns that have been raised surrounding China's Confucius Institutes, namely that they are tools for propaganda, lack transparency, and are a threat to the freedoms cherished by the American higher education system. Though some of these concerns have been heeded as many Confucius Institutes have been closed, many still remain operational.

Also in 2019, the US Senate's Permanent Subcommittee on Investigations recommended that unless "there is full transparency regarding how Confucius Institutes operate and full reciprocity for U.S. cultural outreach efforts on college campuses in China" those still operational in the United States should close. Citing that these institutes are funded "with strings attached that can compromise academic freedom," if the institutes are not shut down, the Senate panel recommended that the US Justice Department should think about making Chinese-hired Confucius Institute teachers register as foreign agents.[53]

So far, the Chinese Communist Party has not shown much

interest in reciprocity with regard to the institutes. As a response to these Confucius Institutes, in 2010 the US Department of State attempted to establish American Cultural Centers throughout China to "tell America's story through explaining U.S. politics, values, culture and history."[54] The State Department noted that the intent was to provide a space for community and allow "interactions that enable Chinese audiences to better understand the United States, its culture, society, government, language, law, economic system, and values."[55]

In 2011, when the number of Confucius Institutes in the United States was at its height, there were only five similar centers in China. Further, these were only operating in American embassies or consulates, which prevented the majority of the Chinese population from attending. Additionally, according to the Senate report, in 2012, the State Department gave more than two dozen American universities grants to establish American Cultural Centers (ACCs) in China, but the Chinese host schools began slow-walking the process. Some canceled the centers altogether without much explanation. The America centers that were established were constantly hamstrung. According to the US Senate report:

> "The ACCs that did open found they needed permission from their Chinese host schools to hold most cultural events. One Chinese host school refused to allow its ACC to host a play about the life of Muhammad Ali. Another denied approval for a lecture series on policy issues facing Americans. One U.S. school official who staffed an ACC told the Subcommittee that members of the local Communist Party often participated in the approval process. Another U.S. school official left the ACC after two sessions of extensive questioning by Chinese police officers regarding her involvement with the ACC and the State Department. When the U.S. school official returned to the United States, a colleague told

her that Chinese police interrogation of school officials was common and that she was now just 'part of the club.' "[56]

Actions taken by the Chinese Communist Party—such as denying American officials from entering China and interrogating American staff members on Chinese campuses—caused many of the remaining ACCs to close down. It is clear that the Chinese Communist Party has no interest in reciprocal cultural education. In the National Association of Scholar's report, Peterson found that in 2015, Yuan Guiren, the Education Minister in China, said that "books highlighting Western values had no place in classrooms" and that Chinese universities must "ensure that Xi's ideology is front and center."[57]

But even if every Confucius Institute within the US is shut down, American academics will still be subject to the Chinese Communist Party's coercion and intimidation. According to the USCC's 2009 Report to Congress, "the Chinese government seeks to shape opinion in elite policy-making circles by influencing the commentary about China and US-China relations that emerges from U.S. academics and think tanks." China accomplishes this by rewarding scholars who are friendly to China with "career-enhancing interviews and documents" and by punishing scholars who say things that the Chinese Communist Party doesn't like by denying visas to conduct research in China.[58]

A declassified page of a CIA report that was obtained in 2018 noted that "The [Chinese Communist Party] provides 'strings-attached' funding to academic institutions and think tanks to deter research that casts it in a negative light."[59] The report stated, "It has used this tactic to reward pro-China viewpoints and coerce Western academic publications and conferences to self-censor. The [Chinese Communist Party] often denies visas to academics who criticize the regime, encouraging many China scholars to preemptively self-censor so they can maintain access to the country on which their research depends."

Dr. Ross Terrill, a former professor of modern Chinese history at Harvard who is now an independent scholar for the Fairbanks Center for Chinese Studies, reiterated this point back in 2009 when he told the USCC that "self-censorship" among journalists in China was "a daily necessity." He said a "diluted form" is pressed upon editors and academics. "Folk worry about their next visa, their access to a sensitive area like Xinjiang for research or take a Beijing point of view because of the largesse available for their projects from the Chinese side," Terrill said.[60]

Dr. Victor Shih, a professor of political science at Northwestern University, also testified before the USCC in 2009 and said:

> "People who do research in Xinjiang in a very serious way are barred from going to China. So many of us avoid that topic…and there [are] the economic interests which face both academic and government officials. They don't want to offend the Chinese government and…close the doors to future opportunities to make money."[61]

INDOCTRINATING THE WORLD

The Chinese Communist Party also uses more traditional methods and organizations to spread its propaganda through official and political channels. China Foreign Affairs University, or CFAU (which was previously the Diplomacy School of the People's University of China), was founded in 1955 in Beijing. According to its website, it is "dedicated to grooming China's most promising young minds with global vision and great learning to work for China's foreign services and for world peace and prosperity." The organization is run by China's Ministry of Foreign Affairs. In the 1950s and 1960s, the CFAU trained more than 100 international students from the USSR, Eastern Europe, and Vietnam. After graduation, some of the students became ambassadors to China or obtained senior positions in their home country's government. Today, the CFAU organizes training programs for diplomats from Asia, Africa, Latin America, Eastern Europe, Central Asia, and Russia—all nations in which China is seeking to build influence. According to the organization, more than 3,000 diplomats from 150 countries have participated.[62] A variety of programs teach courses in "China's basic national conditions and policies," "Diplomacy and international relations," and "Chinese Language." Participants also get the opportunity to attend meetings with Ministry of Foreign Affairs and Ministry of Commerce officials.

Similarly, Beijing Foreign Studies University is run by the Chinese Ministry of Education. In 1959, it merged with the Beijing Russian Institute. The university calls itself the "cradle of diplomats" because more than 400 ambassadors and 1,000 counselors have trained there. The university has 1,326 international students and teaches in 83 languages. It offers postgraduate degrees in Scientific Socialism, International Communist Movement, and Chinese and Foreign Political Systems.

UNCOVERING THE FACTS

The Communist Party's tight control over the domestic and international spread of information is important for Americans to understand. The propaganda machine gives the Chinese Communist Party substantial influence over the perceived image of the party worldwide. By reporting on current events and pop culture, the media and internet play a huge part in shaping the view of modern China and the role it plays in the world today.

The US government and the American media must examine and expose the activities of the Chinese Communist Party's United Front Work Department. In many ways, the United Front Work Department is the modern equivalent of the Soviet Union's Comintern (Communist International) and its successor, the Cominform (Communist Information Bureau). The impact of the United Front Work Department on Chinese media around the world, on academics, and on campuses needs serious in-depth scrutiny.

The role of the Confucius Institutes and Classrooms in infiltrating campuses needs much more study and transparency. These global education systems shape international views of Chinese culture and society (as perceived by the Communist Party) and promote China's soft power. Senator Ted Cruz and Congressman Francis Rooney's SHEET Act (Stop Higher Education Espionage and Theft Act) is a good step in the right direction.[63]

But lastly, we must keep in mind, in the absence of a free press and the freedom of speech in China, there is limited accountability for the failures and tragedies caused throughout the Chinese Communist Party's 70-year rule. The tight control on information gives the Chinese Communist Party the power to write the narrative for China today but also to rewrite the past. It is truly Orwell's *1984* but with Chinese characteristics.

We see a somewhat related debate occurring in the US, as we question whether we should rename streets or tear down statues bearing the persona of Confederate leaders. The Civil War was a painful and tragic part of our American history, but we still teach our children about this period of our country's history to prevent something equally horrible from happening again. What is to be said about what students in China, and what those outside of China studying Communist Party resources, learn about the horrors of the Great Leap Forward, the atrocities of the Cultural Revolution, and the devastation at Tiananmen Square?

Just as we must critically examine the propaganda being spread by the Chinese Communist Party, and objectively analyze such messaging, what's equally important is what's not being told as part of the story—as some of the most revealing truths about the Chinese Communist Party and its turbulent history are shrouded in silence. The Chinese propaganda machine is perhaps the most developed, meticulous agit-prop outfit in the world. It has existed right before our eyes for decades, and we are only now beginning to see it in its full form.

This represents an enormous, ongoing challenge for the United States, because if it prevails, we will have to reteach every generation the real history between China and the world.

CHAPTER SEVEN

THE 5G CHALLENGE

We cannot allow any other country to outcompete the United States in this powerful industry of the future. We are leading by so much in so many different industries of that type, and we just can't let that happen. The race to 5G is a race America must win, and it's a race, frankly, that our great companies are now involved in. We've given them the incentive they need. It's a race that we will win.

—President Donald Trump, April 2019[1]

Our greatest strength lies in our socialist system, which enables us to pool resources in a major mission. This is the key to our success. We have relied on this in making noticeable scientific breakthroughs in the past. And today we will still rely on this in achieving leapfrog scientific and technological innovations. We will develop a new mechanism under the socialist market economy to pool our resources in scientific initiatives.

—General Secretary Xi Jinping, May 2016[2]

The most immediate and pressing challenge that we face with China is the race to develop and deploy the world's 5G communications network. At the time I'm writing this, we are well behind in this effort—and by the time you are reading this, we are likely even further behind. The Chinese Communist Party has been working toward globally dominating in this technology, and the United States is only now waking up to the fact that we are in a serious competition.

This competition is especially important because it is the first head-to-head test case of the Chinese Communist Party's ability to mobilize a society-on-society competition on a grand scale. We must learn how to deal with the 5G challenge both because of its inherent importance and because we are going to face many challenges like this over the next few years.

I feel so strongly about this challenge that I wrote a long report for members of the US House of Representatives and the US Senate on this subject. This chapter is, in part, a summary and an update of that report.

Our major telecommunications companies, namely AT&T and Verizon, in partnership with European companies, led in the deployment of 4G LTE (the current worldwide standard for mobile communication). As a result, the rest of the world adopted an American model for developing the international networks. I know, many of you may be thinking, "Newt, why do I care if the Chinese develop the next generation of mobile networks? Chinese companies already create most of the components in my cell phone. Isn't this just a natural result of global economic competition? What's the big deal?"

The big deal is that whoever leads in this sector globally will likely lead in many other future sectors. The development of 5G (or fifth generation) technology isn't simply an incremental update of 4G LTE. It's not simply going to let you download movies faster or improve your phone's ability to navigate traffic during your commute. This technology is the backbone of what has been called the 4th Industrial Revolution. It will be the groundwork for developing what used to be the stuff of science fiction—fully self-driving cars, smart homes and cities, long-distance surgery, autonomous manufacturing, advanced virtual reality, and many other innovations.

The implications of the capabilities associated with 5G are most clearly communicated on a sign I saw in one of Samsung's South Korean facilities. It says: "5G is to 4G as a computer is to a typewriter." On our current 4G LTE networks, it takes about six minutes to download a movie. With 5G, the download time drops to just over three seconds.[3] Today's 4G networks support only 2,000 connected devices per square kilometer, while 5G will be able to support up to one million devices in the same space.[4]

5G technology will introduce new capabilities—but also security vulnerabilities—as it increases wireless capacity and changes the way our physical and virtual environments interact. The growing Internet of Things (IoT) has already begun to transform the modern world. (Do you know anyone with a smart refrigerator, a home security system, or a thermostat they control with a cell phone app?) 5G will accelerate these changes exponentially across virtually every aspect of our lives.

If American companies are at the forefront of developing this infrastructure, then American companies will be the ones developing the future technologies that interact with this new network. This is exactly what happened with the American-led development of 4G LTE. For example, out of America's 4G dominance, we saw the rise of Netflix, Hulu, and other American streaming services.

The other big reason we need to win the race to 5G dominance is to prevent the internet and communication networks of the future from being controlled—and watched—by a communist totalitarian state. The Chinese Communist Party already censors the internet within China. Websites are routinely blocked, and Chinese citizens are jailed or worse for criticizing the government online. You cannot find a picture of Winnie the Pooh online in China because an internet meme previously compared General Secretary Xi Jinping to the cartoon bear.

Imagine a world in which Chinese totalitarian rules are applied to the internet, your cell phone is monitored by Beijing, your search engine is censored by Chinese communist authorities, and your facial identity is tracked around the world and archived in China. This world is incredibly likely—and perhaps a decade away—if we continue to be confused and disorganized in building a 5G communication system.

The Chinese Communist Party's penetration and manipulation of our free and open American system are happening now. It is not a distant, future problem. One Chinese app, TikTok (which I discussed in the chapter about data collection and big data), has already deeply penetrated the American teen market.[5] TikTok and its Chinese version have been downloaded worldwide more than a billion times. One of my colleagues recently saw a banner advertising TikTok behind home plate at an Atlanta Braves game.

Finally, the vast amount of information that will flow through the world's communication networks could also be up for grabs if the Chinese Communist Party's history of spying and rule-breaking are any indication of how it will conduct itself in the worldwide telecommunications business. If the party controls the infrastructure behind the global internet, personal privacy and individual freedoms will not factor into any equation. The Communist Party will aggressively mine personal data from every device that touches the network. There will be no one to stop them.

HUAWEI AND THE FIGHT FOR 5G DOMINANCE

The contest over 5G is the first great strategic competition in the struggle between the Chinese Communist Party and the United States. As of today, we are losing.

China is succeeding through its champion, Huawei. This telecommunications giant has been aggressively seeking to build out the worldwide 5G network with the help of heavy subsidies from the Chinese government. At the time I'm writing this, Huawei is operating in 170 countries (through existing 4G contracts and new 5G contracts). Meanwhile, the major US telecommunications companies have virtually no international 5G presence. They are focusing exclusively within the United States—and only in urban areas. Similarly, their international 4G business reaches to Canada and Mexico, but that's about it. The gap between Huawei and non-Chinese companies is growing so rapidly that within a few years, we may encounter a tipping point in which the Chinese penetration and saturation of markets enables China to define and dominate the internet and all wireless communications.

The insert map showing the Huawei footprint, created with data from RWR Advisory Group, depicts the technology company's worldwide presence and provides insight to the scale of China's efforts.[6] Visualizing Huawei's immense global footprint reinforces the necessity of, and urgency for, an American strategy to counteract China's worldwide efforts.

In many ways, this contest with Huawei represents our third great contest for the survival of our rule of law and freedom-based civilization. We are as unprepared for the new totalitarian Chinese challenge as we were in 1939 for Nazi Germany and Imperial Japan—or in 1946 for the worldwide challenge of the Soviet Union. Just as those earlier contests required new thinking, new strategies, new institutions, new allocations of resources, and new creativity, the competition with totalitarian China will force all of American society to, as President Lincoln said, "think anew and act anew."[7]

Jeremy Hunt, foreign secretary of the United Kingdom, recently said:

> "We are right to have a degree of caution about the role of large Chinese companies because of the degree of control the Chinese state is able to exercise over them in the way that would not be possible if they were large Western companies.

> "That doesn't mean to say that their role is automatically malign, but there are things like the 2017 law which requires all Chinese companies, whatever their ownership, to co-operate with Chinese intelligence services on any occasion."[8]

So, to trust Huawei is to trust the Chinese totalitarian system.

As Secretary of State Mike Pompeo said on May 23, 2019, "The company is deeply tied not only to China but to the Chinese Communist Party. And that connectivity, the existence of those connections puts American information that crosses those networks at risk."[9]

This point is critical, because China is engaged in an all-of-society competition with the United States in which virtually every Chinese company will support every other Chinese company, and no company can survive if it ignores the Chinese Communist Party's demands. China's communist system enables it to have an integrated effort on all fronts—using economic, diplomatic, military, political, and academic tactics—to advance its hegemonic ambitions at the expense of the United States. The South China Sea campaign, the Belt and Road Initiative, and the Huawei telecommunications strategy are subordinate campaigns within a grand, long-term effort to establish global hegemony with the Chinese Communist Party at the helm.

Huawei as a threat can only be understood within this totalitarian context of an all-of-society and all-of-government effort to reestablish China as the Middle Kingdom at the center of human affairs. The introduction of 5G wireless technology is an opportunity for China to achieve a decisive advantage over all other nations—including the United States.

If Huawei wins the competition to implement 5G, an internet defined by totalitarian China will dominate the globe by 2030. The United States will have lost its place as the leading technological power, and American behavior around the world will be severely constrained by the existence of a Chinese-supplied and totalitarian-controlled communications and computation system.

Even if China's networks don't enter the United States, we will become an island within a sea of controlled communication and information. It is *essential* to get other countries on board. Think what would happen if American tourists, visiting professors and researchers, military operatives, and diplomats were forced to operate on or within compromised 5G networks while overseas. Stopping Huawei's global deployment of 5G technology must be a worldwide effort.

For those who think this position might be too strong, consider the views of some key experts.

According to General Jim Jones, former US national security adviser and NATO supreme allied commander:

> "If China controls the digital infrastructure of the 21st century, it will exploit this position for its national security purposes and be capable of coercive leverage over the United States and allies."[10]

Former Chairman of the House Homeland Security Committee Congressman Michael McCaul reiterated the threat of Huawei entering global markets in a May 2019 interview with *Bloomberg*:

> "Let me just say something about Huawei.... Once they get into these markets with 5G technology capability, they own that data. So it's very much a big national security risk.... I would urge any of our allies, particularly our Five Eyes [Australia, Canada, New Zealand, the United Kingdom, and the United States] not to engage with Huawei because of the national security threat."[11]

Americans must understand that Huawei is massive and has a tremendous head start. Fred Kempe, president and CEO of the Atlantic Council, wrote:

> "The danger is growing of two spheres of tech influence, with many Huawei customers arguing that the Chinese are offering far better prices, with direct and indirect subsidies, while providing better service and fielding more advanced equipment. The company now has 180,000 employees in 170 countries, 80,000 of whom are working in research and development. It counts 45 of the world's biggest 50 wireless carriers as customers."[12,13]

Michael Chertoff, Keith Alexander, and Timothy Keating in an article for RealClearDefense reinforced this warning:

> "Moreover, the global race to 5G is a future-defining geostrategic contest, and it's well underway. Leadership confers not only the pole position on innovation but the ability to set the international norms and standards that will determine what the global future looks like. China knows that this is a Sputnik moment and is refining its strategy and accelerating its investments to seize it.
>
> "According to the latest report from Forrester Research, China is best positioned to win the emerging global race to roll out 5G mobile infrastructure. A recent Deloitte study shows that China is outpacing the U.S.' wireless infrastructure spend by $8–10 billion since 2015. The net effect was summed up by the Defense Innovation Board, 'China is on a track to repeat in 5G what happened with the United States in 4G.' "[14]

At stake is whether the world will adopt the Chinese Communist Party's model that harnesses 5G as a tool for espionage, economic pilferage, coercion, and authoritarian rule; or the US and Western model of using 5G as a platform for prosperity, human development, and privacy protection. It's well known, but not sufficiently appreciated, that global market penetration of made-in-China 5G equipment is part of the country's Belt and Road Initiative. At the same time, Chinese law obligates the country's makers of this equipment to cooperate with national intelligence efforts. All discussions of 5G policy must begin with the understanding that developing a successful program to outpace Huawei in technology, financing, marketing, and sustainment is a matter of life and death for American freedom.

As General Jones has warned:

> "[T]his race, and its outcome, rises to the level of importance of such projects as the Manhattan Project and the 'man on the moon' efforts of the 20th century.... For countries who select the Chinese alternative and the consequences attendant to such a decision, the costs of reversal will increase exponentially as they proceed."[15]

This must be an American effort, not a Republican or Democratic effort, nor a liberal or conservative effort. Just as in 1939 and 1946, the American people will have to discuss, debate, and decide if we are to have a sustainable strategic response to this challenge to our survival as a civilization.

Huawei's aggressive tactics in the 5G sphere is the first test case in this new era of competition with China. But it will be far from the last.

BETAMAX VS. VHS—HOW WE ARE FAILING

The United States is losing this competition largely because we have no concerted effort or strategy to win it. The major American carriers seem happy to slow-walk their own plans to launch 5G domestically—and apparently have no interest in the international markets that Huawei is securing. AT&T has gone so far as to deceptively label their latest service as "5G E" (the E is for evolution) in a desperate attempt to garner early market share without actually doing anything substantial. According to the technology news website Ars Technica, a study of AT&T's farcical 5G network found that its speeds were, in fact, *slower* than 4G networks run by Verizon and T-Mobile.[16]

In addition, the United States is also seeking to use a different band of the electromagnetic spectrum from the rest of the world for its 5G network traffic. I will try to avoid getting too technical, but this is an important part of the problem. The rest of the world plans for its 5G cellular networks to use the sub-6 GHz frequency band of spectrum. It is a relatively low frequency, so it can cover a large area with fewer relay towers. In the United States, the Department of Defense (DoD) controls most of this band for infrequent, albeit important, communications.

The government and industry in the US are eyeing a higher frequency band. This means huge swaths of the country will never get 5G coverage and will lose major opportunities as a consequence of the government's poor choice of spectrum allocation. This will also leave the United States technologically isolated. Countries that build networks on the more widely used lower frequency spectrum will develop entirely new technology ecosystems and standards that will make it difficult for America to catch up and compete. As journalist Josh Rogin summarized in the title of a *Washington Post* article, "On 5G, the United States is Building Betamax While China Builds VHS."[17]

This spectrum dispute between the DoD, the private sector, and federal spectrum regulators is significant—and could determine whether the US wins or loses this competition with China.

First, rural America needs sub-6 GHz spectrum to get the distance and penetration needed for coverage. Higher frequency waves are too short in reach and too easy to disrupt. They are adequate for the Dallas Cowboys football stadium (one of the announced AT&T sites) but hopeless for the forests of Maine or to span across the distances of Montana. In one test, the higher frequency wave antenna dropped off after 600 feet. How would that work in North Dakota or any rural area? Sub-6 GHz spectrum is needed. The Pentagon controls it, and the Pentagon's bureaucracy is crippling the entire American 5G effort.

T-Mobile Chief Technology Officer Neville Ray wrote how this higher frequency millimeter wave spectrum will fail to bring coverage to all of rural America. He noted:

> "Some of this is physics—millimeter wave (mmWave) spectrum has great potential in terms of speed and capacity, but it doesn't travel far from the cell site and doesn't penetrate materials at all. It will never materially scale beyond small pockets of 5G hotspots in dense urban environments."[18]

Similarly, Verizon CEO Hans Vestberg advised that when it comes to millimeter wave spectrum: "We will need to remind ourselves, this is not a *coverage* spectrum."[19] If America's 5G spectrum is only useful in densely populated cities, it will be a profound betrayal of rural communities and will leave these Americans even further behind. This is exactly the opposite of President Trump's goals. At a White House event in April 2019, President Trump said:

> "[5G networks] must cover every community, and they must be deployed as soon as possible.
>
> "As we are making great progress with 5G, we're also focused on rural communities that do not have access to broadband at all....
>
> "We're working closely with federal agencies to get networks built in rural America faster and at much, much lower cost than it is even today....
>
> "No matter where you are, you will have access to 5G."[20]

The purpose of the White House event was to announce the sale of several pieces of millimeter wave spectrum to kick off the American 5G effort. The announcement was wrong, but President Trump's goals are right.

The second big problem with our domestic spectrum conflict with DoD is: The rest of the world is not inhibited by the Pentagon and is moving to sub-6 GHz spectrum. The Defense Innovation Board explained of the cost of focusing on higher frequency millimeter wave spectrum in its April 2019 report titled *The 5G Ecosystem: Risks & Opportunities for DoD*:

> "U.S. carriers may continue to pursue mmWave, but it is impossible to lead in the 5G field without followers. Leadership in wireless networks requires the global market to subscribe to and build to the specifications of the leader's spectrum bands of choice, as these 5G subcomponents and products will ultimately drive interoperability across networks. The rest of the world does not face the same sub-6 spectrum limitations as U.S. carriers, and is subsequently pursuing 5G development in that range. As a result, the United States may find itself without a global supply base if it continues to pursue a spectrum range divergent from the rest of the world.
>
> "If the future 5G ecosystem adopted by most of the world is built on the sub-6 mid-band spectrum, the United States will also be faced with mmWave device interoperability challenges and sub-6 infrastructure security concerns. As sub-6 becomes the global standard, it is likely that China, the current leader in that space, will lead the charge. This would create security risks for DoD operations overseas that rely on networks with Chinese components in the supply chain. Even if the United States were to restrict use of Chinese equipment suppliers domestically, the United States is not a big enough market in wireless to prevent China's 5G suppliers from

> continuing to increase market share globally, resulting in significant pressure on a declining set of vendors that would serve the U.S. market. These vendors will in turn be unable to invest R&D towards future 5G offerings due to decreasing market share, limiting the number of competitive products and depriving DoD and U.S. industries of better and cheaper global supply chains."[21]

Despite the report by the Defense Innovation Board, the Pentagon has done nothing to free up lower frequency 5G spectrum (of which it possesses an enormous amount). The Federal Communications Commission (FCC) has continued to move forward with a higher frequency millimeter spectrum auction pretending that it will help rural America, when such a result is technologically impossible. The defenders of the old telecommunications companies and the FCC try to focus on 5G inside of America, but this is also simply impossible and will have serious consequences. Scale is going to come from worldwide sales. Nortel, Lucent, and Alcatel were once powerful companies with excellent technology, but they couldn't grow to scale and were driven out. Intel just announced it's dropping out of the 5G chip business while Huawei is open to selling its 5G chip to Apple. Trying to defend a 5G strategy focused solely inside the United States is a hopeless denial of the economic realities of the modern world.

In the *Washington Post* article I mentioned, Rogin cited one administration official who said, "So we are winning a race that no one else is running to build a 5G ecosystem that no one else will use."[22]

Unfortunately, April's bureaucratic announcements during the White House 5G event were disastrous and a step in the wrong direction. As I wrote in my 2014 book *Breakout*, during times of change there are pioneers of the future and prison guards of the past. The White House event was a clear example of the lobbyists and bureaucrats who are prison guards of the past protecting their turf and self-serving vested interests at the country's expense. The Defense Innovation Board's April 2019 report captures how badly the old systems have failed. The report notes:

> "The country that owns 5G will own many of these innovations and set the standards for the rest of the world.... [T]hat country is currently not likely to be the United States."[23]

This 31-page report is publicly available and cuts through all of the propaganda of the old telecommunications companies and their captive trade association, CTIA. After all of the hype about how many small sites American companies are launching, this is the Defense Innovation Board's assessment:

> "China plans to deploy the first widespread 5G network, with its first set of sub-6 services becoming available in 2020. First-mover advantage will likely drive significant increases in their handset and telecom equipment vendors market along with their domestic semiconductor and system suppliers. As a result, Chinese internet companies will be well-positioned to develop services and applications for their home market that take advantage of 5G speed and low latency. As 5G is deployed across the globe in similar bands of spectrum, China's handset and internet applications and services are likely to become dominant, even if they are excluded from the US. China is on a track to repeat in 5G what happened with the United States in 4G."[24]

This warning was made even stronger by the recent announcement that the FCC would move ahead with an auction it proposed in September 2018, approved in December 2018, and plans to now hold in December 2019—one year after approval. This 15-month process was the "fast track version." It truly highlights the slow pace of an overbearing bureaucracy.

Finally, if Huawei becomes the dominant provider of telecommunications equipment worldwide, American forces, American diplomats, and American companies will be operating in a sea of Chinese-controlled communication technology and infrastructure. This is not a distant threat. Recently, *The Wall Street Journal* reported that AT&T is using Huawei in Mexico:

> "AT&T doubled down on Huawei over the next four years as it upgraded the infrastructure it acquired to support 4G service. A senior AT&T executive in 2016 told an industry publication that the supplier's performance was 'excellent.' The company has estimated the price of replacing the Huawei electronics it has in Mexico and found the cost prohibitive, according to a person familiar with the matter....
>
> "When AT&T's Mexican headquarters moved into a glassy tower finished in 2016, Huawei moved into a satellite office a floor away to stay close to its client."[25]

Meanwhile, according to the *Financial Times*, even our European allies are embracing Huawei's offers. The article noted:

> "Germany's telecoms regulator has given the clearest signal yet that equipment maker Huawei will not be excluded from the buildout of the country's superfast 5G network, despite fierce pressure from the US to shut out the controversial Chinese supplier for security reasons."[26]

US strategic operations in the former communist bloc of Eastern Europe are also under threat as China's 5G domination continues. On April 16, 2019, Reuters reported that Poland would allow Huawei in its 5G networks, despite the fact a former Huawei employee is under investigation for espionage against Poland.[27] At the time of this writing, the United States is negotiating a deal to establish an American military base in Poland—an outpost the Poles see as a deterrent to Russian aggression.[28]

Where Huawei's 5G is deployed, Chinese surveillance technology follows. When China Telecommunications' consortium was awarded the third telecommunications company license in the Philippines, Huawei swooped in to offer a "Safe Manila" CCTV camera system, deploying more than 12,000 cameras with advanced facial recognition software built in.[29] The United States had just signed an enhanced cooperation agreement with the Philippines on its military presence in the island-nation. Though the project was eventually rejected, Huawei and China are astoundingly quick to offer surveillance systems in countries where a major strategic American military presence exists. How can we protect our troops and our interests if they have to operate within Chinese surveillance technology built on Chinese-powered networks?

HOW WE CAN WIN

The United States must study Huawei and the development of 5G technology as a case study for the kind of sophisticated society-on-society strategy we will see a lot more of from China. It is essential that we force ourselves to think through and solve the Huawei-5G challenge because of the inherent importance of 5G and the need to analyze the Chinese Communist Party's system and develop effective responses. The investment in Huawei, the use of state financing to give Huawei huge advantages, the willingness of the government to provide diplomatic and additional help for Huawei in signing up foreign countries, and the global strategy of dominating the standards that need to be set for the 5G internet, all reflect a coordinated all-of-society, long-term investment approach that we are going to face again and again. The United States must analyze the rise of Huawei, figure out how to overmatch China's strategy, and implement the institutional reforms in both the public and private sector that will be needed for America and her allies to dominate the 5G world and the 5G internet.

President Trump's vision for a powerful and secure 5G network that serves all of rural America, and an American 5G system that successfully competes with and defeats Huawei is the right vision. It parallels his bold vision for a manned space program to the Moon and beyond that will ensure America's leadership in space.

The difference between the space program and the 5G project is the active leadership of Vice President Pence and the momentum fueled by the system built around the National Space Council. With President Trump's vision and Vice President Pence's leadership, a space program that is an all-of-government *and simultaneously* an all-of-society effort is beginning to really take shape.

There is no comparable leadership effort for 5G, and no coordinating system at an all-of-society and all-of-government level. The dominant voices on 5G have been the old bureaucracy and the old corporations who reject change and cling to outdated perspectives. This has left rural America without broadband and cell phone coverage. And even 11 years after Huawei began its investments to dominate the internet and all global communications, the United States is still without a global strategy.

It is as though the trailblazing, entrepreneurial leaders have been excluded, and only the oldest, slowest, businesses and government bureaucracies have been allowed to plan for President Trump's vision for a powerful and secure 5G network. The result, predictably, has thus far been a disaster. To solve this, we need a 5G Implementation Council comparable to the National Space Council. Competing with China is going to take an all-of-government and an all-of-society approach similar to that which President Trump and Vice President Pence have established for getting Americans back into space. The 5G

Implementation Council should have a small staff but a lot of authority to implement its ideas. Its members should include public and private stakeholders including would-be stakeholders with real assets and new start-ups with bold ideas.

However, achieving 5G dominance *does not* require a government-run program. In fact, a government-run program would be a disaster. The government should only provide information, guidance, and public momentum that will enable the private sector to provide the capabilities and implementation mechanisms to carry the project over the finish line. In this vein, the Trump administration should begin coordinating and implementing an aggressive 5G strategy capable of overmatching the Chinese-Huawei effort. The United States must develop a strategy to beat Huawei in technology and financing, so the next generation of worldwide internet (outside of China's borders) will be based on principles of freedom and the rule of law. Further, it must achieve 100 percent 5G coverage for rural America as rapidly as possible. This will require a strong, clear Presidential Executive Order to bring all of government into one operational plan. Time is of the essence. We need to begin executing a serious implementation strategy by the spring of 2020.

Moreover, the US government's decision to stick with higher frequency millimeter wave spectrum for 5G deployment must change. Which bands we allocate will determine whether America can produce alternatives to Chinese equipment to sell around the world and whether the networks that US carriers are building domestically have any long-term value on a global scale. President Trump should order the DoD to make a request for information from the American telecommunications sector. The request should be to find out how the private sector could make use of the sub-6 GHz spectrum the DoD has—while still allowing the DoD to have priority control when necessary. This will get the United States on the same page as the rest of the world in terms of spectrum—and open the discussion to a wider group of entrepreneurs.

This request for information should be followed rapidly by a request for proposals once the information and options have been assessed. On Friday, May 3, 2019, the National Spectrum Consortium issued a Call for Technical Concepts relating to, among other things, "Dynamic Spectrum Sharing" in the 5G context. This could prove to be an extremely important development. The Consortium was originally established by the DoD to "incubate new technologies to revolutionize the way in which spectrum is utilized," so this call, which is equivalent to a request for information, is timely. If the Consortium receives suitable responses and moves quickly toward a procurement, it could provide the vehicle the executive branch needs to share the DoD's sub-6 GHz spectrum with a private 5G rollout nationally in the short term.

Next, the FCC must open up its auction system to include alternative models and new players with new capital and new entrepreneurs. For too long the FCC and the large, bureaucratic, old telecoms have run an insiders' club oligopoly. It has failed, and it is presently failing to serve rural America. A new request for information should go out with the widest possible range of proposals and ideas being accepted for public scrutiny. For too long we have had a bureaucrat- and lobbyist-defined system of insider games in the telecommunications industry. It has served us badly in rural America and in the world market. It has also charged us more than we would pay in a genuinely competitive environment.

Further, in the spirit of competing with China, the Federal Trade Commission should drop its suit against Qualcomm over chip patents and royalties. Congress should amend the law to make responding to competition with China an exemption for collaborating. We need an allied coalition to defeat Huawei which requires rethinking whether companies can work together if their goal is to defeat a Chinese government-sponsored assault on markets worldwide.

On a deeper level, the Joint Committee on China's Activities, that I previously proposed establishing in the Congress, would be useful to help address the 5G challenge and other similar future industry challenges posed by the Chinese Communist Party. China is so large and energetic and has such intelligent and assertive strategies that Congress needs to develop a much deeper understanding of the competition between our two systems. Today, China is buying market share with heavily subsidized prices. The outcome will be catastrophic if we don't find a way to match or beat their prices. We may need to divert one-fourth of the foreign aid budget to matching Huawei's government-subsidized prices in the third world and rethink the Export-Import Bank.

Moreover, as I've described the totality of China's IP theft in an earlier chapter, an aggressive program of patent and intellectual property protection must be implemented to eliminate China's pattern of simply stealing the inventions of other countries. Huawei's research and development endeavors are strongly helped by theft. This must be stopped.

To ensure the US 5G deployment effort benefits all Americans, Congress should insist on a feasible strategy for rural America with deadlines and a real strategy for defeating Huawei. This effort will also require a relentlessly realistic assessment of the key yardsticks of success. This assessment is important because it will force us to truly change and not just kid ourselves with platitudes and promises. In addition, Congress should collaborate with the Trump administration and the private sector to identify laws that need changing so that we can win the competition against Huawei.

Finally, Congress and the Trump administration should work to ensure the new 5G system will be designed with electromagnetic pulse (EMP) hardening and powerful cybersecurity capabilities embedded in the system. It should also have secure, reliable communications even in the presence of unreliable networks. We must prepare for the reality that Huawei will still be operating in some countries, even if we are extraordinarily successful. The US 5G effort must be built for a generation, not for a quarterly report.

A WHOLESALE SOLUTION

Part of the reason we are so behind in this technological competition is that our system is outdated and incentivizes unhelpful behavior.

In the current system, the government auctions off spectrum that the highest-bidding company then uses to build a network. Though still subject to stringent government rules, the auction winners are the license holders of these networks and have the option to contract with other companies to use part of their networks. However, the license holders ultimately set the price and build their networks to optimize their own profits. This incentivizes the license-holding winners to set the highest possible price for wholesale customers and to only build out networks in urban areas with the largest customer bases.

At the present time, there are only four nationwide carriers in the US and two of them—T-Mobile and Sprint—are trying to merge. If this merger is successful, it would leave only three nationwide American wireless network operators. This limited competition creates an oligopoly rather than an intensely competitive system.

Unsurprisingly, the more mobile network operators (MNOs) that compete in the market, the lower the price for consumers. According to a 2019 report by Rewheel, the median gigabyte price of 4G smartphone plans in the European Union (EU28) and Organisation for Economic Cooperation and Development (OECD), another intergovernmental economic organization, markets is lower in 4-MNO markets compared to 3-MNO markets.[30] However, with more competition, a 5-MNO market offers the lowest median price for consumers. As made evident in the chart shown on the next page. US prices are a "*universe apart*" compared to other 4-MNO and the Israeli 5-MNO markets. Prices for US consumers are also *even higher* than the median price for 3-MNO markets. According to the report, "The median smartphone plan gigabyte price…[in] the US was 15 times higher than median prices in 4-MNO competitive large European markets."

MEDIAN GIGABYTE PRICE (SMARTPHONES)—APRIL 2019
Fully allocated median gigabyte price of 4G smartphone plans
(with at least 1,000 mins. and 3Mbit/s for HD video)
MNO: Mobile Network Operator

Source: Rewheel/research, Digital Fuel Monitor

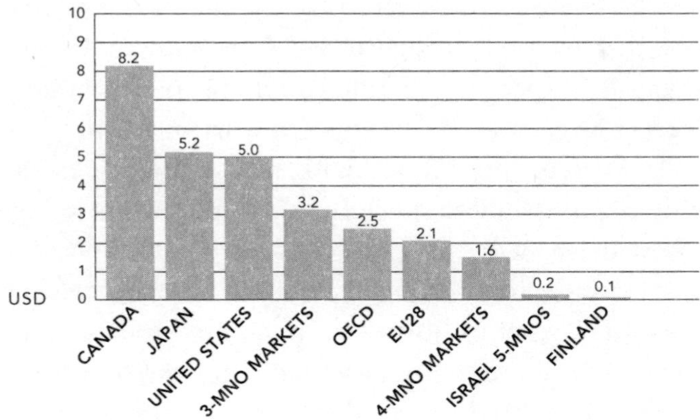

The exorbitant prices are also reflected in US 4G mobile and wireless home broadband plans. According to the Rewheel report, "US and Canadian median mobile broadband gigabyte prices were 6 times higher than the median price in OECD markets and 10 times higher than the median price in EU28 markets."[31]

MEDIAN GIGABYTE PRICE (Mobile Broadband)—APRIL 2019
Fully allocated median gigabyte price of 4G mobile & wireless home broadband plans
(with at least 3Mbit/s for HD video)
MNO: Mobile Network Operator

Source: Rewheel/research, Digital Fuel Monitor

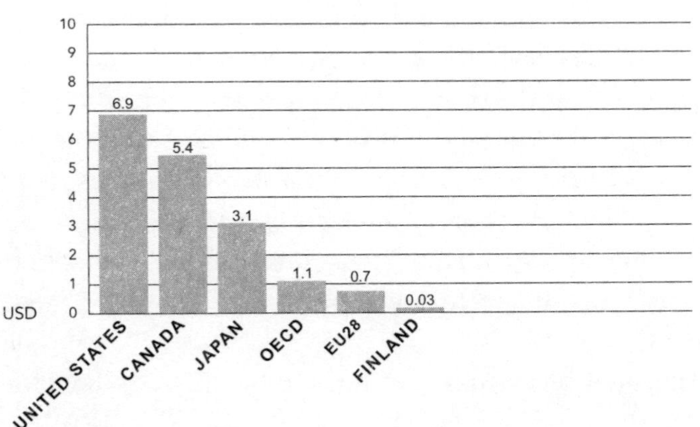

The current system creates substantially higher prices for consumers in the US. Moreover, our current model has significantly disadvantaged rural communities in the United States and has failed to successfully provide the essential telecommunications coverage needed by *all* Americans in the modern digital age. To experience the shortcomings of this system, just drive across large parts of the country with no cell phone coverage at all. Even in small towns with service, device users experience significantly lower speeds compared to users in big cities just a short drive away.

The current system strongly favors building out telecommunications infrastructure in urban areas first and then, *maybe*, building out rural areas. So far with 4G networks, this strategy has not been beneficial for rural and small-town America. The result has been economic growth and prosperity for the connected urban areas and has led rural areas to fall behind from a lack of growth and opportunity. One major result is evident in the migration of young people from disconnected rural areas to the modern, connected cities.

The FCC has attempted to solve the problem through auction design. Spectrum licenses are generally not sold in nationwide blocs, but rather in geographic divisions of various sizes. This is done in part to encourage network build outs in areas that the nationwide carriers are disinclined to serve. There are a few successful regional carriers; however, for the most part, these rural license holders become economic vassals of the major carriers and become dependent on them for roaming agreements. Additionally, rural license holders find themselves subject to punishing disparities in the roaming prices that they can charge and are charged in turn by the nationwide operators. Issuing rural spectrum licenses has helped, some, in those few places with successful local operators. However, these are the exception.

If this auction system continues to be utilized, the development of 5G systems will make the current gap between urban and rural America even greater. If the 5G systems are rolled out first in the cities, then every advantage of speed, latency, and capacity will accrue to urban businesses and urban lives, while the technological development of rural areas falls even further behind.

Current efforts use taxpayer subsidies to lure telecommunications into rural areas. These schemes are slow, cumbersome, and ineffective. The subsidies provide money to the established companies, but ultimately, have had little impact since the financing has not had success in providing full coverage for rural America. Currently, there is no plausible plan for covering all of rural America with 5G in a timely way.

5G will enhance distance learning, distance medicine, autonomous vehicles, and data dense systems of monitoring manufacturing and agriculture. Under current plans, all of these advantages will be made available to urban areas, while rural areas will struggle economically and technologically and find it impossible to progress at the same rate.

WHOLESALE AS A CONCURRENT SYSTEM

Introducing wholesale as a concurrent system could potentially be the most powerful structural change for the rollout of 5G connectivity capabilities that would have enormous impact on rural areas.

In a wholesale model, carriers and others engage in a continuous process of bidding for usage of network capacity using prices based on market principles. Supply and demand—not the spectrum license holders or network owners—set the price and the market is continuously open to all wholesale bidders with equal rights of access.

The idea is not to replace or eliminate the existing carriers, or force them onto a single, mandatory wholesale network. Rather, a wholesale network would operate concurrently with and alongside both the current and future networks of the carriers.

A wholesale system allows multiple service providers to share the same capital investment. It lowers the cost per user and per bit of data produced. Additionally, by maximizing the use of the capital investment, it makes it more profitable to expand coverage rapidly and widely to service less populated areas.

RESISTANCE TO CONSIDERING A WHOLESALE MODEL

The mention of a wholesale market for bandwidth seems to alienate and anger long-time supporters of large telecommunications companies. The hostility to even thinking about adding wholesale to our wireless ecosystem seems to pervade both big companies and their bureaucratic regulators. Part of the resistance to a wholesale model may be the threat of a crash in the prices that heavily indebted companies can charge their customers. It may be impossible to sustain the debt burden of companies, such as AT&T, if the price of connectivity drops substantially.

Furthermore, the big telecommunications companies make plenty of money in urban America and are happy to take taxpayer money to slowly, gradually, develop rural America. They don't seem to be significantly impacted by the economic and social costs of rural America lagging behind in technological access and connectivity.

Meanwhile, the model I'm describing has worked well in other industries. In fact, in both the electricity and natural gas markets, competitive wholesale systems have developed and resulted in dramatic declines in cost and remarkably greater shared usage of capital investments.

Consider just a few examples of the impact of the wholesale system on the cost of electricity.

Citing data from a joint Cleveland State University and

Ohio State University study, Electricity Policy Manager and Senior Fellow Devin Hartman at the R Street Institute wrote:

> "The economic advantages of [electricity] markets have culminated in rates trending in opposite directions in monopoly and restructured states. From 2008 to 2016, the weighted-average price of electricity in monopoly states increased 15 percent, while it decreased 8 percent in restructured states. This national trend holds true in the Midwest."[32]

In fact, Hartman reported that consumer savings for electricity in wholesale markets in Ohio were projected to reach roughly $15 billion through 2020.

The impact of competition has exactly the effect that a free market advocate would expect. Citing the study "The Evolution of the Revolution: The Sustained Success of Retail Electricity Competition," Cheryl Kaften reported in Energy Manager Today:

> "Competition-era price trends in the customer choice jurisdictions have been more favorable to customers than price trends in the 35 traditional monopoly regulation jurisdictions ('monopoly states'), with average electricity prices falling against inflation in customer choice jurisdictions, but far exceeding inflation in monopoly states....
>
> "Customer choice jurisdictions, as a group, have outperformed monopoly states in generation, attracting billions of dollars of investment in new, more efficient generation; and resulting in higher capacity factors than in monopoly states and parity in resource adequacy to meet load."[33]

The competition in the electricity industry actually grew out of the success of a similar pattern in the natural gas market.

According to a National Renewable Energy Laboratory report from 2016:

> "Deregulation of the natural gas industry also increased the impetus for electricity deregulation. The decline in real wholesale and retail natural gas prices in the late 1980s and early 1990s was attributed to the deregulation and introduction of competition in the natural gas industry.... In the mid-1990s, states began to look at competition as a way of increasing the electric power industry's efficiency and lowering electricity rates. By April 2001, 24 states had passed legislation related to electricity market restructuring....
>
> "As of July 2015, 14 states have broad-based customer access to competitive retail markets."[34]

Looking at the successes and lessons learned in these two industries will be essential as we think through how to efficiently and effectively deploy a 5G network.

BUILDING OUT THE SYSTEM

It would be too radical to impose a wholesale telecommunications system as a replacement for the entire current model. A replacement therefore is not being suggested.

However, it is possible to have a wholesale provider existing side by side with the current oligopolists. Then the competition would attract smaller carriers, start-ups, and new distributors using a wide range of innovations.

Just as the electric wholesale model grew and developed in part to accommodate solar, wind, and other power sources, a wholesale model for 5G could potentially liberate customers from the current oligopoly and oligopolistic pricing. Large buildings could form their own co-op and buy network capacity through the wholesaler. Large companies that use a lot of data, such as FedEx, UPS, or major trucking companies, might form purchasing systems to buy through the wholesaler.

There are major private investors indicating that there is a clear willingness to invest billions in a new, competitive, carrier neutral, wholesale network. As a result, it is evident that a new 5G network based on this model can be built in the private sector with no government subsidies.

Instead of government subsidies, the detailed records of the competitive bidding process would allow the wholesale network to pay authorities a royalty in perpetuity. This in turn would create a stream of revenue far greater than that which is received from the current system. Additionally, because the wholesale system is so much more efficient at using spectrum, it could provide low-cost (and in some cases no cost) 5G services to the federal government in perpetuity.

If the prospect of launching a nationwide wholesale network all at once is simply too much for the bureaucratic mindset, an interim step would be to offer individual states or regions the opportunity to develop a wholesale network. A governor who was offered a privately financed 5G network that would put his or her state a decade or more ahead of others might agree that this is a big breakthrough for his or her home state. A governor who could tell all of his or her constituents in rural areas that they would have 5G coverage before most of the big cities in America would receive a significantly positive response.

If the FCC is unwilling to propose the framework for a nationwide wholesale network, it should at least authorize such a network for states who come and request to have it installed by private companies. The construction of a wholesale network would be privately funded with a bonded guarantee of completion, including in rural areas.

If the wholesale network failed to generate enough revenue after it was completed, it would still be a state-of-the-art

5G network, and the entire system could be sold to traditional telecommunications companies or to other entrepreneurs. Ultimately, there is no downside risk from trying this innovative approach to speed up the development of a 5G system.

WE MUST WIN

The case for American-led 5G deployment is a critical matter of national security and should be seriously and urgently addressed. The state or entity that controls 5G will define the essential digital infrastructure of the future. Consequently, if an aggressive totalitarian actor controls this technology globally, it will have dangerous implications for the United States.

Additionally, 5G is essential for developing the economic and technology spheres of America. The US has the opportunity to lead the world in this emerging technology. Also, there has been an obvious failure to bring the same level of technological connectivity that exists in urban areas to rural communities. With 5G, we have the opportunity to correct this error and bring both rural and urban communities in America into the new digital age.

There are clear steps that must be taken to bring 5G to market that will protect America's national security, connect rural America, and ensure the United States' leadership in this industry. The government must provide the leadership and encouragement, while the private sector must install and deploy the necessary, cutting-edge technology. If we fail to implement this all-of-government and all-of-society effort to deploy 5G securely and efficiently, we are risking a totalitarian, Chinese Communist Party-controlled technological future. The time to act is now, and the level of urgency for successfully completing this effort cannot be overstated.

CHAPTER EIGHT

GATHERING SAND

> But trade, and commerce, and making money for our country, it's all very important, but to me the most important job I have is the security of our country, even more important than those other things that I talk about all the time—it's the security of our country.
>
> —President Donald Trump, April 2019[1]

> National security is the cornerstone of peace and stability of our country, and safeguarding it is in the fundamental interests of the Chinese people of all ethnic groups.... We will strengthen efforts to raise awareness of national security among all Party members and all the people, and create a strong synergy of the whole society to safeguard national security.
>
> —General Secretary Xi Jinping, October 2017[2]

When Americans think of espionage and spying, our minds conjure up images of highly trained agents, who speak many languages, artfully insinuating themselves into government institutions. They learn their adversaries' secrets using their wits, skills—and a few high-tech gadgets. Or, we picture spies in catsuits crawling through air ducts as they plan to rappel into a secured server room to secretly copy a hard drive full of classified information. On the darker side, we imagine black-clad snipers on moonlit rooftops waiting for some dignitary or political defector to step into their sights.

Certainly, the spy agencies of the world have special agents who have done missions like these, but the reality of espionage is much broader—and it more often involves regular people who may have no idea they are being used by foreign operatives. There is an analogy used in the intelligence community for understanding the various methods and characteristics of foreign espionage.

Imagine the currency of espionage is sand on an island. Each grain contains valuable information, data, or secrets. Possessing lots of this sand is important to world powers because it can provide significant strategic advantages. Knowing the opposing team's playbook is, after all, helpful for winning. To acquire the valuable secrets of the sand, the United States will capture thousands of high-resolution images of the island with a satellite and beam them to various agencies around Washington, DC. Russia might deploy a submarine in the middle of the night and send a crew of frogmen to steal buckets of sand to bring back to the submarine for analysis. Meanwhile, China will send a cruise ship filled with thousands of tourists to the island. They will spend a long day walking and sunbathing on the island's beaches. Then the tourists will return to the ship and shake the sand out of their towels, clothes, and shoes. In the end, China will have more of the sand—and the valuable information it contains—than any other country.

Of course, many experts would agree that this analogy is an oversimplification. Moreover, I don't mean to give the impression that every Chinese person you meet is secretly a spy. But this is helpful for understanding the way that China's government approaches spying. Communist party leaders don't rely solely on cells of trained agents. The Chinese Communist Party looks for assets in virtually every aspect of modern life. Furthermore,

Chinese spy agencies are not exclusively interested in military or national secrets. They are just as interested in commercial secrets—and information about everyday people.

The Chinese communist leadership has a deep institutional understanding of the merits and uses of espionage. As Chinese military strategist Sun Tzu emphasized in *The Art of War* some 2500 years ago: "[S]pies are a most important element in war because on them depends an army's ability to move." Sun Tzu's treatise, which was written in the sixth century BC, instructs readers to "[b]e subtle! Be subtle! And use your spies for every kind of business."[3]

The Chinese Communist Party tends to follow Sun Tzu's advice. It uses an all-of-government, all-of-society approach to acquire information both domestically and abroad—across politics, commercial industry, media, academics, and other fields. The party's tactics emphasize subtlety and incremental gains—traits that are central to China's strategic thinking.

CHINA'S ESPIONAGE MACHINE

As I've mentioned earlier, several recent Chinese laws require individual citizens and companies to comply with the government in protecting national security. While this may seem typical of any country, in China it is an incredibly broad mandate that carries implications and requirements for American companies operating in China. These laws essentially force Chinese citizens and companies in China to assist and cooperate with the Chinese government (i.e., the ruling Communist Party) to protect against any suspected threats to China or its interests under its legal definition of national security. In practice, this is carte blanche authority for the totalitarian communist regime to threaten everyday Chinese citizens and businesses operating in China with criminal charges if they are seen as anything less than fully patriotic and loyal to the party.

China's 2015 National Security Law defined national security as "the relative absence of international or domestic threats to the state's power to govern and the capacity to protect security in a sustainable manner."[4] According to the law, the concept of national security includes "sovereignty, unity and territorial integrity, the welfare of the people, sustainable economic and social development, and other major national interests."[5] Furthermore, according to a 2015 report by Covington & Burling LLP, the law also institutes "broad obligations on citizens and corporations to assist and cooperate with the government in protecting national security."[6] With this sweeping definition of national security in place and its accompanying mandates, in 2017 China created the National Intelligence Law that obliges individuals, organizations, and institutions to help Chinese intelligence agents in carrying out "intelligence" work or espionage.[7] This law essentially made any company operating in China or Chinese citizen an agent of its espionage machine.

Writing for *Lawfare,* Dr. Murray Scot Tanner unpacked China's 2017 National Intelligence Law. According to Tanner, the law attempts to create an offensive, rather than defensive intelligence gathering machine. He writes that the law creates "affirmative legal responsibilities for Chinese and, in some cases, foreign citizens, companies, or organizations operating in China to provide access, cooperation, or support for Beijing's intelligence-gathering activities."[8]

Two articles within the recent 2017 National Intelligence Law are important. The first is Article 7 that mandates that "any organization or citizen shall support, assist, and cooperate with state intelligence work according to law." The second is Article 14 that gives intelligence agents the authority to demand such cooperation. Murray points out that while these clauses seem to only apply to individuals who are Chinese citizens, they *do not specify that only Chinese* "organizations" are required to abide by such mandates.

Moreover, similar to laws that had previously been passed in China, Murray described concerns that were raised about the law giving intelligence officials the authority to enter restricted facilities, inspect private records, subject personnel to questioning and investigation, and access or requisition equipment owned by organizations or individuals used for communications and transportation.

In a revealing article, *The Wall Street Journal* described how China's laws impact China's largest technology companies—Alibaba, Tencent, and Baidu—and their consumers or users.[9] These companies can be thought of as China's Amazon and eBay (Alibaba), China's Facebook, Apple Pay, and WhatsApp (Tencent), and China's Google (Baidu). Each of these companies has a wealth of data about its customers, and communist officials take full advantage of their intel. The article found that the assistance these companies give to authorities "is far more extensive than the help Western companies extend to their governments, and the requests are almost impossible to challenge." Plus, while operating a business in an authoritarian country where the Communist Party has sole control over protectionist trade and economic policies, businesses are highly incentivized to willingly oblige to investigative demands—however invasive they may be.

For example, *The Wall Street Journal* described a police outpost on Alibaba's campus. It is used to "report suspected crimes to the police" and for the police to "request data from Alibaba for their own investigations." An Alibaba employee recalled an instance in which he was approached by police, who wanted the user ID and information of someone who posted terrorism-related content. He turned it over. As the article noted, compare this sort of compulsory cooperation to the pushback Apple gave the FBI when asked to unlock the iPhone of a San Bernardino mass shooting suspect in 2015. This clearly shows the differences in how companies and the government in the US and China view the protection of consumer privacy.

The Wall Street Journal described another case, in which a Beijing activist, Hu Jia, bought a slingshot online to use as a stress reliever. Hu used the Tencent app, WeChat's, mobile-payment feature. Later, a state security agent interrogated him to find out if he was plotting to shoot out installed surveillance cameras around his apartment. Prior to this incident, Hu sent a message to a friend who was traveling to Taiwan and included names of activists who he might want to meet with while he was there. His friend then received a visit from state security agents at his house, who warned him against meeting with any of the individuals Hu had recommended.

According to Hu, particularly for individuals who are on the party's watch list, "Experience has proven that WeChat is completely compromised." He warned, "Everyone has a spy watching them. That spy is their smartphone."[10] Hu was almost right. With China's recently passed laws, the spy is not just the smartphone—but the businesses and organizations behind it.

CHINA'S SPYCRAFT

Former National Counterintelligence Executive Michelle Van Cleave said in a June 2016 statement to the US-China Economic and Security Review Commission (USCC) that "Chinese intelligence is routinely ranked No. 1 or No. 2 in the hierarchy of foreign intelligence threats to the United States and our interests worldwide."[11]

Indeed, China's espionage efforts have targeted and infiltrated some of the highest levels of our government. In 2013, California Democratic Senator Dianne Feinstein, who was chair of the Senate Intelligence Committee, was approached by the FBI about an employee who had worked on her personal staff for almost 20 years.[12]

The staffer in question was both her personal driver and a worker in her San Francisco office. News of the investigation didn't become public until 2018. For nearly two decades, the spy heard every conversation Feinstein had while he was driving her around—with passengers and people on the phone. He knew her schedule, who she was meeting with, when she was meeting them—and likely what the meetings were about. If she ever left a briefcase, cell phone, or laptop in the car, he had access to these items and could have easily shared them with his communist confidantes. This is incredibly valuable if you are trying to guess what the Senate Intelligence Committee Chairwoman is thinking—or how she could be manipulated.

The San Francisco Chronicle reported that the driver was sharing information with staff at the People's Republic of China consulate in San Francisco—which Feinstein helped open when she was mayor of the city.[13] According to *The Weekly Standard*, "it appears [the spy] had started as a legitimate employee but was at some point, likely on a visit to the East, turned by a member of the Chinese Ministry of State Security." The driver was forced to retire after Feinstein learned of the investigation, and as of this writing, he has not been charged with espionage. According to Fox News, this is because "he was passing on political intelligence rather than classified materials—making the prosecution nearly impossible."[14]

This is an excellent case study in how China conducts espionage operations. Agents targeted someone who had low status but high access—someone who could provide intelligence for nearly 20 years before being discovered. It's likely that most of what he shared wasn't top secret information—but this was a long game to gather political intelligence and created a serious security vulnerability within our government. This scheme was about being patient to catch valuable information whenever and however it came by having a Chinese agent in place with close access to a high-level official. As a consequence of this breach, it is impossible for us to know how seemingly innocent material or information the spy gathered from Senator Feinstein might have been matched to other seemingly innocent information back in Beijing to suddenly provide really useful insights to be used against the United States.

However, China's spy machine has also fully embraced the capabilities of the twenty-first century. Dennis F. Poindexter, author of *Chinese Information War, Espionage, Cyberwar, Communications Control and Related Threats to United States Interests*, spoke at a hearing before the USCC on June 15, 2015:

> "They aren't just hacking businesses. They have hacked industries that support our government and contractor personnel, like processors of security clearances, insurance companies, health care, defense, computer security, educational institutions, and information technology at all levels. They probably know more about our military, business, and government personnel than we do.... They are perfectly willing to use stolen technologies to set up competition for our business sectors. They use their intelligence and military functions, university research centers, enhanced with state-owned businesses, to gather the information and apply it. Then, they deny everything, and say, 'Prove it.'"[15]

In 2014, the Chinese government hacked the records of the US Office of Personnel Management (OPM), the custodian of federal employee files. In two different cyberattacks, the records of more than 22 million Americans were potentially stolen. Calling the hack one of "the most potentially damaging cyber heists in U.S. government history," *The Washington Post* reported that "hackers accessed not only personnel records of current and former employees but also extensive information about friends, relatives and others listed as references in applications for security clearances for some of the most sensitive jobs in government."[16]

In addition to potentially helping the People's Republic of China identify American spies working within its area of influence, the Chinese Communist Party could also sell or trade this information to Iran, North Korea, Russia, and other less-than-friendly countries. This puts American lives in serious peril. For those US employees who aren't viewed as high-value targets, the party might simply use their information for blackmail, identity theft, or some other nefarious activity.

China faced no obvious or immediate consequences for the OPM hack at the time. The Obama administration did almost nothing to definitively solve the larger, persisting problem of China's espionage and infiltration. (Although then-FBI Director James Comey called it "a very big deal" and former Director of National Intelligence James Clapper told CNN: "You have to kind of salute the Chinese for what they did.") The Obama administration eventually indicted five People's Liberation Army (PLA) hackers for breaching US businesses unrelated to the OPM hack. Ultimately, in September 2015, Obama signed an agreement with China that said both countries would not engage in cyber-enabled intellectual property theft. Moreover, according to CNBC, the agreement specified that "both countries are committed to finding appropriate norms of state behavior in cyberspace within the international community."[17]

As I've mentioned earlier, this agreement did not solve the problem. With this kind of response for hacking the most powerful nation on Earth, it's no surprise China kept doing it. The Obama administration failed to apply any real pressure on China.

President Trump has taken a much different approach. In September 2018, National Security Adviser John Bolton released a new cybersecurity policy—specifically citing the Chinese OPM hack as a reason for the US to be more vigilant. "For any nation that's taking cyber activity against the United States...we will respond offensively as well as defensively," Bolton said at the White House.[18]

Further, in May 2019, the Trump administration unsealed its fourth round of indictments against Chinese hackers in 18 months. *The Washington Post* reported that the May indictments targeted two PLA-linked hackers apparently responsible for the 2015 hack of Anthem, a large American health insurance company. In that cyberattack, hackers potentially stole the private information of 78 million people. The newspaper quoted former Department of Commerce cybersecurity official Jim Lewis as saying: "The Chinese thought they could get away with anything. This is part of a larger administration strategy to be more aggressive and assertive...to find and make public Chinese hackers and punish them for their activities."[19]

Indictments alone will not fix the problem of cyber espionage, but they will play an important role in sending a message to China and many other countries that the US will not tolerate such intrusions. Luckily, the Trump administration is taking the threat of cyberattacks and espionage from China seriously.

On January 29, 2019, former Director of National Intelligence Dan Coats testified to the Senate Select Committee on Intelligence that "China presents a persistent cyber espionage threat and a growing attack threat to our core military and critical infrastructure systems" and that the country "remains the most active strategic competitor responsible for cyber espionage against the US Government, corporations, and allies."[20]

The US government is not the only foreign government that China has successfully infiltrated electronically. According to *The Intercept*, the surveillance technology firm Hikvision, that I previously mentioned has been installing its systems in Xinjiang, has also "supplied its surveillance cameras for use on the British parliamentary estate, as well as to police, hospitals, schools, and universities." The company is "generating millions of dollars in annual revenue" by selling to British companies, the news outlet reported.

British politicians are raising concerns and fears that Chinese intelligence could use the estimated 1.2 million cameras to spy on its citizens. Some of the cameras are reportedly in sensitive locations, and some are connected to the internet.[21]

Thankfully, Congress added an amendment to the 2019 National Defense Authorization Act that essentially bans government agencies from purchasing video surveillance products made by the Chinese companies Hikvision and Dahua.

ECONOMIC ESPIONAGE

In addition to traditional spying activity to "[p]enetrate, collect, and compromise US national security secrets (information, plans, technology, activities, operations, etc.), in order to advance their interests and defeat US objectives," Van Cleave told the USCC in June 2016 that Chinese spies seek to steal commercial secrets from US companies, so they can bolster China's military capabilities.

In fact, she said the "FBI estimates that the Chinese Army has developed a network of over 30,000 Chinese military cyberspies, plus 150,000 private-sector computer experts, whose mission is to steal American military and technological secrets."[22]

The obvious commercial sector target for China has been our nation's defense contractors. In 2014, the US government arrested a Chinese national who was employed by a US defense contractor. The operative was caught heading to China with "sensitive proprietary documents containing equations and test results used in the development of technologically advanced titanium for U.S. military aircraft."[23] Earlier that year, US Customs and Border Protection found him with "undeclared cash, Chinese corporation-establishment documents and a mostly complete application for a Chinese state-controlled aviation and aerospace research center."[24]

Furthermore, the Foundation for Defense of Democracies found in a 2018 report on China's use of cyber-enabled economic warfare that in 2012, "Chinese hackers gained access to the U.S. Transportation Command, conducting at least 20 intrusions into the U.S. military's logistics and supply systems through defense contractors."[25]

Recently, China's intelligence agencies have even been using LinkedIn to recruit non-Chinese citizens to betray their home countries and provide the Chinese Communist Party with information. According to Cyberscoop.com, Dean Boyd, the spokesperson for the National Counterintelligence and Security Center, warned about China's newest way to recruit.

> "They may pose as a job recruiter or someone with a shared interest to make a connection to a target and lure them into a relationship, concealing their role in Chinese intelligence, they often attempt to elicit personal and professional information for their targets to gauge their value. With the most promising targets, they may offer all-expense paid trips to China for an interview, a speech, or an exchange of research."[26]

China's intelligence operatives used this method to entice Keven Mallory, a former CIA officer, to spy for them. In early 2017, Mallory was sent a message about contracting work, and he responded. At the time, *The New York Times* reported that Mallory was "thousands of dollars in debt and behind on his mortgage."[27] He was reportedly given $25,000 by the Chinese operative. According to the newspaper, Mallory was fluent in Mandarin, and he traveled to Shanghai over the course of four months and "had covert communications with the operative on a Chinese provided phone."[28] While there, the paper reported he also passed along information such as "an unclassified white paper on American intelligence policy."[29] In 2018, he was found guilty of espionage and lying to the FBI.[30]

The Mallory case is interesting because it shows how the Chinese Communist Party uses many layers of espionage to find vulnerable targets. In this case, Chinese spies might have started with a mountain of personal financial data about millions of Americans. (This could have come from the OPM breach, the Anthem hack, or any major cyberattack China has initiated.) After zeroing in on those Americans in the dataset who were in dire financial straits, agents could then determine who might be valuable. In this case, they found a former CIA officer. That's a fairly high-value target.

The United States is not the only country in which the Chinese Communist Party has used LinkedIn to get citizens to spy. On October 22, 2018, French newspaper *Le Figaro* reported a

Chinese spy program had targeted France. According to the paper, "a few thousand managers and employees of the public services, employees of strategic companies and circles of influence have been 'approached' by China via professional social networks, in particular, LinkedIn."[31]

Finally, the Chinese Communist Party has established business fronts in the United States to "create companies designed to bring in needed defense technology,"[32] according to Larry M. Wortzel, PhD, in a 2005 lecture at The Heritage Foundation. This practice probably started in the late 1970s and 1980s, Wortzel said. Some estimates for the number of these front companies at that time totalled 3,200, and their goal is to "produce defense goods for the [People's Liberation Army] and for sale to other companies."[33]

Wortzel highlighted three examples of the PLA establishing these fronts.

> "The General Political Department of the People's Liberation Army started a proprietary company, Kaili, or Kerry Corporation that for years operated in the U.S. as a real estate and investment company.[34]
>
> "The General Equipment Department of the PLA operated a proprietary company, Polytechnologies, or Baoli, that had offices here in the U.S.[35]
>
> "The General Logistics Department operated a proprietary called Xinshidai, or New Era that had offices in our nation and continues to be responsible for a network of PLA manufacturing plants in China."[36]

Wortzel noted that according to Chinese law, "these technically are independent legal entities" although the "Central Military Commission of the Chinese Communist Party established them" to "serve the interests of the PLA and the military-industrial complex."

INFILTRATING ACADEMICS

China's spy service also has specifically honed its ability to steal knowledge and cultivate assets in our nation's colleges and universities.

Van Cleave told the USCC that the vast spy network of government and private sector tech experts China employs also focuses on garnering information from "hundreds of thousands of students and academicians." These students, professors, and researchers (along with government and private sector actors) help "potentially extend the reach of Chinese intelligence into the core structures of our nation's security."[37]

Indeed, the National Counterintelligence and Security Center's 2018 Foreign Economic Espionage in Cyberspace report found that China's espionage activities specifically target "individuals for whom science or business is their primary profession" to surreptitiously learn secret or proprietary technology. Similarly, they often use academic collaborations with higher education institutions "to acquire specific research and gain access to high-end research equipment."[38] In 2018, Katherine Hille of the *Financial Times* described this spying system as "a web of research collaborations that could boost Beijing's military technology development."[39]

Peter Harrell, senior fellow at the Center for a New American Security, told the Senate Judiciary Committee in 2018 that China also conducts missions "aimed at intimidating Chinese students and professors critical of Chinese policies, and to a lesser extent American students and academics."[40]

Further, *Radio Free Asia* reported that China's state security police recruit Chinese students studying abroad as agents or long-term moles to monitor overseas activities and ensure they align with the interests of the Chinese Communist Party. China's secret police aim to infiltrate dissident groups of overseas Chinese, particularly those fighting for democracy in China, or migrant Tibetans and Uyghurs.

Chinese students at the University of Georgia experienced

such aggressive recruitment tactics firsthand. Sulaiman Gu, a US-based rights activist and student at the University of Georgia, told *Radio Free Asia* that he was a target of the state security police's recruitment efforts. He received a phone call from China's state security police. The voice from the recording of the call intimidates Gu by saying:

> "According to my understanding, you wouldn't be taken straight to prison the moment you came back to China.... But seeing as you are pretty active and you have said various things that have had a negative impact on the country and the government, you are definitely a person of interest.... We are interested in [exiled Chinese billionnaire] Guo Wengui, also in the activities of that little circle of yours.... Such as how many people are involved in pro-democracy groups in the U.S., what the current situation is, what their events usually consist of.... If you were able to send [such information] to the higher-ups, using me as a channel, you could end up better off than the majority of people just from doing that little bit of work."

Imagine being in college, on your own, in a foreign country, far from home, and receiving this phone call. Knowing you were being watched and monitored by an increasingly repressive government would be terrifying for anyone. But the threats didn't stop with Gu. The police even harassed those closest to him back home in China. He told *Radio Free Asia*, "The secret police have harassed my family and friends on many occasions, frightening them by saying they have a blacklist of all dissident youth studying overseas, and that I am on the list of people to be charged with 'incitement to subvert state power outside China.'"

Similar incidents happened to another University of Georgia student, Wu Lebao, who said that he and his family and friends have all been the recipients of intimidating phone calls.

"They have harassed me repeatedly and asked me to give them information about the activities of overseas democracy activists and dissidents," he said to *Radio Free Asia*. "They are particularly interested in the activities of Uyghurs and Tibetans," he added. "This would be a requirement if I wanted to return in [sic] future," Wu noted. "I told them I wasn't going back, and they said I would have to come back to see my aging relatives. This is coercion."

Xi's administration has been increasingly tightening controls on information, society, culture, and citizens. It appears likely that cases such as these will continue.

Still in other situations, Chinese scholars and scientists coming to universities are Chinese operatives that exploit the free and open exchange of ideas in institutions of higher education. Alex Joske published a report for the Australian Strategic Policy Institute (ASPI) in 2018 on the Chinese military's collaboration with foreign universities. Joske found that China's People's Liberation Army "has sponsored more than 2,500 military scientists and engineers to study abroad," and that "[s]ome of those traveling overseas have actively used cover to disguise their military affiliations, claiming to be from non-existent academic institutions."

The Chinese military keeps a close eye on these overseas students and ensures that they maintain absolute loyalty to the party. The *PLA Daily* refers to China's advancing of its domestic military capabilities by using overseas expertise, research, and training as "Picking flowers in foreign lands to make honey in China."[41]

Joske writes that China's military encourages scholars studying abroad "to work on areas of interest to the military." Joske summarized a 2016 article written by specialists associated with the PLA National University of Defense Technology, which recommended:

> "[I]n choosing where to study overseas, students' first priority should be the relevance of the research direction of an overseas institution to their work in China, as

> they 'must comprehensively consider the continuity of their research work when in China with that when they are studying overseas.' When students are overseas, the report adds, they should 'fully take advantage of the cutting-edge research conditions and environment abroad' and 'map out the arrangements of their overseas research and their plans for research after returning to China.' "[42]

The United States is one of the primary countries of which Chinese military-affiliated scientists have been taking full advantage. In 2017, the United States, according to Joske, was the number one country "engaged in research collaboration with the PLA." This was calculated based on the number of peer-reviewed publications that were coauthored by Chinese military and overseas scientists. Using this metric, the UK, Canada, Australia, and Germany followed the US for 2017.

In some cases, foreign government funding is used for collaboration with the PLA. In one example, Joske's report finds that grants from the US Air Force and Navy were used as sources of funding for a paper authored by scientists at the University of Manchester and the PLA National University of Defense Technology.

To recap, not *all* students studying abroad from China are agents of the Chinese Communist Party or its military. Oftentimes, many Chinese scientists and scholars contribute to the vibrant diversity of our American institutions. However, the US and our universities need to work together and recognize that in some cases the openness of our institutions is exploited. Students studying in the United States from China can be intimidated and coerced by their home government—a clear and deliberate violation of their individual freedoms and rights that are protected in our free country. Institutions of higher education need to take on stronger initiatives to counteract these violations targeting their students and protect the integrity of the American education system. Further, universities in the United States, in effect, are sometimes helping to build up China's military capabilities. In some cases, the US is funding the buildup, and in other cases where scholars conceal their affiliations, universities and scientists don't have full knowledge of the larger purposes that their research and discoveries are being used to fulfill.

In addition to co-opting and sending students abroad, the Chinese Communist Party also seeks to convince US students to apply for jobs with the CIA and the US State Department.

Glenn Duffie Shiver, a college student, was sentenced to 48 months in prison for "conspiring to provide national defense information to intelligence officers of the People's Republic of China," according to the US Department of Justice.[43] Shiver majored in international relations and attended a study abroad program in Shanghai his junior year.[44] In 2004 while living in Shanghai, he saw an English ad seeking English speakers to write political papers. He responded and was paid $120 to write a paper. Just a few months later, he was asked if he would be interested in meeting with the advertiser's associates. He agreed, and the Chinese intelligence officers offered to pay him to apply to US intelligence and defense jobs. In the end, he had accepted $70,000 before he was caught in 2010.

Shiver told his story and warned students going abroad in the 2010 FBI video *Don't Be a Pawn: A Warning to Students Abroad.* He described how the Chinese government manipulated him to commit espionage and what students should look out for. His core message: "the recruitment is active, and the target is young people."[45]

> "The biggest thing was how friendly they were you know just, 'Hey no problem; you want some money? Hey, don't worry about it. We just want to be friendly with you, we're friends, it's important for China and America to have strong relations, and the more people who are friends the better off that will be.'

> "At that point, I kind of realized wow I can just go to Shanghai, they'll give me a huge wad of Chinese money when I get there and then when I leave, they'll give me another huge wad of American currency. The motivation behind it was definitely greed and money. You know, when you're having money thrown at you, especially when you're at a place like Shanghai, you know, it's a hard tap to turn off."[46]

There is no doubt, China is definitely using the Sun Tzu model for espionage. They are subtle—and they use their spies in every kind of business. Any American strategy toward China must begin with an understanding of how comprehensive and pervasive espionage is in the Chinese Communist Party's way of doing business.

SECTION TWO

UNDERSTANDING CHINA

The main reason America finds itself in this intense competition is our leadership has continually misunderstood China, its history, and its intentions. The following section seeks to correct this misunderstanding and explain how the US should approach China going forward.

CHAPTER NINE

THE RETURN OF THE MIDDLE KINGDOM

> As long as we know our history, we will know how to build our future.
>
> —President Donald Trump, July 2017[1]

> It is a great blessing for China, the Chinese people and the Chinese nation to have the CPC [Chinese Communist Party] as the ruling party. As long as we read and understand the history of modern China and that of its revolution, it is readily apparent that without the leadership of the CPC, our country and our nation would not have made such great progress, nor would we have achieved such high international standing.
>
> —General Secretary Xi Jinping, December 2015[2]

For most of China's history there has been a deep assumption among its people that China is the "Middle Kingdom." The actual translation of the Chinese word for "China" is more accurately translated as "Central States," but while dynasties rose and fell, there was a general sense of continuity. Then for more than 100 years, during the "Century of Humiliation"—which began with the First Opium War (which resulted in Chinese defeat in 1842) and ended with the establishment of the People's Republic of China in 1949—the very concept of Chinese superiority and Chinese centrality was shaken to its core.

The primary reason for the collapse of Chinese confidence was that great powers in Europe, and then Japan, had modernized much faster than China. To China, European and Japanese military power was unstoppable. The result was a steady series of disasters. Then, Britain, France, Germany, Russia, and Japan preyed upon China's weaknesses and extorted huge advantages, including massive reparations payments for military conflicts. China's imperial government was financially and psychologically weakened until it collapsed in 1911. In the power vacuum, a wave of regional warlords sprang up. The warlords had their own separate armies, approaches to raising money, and ideas about China's future.

In response to this chaos and widespread violence, two modernizing movements sprang up. The first was the Kuomintang, or Nationalist movement. The second was the Chinese Communist Party. Ironically, both were helped by the Soviet Union—and both were centralized organizations based on methods created in Leninist Russia. The Kuomintang was originally the more powerful. It focused on destroying the urban Communist Party in places like Shanghai. Ironically this created a new power vacuum within the Communist movement. Mao Zedong, who had radical—indeed heretical—ideas about organizing the peasants in the countryside instead of the urban proletariat is the man who filled it.

The Kuomintang might have ended up destroying the Chinese Communists. There was a period in the 1930s when they were clearly on offense and Mao's Communists were desperately trying to survive. However, when the Japanese attacked in 1937, the Kuomintang had to divert their resources into a war for national survival. During that war, their system grew more and more corrupt. By contrast, the Communists kept gaining ground in rural China and, by 1945, had a large, effective military. Within four years of the end of World War II, Mao's Communists had won the decades-long power struggle, and the Kuomintang were forced to flee to Taiwan, where they survived but had no ability to influence China.

When Mao proclaimed the establishment of the People's Republic of China on October 1, 1949, China was once again unified. It was thoroughly war-torn and impoverished. It would take years for Mao to consolidate power in rural areas, but China was clearly one country again, and the Century of Humiliation had come to an end.

However, the end of the Century of Humiliation and the establishment of the People's Republic of China in 1949 marked the beginning of a *new era* for China—not a *new* China.

Mao, and every Communist Chinese leader since, has focused on the central goal of making China the Middle Kingdom again. According to China's leaders since the establishment of the People's Republic of China, under the rule of the Chinese Communist Party, China will once again become the strong and powerful nation it once was. After all, China has the largest population in the world. It has an extraordinarily rich history and culture. At one time, it was the most technologically advanced nation and had the largest economy. From China's perspective, it was historically the Middle Kingdom around and through which the rest of the world operated. Given this reality, it is perfectly natural for General Secretary Xi Jinping to think of himself as the leader of the inevitable Middle Kingdom of the future. It is helpful to get a deeper sense of what that means in the context of Chinese history.

CHINA'S ANCIENT PAST

China's ancient history dates back approximately 5,000 years. There were many emperors, wars, successes, failures, developments, and declines. To say China's long history is complex would be a serious understatement. The history of China is dynamic, fascinating, and worthy of careful study. However, for the purposes of this book, we will look into three lessons from China's ancient past. The first is the patterned rise and fall of dynasties, the second is China's perception of itself as the "Middle Kingdom," and the last is China's ancient capabilities.

THE INEVITABLE CYCLE

Legend describes Huangdi, or the Yellow Emperor, as China's founding ruler. The Yellow Emperor lived during a time when many tribes were fighting each other for control over coveted farmland. The Yellow Emperor recognized the suffering that was caused by the chaos and warfare. To put an end to the violence, he created a moral code and trained an army to put an end to the disunity. After fighting 56 battles, his army emerged victorious. He became chief of the unified tribes and was given the name Yellow Emperor to represent the yellow color of the earth, which symbolized farming.[3]

Note the emphasis on the human cost of chaos and decentralization and the desirability of a unified system with conformity and safety. This model is deeply ingrained in Chinese history, with roots going back to the mythical period five millennia ago. The idea that order is better than anarchy and chaos is central to much of Chinese culture and psychology. It is amazingly different from the Western emphasis on individuality.

In the legend of the Yellow Emperor, we see a strong leader emerging to restore order and unity to a violent, chaotic, and warring people who had no kingdom to organize them and provide security. This series of events is one of the most prevalent patterns of Chinese history. Associate Professor Michael Tsin from the University of North Carolina at Chapel Hill described this recurring pattern. While studying events throughout China's history, Tsin says to "[n]ote the pattern of dynastic formation, ascendance, and decline.... The last years of many dynasties were marked by inefficient administration and corruption, which, when compounded by natural calamities such as flood or droughts, led to social unrest among the population." Tsin also observed that various movements and rebellions, some religiously or politically motivated, led to the downfall or collapse of dynasties throughout China's history.[4] This continual cycle is a hallmark of Chinese history that has endured over the millennia. The *Romance of the Three Kingdoms*—the famous fourteenth-century epic novel that Mao often quoted in his speeches and probably reread far more than any political document—opens with, "The empire, long divided, must unite; long united, it must divide. Thus it has ever been."[5,6]

Furthermore, in the historic Chinese view, a major part of what gave each dynasty its power to establish or continue its rule is a concept known as the "Mandate of Heaven." Using the Mandate of Heaven to explain a leader's legitimacy in China began during the Zhou Dynasty (1046–256 BC) and was used until the collapse of the last emperor in 1911.[7] Under the Mandate of Heaven, only rulers who were virtuous and just were permitted to maintain power. If the current ruler was corrupt, cruel, or overly indulgent, for example, the ruler would lose the mandate, chaos would erupt, and a new ruler would take the corrupt one's place. For leaders, the Mandate of Heaven provided power, but also required an adherence to a moral code. This concept of a mandate helped the Chinese people understand the reason for the rise and fall of dynasties throughout their long history. It also provided divine legitimacy to a dynasty that was doing well.

One of the most notable examples of this cycle started with the decline of the Zhou Dynasty. The dynasty's loss of power led to the Spring and Autumn Period (approximately 770–476 BC) and the Warring States Period (approximately 475–221 BC). The first was later named by historians after a Confucian book. The latter's name is self-evident. These two periods of conflict were highly creative—intellectually and culturally. Both Confucius and Sun Tzu developed their solutions in the middle of the chaos. One was trying to solve the problem of how to win and impose order. The other was trying to develop a moral code which, in effect, would sustain order once it was imposed. Ultimately, these periods of violence and disorder were replaced by the rise of the Qin Dynasty (pronounced "chin").

In the course of these Spring and Autumn, and Warring States periods, nobles increased their power and expanded their control over surrounding smaller states. This created larger, more powerful, semiautonomous states—some of whom declared their independence from the ruling Zhou Dynasty. Violence ensued as the quest for power and control erupted throughout the empire. At the beginning of the fourth century BC, during the Warring States Period, seven major states emerged (though some smaller states still existed). By 221 BC, one of the states, the Qin, conquered all of the other major powers and established the Qin Dynasty.[8] The leader, Ying Zheng, also known as Qin Shi Huang Di, which translates to "the first emperor of Qin,"[9] united the conquered people and is known as the first emperor of a united China.[10] In fact, the word "China" comes from his name.

Significant advancements were made during the new Qin Dynasty, such as the standardization of the writing system, the unification of the people, and the construction of a series of large infrastructure projects. Of all of the advancements that were undertaken during the Qin Dynasty, perhaps the best known by people across the world today is the First Emperor of Qin's massive tomb and terra-cotta army. The tomb (even by today's standards) is truly remarkable. The First Emperor of China was preoccupied with trying to live forever and his life after death. He built an incredible tomb that is an estimated 38 square miles. The mausoleum has a terra-cotta army of approximately 8,000 soldiers and horses to protect the emperor in the afterlife. The attention to detail is incredible; the soldiers all have different facial expressions and are arranged throughout the tomb according to their rank. Archaeologists today haven't even begun to excavate the entire tomb. The emperor's final resting place is housed inside a tall mound that is sealed from the rest of the complex. A historical account describes what may be inside. Allegedly, the tomb contains replicas of China's rivers, with mercury that flowed through them all the way to the sea. Hills and mountains were made of bronze, and pearls and other valuable stones were used to symbolize the sun, the Moon, and stars.[11] This was a taxing project, however, as archaeologists have also uncovered massive graves at the site of the emperor's mausoleum that are thought to belong to craftsmen, laborers, and prisoners in chains, who died during the creation of the tomb.[12] So, even in the midst of this grandiose project, in reality, the rule of the First Emperor of Qin was one of fierce tyranny and brutality that led to resistance from many people. Following the First Emperor of Qin's death, a civil war erupted and was made worse by floods and droughts. The Qin Dynasty officially collapsed after the First Emperor of Qin's son was killed. Chaos continued until the Han Dynasty reunited China and restored order once again in 202 BC.

This example notes two iterations of the cycle of the rise and decline of China's dynasties. The Zhou Dynasty declined, and chaos followed during the Spring and Autumn, and Warring States periods. The Qin Dynasty then consolidated power, developed and made advancements during its 15-year reign, and then declined. This resulted in more chaos and made room for the rise in power of a replacement dynasty, the Han.

This pattern is repeated again and again throughout China's past. It sends a message that no matter how powerful or sophisticated any regime may be at a given time, the threat of decline and collapse always looms overhead. This cycle, and with it the question of not *if* but *when* a dynasty will fall, has become a fundamental part of China's historical narrative.

THE MIDDLE KINGDOM WORLDVIEW

In addition to the ancient patterns of the rise and fall of China's dynasties, for many millennia China has considered itself to be the "Middle Kingdom." This is central to its worldview. This was because in ancient China, the sophistication of Western civilizations was virtually unknown, and the people believed that their empire was situated in the middle of Earth. Especially with China's vast territory, for much of its history, the empire did not regularly encounter other countries or civilizations that matched its capabilities, scale, or sophistication. This helped to foster a sense of China's preeminence among its neighbors and greatly influenced the empire's worldview. Former Secretary of State Henry Kissinger explains this in his book *On China*:

> "[China] was never engaged in sustained contact with another country on the basis of equality for the simple reason that it never encountered societies of comparable culture or magnitude. That the Chinese Empire should tower over its geographical sphere was taken virtually as a law of nature, an expression of the Mandate of Heaven....
>
> "The Chinese Emperors felt it was impractical to contemplate influencing countries that nature had given the misfortune of locating at such a great distance from China. In the Chinese version of exceptionalism, China did not export its ideas but let others come to seek them. Neighboring peoples, the Chinese believed, benefited from contact with China and civilization so long as they acknowledged the suzerainty of the Chinese government. Those who did not were barbarian. Subservience to the Emperor and observance of imperial rituals was the core of culture."[13]

The approach Kissinger described—China versus the "barbarians"—resulted in the Chinese tribute system, which became a key part of Chinese foreign relations. Some form of China's tribute system can be traced back to the Han Dynasty

(206 BC–220 AD) and lasted until the end of the nineteenth century. Although, how stable and consistent this system was throughout China's long and turbulent history is debated.[14] However, the tribute system established a highly ritualized and regulated process for exchanges between China's imperial court and other Asian polities. People from independent polities would come to China to pay tribute and, in doing so, would recognize the ultimate and supreme authority of the emperor. Oftentimes, exchanges such as these were required in order for the tribute-giving polity to establish other commercial or political relations with China. Polities from what are now present-day Korea, Vietnam, Thailand, Burma, and others were a part of this system.[15]

The tribute system was key in reinforcing the idea that China was the Middle Kingdom through diplomatic relations, but China's highly regulated and restrictive oceanic trade system also helped to preserve this notion of centrality and superiority. Trade between Europe and China using direct oceanic routes started in the sixteenth century. In the beginning, multiple ports on China's coast were permitted to be used by Western powers for trading; however, this eventually changed. China later restricted trade with Western nations to one location—the southern port of Canton (Guangzhou). This restrictive Canton System was acceptable for Europe and China for a time. However, for Britain, as soon as the Industrial Revolution produced more goods that needed to be sold and the demand for Chinese tea increased, tensions rose. Britain wanted to expand its trading privileges and diplomatic relations with China outside of the established system.

So, in 1793, a British mission led by Lord Macartney arrived in China to issue a series of requests to the Chinese emperor—namely, to permit more trade privileges between the nations. The Chinese saw the British demands as a direct challenge to their policies and went so far as to call the British mission and gifts "tribute."[16] In a defiant letter to King George III, the emperor rejected the British requests and clearly conveyed how he viewed Britain's inferior position:

> "You, O King, live beyond the confines of many seas, nevertheless, impelled by your humble desire to partake of the benefits of our civilization, you have dispatched a mission respectfully bearing your memorial. Your Envoy has crossed the seas and paid his respects at my Court....
>
> "I have perused your memorial: the earnest terms in which it is couched reveal a respectful humility on your part, which is highly praiseworthy. In consideration of the fact that your Ambassador and his deputy have come a long way with your memorial and tribute, I have shown them high favour and have allowed them to be introduced into my presence....
>
> "Our dynasty's majestic virtue has penetrated unto every country under Heaven, and Kings of all nations have offered their costly tribute by land and sea. As your Ambassador can see for himself, we possess all things. I set no value on objects strange or ingenious, and have no use for your country's manufactures.... It behoves you, O King, to respect my sentiments and to display even greater devotion and loyalty in future, so that, by perpetual submission to our Throne, you may secure peace and prosperity for your country hereafter."[17]

The emperor's response clearly lays out his view of the late eighteenth-century world order. From the Chinese perspective, the empire was truly the Middle Kingdom—situated at the center of the world—and through the Mandate of Heaven possessed the ultimate right to rule. As a result, it would "behove" other nations to recognize China's superiority.

CHINA'S CAPABILITIES

China's notable technological advancements throughout its ancient history also contributed to the idea that the empire was the Middle Kingdom. From groundbreaking infrastructure and research projects, to complex bureaucratic systems, to goods such as silk, porcelain, tea, bronze, and gunpowder, China's innovative capabilities were remarkable and (specifically in the case of gunpowder) significantly impacted the world.[18]

The incredible size and scale of ancient China is one of the reasons the empire was so successful in instituting such advancements. Since GDP was closely related to population size prior to the Industrial Revolution, these two figures reveal just how large a power China historically was. According to Angus Maddison in *The World Economy: Historical Statistics*, China had 26 percent of the world's population in 1 AD and accounted for 26 percent of the world's total GDP. The trend of China's capacity continued into the next millennium. In 1600, China dominated 29 percent of both the world's total GDP and population.[19] Also referencing Maddison's work, Kissinger wrote, "China produced a greater share of total world GDP than any Western society in 18 of the last 20 centuries. As late as 1820, it produced over 30 percent of world GDP—an amount exceeding the GDP of Western Europe, Eastern Europe, and the United States combined."[20]

However, one of the most interesting examples of China's historical capacity for making incredible technological strides occurred much earlier. From 1405–1433, Admiral Zheng He traveled in a fleet of "treasure ships" to distant lands such as India, Java, the Strait of Hormuz, and the Horn of Africa. As if successfully embarking across such incredible distances wasn't enough of an accomplishment at the time, the treasure ship fleet was so technologically advanced that there was no other fleet comparable. The European age of exploration had not even started when Admiral Zheng left China. The Spanish Armada was still 150 years away from sailing. Even so, as Kissinger wrote, it would have been outmatched by the sheer size and sophistication of China's treasure ship fleet.[21]

No one knows for sure why Admiral Zheng embarked on such monumental missions at this time. Kissinger said the travels of the treasure fleet resembles "a kind of early exercise of Chinese 'soft power.'"[22] While stopping at each destination during his missions, Admiral Zheng formally exalted the Chinese emperor, gave extravagant gifts, and invited rulers (or their designated envoys) to visit China. The foreigners during these reciprocated visits to China would perform the "kowtow"—the practice of laying prostrate on the ground and touching one's forehead to the ground three times—upon meeting the emperor. Doing so would represent the foreigners' recognition of the supreme authority of the emperor and their own subjugated position in what Kissinger terms the "Sinocentric world order."[23]

Interestingly, on these missions, Admiral Zheng didn't lay claim to any territories, conquer any peoples, or assert any control over resources. He only brought back "tribute" (gifts) from his journeys, which came to a halt in 1433. The next emperor destroyed the records from the three decades of the treasure ship voyages and disassembled the ships (much to China's later detriment). This decision resulted in China backing away from the infusion and exchange of new ideas and new attitudes. The world would have been very different if the next emperor had embraced the ocean opportunity. However, though the quests did not occur again, and China's seafaring capabilities declined, the treasure ship voyages and capabilities were so remarkable for the time that it proved China had the capacity to make incredible achievements in technological developments.

These three aspects of China's history (its long historic cycles, its self-centric worldview, and its ability to take leaps in technology) lead to fundamental lessons that have helped to shape China's national identity and influence China's leadership today—made up of people who are both Communist *and*

Chinese. The inevitable cycle teaches China that the decline of unity and power is always possible and imminent. More importantly, however, that following these periods of uncertainty and chaos, the empire will rise, unite, and regain its strength. The Middle Kingdom worldview teaches China that the empire is the influential and superior entity, compared with outside "barbarians." Finally, China's capabilities reinforce China's notion that it was the Middle Kingdom. Such advancements teach China that regardless of whatever challenges may arise, the empire can continue to grow and develop at a level that competes with or supersedes Western powers. All of these lessons that we learn *from* China's ancient history were put to the test as China entered yet another period of decline and chaos in the mid-nineteenth century. This downcycle dramatically influenced and shaped the China that we know today.

THE CENTURY OF HUMILIATION

Because this period so decisively shaped the thinking of Mao and the founding generation and is still vivid for the current Chinese leadership, it is worth examining in more detail. China's reign as the dominant power in its world came to a grinding halt during the Century of Humiliation at the time of the rule of the Qing Dynasty. This period, which lasted from the mid-1800s until the establishment of the People's Republic of China in 1949, consisted of multiple rebellions as well as invasions from foreign and regional powers. This led to heightened instability and chaos within China and the eventual collapse of China's last dynasty in 1911. The Century of Humiliation began with the First Opium War—a war that resulted from trade imbalances between China and Britain. The First Opium War lasted from 1839–1842 and ended in Chinese defeat.

Prior to the outbreak of the war, Chinese products, such as porcelain and silk, were in high demand in the West. However, the demand for Western products was not equally reciprocated in China. This resulted in many payments in the form of silver currency flowing into China. Since at the time there was a global shortage of silver, and silver currency was the only currency that China would accept, a solution to the trade imbalance was needed to allow the exchange of goods to continue.[24] To counteract the influx of silver being sent to China, British—and also American—traders found that opium from India was highly addictive and there could be a demand for this drug in China. British traders saw opium as a potential opportunity for massive profits and began shipping the drug to China.

The leaders of the Qing Dynasty recognized how destructive opium was for the Chinese people. (The same notion holds true today, as drugs that we recognize as being dangerously addictive and potentially devastating—such as morphine, codeine, heroin, and oxycodone—are made from the opium plant.) As a result, the Chinese government banned the importing and producing of the drug in 1800. In 1813, smoking opium was made illegal and was punishable by 100 beatings. Despite opium being outlawed by the government, a complex system of smuggling the drug into China continued. Opium was shipped in large containers, or chests, and from 1810 to 1838, the number of chests imported into China multiplied from 4,500 to 40,000. Silver flowed out of China to finance the population's addiction and rose from approximately two million ounces of silver during the early 1820s to more than nine million ounces in the early 1830s.[25] The US Office of the Historian notes the significance of the imports of opium to China and states that "the increasing opium trade with Western powers meant that for the first time, China imported more goods than it exported."[26]

The war to stop the illicit flow of opium into China officially broke out in 1839 and ended with a British victory and a Chinese defeat in 1842. As a result of this loss, China was forced to agree to the first of a series of "unequal treaties." China agreed to open ports to foreign trade and inhabitance by Westerners, which destroyed the "Canton System"—China's highly regulated and restrictive trade system that had been in place that I previously described. Moreover, China paid substantial reparations and gave control of Hong Kong to the British.

Interestingly, Kissinger noted in *On China* that "the most bitterly contested provisions" were related to the issue of the "equality of status" between China and the British. Kissinger wrote, "The leaders on both sides understood that this was a dispute about far more than protocol or opium. The Qing court was willing to appease avaricious foreigners with money and trade; but if the principle of barbarian political equality to the Son of Heaven [the Emperor] was established, the entire Chinese world order would be threatened; the dynasty risked the loss of the Mandate of Heaven."[27]

In order to resolve this dispute, Kissinger wrote that the Chinese and the British agreed to include "a clause explicitly ensuring that Chinese and British officials would henceforth 'correspond...on a footing of perfect equality'; it went so far as to list specific written Chinese characters in the text with acceptably neutral connotations. Chinese records (or at least those to which foreigners had access) would no longer describe the British as 'begging' Chinese authorities or 'tremblingly obeying' their 'orders.' "[28]

The Chinese historic "Sinocentric" world order began to unravel upon the conclusion of the First Opium War. Throughout the rest of the nineteeth century, Western powers and Japan encroached on China, particularly during the Second Opium War (1856–1860) and the Sino-Japanese War (1894–1895). The cession of Chinese power and control to foreigners was met with resistance by the Chinese people and resulted in an uprising in 1900—known as the Boxer Rebellion.

A secret group composed primarily of peasants was organized calling itself the Society of Righteous and Harmonious Fists. The group received the nickname "Boxers" because of the martial arts and calisthenics practices they performed to prevent injury from bullets or attacks. These rituals were referred to as shadow boxing by Westerners, hence the name

"Boxers." Many members were from the Shandong province, an area in China that had witnessed devastating floods and famine and that had made territorial and economic concessions to multiple European nations—who they blamed for the bad living conditions. Consequently, the Boxers were opposed to the increasing foreign influence in China and were also staunchly anti-Christian. The Boxers increased in popularity in the late 1890s and led frequent attacks on foreigners and Chinese Christians. The movement spread to the area surrounding Beijing in 1900. Chinese Christians and missionaries were murdered by the Boxers, and churches and railroad stations were obliterated. The Boxers initiated a siege of the foreign legation district—an area where foreign diplomats lived—in Beijing on June 20, 1900.[29] The Qing Empress responded to the Boxer siege by praising the "the brave followers of the Boxers" and declaring war on every foreign nation that had diplomatic ties in China.[30]

A multinational force was established to put an end to the siege while diplomats, their families, and guards endured hunger and difficult conditions. Hundreds of foreigners and thousands of Chinese Christians are estimated to have died during the rebellion. The multinational force made up of around 20,000 troops from the US, Austria-Hungary, France, Germany, Italy, Japan, Russia, and the United Kingdom liberated the foreigners and Chinese Christians from the Boxers on August 14, 1900.

The Boxer Protocol was signed on September 7, 1901, which marked the official end of the uprising.[31] The Boxer Rebellion was yet another example of China's failed attempt to prevent the increasing influence of foreigners. In fact, the problem was only exacerbated by the Boxer Protocol that came as a consequence of the revolt. Under this agreement, China was required to destroy forts that were protecting Beijing, was not allowed to import arms for two years, and was forced to pay more than $330 million to the involved foreign nations—approximately $9 billion in today's currency. Moreover, punishments were mandated for all government officials and Boxers who participated in the rebellion. For defensive purposes, troops were allowed to be deployed to foreign legations in Beijing.[32,33]

The consequences from the Boxer Rebellion were catastrophic for China. It further diminished China's global position and severely weakened the Qing Dynasty. Following the cycle typical of China's dynasties, an uprising occurred in 1911 (which was also caused in part by the government's failure to modernize, a quadrupling of the population size since 1644, and the depletion of government resources). The Qing Dynasty collapsed.[34]

A power vacuum emerged in China throughout much of the first half of the twentieth century. Establishing a replacement strong, centralized government proved challenging, particularly with such a vast territory, large population, and warlords controlling various areas and armies throughout China (note the fragmentation parallel to the Warring States period). By the 1920s, two major political party movements had gained popularity and took hold in China: the Kuomintang and the Communist Party of China.

The Kuomintang, also known as the Nationalist Party, was established by Sun Yat-sen following the revolution in 1911. Sun Yat-sen ultimately aimed to establish a Chinese republic that was strong, united, and modernized while focusing on the "Three Principles of the People": nationalism, democracy, and livelihood.[35] The Kuomintang did not receive assistance from the West, resulting in the Kuomintang looking to Moscow for aid. The Kuomintang was not communist; however, it relied on and welcomed support from the Soviet Union. Sun Yat-sen even praised Lenin for the successful Bolshevik revolution, and in the 1920s, the Soviets agreed to provide military, political, and organizational aid.[36]

The Chinese Communist Party, on the other hand, began when the head librarian at Beijing University—Li Dazhao—established a Marxist study group upon realizing that the model being used for Russia could also be useful for China. The party was formalized in 1921 with Mao Zedong as one of its founding members.

For a period of time, there was cooperation between the Kuomintang and the Chinese Communist Party to unify China. In fact, Chinese Communist Party members were ordered by the Soviet Union (Lenin and then Stalin) to join the Kuomintang, though they were still able to have their separate Chinese Communist Party membership. Leaders such as Mao and China's first foreign minister, Zhou Enlai, obliged.[37] This alliance to unite China became known as the First United Front. However, a couple of years after the death of Sun Yat-sen in 1925, a civil war in China erupted between the two parties.

The conflict was put on pause when the Kuomintang and Chinese Communist Party established the Second United Front alliance to fight against the Japanese invasion during World War II. After the end of the war in 1945, talks to establish a post-war government between Kuomintang leader Chiang Kai-shek and Chinese Communist Party leader Mao Zedong were unsuccessful. Fighting between the two sides broke out once again. The Communists defeated the Kuomintang and Mao Zedong formally declared the establishment of the People's Republic of China in October 1949. The Chinese Communist Party's declaration of the People's Republic of China ended China's Century of Humiliation. In the wake of the Communist victory and consolidation of power, the Kuomintang was forced to retreat to Taiwan. After seizing power, the Communist Party had a daunting task in front of it. The Chinese Communist Party had to unite the Chinese people and strengthen the country once again, following more than a century of violence, war, and infiltration by foreign powers.

One important attribute of the new ruling Chinese Communist Party "dynasty," however, is that it no longer obtains its legitimacy to rule from the Mandate of Heaven and divine forces. Instead, the Communist Party maintains its authority by visibly pushing China forward toward a better future following a century of tragedy. Successors are not chosen by blood. They rise through adherence and loyalty to the totalitarian Chinese Communist Party and its objectives. This preserves unity and the power of the party—which in turn fends off or eliminates chaotic, entropic forces within the Chinese communist system.

In a speech given by Mao in 1949, he describes the decline of China during the Century of Humiliation and the People's Republic of China's goal for restoring the strength of the nation:

> "The Chinese have always been a great, courageous and industrious nation; it is only in modern times that they have fallen behind. And that was due entirely to oppression and exploitation by foreign imperialism and domestic reactionary governments. For over a century our forefathers never stopped waging unyielding struggles against domestic and foreign oppressors.... Our forefathers enjoined us to carry out their unfulfilled will. And we have acted accordingly.... Ours will no longer be a nation subject to insult and humiliation. We have stood up....
>
> "Our state system, the people's democratic dictatorship, is a powerful weapon for safeguarding the fruits of victory of the people's revolution and for thwarting the plots of domestic and foreign enemies for restoration, and this weapon we must firmly grasp....
>
> "There are indeed difficulties ahead, and a great many too. But we firmly believe that by heroic struggle the people of the country will surmount them all. The Chinese people have rich experience in overcoming difficulties. If our forefathers, and we also, could weather long years of extreme difficulty and defeat powerful domestic and foreign reactionaries, why can't we now, after victory, build a prosperous and flourishing country?...
>
> "Let the domestic and foreign reactionaries tremble before us! Let them say we are no good at this and

no good at that. By our own indomitable efforts we the Chinese people will unswervingly reach our goal."[38]

However, this optimism for the future of a new direction for China under the leadership of the Communist Party would be short-lived. With the ideological split between China and the Soviet Union, followed by chaos caused by Mao's failed policies during the Great Leap Forward that resulted in up to 45 million deaths from 1958–1962, followed by the Cultural Revolution (1966–1976) that caused an estimated 500,000–8 million deaths, the possibility of the revitalization of China remained uncertain.[39,40] That is, until the continuous surge of the Cold War and, later, the rise of the reformist Chinese leader, Deng Xiaoping. Deng saw an unlikely strategic opportunity for the People's Republic of China—to align with an estranged superpower across the Pacific—the United States.

CHAPTER TEN

ALLY, ENEMY, STRATEGIC PARTNER

[W]e are standing up to China's chronic trading abuses and theft of intellectual properties and so many other things that they've done to us. I don't know how you people allowed this to happen for so many years.... But they really have, they've taken advantage of our country... I get along with [Xi] great, but I really hit him hard about how they've hurt our country.... I blame the leaders of our country for allowing it to happen.

—President Donald Trump, April 2019[1]

Sound China-US relations will be of benefit not only to our two countries and our two peoples, but also to the world at large. There are a thousand reasons to make the China-US relationship a success, and not a single one to harm it. Since the normalization of China-US relations 45 years ago, in spite of ups and downs, they have made historic progress, which has delivered enormous practical benefits to our two peoples.

—General Secretary Xi Jinping, April 2017[2]

Americans have had a variety of views of China. Those views have evolved over time. It helps to put the current shift in our perception of China into perspective by looking at the long pattern of change. The earliest American attitudes toward China changed significantly by the time we reached the strategic partnership which had greatly evolved by the end of the Cold War.

Early on, from the American Revolution to the late nineteenth century, Americans saw China as a market, an exotic destination, and a dramatically different culture. As the Chinese government lost power, the country became more violent, unstable, and uncontrollable. A substantial number of largely Protestant missionaries began to go to China including a significant number of missionary doctors and nurses. There was a sense of "civilized, modern Americans" helping "poverty stricken backward Chinese." Specific violent events, such as the Boxer Rebellion, defined a lot of our thinking about China toward the end of the nineteenth and beginning of the twentieth centuries. Movies like *55 Days at Peking* later sought to capture that era. A similar sense of violence was conveyed in the novel and movie *The Sand Pebbles*. The author, Richard McKenna, enlisted in the US Navy in 1931 and served for 10 years in the Far East, two of which were spent on a gunboat on the Yangtze River.[3]

By contrast, we initially admired the Japanese for their dramatic transition to modernity and their demonstrated military effectiveness in annihilating the Russian Baltic fleet in the Battle of Tsushima Strait in 1905.[4] In fact, President Theodore Roosevelt became the first American to win the Nobel Peace Prize for his mediation between Russia and Japan to end the Russo-Japanese War. Our admiration of Japan continued through World War I when it was our ally against Germany. The Japanese were treated as one of the five major powers at the Versailles Peace Conference in 1919. Meanwhile, the Chinese were so ignored and their interests were so neglected that China became the only country at the Paris Peace Conference at Versailles that refused to support the Treaty.[5] (President Woodrow Wilson advocated for the Treaty, but the US ultimately did not ratify the treaty after a failed vote in the Senate.)

American admiration for Japan began to turn into hostility toward Japanese militarism. Each step by the Japanese in wanting to build a navy to dominate the Pacific inevitably posed a threat to us as the only other major naval power in that ocean at that time. Japan's aggression in beginning to occupy first Manchuria, attacking into China proper, and controlling large sections of the country by 1937 turned American sentiment against Japan and toward a more favorable view of China.[6]

The rise of the Kuomintang and the brilliance of Chiang Kai-shek's wife, Soong Mei-ling, who worked as a propagandist and diplomat, created a "China lobby." Henry Luce, the creator of *Time* and *Life* magazines and one of the most prominent communicators in America, became a powerful advocate of helping China defend itself against Japanese aggression. He was also passionately anti-communist and built up Chiang Kai-shek and the Kuomintang. This pro-Chinese sentiment was captured in a series of novels by Pearl Buck, the daughter of missionaries who spent most of her first 40 years living in China. Her novel, *The Good Earth*, won the Pulitzer Prize and was the bestselling book in both 1931 and 1932. Her China was a romanticized country of good people who needed and deserved our help.[7]

From 1937 to 1945, Americans saw the underdog Chinese as courageously fighting the invading Japanese. Events like the Rape of Nanking (a truly horrifying orgy of rape, torture, and murder on a citywide scale) made the Americans steadily more pro-Chinese and anti-Japanese. By 1941, while the United States was still at peace with Japan, President Franklin Roosevelt authorized the development of the American Volunteers Group, popularly known as the Flying Tigers, to help China defend itself against Japanese airpower.

The Japanese surprise attack at Pearl Harbor guaranteed

an anti-Japanese fervor and consequently a very big pro-Chinese attitude. As the war went on, Americans became more and more committed to helping China. The US Army Air Force and China National Aviation Corporation flew 650,000 tons of supplies over the Himalayan Mountains, called the "Hump."[8] The route was so dangerous that there are records of close to 700 fatal crashes.[9] This was just one example of the extraordinary effort President Roosevelt went to strengthen China and keep it in the war. In 1943, Chiang Kai-shek was invited to the Cairo Conference with President Roosevelt and Prime Minister Winston Churchill as proof he was now the head of a great power. This same sentiment would lead China to be given a permanent seat on the United Nations Security Council.

In America, Chiang Kai-shek was steadily built up as the hope of a pro-American "Westernized" China. Luce was so committed to the Nationalist Chinese that he rejected warnings from his reporters in China (Theodore H. White being the most famous) that the Kuomintang was corrupt and unpopular and the Communists were likely to win the civil war once the Japanese were gone.[10] After the war, America tried to find a compromise between the Communists and the Kuomintang, but even the effort of General George Marshall from 1945–1947 failed. When the Nationalists were driven off the mainland to exile in Taiwan, most Americans' loyalty and friendship went with them. The Chinese Communists were portrayed as dangerous, destructive people who were natural enemies of the West. They were also seen as allies of the Soviet Union in the new Cold War—which had followed all too rapidly after the end of World War II. (As I've noted, this is ironic since the Kuomintang actually had Soviet support initially.)

In America, the shock at the victory of the "Reds" was so great that the question of "Who lost China?" became a major political issue. We were committed to defending Taiwan against any communist invasion. Suddenly, we found ourselves in a totally different war when North Korea invaded South Korea.

When we went to the defense of our ally and fought to stop communist aggression, the Chinese Communists decided they had to enter the war to stop us from getting too close to their border.

Our image of inefficient or incompetent Chinese troops was shattered in November 1950 when they moved as many as 300,000 troops into position secretly and surprised the Americans in a shattering attack that drove us out of North Korea.[11] For the next three years we fought a bitter, intense conflict. We lost almost 40,000 Americans.[12] The Chinese lost more than 400,000.[13] The Korean people lost 10 percent of their population in a larger civilian casualty rate than World War II.[14] Coming out of the Korean War in 1953 we had a new vision of a tough, dangerous communist-ruled China that was clearly an implacable enemy. We saw them closely allied with the Soviet Union, and we maintained an aggressive effort to contain them.

The Vietnam War shifted our attention south of China. We knew a lot of supplies for the Vietnamese Communists came through China, but we were careful not to slide into a new war with the neighboring giant. The 1950s saw the Communists consolidating power and mutual paranoia rising between the Americans and the Chinese. Toward the end of Vietnam War, our view of China and their view of America began to shift.

A deep split had developed within the communist world—between Beijing and Moscow. Mao and his leaders saw themselves as true Communists following the principles of Lenin and Stalin. They saw the Khrushchev leadership as heretics who were betraying those true principles. Later, they increasingly saw Khrushchev's successor, Brezhnev, as a Russian nationalist who no longer represented the international interests of communism. China felt further alienated by what it saw as the Russian mismanagement of Eastern Europe and the unrest in that region. Chinese suspicions of Moscow increased beginning in the mid-1960s as the Soviets began increasing their military strength in Asia. According to a declassified Top Secret CIA Special Memorandum from 1968:

> "The past two and a half years have witnessed a significant quantitative as well as qualitative improvement of the Soviet military posture near China. There has been a steady increase in the strength of regular combat units along the Sino-Soviet border. For the first time in two decades, a significant Soviet combat force is taking shape in Mongolia. Certain units of the Strategic Rocket Forces have almost certainly been earmarked for potential missile strikes against Chinese targets. [redacted] the types of Soviet units involved in the reinforcement [redacted] indicate that the Soviets are preparing their forces not just for containing local outbreaks of fighting, but even for the eventual possibility of major military operations—either conventional or nuclear—against the Chinese."[15]

By 1969, tensions were high enough that there were serious border clashes between the two countries. A genuine fear was building that the Soviets might try to solve the global leadership of communism question by launching a preemptive strike against China. American fears of China were declining as the effect of the Great Leap Forward in the late 1950s and the Cultural Revolution of the late 1960s convulsed the country and weakened its ability to project power. The real fear was that China would be dominated by the Soviet Union. Popular opinion between the two countries had not changed dramatically, but the governing leaders in both Washington, DC, and Beijing were beginning to see that some kind of rapprochement might be strategically helpful to both countries.

Nixon, before being elected as president, also expressed similar concerns about an isolated China. He wrote an article that was published in *Foreign Affairs* in October 1967. "We simply cannot afford," he wrote, "to leave China forever outside the family of nations, there to nurture its fantasies, cherish its hates and threaten its neighbors. There is no place on this small planet for a billion of its potentially most able people to live in angry isolation."[16] Nixon compared the diplomatic challenge the United States faced at that time to inner city social reform. He argued, "In each case dialogues have to be opened; in each case aggression has to be restrained while education proceeds; and, not least, in neither case can we afford to let those now self-exiled from society stay exiled forever."[17] Later, when Nixon became president in 1969, he carried with him these concerns but also recognized the strategic opportunities associated with establishing relations with the People's Republic of China. He wanted to end the Vietnam War through a phased withdrawal of US involvement, but also was committed to ensure that America had a role in shaping the new emerging Indo-Pacific order. As Kissinger wrote in *On China*:

> "Nixon was committed to ending the [Vietnam] war, but equally strongly to giving America a dynamic role in reshaping the international order just emerging piece by piece. Nixon intended to free American policy from the oscillations between extremes of commitment and withdrawal and ground it in a concept of the national interest that could be sustained as administrations succeeded each other.
>
> "In this design, China played a key role. The leaders of the two countries viewed their common goals from different perspectives. Mao treated the rapprochement as a strategic imperative (due to the severe threat of continued Soviet aggression) Nixon as an opportunity to redefine the American approach to foreign policy and international leadership. He sought to use the opening to China to demonstrate to the American public that, even in the midst of a debilitating war, the United States was in a position to bring about a design for long-term peace."[18]

Despite Nixon's and Mao's conclusion that rapprochement was both beneficial and necessary, tactically establishing diplomatic relations would prove difficult because of historic tensions and domestic hurdles. Mao's position as leader of the Chinese Communist Party allowed him to dictate any direction for China that he wanted, while President Nixon had to be more cautious. When Nixon became president, the American embargo on China had been in place for 20 years (since the US supported the Kuomintang exiled government in Taiwan, wanted to contain communist-ruled China, and was fearful of a Sino-Soviet partnership). Changing long, deeply held beliefs within the American bureaucracy is challenging, as is shifting the tides of the opinions of the American people. Making this all the more difficult was the continuation of the Cold War, widespread opposition to communism, and America's involvement in the Vietnam War.

This made traditional diplomatic engagement challenging for the US and China and added to the vast cultural and political differences between the two powers. How to convey the beginning stages of rapprochement between the US and China was uncertain—the US didn't have a way to effectively communicate Nixon's strategy as a formal position, and China didn't want to seem weak amid the mounting threats they faced as a nation.

Nonetheless, between 1969 and 1970 a series of back-channel and secret communications occurred between the two countries. In December 1970, Kissinger, who was President Nixon's assistant for national security at the time, received a message (by route of the Pakistani government) from Chinese Premier Zhou Enlai. The message was an invitation for a US emissary to come to Beijing to talk about "the vacation [sic] of Chinese territories called Taiwan" that "have now been occupied by foreign troops of the United States for the last fifteen years."[19]

The White House issued a reply to China. It accepted the invitation for an emissary to visit but defined the agenda of the discussions to include not just Taiwan but also "the broad range of issues which lie between the People's Republic of China and the US."[20] To the Nixon administration's disdain, a three-month-long silence from the Chinese government followed. When the United States did finally hear from China in April 1971, it was through an avenue that no one expected—during the World Table Tennis Championships.

In Nagoya, Japan, three-time world champion Zhuang Zedong sat in the back of his Chinese team's bus. Nineteen-year-old Santa Monica College student Glenn Cowan—possibly by accident—stepped onto the bus. The Chinese athletes were confused by the arrival of the long-haired American opponent in a USA uniform on their bus. Zhuang later said in a CNN interview, "We were all tense." He added, "Our team had been advised not to speak to Americans, not to shake their hands, and not to exchange gifts with them."[21]

Despite the instructions, Zhuang believed that ignoring Cowan contradicted the Chinese practice of hospitality. After weighing his options for about 10 minutes, he approached Cowan and began conversing with him through a translator. Zhuang gifted Cowan a silk screen picture of the Huangshan mountains in China, and the following day, Cowan gave Zhuang a T-shirt with a peace sign and the words "Let It Be." The exchange was widely reported by the press, and news of the event reached Beijing and Washington, DC.

"Zhuang Zedong is not just a good table tennis player," Mao said, "he's a good diplomat as well."[22] Mao then invited the American team on an all-expense paid trip to China, which was approved by the American Embassy and accepted by the athletes.

On April 10, 1971, the 15 American ping-pong athletes, as well as team officials and spouses, passed through the "Bamboo Curtain" by way of a Hong Kong bridge into China. It had been more than 20 years since an American delegation had visited China. President Nixon later wrote about the significance of this "Ping-Pong diplomacy"—the first public indication of thawing relations—in his memoirs. "I was as surprised as I was pleased," he wrote, "I had never expected that the China initiative would come to fruition in the form of a ping-pong team."[23]

For the United States, this interaction was reassurance that the Chinese were publicly committed to rapprochement. In late April, the Nixon administration received another letter from Premier Zhou Enlai, in response to the US acceptance of the invitation to send an emissary to Beijing. Zhou requested that the emissary be Kissinger, Secretary of State William Rogers, or "even the President of the US himself."[24] As Kissinger recalls in *On China*, "Nixon had decided that the channel to Beijing should be confined to the White House. No other agency had been told of the . . . communications from Zhou Enlai."[25]

Nixon accepted the invitation on May 10, 1971, and secretly sent Kissinger to Beijing in July to begin preparations for a presidential visit. This was one of two trips to China Kissinger made in 1971. In February 1972, President Nixon visited China, where he met Chairman Mao and Premier Zhou. From this visit emerged the Shanghai Communiqué—agreed to by the US and China. This document was critical in beginning the normalization of US-China relations and ending more than 20 years of hostility. Relations continued to thaw and improve between the United States and China in the years following. Full diplomatic recognition was given to the People's Republic of China by President Jimmy Carter in 1979, severing formal US ties with Taiwan.

BUILDING UP CHINA: MILITARY, SCIENCE, AND TECHNOLOGY

Throughout much of the twentieth century, the US policymakers commonly thought that China was a "backward" country, did not have an aggressive military, was limited in its capabilities, and didn't see America as a major military threat. It's easy to wonder now how this belief began and why it persisted for so many decades. It is more important, however, to recognize that this belief led the US to help build up China's economy through technology transfers, exchanges, and education efforts—and boost China's military by providing intelligence and weapons systems. Since the early phases of rapprochement in the 1970s, China's communist leaders emphasized that China was not a threat to the United States. Instead, Beijing argued, America should help China grow and develop to become a strong nation. When Kissinger was in China in 1971 preparing for President Nixon's visit, Premier Zhou Enlai made this exact point:

> "We do not consider ourselves a power. Although we are developing our economy, in comparison to others we are comparatively backward. Of course, your President also mentioned that in the next five to ten years, China will speedily develop. We think it will not be so soon, although we will try to go all out, aim high, and develop our socialist construction in a better, faster, and more economical way....
>
> "When our economy is developed, we will still not consider ourselves a superpower and will not join in the ranks of the superpowers."[26]

Referring to American concerns, Mao reiterated this notion during his meeting with President Nixon in February 1972: "They are concerned about me?" He added, "That is like the cat weeping over the dead mouse!"[27] In this way, China's communist leaders positioned themselves perfectly. Communicating to the Americans that China viewed itself as a substantially weaker power influenced US perceptions of their intentions. Rather than seeking any sort of expansion or regional dominance, China appeared to be a nonthreatening country, struggling to learn and grow. This perception led to a flood of US intelligence, technology, weapons, exchanges, and deals being sent to China in the following years and succeeding presidential administrations that just a short time before would have been incomprehensible.

The Hundred-Year Marathon, authored by the director for Chinese strategy at the Hudson Institute and one of President Trump's leading advisers on China, Michael Pillsbury, describes these transfers at length. As Pillsbury describes, the first significant covert offer of assistance to the Chinese was made before President Nixon even visited China. Kissinger secretly provided classified intelligence to the Chinese that described the movements of Indian troops against Pakistan. The second was made by Alexander Haig, Kissinger's deputy, who visited China in January 1972 in preparation for Nixon's visit. Instructed by Nixon, Haig promised the Chinese that the US would cooperate with China in efforts directed against the Soviet Union.

These two offers were a clear sign of America's optimism toward a future US-China relationship. Though they were covert, considering the lack of cooperation and relations that had been the norm for the preceding two decades, they were groundbreaking. Continuing these promises of American cooperation with China against the Soviet Union, during a meeting with Mao in February 1972, President Nixon stated that the US would stand against any "aggressive action" taken by the Soviets against China.[28] Also, during this visit, Kissinger provided a briefing to two Chinese officials where he described critical information about the positions of Soviet forces along the shared border between China and the Soviet Union—including intelligence of Soviet ground forces, aircraft, missiles, and nuclear forces. The nuclear targeting information provided during Kissinger's briefing was seen by one of the Chinese officials, according to Yale Professor Paul Bracken in his book *The Second Nuclear Age*, as "an indication of your wish to improve our relationship."[29]

The idea that China was the missing link in the United States' strategy against the Soviet Union persisted. The US began to see China as a possible partner, as evidenced by Kissinger's comment to Nixon when he said, "with the exception of the UK, the PRC might well be the closest to us in its global perceptions."[30] The Nixon administration wanted to find a way to capitalize on this engagement with China and use it as a counterbalance against the Soviet Union. A year after Nixon's visit, Kissinger told Chinese officials that Nixon wanted to establish "enough of a relationship with [China] so that it is plausible that an attack on [China] involves a substantial American interest." Pillsbury calls this concept a sort of "symbolic trip wire."[30] In effect, it would create a deterrent from Soviet expansion into China—a situation that the United States was concerned with avoiding.

The promises the United States offered to China up until this point, though significant, were not tangible. As normalization of bilateral relations progressed, the issue of whether or not the United States should continue to provide only diplomatic promises and gestures to China, or begin to provide tactical assistance, became apparent. The US decided to supply China with tactical aid in November 1973 (indicative of real progress in rapprochement) when Kissinger offered US supply of "equipment and other services" to China if the Soviets attacked. "Under some guise," he also offered US help to improve communication capabilities between Beijing and Chinese bomber bases. He also said the US would supply the technology necessary for China to build "certain kinds of radar."[32] This emphasized US willingness to prop up China against its mutual adversary. These November tactical propositions to provide US aid to the People's Liberation Army were also kept secret, and according to Pillsbury were not revealed—even to the CIA—for three decades.[33]

The American offers to China and the progression of rapprochement between the two countries continued to move forward after the Chinese and US leadership changed. Following Mao's death in September 1976, Deng Xiaoping rose to power and consolidated his authority over the Chinese Communist Party in the late 1970s. Deng was a leader who greatly appealed to the West, both with his tranquil personality as well as his reform-oriented policy goals. Deng believed China's modernization and development had fallen behind and had not progressed as substantially as it should have. In order to propel China forward on a path of development, Deng adopted the "Four Modernizations" of agriculture, industry, science and technology, and national defense. The goal of the Four Modernizations was to transform China into a relatively modern state by 2000. The Chinese Communist Party was so committed to this directive that it was enshrined in both the party and state constitutions.

Among these four areas, Deng recognized the significant power that science and technology possessed to increase a country's economic strength and capabilities. In terms of economic growth, he later put forth the theory in 1988 that "Science and technology are primary productive forces."[34]

To aid with China's technological development, President Carter in July 1978 sent, according to Pillsbury, "the highest-level delegation of US scientists ever to visit another country."[35] The delegation was led by a science adviser for President Carter, Frank Press, who was previously a professor at MIT. Press gave a speech that emphasized the benefits of globalization that was published by the *People's Daily*. The publication of his speech was significant, as it was especially rare for the Chinese state-sponsored media outlet to publish a speech made by a foreigner. Reportedly, Deng was also very engaged with the American delegation, showing curiosity and interest in their discussions, while also sharing with the delegates his vision for the future of China. According to Pillsbury, Deng also conveyed to the Press delegation that "China's all but hopeless backwardness in science and technology and expressed his concerns about American constraints on high-tech exports to his country."[36] This continued China's narrative of US superiority, and China's need for improvement.

Deng also proposed to the Press delegation that the United

States should immediately bring 700 Chinese science students to America and throughout the course of the next few years, aim to accept tens of thousands more. (China previously exerted strict control over scientists allowed to venture to the US for fear of their defection to the US.) Press was so excited about this groundbreaking offer that he called President Carter at 3:00 a.m. to convey the message. Also in 1978, Presidential Directive 43 was signed. Various programs were created under this directive that sent science and technology advancements from the US to China in fields including education, energy, agriculture, space, geosciences, commerce, and public health.

The following year, Deng's highly publicized visit to the United States was monumentally successful. Not only did he tour Disney World, Houston's Johnson Space Center, Coca-Cola's headquarters, and take an iconic picture wearing a ten-gallon cowboy hat, he also signed numerous agreements with the US to increase the rate of scientific exchanges. Approximately 19,000 students from China came to study in America during the first five years of these exchanges. These students focused primarily on mastering the physical sciences, health sciences, and engineering while at American universities. More agreements related to consular offices, trade, and science and technology were signed by Carter and Deng during the 1979 trip. Collectively, the information the United States provided to China related to the fields of science and technology was the largest historical transfer of US expertise in these fields.[37]

Around this same time, President Carter approved the creation of signal intelligence collection sites to be located in northwest China. In his memoir, *China Hands*, James Lilley—a CIA operative and later the US ambassador to China—wrote, "Part of the reason I was awarded a medal from the CIA was my work setting up the first CIA unit in Beijing." He described, "Another contributing fact was my role in developing intelligence sharing with China.... It sounded like a far-fetched idea—the United States and China, who had been fighting each other through surrogates just a few years earlier in Vietnam, working together to collect strategic intelligence on the Soviet Union."[38]

Years later, though he was more skeptical of Chinese communist intentions than his predecessors, President Reagan continued to foster increased US-China military cooperation and science and technology exchanges, following the trajectory set by the previous presidential administrations. President Reagan signed the National Security Decision Directive (NSDD 11) in 1981. This directive gave the Pentagon permission to sell to China advanced air, ground, naval, and missile technology, which provided the capabilities the People's Liberation Army needed to become dramatically more powerful. In 1982, one year later, President Reagan signed NSDD 12, which initiated the increase of Chinese military and civilian nuclear programs through US-China nuclear cooperation and development.[39] Later, for the price of more than $1 billion, the Reagan administration agreed to sell six major weapons systems to China.[40] Now, the US was providing China with not only military intelligence and technological knowledge but also the physical weapons needed to build up China's forces.

Moreover, institutions run by the Chinese government obtained funding and training resources from the Reagan administration. These institutions focused on fields of study such as genetic engineering, automation, biotechnology, lasers, space technology, manned spaceflight, and intelligent robotics. After receiving approval from Reagan, a military delegation from China came to the US to visit the Defense Advanced Research Projects Agency (DARPA), a central institute for American national security–related projects and initiatives that is credited with inventing the internet and cyber operations, in addition to a variety of other high-tech breakthroughs.

In March 1986, the US helped China with developing eight national research centers, specializing in genetic engineering, intelligent robotics, artificial intelligence, automation, biotechnology, lasers, supercomputers, space technology, and manned spaceflight. As a result of this assistance, China made substantial strides in its initiatives on more than ten thousand projects.[41]

So, for decades, significant steps were taken to build up China's military and science and technology capabilities. With China's leaders continually reinforcing the message that the United States was dealing with an underdeveloped, growing, "backward" country, coupled with the incentive to build up China's capability to deter and defend against the Soviet Union, it makes sense why multiple presidential administrations would support an outpouring of engagement and assistance to China.

In 1991, the Cold War ended, but US engagement with China did not. Clearly, for the United States, the still-developing (but, as of 1979, official) relationship with China was based on something more than just a strategic ploy to defeat the Soviet Union and end the Cold War. Rather, US officials saw a window of opportunity to engage with a nation that had a real possibility—or so we thought—to shift course from one of communism to one of democracy, freedom, and liberalization.

CHAPTER ELEVEN

SOBERED REALISM

I do not blame China or any other country, of which there are many, for taking advantage of the United States on trade. If their representatives are able to get away with it, they are just doing their jobs. I wish previous administrations in my country saw what was happening and did something about it. They did not, but I will.

—President Donald Trump, November 2017[1]

During the early period of reform and opening up, when we lacked strength and experience, many people doubted whether we could benefit from reform and opening up without becoming corroded and being swallowed up by the dominant Western countries.... Looking back today, we chose the correct direction of development by opening up the country and going global.

...Today, China is considered the biggest driver of global trade liberalization and facilitation, resisting various forms of Western protectionism.

—General Secretary Xi Jinping, January 2016[2]

The final convulsions of Mao's leadership, as he was frustrated at the pace of progress, led to the economic disaster of the Great Leap Forward. This failure was followed less than a decade later by the Cultural Revolution, during which time Mao attempted to mobilize Chinese youth into fanatic groups who would purge society of those who were inadequately committed to his vision of a Communist China. The turmoil that came as a result was so great—and the damage to China so obvious—that the army had to step in and repress the student movement that had grown out of control. It was a disaster as during this period, an entire generation of future leaders was sent from the cities to work in the countryside and be "reeducated."

Following Mao's death and the end of the Cultural Revolution, China's economy and society were left in shambles. The majority of China's population was living in extreme poverty, with more than 88 percent of people surviving on fewer than two dollars per day. In 1978, China represented only 1.8 percent of the total global economy (a dramatic decline since the onset of the Industrial Revolution).[3]

Under the leadership of the more moderate and pragmatic Deng Xiaoping, China instituted a series of economic and political reforms to correct course. This period of reform and opening up began during the Chinese Communist Party's Third Plenum of the 11th Central Committee in Beijing. The Third Plenum began a shift away from failed Maoist ideology and declared the beginning of a new era that would ultimately lead to the exponential growth and strengthening of China's economy. Professor Klaus Mühlhahn, in his book, *Making China Modern*, describes the impact of the Third Plenum:

> "The Third Plenum was a watershed event in China's political, economic, and social development. The leadership formally announced the epochal change of policy from Maoist class struggle to economic development. A

> new tone was set, one that encouraged new thinking and a focus on practice and concrete improvement of living standards. It marked a sharp departure from the Mao era's insistence on doctrinal purity. There was an atmosphere of a new beginning, a turning point that fueled optimism and enthusiasm in China and abroad. Deng became the de facto head of the party and was now able to embark on the reform and opening that would lay the foundation for China's rapid economic development in the following three decades."[4]

This transition was beneficial for China. According to Senior Brookings Fellow Nicholas Lardy, "No other country has ever increased its share of world trade so rapidly."[5] Under Deng, development and growth were key elements of China's mission. This happened through the integration of a planned, controlled economy with a globally focused market-based economy—while still maintaining the centrality of the Chinese Communist Party. With Deng's leadership, China's emphasis on economic development and the implementation of various reforms brought about significant changes following the chaos of the Cultural Revolution. There was an easing of policies (though the Chinese Communist Party still exerted strict control over the Chinese people) and as more engagement with the outside world occurred, more knowledge and ideas came to China that encouraged intellectual debates. Moreover, China attracted innovation and advancements, as well as foreign investment and expertise, by establishing Special Economic Zones (SEZs). In 1980, cities such as Shenzhen, Zhuhai, and Xiamen were designated as SEZs. These zones provided legal protections for foreign investors that were unavailable to Chinese companies. China's efforts to attract foreign capital were extremely successful, and according to Professor Mühlhahn, between 1979 and 1982, foreign investors made a total of 949 agreements for the economic zones that amounted to more than $6 billion.[6]

Despite all of these positive steps, Deng's unprecedented reforms still led to internal tensions and uncertainty. The reforms and global opening led to greater expectations of liberties and living standards among the Chinese people, as well as disparities of wealth and success distribution. This led to some existential questions for the Chinese Communist Party. Kissinger wrote in *On China*, "By turning outward, was China fulfilling its destiny, or was it compromising its moral essence? What, if anything, should it aim to learn from Western social and political institutions?"[7]

These questions surfaced during the student protests and occupation of Tiananmen Square in 1989. During this movement, demonstrators advocated for further political liberalization and protested against corruption, inflation, media restrictions, conditions of universities, and party elders' pervasive control and influence. These anti-government protests directly challenged the authority of the Chinese Communist Party. By June 1989, demonstrations across 341 cities were protesting against China's leadership. In a tragic confrontation, the Communist Party's People's Liberation Army violently suppressed the protests in Tiananmen Square on June 4, 1989. The total number of victims is uncertain, but estimates of the casualties range from hundreds to thousands.[8]

Following the massacre, Deng gave a speech on June 9 where he said, "The incident became very clear as soon as it broke out. They [the demonstrators] have two main slogans: One is to topple the Communist Party, and the other is to overthrow the socialist system. Their goal is to establish a totally Western-dependent bourgeois republic."[9] Based on patterns from China's long past, the threat that the country could once again descend into a period of chaos and civil war is always a primary concern of Chinese communist leadership (as is losing their grip on power). After the challenge to communist control was brutally eliminated, Deng was still convinced that the policies of economic reform and opening up to the world were correct. In the June 9 speech, Deng provided an answer to the question that China now faced following the protests and massacre:

> "Is our basic concept of reform and openness wrong? No. Without reform and openness, how could we have what we have today? There has been a fairly good rise in the people's standard of living in the past ten years, and it may be said that we have moved one stage further. The positive results of ten years of reforms and opening to the outside world must be properly assessed, even though such issues as inflation emerged. Naturally, in carrying out our reform and opening our country to the outside world, bad influences from the West are bound to enter our country, but we have never underestimated such influences."[10]

Deng was still resolute in his conviction that reform and openness would bring prosperity and progress to China. He held on to this belief even after stepping away from the central Chinese Communist Party leadership. In 1992, Deng had become frustrated watching the slowing of the reform initiatives that he had put in motion while in power. Traveling to the south of China, under the guise of a family vacation, Deng sought to revitalize China's reform efforts. On his way south from Beijing, he publicly told party officials in Wuhan that "whoever is against reform should leave office," and ordered officials in Changsha to be, "bolder in carrying out reform and opening."[11]

While on his famous Southern Tour lasting just over a month, he toured factories and offices and was warmly welcomed by crowds calling him "Uncle Deng." Despite conservative efforts in Beijing to prevent Chinese media coverage of Deng's visit to the south, the Hong Kong media reported on his travels to the global community. At this time, Jiang Zemin, Deng's successor, was still securing his position as leader of the

Communist Party. Though retired, Deng still maintained significant influence throughout China. Based on the reactions from Deng's Southern Tour, Jiang recognized that he needed to also push China's reform and opening-up policy. According to a biography by Harvard professor Ezra Vogel, "Jiang realised that Deng was determined to remove him if he did not boldly promote reform and opening. Jiang could see from Deng's visit to the south that he had attracted a great deal of support from key leaders in Beijing and from local leaders. Later Jiang acknowledged that he had concluded that Deng's views would prevail and that he, Jiang, would be wise to support them."[12] Now with Jiang's leadership, the Southern Tour provided the platform for a revival of Deng's reform and opening-up initiatives that had led to China's recent substantial growth. It effectively jumpstarted a period of development with the new leadership and allowed China to continue on its trajectory toward progress.

Regardless of the resurgence of China's focus on reform, US policymakers were certainly not indifferent to the horrific atrocities committed at Tiananmen Square. After the collapse of the Soviet Union in 1991, the United States no longer needed to work with China to offset the expansion of the Soviets. However, the reform and opening-up period that was started by Deng in the late 1970s brought a new dimension into the relationship with China. It appeared there was a possibility that freedom, liberty, and democracy could evolve within a communist regime. Following the clear setback of Tiananmen, the idea that China transforming into a more free and open society was reinvigorated with Deng's Southern Tour and China's commitment to reform and continual economic growth throughout the 1990s.

Economically, China continued on its path of reform. In 1995, new economic and trade policies were created that allowed the establishment of joint venture companies and slashed tariffs on imports by 30 percent.[13] The economy continued to grow as a result of such reforms. Starting with a total GDP of $149.54

billion in 1978, the economy exploded to a total GDP of $1.211 trillion in 2000—a nearly 710 percent increase in just over two decades.[14] By comparison, the US had a total GDP of $2.35 trillion in 1978 and rose to $10.25 trillion in 2000, amounting to almost a 340 percent increase.[15]

Additionally, with a growing economy and a population of 1.25 billion in 1999, the opportunity for increased trade with China was immense. Negotiations for China's admission to the World Trade Organization (WTO) were in full swing leading into the twenty-first century.[16] On November 15, 1999, the US and China agreed to a WTO pact where China agreed to open a variety of markets, spanning from agriculture to telecommunications and to slash tariffs. Simultaneously, the issue of normalizing trade relations with China had also been raised in Washington, DC.

Examining China's 20-year trend toward reform and opening up—and the vast economic opportunities—gave US policymakers an optimistic outlook toward what the normalizing of trade relations with China and its entry into the WTO could mean for America. Further, a bipartisan consensus was formed that economic engagement was an effective tactic for steering China toward freedom and democracy—a development that would further American interests. President Bill Clinton made this precise point during a speech on March 8, 2000:

> "Supporting China's entry into the WTO, however, is about more than our economic interests; it is clearly in our larger national interest. It represents the most significant opportunity that we have had to create positive change in China since the 1970's, when President Nixon first went there, and later in the decade when President Carter normalized relations."[17]

Alan Greenspan, chairman of the Federal Reserve, similarly argued that establishing permanent normal trade relations and admitting China to the WTO would lead to better standards of living for the Chinese people and strengthen the rule of law. Greenspan said in May 2000:

> "The addition of the Chinese economy to the global marketplace will result in a more efficient worldwide allocation of resources and will raise standards of living in China and its trading partners. . . .
>
> "As China's citizens experience economic gains, so will the American firms that trade in their expanding markets. . . .
>
> "Further development of China's trading relationships with the United States and other industrial countries will work to strengthen the rule of law within China and to firm its commitment to economic reform. . . .
>
> "I believe extending [permanent normal trade relations] to China, and full participation by China in the WTO, is in the interests of the United States."[18]

Moreover, then-Governor George W. Bush also argued during his presidential campaign that more trade with China would inevitably lead to more freedom for Chinese citizens and would promote America's values and agenda:

> "First, trade with China will promote freedom. Freedom is not easily contained. Once a measure of economic freedom is permitted, a measure of political freedom will follow. China today is not a free society. At home, toward its own people, it can be ruthless. Abroad, toward its neighbors, it can be reckless.
>
> "When I am president, China will know that America's values are always part of America's agenda. Our advocacy of human freedom is not a formality of diplomacy. It is a fundamental commitment of our country.

It is the source of our confidence that Communism, in every form, has seen its day."[19]

On October 10, 2000, a law was signed by President Clinton that granted China normal trade status with the United States. One year later, China was admitted to the WTO. Let me admit that I was one of those who thought admitting China to the WTO would be a big step forward. Naively, I thought it would teach the Chinese Communist Party leaders how to operate within the rule of law. There was this prevalent sense among American elites that a supposedly backward China could be brought into the modern world and learn from our supposedly more advanced way of doing things. Boy, were we wrong.

Almost 20 years later, the future version of China that Clinton, Greenspan, and Bush described has failed to become a reality. The world we now live in is vastly different than the world we knew during the 70s, 80s, 90s, and early 2000s. The US-China relationship that began in part to counter the expansion of the Soviet Union, and that was later seen as an opportunity to create growth for the American economy and promote American values, now needs to be critically reexamined.

As Michael Pillsbury reflected in *The Hundred-Year Marathon*, "We believed that American aid to a fragile China whose leaders thought like us would help China become a democratic and peaceful power without ambitions of regional or even global dominance."[20] Perhaps we were naive, perhaps we were blinded by optimism, or perhaps we let self-interest stand in the way of objectivity. Whichever the case, we now know that the American vision for China's future was rooted in nothing more than fantasy. Instead of continuing to pursue the China fantasy, we must look at our world with sobered realism.

The reality is the United States now finds itself in a fierce competition with a modern communist-ruled China that, instead of *emulating* American values as we predicted, is *challenging* them. How could we have been so wrong?

THINKING DIFFERENTLY

It is clear that the US is in need of a course correction. Positive actions have already been taken by the Trump administration, but in order to prevent further misdirection in the future, Americans must study what the Chinese Communist Party is doing *and* understand different approaches to Chinese strategic thinking.

One of the most revealing ways to study Chinese strategy is by playing the game *wei qi*, also known as "go." Henry Kissinger wrote about this in *On China*. Go has been a game beloved by China for centuries, and its popularity has spread around the world. Today, there are tens of millions of go players, as well as schools in China that train go masters.

A professional go player and coach, Wu Yulin, described what players can learn from the game: "In go, you can find the application of dialectics and military stratagems. It can also cultivate your character and improve your intelligence. There are numerous variations within the game of go and you can never reach the bottom of it."[21]

Go is said to have originated thousands of years ago in China. It is one of the oldest games in the world that is still played in its original format. Though there are few rules and it uses simple game pieces, go is the world's most difficult game. As the saying goes: go takes minutes to learn but a lifetime to master. The game is played on a square, 19-by-19 lined checkered board. One player gets 180 white round stones, and another gets 181 black round stones. All pieces possess equal power. The flat, square board represents Earth—which was historically believed to be flat and square. The square, solid shape of the board also symbolizes stability. The four seasons and time's cyclical changes are symbolically represented by the four corners on the board. The placement of the stones on the board represents activities on Earth and their round shape reflects a sense of mobility.[22]

The board begins empty, and black goes first. Each player

GO VS. CHESS

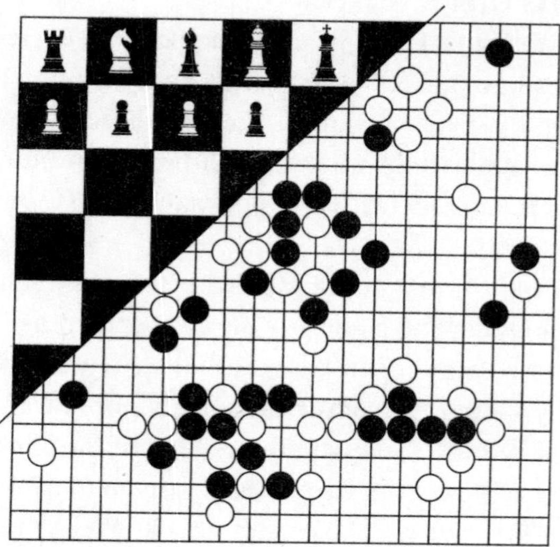

Chess is a linear, force-on-force focused game. By contrast, in a game of go (a game that is thought to have originated thousands of years ago in China and is still popular today), the balance of power is constantly evolving through subtle, incremental victories. It is nearly impossible to tell who is winning at any given time.

takes turns back and forth placing one stone on the board on an intersection of two lines (not in the middle of the squares). The object of the game is to capture as much territory (spaces) as possible, either by encircling vacant spaces, or by encircling and capturing your opponent's pieces. Points are awarded for each space of territory that is captured. The player with the most points after all stones have been played, or when both players pass on their turns, wins. The rules are straightforward; however, the complexity of the game arises from the sheer number of moves available for each player. According to Hua Yigang with the China Go Association, "An ancient scientist once calculated that the board positions in a single game can be a number that is 768 digits long."[23] This level of complexity leaves a lot of room for players to be creative, intentional, and strategic.

The quest for and defense of multiple realms of territory

across the board result in various complex scenarios that require invasion, engagement confrontation, and fighting between players. It is a lengthy game with many turns that requires each player to constantly think about short-term victories and long-term strategy. The apparent control of one player's territory can be challenged, weakened, or totally obliterated with just one move from his or her opponent. Go is dynamic, and control of the board is often uncertain—constantly fluctuating back and forth between players. In a game of go, when selecting a move, players are always required to alter their thinking from one's own perspective to their opponent's, from offensive to defensive mode, and from a risk-taking to a risk-averse mind-set to determine the best play for a constantly evolving board.

In 2004, Dr. David Lai, now the research professor of Asian Security Studies at the Strategic Studies Institute of the US Army War College, wrote a paper that equated go to Chinese strategy. Lai argues, "This game bears striking resemblance to the Chinese way of war and diplomacy. Its concepts and tactics are living reflections of Chinese philosophy, strategic thinking, stratagems, and tactical interactions. This game, in turn, influences the way Chinese think and act."[24] Lai also argued that American strategy closely resembles chess. American strategy is centered around the idea of force-on-force competition that is focused on battlefields. The United States engages in warfare using massive power, possesses exceptionally advanced technology, and uses both to pursue complete, total victory against an opponent. When engaging in warfare, Americans rely heavily upon capability and technological superiority. This means we rely less upon sophisticated, skilled strategies and maneuvers. Chess reflects this notion of a "power-based competition."[25] Each piece carries a different capacity for power and a different sort of capability. However, we know that the queen is significantly more powerful than a pawn, just as the rook is more powerful than a knight. So, when stronger pieces are eliminated from the board as the game continues, the balance of power shifts, tilting the chances of victory in favor of the player with the stronger pieces still in play.

Each piece in a game of chess therefore can be seen as a military or political entity. Some are substantially more powerful than others. In a game of chess, by looking at the number and strength of the individual pieces still in play for each player, one can likely predict who will win and who will lose. On the other hand, Lai explains that go is a game based largely upon skill and the ability to adapt quickly. Lai writes:

> "In the game of *go*, each piece has the same tangible power, but their intangible and potential power, based on the near-infinite combinations and alternative ways of engagement, is situational and limitless. The stones on the board work collectively and always in concert with one another to fight battles. It is difficult to predict victory with a casual look at the individual pieces."

So, while chess players focus on the balance of power and clear capabilities of the individual pieces, go players must figure out how to get multiple stones of equal rank to work together to create strength and unleash a player's full capability. Ultimately, one of the key differences between these two games is visible versus potential power. In the real-world competition with China, Americans may not see, understand, or recognize the ways by which China is strategically deploying stones across the world. The potential strength that these stones will have in the short run—and, more importantly, over the course of the long term—is outside the American system of analysis. Additionally, Lai notes, the decisions regarding resource allocation are different between chess and go. At the beginning of a chess game, all resources (pieces) are on the board and players take turns eliminating their opponent's resources one by one. In go, the game starts with an empty board. The possibilities are endless, and players have the option to deploy their resources (stones) anywhere they choose on the board. There are so many spaces on the board and near-infinite options for players; as a go game progresses, there are multiple campaigns, competitions, and battles going on in different places across the board at one time. All of this means that go players must be strategic and intentional about where they allocate their resources. There are many times when a player must make a decision to continue to invest resources in a particular battle or quest, or if it would be more beneficial to allocate resources elsewhere if the battle or quest seems impossible to complete successfully.

Go players, just like political and military leaders and strategists, are constantly having to do a cost-benefit analysis to determine which moves and pursuits are most efficient and advantageous given the finite number of resources available to each player (one stone per turn). Knowing when to surrender or let go of a territory for the sake of the larger, longer-term victory is a key to mastering go. In order to know how to effectively use resources across the multiple battlefields in go, players must be able to see the bigger picture. A player cannot get too focused on one area of the board, as their opponent may strengthen their position in the other areas, capture a swath of territory, and ultimately emerge victorious. The entirety of the go board, the continuous changes and shifts in players' positions, and the potential for increasing the power of the stones that have already been played must always be kept at the forefront of each players' mind. According to Lai, this is the reason that attacking the strategy of your opponent is effective.

Chess, however, requires players to be more focused on the king. Every single move is made with the objective of placing your opponent's king in checkmate. Additionally, the more powerful chess pieces create a center of gravity and encourage players to focus more intently on these pieces rather than those of lesser power.[26] These types of conditions require chess players to be more narrowly focused and single-minded. Further, chess is a game where the victor wins dramatically and decisively—through the capturing of his or her opponent's king. There is no other objective for both players, besides protecting and keeping your king alive while eliminating your opponent's. Any pawn, rook, or knight that stands in a player's way of achieving victory will be removed.

Typically, in a game of go between two equally matched players, victory is not nearly as decisive. It usually is decided by a small margin, often one of just a few points. Total annihilation of one's opponent is not the goal of go. Instead, players compete for multiple smaller, incremental gains at the same time across the board. Winning at go is about creating advantage for one's stones in many smaller arenas that lead to the acquisition of territory (one square a time). Collectively, successes in these small arenas add up to victory at the end of the game.[27] As Kissinger writes in *On China*, "If chess is about the decisive battle, wei qi is about the protracted campaign." Playing go with the same strategies that are used in chess can result in loss. As Lai writes, "It is dangerous to play *go* with the chess mindset. One can become overly aggressive so that he will stretch his force thin and expose his vulnerable parts in the battlefields."

At our Gingrich 360 offices, we decided that we had to experience playing go to get a better feel for how different the game was. The go players from the National Go Center in Arlington, Virginia, joined our team for an introductory evening. They insisted we play and learn from playing. They matched an experienced go player, including a professional go player from China, with every two of our folks.

Learning by playing was a revelation. It is difficult to overstate how fundamentally different thinking about go is from thinking about checkers or chess. In go, you have to look at the entire board for every move. You have to try to understand your opponent's strategy (which is much more difficult to intuit than in chess). The game has a series of back-and-forth patterns in which you can be on offense one minute, on defense another, and in a state of mutual avoidance in a third.

My two biggest takeaways were that first, you must always look at the whole board. You must never narrowly focus on only one area of the board because letting your mind get trapped into one tactical situation could give your opponent an opportunity to create a decisive breakthrough. Second, you must always think about gaining territory as the primary objective, not killing your opponent's pieces.

Playing go gave me a new appreciation of the Chinese Communist Party's South China Sea strategy and the Belt and Road Initiative—slow, steady, seemingly harmless, yet steadily gaining dominance. I will discuss both of these in greater detail.

At different times throughout America's history, the global challenges we faced, such as those during World War II, could be conquered using a chess player's mentality. At other times, for example during the Cold War, the United States needed to employ a strategy more closely resembling those used during a game of go. It is important to recognize that the competition we face with China today needs to be strategically approached like a game of go—not chess. If we play chess with the Chinese Communist Party, it will be dangerous. The era of competition we are now in can only be navigated using go-based thinking and strategy. We need an American approach to this type of strategy. We must capitalize on US strengths and capabilities. However, we need to also fully understand the nature of our competitor, and the strategies the Communist Party will use to achieve their final objectives.

We must not treat the various challenges with China in isolation. We must look at the larger board and see how all of China's stones and their respective campaigns (5G, South China Sea, Belt and Road Initiative, IP theft, aggressive business practices, espionage tactics, propaganda initiatives, etc.) work together in concert. Otherwise, we won't recognize the small, relatively incremental gains China seeks across various areas and how they all play into a bigger, long-term strategy—that is, until the game is over, and we have lost.

SECTION THREE

GLOBAL CHALLENGES

The following section describes ways in which China is seeking to be the modern Middle Kingdom by growing its regional power, using its economic might to influence other nations, and advancing its technology to project power globally.

CHAPTER TWELVE

STEALING THE SEA

> We must uphold principles that have benefitted all of us, like respect for the rule of law, individual rights, and freedom of navigation and overflight, including open shipping lanes.... [T]hese principles—create stability and build trust, security, and prosperity among like-minded nations.
>
> —President Donald Trump, November 2017[1]

> The Chinese people love peace. We will never seek aggression or expansion, but we have the confidence to defeat all invasions.... We will never allow any people, organization or political party to split any part of Chinese territory out of the country at any time, in any form.... No one should expect us to swallow the bitter fruit that is harmful to our sovereignty, security or development interests.
>
> —General Secretary Xi Jinping, August 2017[2]

The South China Sea is a perfect example of the application of the principles of go to national policy. China has a multigenerational plan to gradually claim control of the South China Sea. This policy began with the Republic of China Land and Water Maps Inspection Committee of 1935 drawing a map—which was later expanded upon in 1947 and picked up and revised by the Communists after they won the civil war.[3]

Remember, the essence of go is to look at the whole board, use patience, and focus on acquiring territory rather than killing your competitor's pieces. Sun Tzu described again and again the virtue of planning and preparation while avoiding conflict until the advantages (what we call the correlation of forces) are overwhelmingly on your side.

The steady nonviolent—but determined and aggressive—strategy China has executed in the South China Sea is a case study from which we can learn a lot. There are many areas in which China is applying the same pattern of long-range goals, patient planning, and implementation designed to minimize violence.

The South China Sea is also worth studying in its own right because it is strategically so important. The South China Sea is a part of the western Pacific Ocean and borders southern China, Taiwan, Vietnam, the Philippines, Malaysia, Indonesia, and Brunei. It is home to multiple islands, reefs, submerged shoals, and rocks that have been disputed, claimed, or occupied by neighboring nations for decades.[4] It is regularly disputed, because the South China Sea is filled with resources, trade routes, and advantageous military positions. The country that controls (or has significant influence over) the South China Sea has a serious strategic advantage in the region and a huge increase in influence over global seaborne trade.

China is presently defying long-standing international norms by building militarized, artificial islands throughout the South Sea and staking claims on existing features—all in an effort to assert control over the region, weaken the US position, and bully its neighbors into accepting its dominance as a regional hegemon. In *China's Vision of Victory,* author Dr. Jonathan Ward writes, "[T]he South China Sea, for a maritime China, is the heart of the Indo-Pacific Region. It is the maritime fulcrum where two great oceans meet, and which China *must control* in order to project military power around the world."[5] To gain that control, China began building artificial islands in December 2013, when the first Chinese dredger arrived at Johnson Reef in the Spratly Islands.[6,7] Keep in mind: The Spratly Islands are more than 500 miles from China. They are actually closer to the Philippines, Vietnam, and Brunei than they are to China.[8] Still, China's dredgers began building artificial islands by grinding up material on the bottom of the seabed, layering the new sand on top of existing seabed or reefs, then adding thick layers of rocks and cement to create a base on which facilities and infrastructure could be built.[9]

The Chinese Communist Party routinely asserts the implausible and then refuses to admit what it is really doing. For years, China has claimed that their constructed artificial islands would not be used for military purposes. In a 2015 joint press conference with President Obama in the Rose Garden, General Secretary Xi Jinping said, "Relevant construction activities that China are [sic] undertaking…do not target or impact any country, and China does not intend to pursue militarization."[10] This was a demonstrable lie. China has been focused on building infrastructure on both the Spratly and Paracel islands. (The Paracel Islands are located northwest of the Spratlys and are closer to the coasts of China and Vietnam.) US Navy Admiral Philip Davidson (before being confirmed as Commander, US Indo-Pacific Command), reported to the Senate Armed Services Committee in April 2018 that:

> "China has constructed clear military facilities on the islands, with several bases including hangars, barracks, underground fuel and water storage facilities, and bunkers to house offense and defensive kinetic and non-kinetic systems.…Today these forward operating bases appear complete. The only thing lacking are the deployed forces."[11]

Later, in November 2018, during remarks given at the Halifax International Security Forum in Canada, Admiral Davidson told the audience:

> "[T]he [People's Liberation Army] secretly deployed anti-ship missiles, electronic jammers, and surface to air missiles (also known as SAMs) earlier this year.
>
> "So what was a 'Great Wall of Sand' just three years ago is now a 'Great Wall of SAMs' in the South China Sea, giving the [People's Republic of China] the potential to exert national control over international waters and airspace through which over 3 trillion dollars in goods travel every year, along with commercial air traffic, as well as information and financial data through undersea cables."[12]

This military buildup is not simply an assertion of vaguely historic or traditional territorial rights. It should be viewed as a clear act of aggression. This is also a powerful cautionary tale for everything dealing with the Chinese communist government. They routinely lie and do so with such enthusiasm that you are tempted to believe them. I have had Chinese officials tell me things that were so unbelievable you had to wonder why they would even bother. Yet, while adhering to the party line, they calmly maintain obviously dishonest statements. Remember this the next time you read a statement by Xi Jinping or any other Chinese Communist Party leader.

According to the Center for Strategic and International Studies Asia Maritime Transparency Initiative, China has seven outposts and has created more than 3,200 acres of new land in the Spratly Islands since 2013.[13] Across the Spratly Islands, China's military has built radar, electronic attack, and defense capabilities.[14] In the Paracel Islands, CSIS reports that China has 20 outposts. Woody Island—which has been expanded to include the neighboring Rocky Island—is the largest island in

MAP OF CHINA

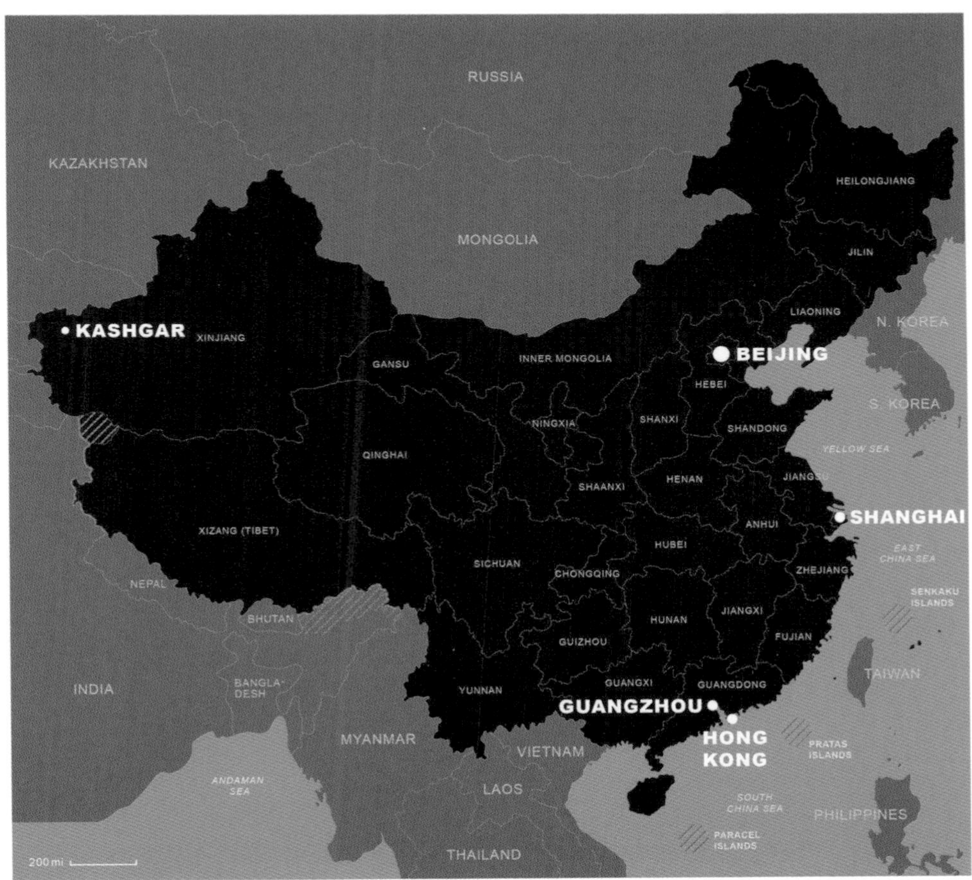

This map of China emphasizes some of the major cities and regions discussed throughout this book. Shaded areas and borders are disputed.

HUAWEI

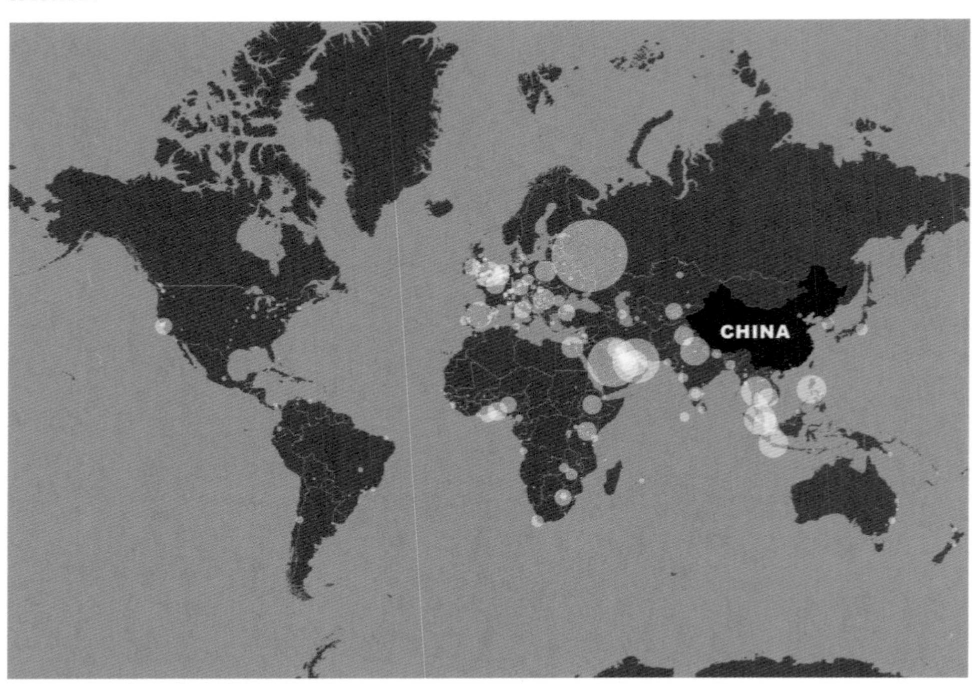

Source: RWR Advisory Group IntelTrak

Huawei's global activity is widespread, as shown in this map, in which larger circles correlate with increased activity.

GLOBAL CONFUCIUS INSTITUTES AND CLASSROOMS

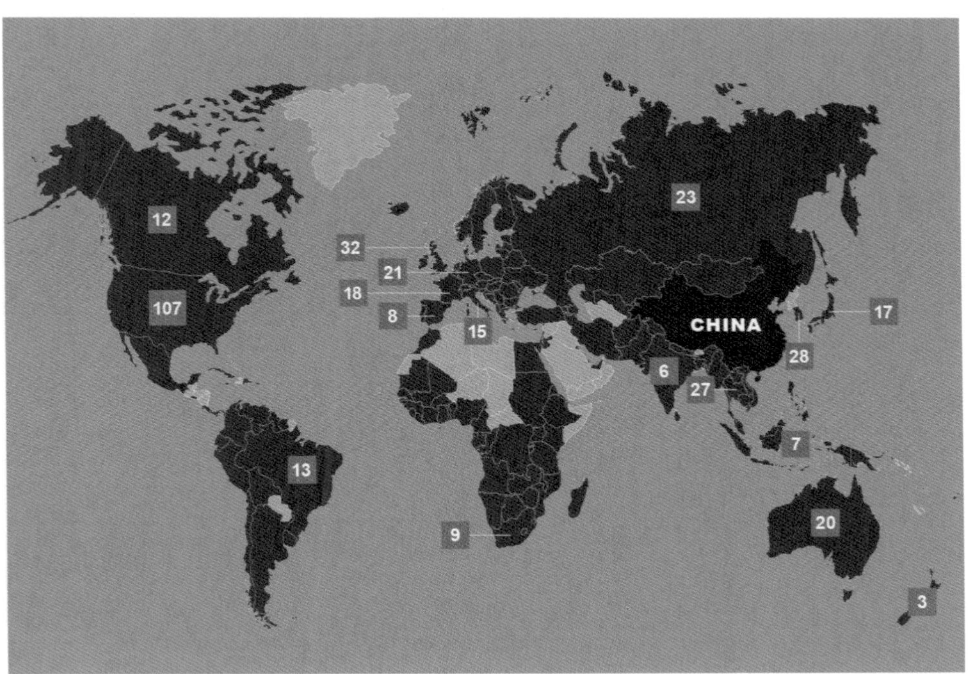

Source: Hanban (*Reported figures from other sources may vary)

Countries with a Confucius Institute and/or Confucius Classroom

Number of Confucius Institutes and Confucius Classrooms

Confucius Institutes and Confucius Classrooms are a primary method for the Chinese Communist Party to export its soft power and influence worldwide.

BELT AND ROAD INITIATIVE

Source: World Bank and the Council on Foreign Relations. (Reported BRI countries from other sources may vary.)

China's proposed global infrastructure effort, the Belt and Road Initiative, is focused on developing the water-based 21st Century Maritime Silk Road, the land-based Silk Road Economic Belt, and the Digital Silk Road. This map aims to convey the general scope of the plan, as projects that are a part of the Belt and Road Initiative are vague and constantly evolving. This map does not depict proposed plans for expanding into Latin America, the Arctic, the Caribbean, and space.

SOUTH CHINA SEA

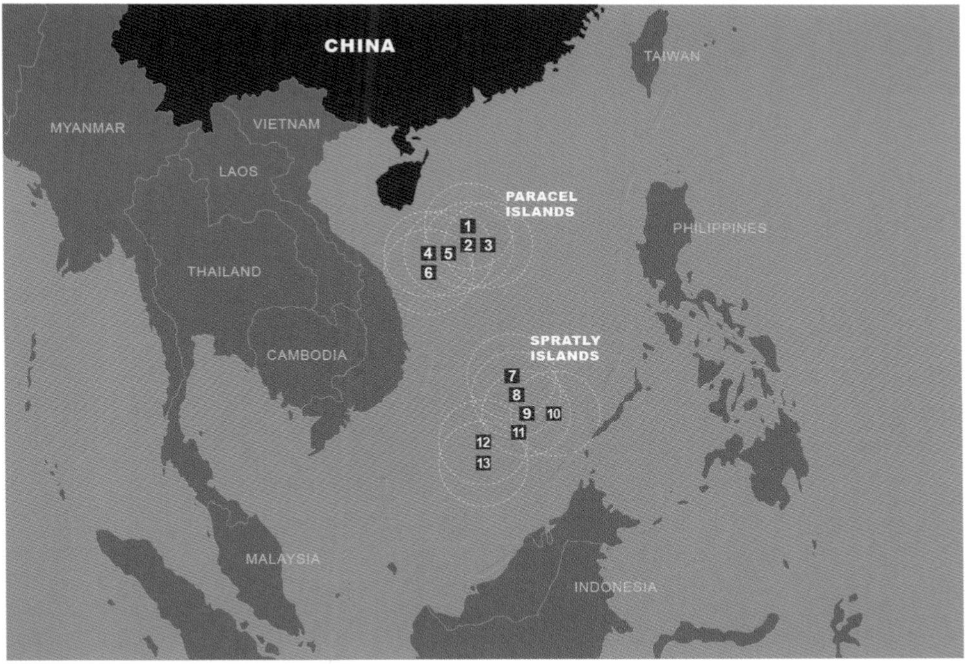

Source: AMTI (Asia Maritime Transparency Initiative)

China claims the area within the 9-dash line as its sovereign territory. Depicted above are some of the outposts in the South China Sea that China has developed. The Chinese Communist Party has been militarizing natural and artificial islands and land formations within the region, leading to increased tensions with the United States, surrounding claimant states, and neighboring nations.

Chairman Mao Zedong proclaiming the founding of the People's Republic of China on October 1, 1949. *(Getty Images)*

Deng Xiaoping puts on a cowboy hat given to him at a rodeo in Texas during his 1979 visit to the United States. *(Getty Images)*

President Trump shakes hands with General Secretary Xi while attending the G20 Summit in Hamburg, Germany, on July 8, 2017. *(Getty Images)*

President Donald Trump and General Secretary Xi Jinping address the press in Beijing after their meeting on November 9, 2017. *(Getty Images)*

the Paracels and serves as China's primary military base in the island chain.[15] A Chinese Communist Party official said that China aims to turn Woody Island and two smaller islets into a "national key strategic service and logistics base."[16] In case anyone was unclear about China's intention to stay, Woody Island was declared the administrative capital for all the island chains that China claims in the South China Sea.

China's objective in asserting its territorial claims in the South China Sea, to project power, and exert control in the region, is clear. And these moves will come with real consequences for the entire region—and the world. As Admiral Davidson described to the Senate Armed Services Committee:

> "Once occupied, China will be able to extend its influence thousands of miles to the south and project power deep into Oceania. The [People's Liberation Army] will be able to use these bases to challenge U.S. presence in the region, and any forces deployed to the islands would easily overwhelm the military forces of any other South China Sea claimants. In short, China is now capable of controlling the South China Sea in all scenarios short of war with the United States."[17]

If anything, Admiral Davidson's testimony understates the problem. Once China finishes putting its assets in place on the islands, it will have driven American power projection hundreds of miles further away from China. It will take a substantial—and possibly unsustainable—American effort to fight our way through the islands and back to the mainland. Considering that prior to the islands being built, we could project power all the way to China, this is a substantial problem and a strategic defeat for the United States and its allies. All of this positioning was achieved without firing a shot in precisely the manner Sun Tzu prescribes. This aggressive strategy of unilateral expansion represents a significant threat to the United States and the world.

In a follow-up testimony to the Senate Armed Services Committee in February 2019, Admiral Davidson made clear that China's goal is to unmake and rewrite international law "through fear and coercion." Admiral Davidson said, "In its place, Beijing seeks to create a new order, one with Chinese characteristics, led by China, an outcome that displaces the stability and peace in the Indo-Pacific that has endured for over 70 years."[18]

A Congressional Research Service (CRS) report published in January 2019 titled *China's Actions in South and East China Seas: Implications for U.S. Interests—Background and Issues for Congress* outlined the threats that could arise if China controls its militarized bases in the South China Sea and dominates the surrounding sea region.[19]

First, according to the CRS, if China controls the region, Chinese military strength and political influence will be increasingly projected into the Western Pacific and establish China as a regional hegemon. Moreover, China could initiate and enforce a blockade around Taiwan. If China controls the surrounding seas, in the case of a crisis or conflict between China and Taiwan, it could complicate capabilities of military intervention by the US. China could also continue to intimidate, pressure, or coerce its neighbors in the South China Sea. As noted by the CRS, China's actions in the South China and East China seas could establish the principle of "might makes right" in the region.[20] (The East China Sea is off of the east coast of China—near Japan, South Korea, and Taiwan—where China is engaged in additional territorial disputes.[21]) Moreover, the capability for US forces to operate in the Western Pacific for "maintaining regional stability, conducting engagement and partnership-building operations, responding to crises, and executing war plans" could be complicated with Chinese control of the near seas and their continued base buildup in the South China Sea.[22]

Another concern is that if a crisis or conflict were to erupt between China and another country bordering the South or

East China Seas, there is a chance that the United States could get drawn into the dispute. The United States has defense treaties with Japan, the Philippines, and South Korea that in the case of a crisis or conflict could result in US involvement as a result of obligations under such agreements.[23] For example, specifically, in March 2019, Secretary of State Mike Pompeo said, "any armed attack on Philippine forces, aircraft, or public vessels in the South China Sea will trigger mutual defense obligations under Article 4 of our Mutual Defense Treaty."[24]

Indeed, prior to 2014, the United States was concerned that as tensions rose in the South China Sea, incidents or a regional conflict could erupt between neighboring territories and US allies. The United States is now concerned with how China's increasing stronghold in the region and aggressive tactics may affect the risk of a conflict between the US and China, influence the strategic competition between our two countries, and impact global US operations.[25]

Furthermore, as China continues to build up its maritime stronghold through aggressive tactics and intimidation, the position, influence, and capabilities of the United States in the region will decline. The CRS report states, "Some observers believe that China is trying to use disputes in the [South China Sea] and [East China Sea] to raise doubts among U.S. allies and partners in the region about the dependability of the United States as an ally or partner, or to otherwise drive a wedge between the United States and its regional allies and partners, so as to weaken the U.S.-led regional security architecture and thereby facilitate greater Chinese influence over the region."[26]

CHINA'S GAMBLE AND THE VAST LEVERAGE THAT IS AT STAKE

Deploying a great deal of military infrastructure across several island chains is already expensive and time-consuming—even when you don't have to build the islands first. But compared to the amount of capital and resources that flow through—or exist beneath—the South China Sea, China's gamble begins to make sense.

Gregory Poling, Director of the Asia Maritime Transparency Initiative and a fellow with the Southeast Asia Program at CSIS, noted that in 2015, 12 percent of the global fish catch came from the South China Sea. Fisheries there officially employ close to 4 million people.[27]

Additionally, there are an estimated 11 billion barrels of untapped oil and 190 trillion cubic feet of natural gas beneath the ocean's surface.[28] However, even if these resources are left in the depths, the South China Sea is already critical for the transportation of liquified natural gas (LNG) and crude oil. The US Energy Information Administration noted that in 2016, almost 40 percent of LNG worldwide was transported through the South China Sea.[29] Additionally, in 2016 more than 30 percent of global maritime crude oil trade was carried through the region.[30] This is equivalent to 15 million barrels per day. The same year, approximately 90 percent of crude oil that was imported by Japan and South Korea—two of the United States' critical Pacific allies—was transported by way of the South China Sea.

This is far from the only commerce that passes through the South China Sea. According to a 2017 report by CSIS's China Power Project, an estimated one-third of global shipping is transported through the South China Sea. In 2016, this amounted to $3.4 trillion worth of trade, making up 21 percent of global trade. Chinese exports accounted for $874 billion, while Chinese imports totaled $598 billion. Compare this to neighboring claimant Vietnam's South China Sea exports and imports ($158 billion and $161 billion, respectively).[31]

Now, imagine a world in which China has direct control over 12 percent of the global fish catch and the trade of 40 percent of liquid natural gas and 30 percent of maritime crude oil. Not only could China begin to deny important resources to some of our key regional allies—such as Japan and South Korea—but they could cause significant damage to the global economy.

The Chinese Communist Party's apparent reasoning behind building and occupying militarized islands is based on its own unique view of history and a warped interpretation of a United Nations law. China's claims in the South China Sea actually predate the founding of the People's Republic of China. Expanding upon a map from 1935 that was drawn by the Republic of China Land and Water Maps Inspection Committee, the Kuomintang nationalists outlined their territory in the South China Sea using an 11-dash line in 1947. The map the nationalists drew set the boundaries of China with this line and mapped out hundreds of rocks and reefs in the sea.[32] However, in the early 1950s, Mao ceded claims to the Gulf of Tonkin, which eliminated two dashes from China's territorial claims and evolved the arbitrary boundary into what we know now as the nine-dash line. The demarcation of the nine-dash line has yet to be officially defined by China. There are gaps in between the dashes, multiple analysts have replotted the line over the years, and even China has periodically reinterpreted its location.[33]

Nonetheless, according to Reuters, China believes the legitimacy of these claims in the South China Sea date back thousands of years—as early as the Xia Dynasty that ruled from the twenty-first to the sixteenth centuries BC.[34] In an interview with *TIME*, Chinese marine geographer Wang Ying (who was a "disciple" of one of the geographers behind the original 11-dash line) noted that there is not much cartographic evidence due to a general lack of maritime ambition throughout much of China's history. However, she pointed to items, such as navigational handbooks that Chinese fishermen used, as proof of the legitimacy of China's claims. Based on these handbooks, Wang said, "The dash lines mean the ocean, islands and reefs all belong to China and that China has sovereign rights."[35]

It is also ambiguous what the Chinese Communist Party is now claiming as sovereign within the already vague nine-dash line. It remains unclear whether claims within the nine-dash line include all or some of the land features, and if these claims also include the ocean itself. In the *TIME* article, former East Asia Bureau Chief Hannah Beech wrote, "For the average Chinese, every drop of sea within the dashes is clearly China's." Wang echoes this point, but says the dashed lines are "discontinuous, meaning that other countries can pass through the lines freely."[36]

Even following a 2016 international tribunal ruling that determined China's historical claims within the nine-dash line have no legal basis, China continues to assert control of the region using aggressive and intimidating tactics.[37] China dismissed the ruling with a statement from the Foreign Ministry saying the decision was "invalid and has no binding force" and that "China does not accept or recognize it."[38] Further, in a June 2018 meeting with former Secretary of Defense Jim Mattis, General Secretary Xi Jinping said, "Our stance is steadfast and clear-cut when it comes to China's sovereignty and territorial integrity.... [A]ny inch of territory passed down from ancestors cannot be lost while we want nothing from others."[39]

China's position is further complicated by the Chinese Communist Party's willful misinterpretation of international customs and laws. Freedom of operations in international waters is a foundational principle of the modern, US-led international order. This concept is also known as freedom of the seas, freedom of navigation, or freedom of passage. Freedom of the seas is not technically defined in international law, but according to the Department of Defense's Freedom of Navigation Report, the concept refers to "all of the rights, freedoms, and lawful uses of the sea and airspace, including for military ships and aircraft, guaranteed to all nations under international law."[40] In short: International waters are global commons, and all nations and peoples are permitted to operate lawfully within them.

However, under the United Nations Convention on the Law of the Sea (UNCLOS)—which the US has not ratified—coastal countries are given control over a specified area of water adjacent to their territorial seas. The law conceptualized and created exclusive economic zones countries can claim off of their shores. Such zones must be adjacent to a country's territorial sea—and can extend up to 200 nautical miles from the coastline of said territorial sea.[41,42] Within these zones, countries have regulatory rights over the economic activities that occur (i.e., fishing, oil exploration, or offshore energy generation from waves or wind).[43,44] Most UN member countries agree (the US and even Russia included) that coastal states *do not* have exclusive control over foreign military activities within exclusive economic zone waters. However, China and a minority group of nearly 30 other countries—including Iran and North Korea—have determined that coastal states have the right to control both economic *and* foreign military activities within these zones. This corrupt interpretation sheds light on China's island-building plan.[45] Once it is accepted that China has sovereign authority over these fabricated islands, Beijing, according to its current position, can claim military and economic control over up to 200 nautical miles of water surrounding each of them. This would allow China to eventually claim as much territorial water as it is willing to build islands. As the Congressional Research Service report on China's South China Sea activity points out, the larger exclusive economic zone dispute in the UN is just as important as the issue regarding territorial sovereignty over the human-made and claimed islands. Resolution of the economic zone issue will establish a precedent that could greatly impact US military operations throughout the South China Sea and the East China Sea—and also throughout the rest of the world.[46]

BREWING CONFLICT

This dispute has created serious tension between the US and China. There is an established international protocol for maritime confrontations (the Code for Unplanned Encounters at Sea). It was signed by both the United States and China in 2014, but it is voluntary and fails to clarify the issue of which countries have a right to go where in so-called territorial waters. According to Collin Koh, a maritime specialist at the Rajaratnam School of International Studies, "It's more like a gentleman's agreement."[47] Additionally, the Department of Defense's *Asia-Pacific Maritime Security Strategy* released in 2015 depicted an increasingly dangerous picture:

> "The growing efforts of claimant States to assert their claims has led to an increase in air and maritime incidents in recent years, including an unprecedented rise in unsafe activity by China's maritime agencies in the East and South China Seas. U.S. military aircraft and vessels often have been targets of this unsafe and unprofessional behavior, which threatens the U.S. objectives of safeguarding the freedom of the seas and promoting adherence to international law and standards. China's expansive interpretation of jurisdictional authority beyond territorial seas and airspace causes friction with U.S. forces and treaty allies operating in international waters and airspace in the region and raises the risk of inadvertent crisis."[48]

To answer China's aggression, the Trump administration has been (rightly) performing regular freedom of navigation operations. These exercises enforce the principle of the freedom of the seas—and make clear the United States' position to the international community. The Trump administration began conducting these exercises on May 25, 2017. They often include having US Navy ships sail through the Taiwan Strait. China has objected to these operations and on multiple occasions has deployed Chinese navy ships to warn the US to depart from the disputed areas.[49]

On September 30, 2018, a close call occurred between two destroyers. The USS *Decatur* and a Chinese destroyer came within 45 yards of each other as the *Decatur* was doing a freedom of navigation operation in the Spratly Islands. The US destroyer came within 12 nautical miles (what would be considered the territorial sea of a recognized sovereign territory) of the Gaven and Johnson reefs during the execution of the operation. Reportedly, the Chinese ship issued a direct warning. "You are on [sic] dangerous course," the ship declared. "If you don't change course your [sic] will suffer consequences."[50] Former US Navy Captain Carl Schuster told CNN the destroyers were possibly just seconds away from colliding with one another. Schuster noted that these tactics forced the US captain to make a "radical maneuver" that was "like slamming on the brakes and turning to the right to avoid a crash on the road."[51] Had this encounter not been avoided, we could have seen a serious military exchange. The US would not turn a blind eye to a sunk or badly damaged destroyer.

In February 2019, Admiral Davidson told the Senate Armed Services Committee that the US will continue to conduct freedom of navigation operations in the South China Sea and will involve US allies and partners.[52]

The Trump administration has undertaken numerous other efforts to challenge China's aggression in the South China Sea. Namely, it has continued to implement the Indo-Pacific Maritime Security Initiative (formerly called the Southeast Asia Maritime Security Initiative when announced by the Obama administration), which is a capacity-building effort for countries in the region to address the significant maritime challenges they face.

Furthermore, the US continues to conduct joint military exercises with allies and partners. Every two years, the US leads a multilateral naval exercise in the Pacific with participants from more than two dozen countries. This exercise is called the "Rim of the Pacific" exercise, or RIMPAC. China participated in the 2014 and 2016 exercises, but on May 23, 2018, the Department of Defense revoked China's invitation to the multinational exercise. Citing "strong evidence that China has deployed anti-ship missiles, surface-to-air missile (SAM) systems, and electronic jammers" in the South China Sea, Department of Defense spokesman Marine Lt. Col. Christopher Logan said at the time, "China's continued militarization of disputed features in the South China Sea only serve to raise tensions and destabilize the region.... China's behavior is inconsistent with the principles and purposes of the RIMPAC exercise." Logan went on to urge China to cease and reverse its militarization efforts.[53] Supporters of the decision to exclude China from RIMPAC argued that inviting China's participation would essentially reward China for its aggressive tactics in the South China and East China seas. Moreover, China would potentially gain valuable intelligence by witnessing the operations.[54]

The Trump administration has additionally taken actions to bolster the maritime security capabilities of Vietnam and Indonesia and provide additional defense and intelligence cooperation with both countries.[55] Despite these positive steps to deter further Chinese control and militarization of the South China Sea, more can still be done. The United States must maintain a strong position against China's expansive territorial claims and continue to uphold the principle of the freedom of the seas. The US needs to boldly stand by our allies and partners and promote the rule of law in the region and halt China's further attempts at militarization and control of trade routes and resources.

CHINA'S PIVOT TO THE SEAS

Ignoring the South China Sea challenge could be a disaster. There is no indication that China's present aggression will abate. The country is clearly turning away from its historic behavior and is actively trying to gain control of the 1.4 million square miles of the South China Sea. This would increase China's area by almost than a third of its current land size.[56]

For much of China's ancient history, the empire was a land-based power. Center for Strategic and Budgetary Assessments senior fellow Toshi Yoshihara lectured on this point at the Institute of World Politics in Washington, DC. Generally, China has historically been focused on preventing land-based barbarians from infringing on their expansive physical borders, rather than projecting their power outward through the seas. The Great Wall of China is an example of a land-focused defensive system.[57]

However, according to a 2019 report by the US Defense Intelligence Agency titled *China Military Power,* in the 1980s, Chinese leaders recognized that modern threats and economic interests required a shift in their maritime strategy. Specifically, naval strategists decided to expand their capabilities outward, beyond the protection of coastal boundaries.[58]

Admiral Liu Huaqing was the head of the People's Liberation Army Navy and is known as the "father of the modern Chinese Navy." In the 1980s, he created an ambitious strategy to grow China's navy so it would have the capability to operate on a global scale complete with groups of battle-ready aircraft carriers by 2050.[59] Today, General Secretary Xi Jinping's ambition for growing Chinese naval capabilities has intensified. In 2015, the Chinese Ministry of Defense published its first public *Chinese Military Strategy* white paper, which stated:

> "The traditional mentality that land outweighs sea must be abandoned, and great importance has to be attached to managing the seas and oceans and protecting maritime rights and interests. It is necessary for China to develop a modern maritime military force structure commensurate with its national security and development interests, safeguard its national sovereignty and maritime rights and interests, protect the security of strategic [sea lanes of communication] and overseas interests, and participate in international maritime cooperation, so as to provide strategic support for building itself into a maritime power."[60]

Xi sees military modernization as essential to protect and defend China's national interests around the globe. He made this clear during a 2017 speech marking the 90th anniversary of the founding of the Communist Party's People's Liberation Army. He said, "We feel more strongly than ever that in order to achieve national rejuvenation and better lives for the people, we must speed up the building of the people's military into a world-class force."[61] Indeed, in 2017, Xi outlined a new time line for the modernization of the Chinese Communist Party's military that moved the deadline up by nearly 15 years. Under this new direction, the People's Liberation Army is targeted to develop into a fully "modern" military by 2035. By mid-century, the plan envisions China as a "world-class" military.[62]

Again, in April 2018, after overseeing the largest review of the Chinese Communist Party's navy since the People's Republic of China's founding in 1949, Xi said building a strong navy "has never been more urgent than today," and he pledged to speed up the modernization effort. By every indication, Xi's plan is being implemented. According to the 2019 *Worldwide Threat Assessment of the US Intelligence Community* published by the Director of National Intelligence:

> "As China's global footprint and international interests have grown, its military modernization program has become more focused on investments and infrastructure to support a range of missions beyond China's periphery, including a growing emphasis on the maritime domains, offensive air operations, and long-distance mobility operations."[63]

The US Defense Intelligence Agency reported that China's navy is the largest in Asia and has a system with more than 300 surface combatants, amphibious ships, patrol crafts, submarines, and specialized units.[64] Moreover, the US-China Economic and Security Review Commission's (USCC) *2018 Report to Congress* found that the modernization may be ahead of schedule.

> "China's rapid buildup of the [People's Liberation Army's] Navy as a blue water force through its continued commissioning of highly capable, multimission warships will give Beijing naval expeditionary capabilities deployable around the globe as early as 2025, well ahead of the [People's Liberation Army's] broader 2035 modernization goal."[65]

A WHOLE-OF-SOCIETY EFFORT

While the Chinese Communist Party is growing its navy, it is also harnessing paramilitary forces to advance its goals. In 2018, China's Central Military Commission brought the China Coast Guard under its direct control. This was no harmless, bureaucratic reshuffling. It eliminated the Chinese Coast Guard's civilian status. The USCC noted that the move "places added importance on the China Coast Guard as an instrument to police, enforce, and advance China's domestic maritime law."[66]

In addition to the Coast Guard, China employs the People's Armed Forces Maritime Militia (PAFMM), which is primarily composed of fishing boats with crew members who are armed.[67] The maritime militia is often overlooked; however, it is one of the most significant components in the Chinese Communist Party's overall strategy to control the South China Sea. A 2019 report published by CSIS's Stephenson Ocean Security Project examined the activities and size of these fishing fleets in the South China Sea's Spratly Islands. The report found that "a significant number of fishing vessels in the area forgo fishing full-time to serve as a direct arm of the state through official maritime militia." Using imagery of the Subi and Mischief reefs in the Spratly Islands, the report concluded that the fishing boats depicted were rarely *actually engaged in fishing.* More often, they idly anchored near Chinese-controlled outposts or simply sailed without nets in the water.[68]

In fact, the CSIS report indicated if militia boats had been fishing, the size and number of Chinese vessels observed would represent a "massive overcapacity." The report wrote:

> "Based on published Chinese catch levels, a 550-ton light falling net fishing vessel could catch about 12 metric tons per day. That means the more than 270 fishing boats present at Subi and Mischief Reefs in August [2018] could catch about 3,240 metric tons per day or nearly 1.2 million metric tons per year. That is between 50 and 100 percent of the total estimated catch in the Spratly Islands.
>
> "This gross overcapacity combined with their tendency to congregate around both Chinese-occupied reefs and those held by other claimants leads to the conclusion that most of these vessels serve, at least part-time, in China's maritime militia."[69]

A 2019 report by the Defense Intelligence Agency suggested that the maritime militia is an extension of the main national military. Militia members train with the Chinese Communist Party's military specifically for "safeguarding maritime claims, protecting fisheries, and providing logistic support, search and rescue (SAR), and surveillance and reconnaissance." The Chinese government actually subsidizes commercial fishing outfits, or rents fishing boats, to perform militia duties, but the Defense Intelligence Agency report also found that "it appears that China is building a state-owned fishing fleet for its maritime militia force in the South China Sea."[70]

This ad hoc militia represents a significant force of the Chinese Communist Party's military might. Some analysts argue that the militia "is the leading component of China's maritime forces for asserting its maritime claims, particularly in the [South China Sea]."[71] We will presently see American warships trying to exercise their maritime rights of passage being surrounded by small so-called fishing vessels with TV cameras on board. It will be a difficult public relations problem if a big American warship starts sinking small Chinese militia vessels disguised as fishing boats.

AMERICA AT THE CROSSROADS

The South China Sea is one of the battlefields on which the competition between the United States and China will be played out. The Chinese Communist Party has won the first round in this region. They have built and occupied islands. They have moved in military equipment. They have developed a fishing fleet militia far beyond the capacity needed for fishing that is clearly being used as seagoing militia for national security purposes. We can complain, but what we are going to *do* about it?

In the absence of a dramatically more imaginative strategy, we are ultimately going to have a Chinese fait accompli. We talk—they build. We talk—they move in military equipment. Occasionally running freedom of navigations operations to assert our right of passage and reinforce our claim that the South China Sea is international water is a losing strategy in the long run. Sooner or later, the Chinese Communist Party will force a humanitarian public relations disaster on us, and the world will sympathize with China. Legal arguments will never win against images and videos of people in a small boat being crushed by an American warship. Forcing China off of these islands will take a war—a fairly serious war, with real risks of escalation.

Therefore, the United States must develop a serious strategy for the long-term Chinese Communist Party's offensive in the South China Sea. In the long run, China's developments will get stronger and our claim will become harder and harder to sustain. We must place a high priority on developing a strategy that can break up China's momentum toward control of the South

China Sea. Until we have such a strategy, we are just allowing China to invest in a stronger and stronger fortress network from which it can control an amazing percentage of the world's ship-borne commerce. Every year that passes without an effective American strategy—including gathering up the allies necessary to make it succeed—the South China Sea moves closer to a becoming an area of strategic defeat of historic proportions.

This American strategy might include an option to build islands of our own west of the Chinese islands, and therefore closer to China than they are.

Twenty years ago, Admiral Bill Owens, then vice chairman of the Joint Chiefs, proposed floating islands that combined huge oil platforms into an airfield that could move at about five knots and gradually get to places where we wanted to influence development. Just the act of announcing that we were going to build five of these and move them to a position to interdict movement between the mainland and the illegal islands would cause the Chinese Communist Party to pay attention. The goal might be to demilitarize the existing islands and put them under joint occupation by the regional countries in addition to China.

However, getting anywhere in the South China Sea is going to be somewhere between hard and impossible. Note: I am saying that this is going to continue to be a difficult problem, but I am not saying that we should ignore this challenge and simply resort to what we've been doing thus far. Clearly, that hasn't worked. The disputes in the South China Sea are a good example of the seriousness with which the Chinese Communist Party is building up its strength and positioning itself for the future. In the course of this book, you will encounter, or have already encountered, a number of equally sobering challenges in dealing with the emergence of China as a serious world power.

CHAPTER THIRTEEN

BELT & ROAD TO EVERYWHERE

> [W]e understand that we have nothing so precious as our birthright, our treasured independence, and our freedom....
>
> [L]et us never forget the world has many places—many dreams, and many roads. But in all of the world, there is no place like home.
>
> So, for family, for country, for freedom, for history, and for the glory of God, protect your home, defend your home, and love your home today and for all time.
>
> —President Donald Trump, November 2017[1]

> China is the initiator and propeller of the Belt and Road Initiative, but the initiative is not China's business alone. Therefore, focusing on China's own development, it should also welcome other countries to board China's express train of development, and help them realize their own development objectives.
>
> —General Secretary Xi Jinping, April 2016[2]

In April 2019, almost 40 heads of state and government from countries around the world gathered in Beijing for the Second

Belt and Road Forum for International Cooperation. The US sent no high-level delegates while Russian President Vladimir Putin was the guest of honor.[3,4] As Axios executive editor Mike Allen wrote, "When you can get that many powerful people to come to you in Beijing, you're starting to look a lot like a superpower."[5] The delegates gathered to discuss the most ambitious worldwide infrastructure investment effort undertaken in history—the China-led Belt and Road Initiative. Announced in 2013 by General Secretary Xi Jinping (and formerly known as One Belt, One Road) the Belt and Road Initiative is a huge project primarily focused on connecting Eurasia and the Indo-Pacific region.[6,7] However, China is expanding the Belt and Road Initiative into Latin America, Africa, the Caribbean, the Arctic, and up to space.[8]

The initiative calls for the development and installation of railways, ports, energy pipelines, highways, digital infrastructure, special economic zones, and more projects, across multiple continents. Clearly, this will have tremendous economic and strategic impact everywhere it touches—most of them benefiting China. The Chinese Communist Party is undoubtedly accumulating power and influence by leading this worldwide project. According to the US-China Economic and Security Review Commission (USCC), as of 2018, more than 80 countries have signed on to participate in the Belt and Road Initiative (at the time of this writing, the Chinese government claims that 137 countries have joined).[9,10] Collectively, these approximately 80 countries account for about 30 percent of the global gross domestic product—and more than two-thirds of the world's population.[11,12]

As inspiration for this project, China looked to its past. The ancient Silk Road connected Asia, Africa, and Europe. It was established during the Han Dynasty. For more than 1,000 years, these trade networks transported goods, ideas, beliefs, and cultures across continents.[13] Today, China is working to create a modern version of the Silk Road. China is so serious about this project that it has been prioritized as General Secretary Xi's signature economic and foreign policy initiative—and it has been written into China's constitution.[14]

Back in August 2018, while commemorating the fifth anniversary of the Belt and Road Initiative, Xi said the initiative "serves as a solution for China to participate in global opening up and cooperation, improve global economic governance, promote common development and prosperity, and build a community with a shared future for humanity."[15] This sounds good, but the USCC pointed out in its 2018 report to Congress later that year that "the phrase 'community with a shared future for humanity' is used by Chinese leaders as coded shorthand for what may be a China-led global order."[16] In fact, the USCC's 2018 Report to Congress described China's objectives for the Belt and Road Initiative fairly clearly:

> "[F]ueling domestic development and increasing control in China's outer provinces, expanding markets while exporting technical standards, building hard and digital infrastructure, bolstering energy security, expanding China's military reach, and advancing geopolitical influence by moving China to the center of the global order."[17]

The Belt and Road Initiative is also a way for China to break into markets in other countries by exporting excess industrial capacity. China claims the Belt and Road is open to all nations and companies who are willing to join, but the majority of contracts associated with Belt and Road projects are being awarded to China. Citing data from the Center for Strategic and International Studies's Reconnecting Asia Project, the USCC writes that 89 percent of transportation infrastructure projects funded by China are given to Chinese contractors.

Comparatively, in projects funded by multilateral development banks, only 29 percent of projects are given to Chinese contractors.[18] There is not a level playing field for foreign businesses to compete for contracts in the Belt and Road Initiative. Randal Phillips, managing partner at the Mintz Group, said in his testimony to the USCC that in these projects, foreign companies have the opportunity to play the role of "best supporting actor." Essentially, foreign companies will act as subcontractors to large Chinese enterprises, specifically in service sectors such as commercial insurance, consulting, and logistics.[19]

Many countries that joined the initiative early have been optimistic about the opportunities and prospects of the Belt and Road. However, many projects have experienced problems, pushback, and protest. Increasingly, the world is becoming skeptical of China's intentions and methods. The USCC writes that, "Political and security risks, financing difficulties, environmental concerns, and a lack of political trust between China and some host countries pose considerable challenges for Beijing and have stalled some of [Belt and Road Initiative's] most high-profile projects."[20] Citing data from RWR Advisory Group, the USCC said in the 2018 report that problems have been reported in 66 countries for approximately 270 of the 1,814 Chinese infrastructure projects announced since 2013. This means that 32 percent of the total value of these projects have reported difficulties.[21] These problems have been followed by widespread criticism. For example, in Malaysia, the prime minister was elected in 2018 after questioning China's investments as part of his platform (this was a stark contrast to his incumbent opponent). Once in office, he criticized the Belt and Road as a "new version of colonialism" and suspended tens of billions of dollars of Chinese-backed projects pending review.[22,23] (After discussions with China, he changed his views.)

In Bangladesh, a major highway project was canceled after the Chinese firm that was going to build the infrastructure allegedly offered a bribe to a government official.[24] While in Sri

Lanka, massive numbers of citizens protested the Sri Lankan government ceding control of a port in Hambantota to pay off debts to China.[25] Evidently, serious problems associated with the Belt and Road Initiative are emerging. But to understand the challenges these countries face and what they mean for the interests and security of the United States, we must first understand China's ambitious goals affiliated with the Belt and Road Initiative.

THE SILK ROADS TO HELL

The primary phase of the Belt and Road Initiative includes three main components: the land-based Silk Road Economic Belt, a sea-based 21st Century Maritime Silk Road, and a worldwide Digital Silk Road. These components can work independently, but often work together to reinforce China's position.

In broad terms, the Silk Road Economic Belt plan connects China with Central and South Asia, the Middle East, and Europe.[26] One of the most significant elements of this belt is the China-Pakistan Economic Corridor (CPEC), which spans from China's western Xinjiang region through the entire country of Pakistan. It includes highways and railways—but also ports, aviation, and information networks (working with the maritime and digital silk roads).[27] As such, the CPEC is an ambitious and broad-reaching proposal with an aggressive goal for completion. The Long-Term Plan for [the] China-Pakistan Economic Corridor also proposes collaboration in "energy related fields," "trade and industrial areas," "agricultural development and poverty alleviation," "tourism," "areas concerning people's livelihood and non-governmental exchanges," and "financial cooperation." It envisions creating enough economic activity in Central and South Asia so that the region becomes "an international economic zone with global influence."[28] The public goal of this project is "shared prosperity" for China and Pakistan, but the reality is much different. This plan could create a land-based corridor connecting China with the Indian Ocean. This presents China with huge economic opportunities and access to important trade routes to the Middle East.

Further, the plan has already created serious problems for Pakistan. This is due in part to a change in Pakistan's government. But, more significantly, it is a result of Pakistan accepting massive Chinese loans while its economy is crumbling. Nearly the entire project is financed by China—and much of the immediate economic benefit for the work is going to Chinese companies. While long-term economic advantages for Pakistan potentially exist, at the moment, the nation's economy is struggling. With each day, it is falling further into debt to its partner. Meanwhile, certain CPEC projects are making Pakistan's financial situation worse. According to *The Wall Street Journal*, various energy-related infrastructure projects such as hydroelectric, wind, and coal power plants are being developed in the CPEC. However, as a condition for this project, China requires Pakistan to pay for the use of the produced electricity "at a price that covers a hefty return on investment."[29] Taken with the initial financing debt, Pakistan is already failing to keep up on the payments.

When it comes to the Belt and Road Initiative, Pakistan's debt predicament is the rule rather than the exception. This sort of debt-trap diplomacy can ultimately undermine Pakistan's ability to run its own country without influence from the Chinese Communist Party. According to the USCC's 2018 Report to Congress, many of the Belt and Road infrastructure projects are covered by Chinese financing and commercial banks:

> "Chinese lending poses debt sustainability problems for a number of [Belt and Road Initiative] countries while providing Beijing with economic leverage to promote Chinese interests, in some cases threatening the sovereignty of host countries. Beijing's response to problems of debt distress in [Belt and Road Initiative] countries

has ranged from offering borrowers additional credit to avoid default to extracting equity in strategically important assets."[30]

Moreover, China's lending practices don't comply with international standards, and opaque loans make it challenging for observers to understand China's full involvement. The USCC's 2018 report pointed out:

> "[A]ccording to Aid Data—a research lab at the College of William & Mary—only a fifth of China's development finance met the OECD Development Assistance Committee's criteria for official development assistance (ODA) between 2000 and 2014. In addition, multilateral institutions and most bilateral development finance institutions disclose the financing terms for loans to sovereign governments; however, Chinese policy banks do not report their loans to individual countries—much less disclose the terms of their loans—making it difficult to assess the present value of the debt owed by a country to China."[31]

A March 2018 report by the Center for Global Development identified "23 [Belt and Road Initiative] countries at risk of debt distress [at that time] according to standard measures of debt sustainability." All 23 countries were at either "significant" or "high" risk for debt sustainability issues. From the list of 23 countries, the report found "eight countries where [the Belt and Road Initiative] appears to create the potential for debt sustainability problems, and where China is a dominant creditor in the key position to address those problems." Notably, Pakistan is one of these eight countries and was determined to be at high risk.[32]

DROWNING IN DEBT

Just as Pakistan's land-based projects are being drowned in debt, China is also eyeing the country for maritime projects. China is interested in developing ports, pipelines, and transportation infrastructure that would allow the shipment of energy and goods directly from the Indian Ocean, through Pakistan, and into China. This is enticing for China, as the country is concerned with energy security.[33] Citing 2016 data by the US Energy Information Administration, the USCC reported that every day, 19 million barrels of oil are shipped through the Strait of Hormuz (just west of Pakistan), and 16 million barrels are shipped through the Strait of Malacca. (When shipping from the Middle East, oil is transported around India and Sri Lanka before passing through the strait and arriving in China.[34]) These sea routes are significant to China. Both the Strait of Hormuz and the Strait of Malacca overlap with major Belt and Road Initiative routes.[35] Similar passages include Bab el-Mandeb off the coast of northeast Africa and the Suez Canal that cuts through Egypt.

In the first half of 2019, Pakistan began to pump the brakes on some of the CPEC-related initiatives.[36] Pakistan's new prime minister has been critical of some of the projects undertaken by his predecessor. With the challenging economic situation in Pakistan and the country's debt to China, critics are concerned whether Pakistan's economy will be able to successfully recover. And Pakistan is not alone. Countries vulnerable to China's debt-trap diplomacy are also located along the 21st Century Maritime Silk Road. This water-based metaphorical road refers to planned oceanic routes and ports broadly connecting China to South Asia, the Middle East, East Africa, and Europe.[37]

Sri Lanka was also one of the 23 at-risk countries mentioned in the Center for Global Development report. In fact, the small island nation has already encountered significant consequences after accepting Chinese funding for infrastructure projects.

In the early 2000s, Sri Lanka announced plans to build a

port in Hambantota—located on the southern tip of the island. Former Sri Lankan President Mahina Rajapaksa sought to develop a series of ambitious projects and was especially optimistic about developing a port along one of the world's busiest maritime shipping lanes. According to the report *Game of Loans* by Jonathan Hillman at the Center for Strategic and International Studies, "Many of these big-ticket projects—including an international airport, a cricket stadium, and the port—had three things in common: they used Chinese financing, Chinese contractors, and Rajapaksa's name."[38] According to the Hillman report, the loans offered to Sri Lanka often carried high interest rates. In the first phase of the Hambantota port project, China gave Sri Lanka a $307 million loan that was later renegotiated to a higher 6.3 percent fixed interest rate (as a step toward providing more funding).[39] Comparatively, multilateral banks usually offer loans with a 2–3 percent interest rate—and sometimes interest rates are closer to zero. Hillman also reported there weren't any other competing offers made for the Hambantota port. Hillman suggested it's possible "that other potential lenders did not see rewards commensurate with the project's risks."

Though the Belt and Road Initiative project was not officially announced until 2013, China folded the Hambantota construction under the initiative's umbrella. After all, it contained all of the characteristics and goals of a typical Belt and Road–related venture. As Jean-François Dufour, economist and director of DCA China-Analysis, put it, "Chinese funds and engineers are mobilized to build infrastructure outside China, as part of a partnership that was meant to be win-win: this is the very definition of the rationale of the Silk Road."[40] Phase 1 of the port opened in 2010. After political leadership changes in Sri Lanka in 2015, the island revisited some of the deals the previous administration had made. Roughly 10 years after the project was conceived, Sri Lanka halted further construction on the port. In effect, this delayed the beleaguered port's ability to generate revenue for Sri Lanka. Hillman reported that by 2015, approximately 95 percent of Sri Lanka's government revenue was being used to service its debt. Eventually, Sri Lanka had to solicit and enter talks with China (its creditor).

According to Hillman, the Hambantota port failed to live up to its predicted success. In 2017, only 175 cargo ships arrived at the port. Since it couldn't pay off its crippling debt, Sri Lanka gave China a controlling equity stake of the Hambantota port and handed over control of its operations and 15,000 surrounding acres as part of a 99-year lease in December 2017.[41] (Ironically, China in 1898 had leased the "New Territories" around Hong Kong to Great Britain for 99 years.) When the Sri Lankan port was handed over to China, the official news agency of China tweeted, "Another milestone along path of #BeltandRoad."[42]

PILFERING THE WORLD'S PIGGY BANK

Despite the horror stories from Pakistan, Sri Lanka, and other countries, the Chinese Communist Party's Belt and Road Initiative continues to entice many countries. Unfortunately, the debt generated by China's aggressive lending schemes is starting to cost the US, our allies, and other countries that haven't agreed to China's offers. When host countries can't keep up with Chinese loans, they often enter debt renegotiations. The Rhodium Group issued an April 2019 report that found that renegotiations and debt distress were common for Belt and Road Initiative host countries. The report found "[t]he sheer volume of debt renegotiations points to legitimate concerns about the sustainability of China's outbound lending." The group predicted more renegotiations were soon to come. Many Belt and Road loans were taken from 2013 to 2016 and will soon come due. Though the report notes that asset seizures, such as Sri Lanka, "are a rare occurrence," it could potentially be the first of many more to come.[43]

Further, the Chinese Communist Party could concoct other

draconian means of repayment. With its significant leverage, China can alter the terms of the deals, extract painful economic or strategic alternative payments—or indirectly garner international funds apportioned to indebted countries. In August 2018, a bipartisan group of 16 US senators wrote a letter to Treasury Secretary Steve Mnuchin and Secretary of State Mike Pompeo. They expressed concerns about countries requesting bailouts from the International Monetary Fund that have "accepted predatory Chinese infrastructure financing." According to the letter, the spiraling debt and financial crises of recipient countries "illustrate the dangers of China's debt-trap diplomacy and its Belt and Road Initiative."[44] Countries sometimes turn to institutions such as the International Monetary Fund (IMF)—which taxpayers from member countries support—for help with unmanageable debt. According to the senators' letter, because of "unsustainable debts to China," the IMF agreed to provide a $1.5 billion bailout loan to Sri Lanka in 2016. Given Sri Lanka's massive debt service, a significant portion—if not all—of this money probably went to China.[45]

And Sri Lanka is not the only one. In May 2019, Pakistan accepted a $6 billion IMF bailout.[46] Since the United States is the largest contributor to IMF funding, American taxpayers are indirectly funding the Chinese Communist Party's global efforts to supplant the traditional world order through the Belt and Road Initiative.[47] In July 2018, Secretary Pompeo said, "There's no rationale for IMF tax dollars—and associated with that, American dollars that are part of the IMF funding—for those to go to bail out Chinese bondholders or China itself."[48] Many more countries are at risk of being deeply indebted to China. Other struggling countries could make similar appeals to international institutions. This would further increase China's ability to extract money from uninvolved nations to advance its own global goals.

Alternatively, if China instead decides to take control of assets in other countries (as it did in Sri Lanka), this could expand China's global control of critical infrastructure and the flow of resources and trade. If leveraged aggressively, this could diminish the free and open flow of goods between countries that don't follow the Chinese Communist Party's will.

TERABYTES OF TYRANNY

The Digital Silk Road, or Information Silk Road, is a less analyzed (but potentially more insidious) element of the Belt and Road Initiative. This component focuses on the integration of digital sectors, such as telecommunications, the Internet of Things, and e-commerce. Specifically, it encourages investment in technology sectors that would boost China's capability to lead these industries and set the standards for future implementation and development.[49] Many intelligence experts are concerned this is a thinly veiled effort to enhance China's spying capability—and help spread its version of authoritarian rule around the world.

The Digital Silk Road spans the globe and incorporates multiple technology sectors. Citing data from RWR Advisory Group, *Bloomberg* reported that since 2012, Chinese companies have sold or installed broadband infrastructure in 76 countries, developed "smart city" and surveillance capabilities in 56 countries, installed telecommunications equipment in 21 countries, and established internet-connected appliances in 27 countries as a part of the digital Belt and Road Initiative efforts. Importantly, in each of these completed or initiated sales or installations, the United States has also been a participant.[50] The *Bloomberg* article, titled "China's Digital Silk Road Is Looking More Like an Iron Curtain," reports that the United States and China are engaged in a massive competition for control of the critical technology sectors of the future and for global influence. Both the US and China sell their technology across the globe. China has an advantage with cheap financing—which is appealing to developing countries with limited funds to update technology infrastructure. In effect, this competition is developing a "digital iron curtain" between two different countries with contrasting views for how the digital world should operate.[51]

In March 2015, China's communist government issued "Vision and Actions on Jointly Building [sic] Silk Road Economic Belt and 21st-Century Maritime Silk Road," which outlined some key priorities for the Digital Silk Road. Among other things, the document calls for advancing construction on cross-border communication infrastructure. The goal is for China to quickly increase multinational cooperation in "new-generation information technology, biotechnology, new energy technology, new materials and other emerging industries, and establish entrepreneurial and investment cooperation mechanisms."[52] The joint communiqué that was signed during the 2017 Belt and Road Forum also described plans for boosting "e-commerce, digital economy, smart cities, and science and technology parks."[53]

Imagine a world in which there is an iron curtain-like digital wall bisecting the globe creating separate Western and Chinese Communist Party versions of the internet, the digital economy, information technology—and all the industries of the future. Add to the list telecommunications—which appears to be the heart of China's Digital Silk Road. As I mentioned in the chapter on 5G, China is eager to supply internet and mobile phone service to as many countries as it can. Since American carriers have no apparent interest in the international market—especially developing markets—and since the US mobile and internet vendors have been wiped out, many Belt and Road countries are happy to accept China's offer.

Africa has been a prime target for China's ambition for digital supremacy. As a part of China's Digital Silk Road efforts, according to data from RWR Advisory Group, China's digital project spending in Africa since 2012 totals at least $2.4 billion in Ethiopia, $1.8 billion in Nigeria, $1.8 billion in Zimbabwe, and $1.7 billion in Angola.[54] Speaking about China's broader

Belt and Road efforts in Africa, National Security Adviser John Bolton said in a December 2018 speech that China is "deliberately and aggressively targeting their investments in the region to gain a competitive advantage over the United States."[55]

With this in mind, the US needs to create and implement a coherent Africa strategy. Africa is going to be an extraordinary center of competition between the United States and China. The 54 countries of Africa include a number that are poor, a number with autocratic governments or dictatorships, and a number that have no particular affection for the United States or the West. All of this creates a substantial opportunity for the Chinese Communist Party to create ties that could become a virtual recolonization on Chinese communist terms. Creating the Africa Command was a useful start, but much more needs to be done. We also need to look at space-based assets that might enable the United States to provide both communications and electricity on a continent-wide basis.

Bolton's description of China's methods underscores the importance of a US strategy for Africa. "China uses bribes, opaque agreements, and the strategic use of debt to hold states in Africa captive to Beijing's wishes and demands. Its investment ventures are riddled with corruption, and do not meet the same environmental or ethical standards as U.S. developmental programs," Bolton said. "Such predatory actions are subcomponents of broader Chinese strategic initiatives, including 'One Belt, One Road'—a plan to develop a series of trade routes leading to and from China with the ultimate goal of advancing Chinese global dominance."[56]

According to *Bloomberg*, there have already been consequences for African nations—namely in democratic Zambia. Zambia is spending approximately $1 billion on Chinese telecommunications, surveillance, and broadcasting technology. While some support China's involvement with Zambia's technology infrastructure development as a cheap way to stimulate the country's modernization efforts, others have expressed fears that this could lead to serious repression.[57] Citing information from the Open Observatory of Network Interference, *Bloomberg* reported that in 2013 and 2014, at least four websites were blocked by Zambia's government "by using a technique typically associated with censorship in China." Though it wasn't proven that equipment from China was involved, ZTE and Huawei equipment used for internet monitoring and blocking had been installed by Zambia.[58]

Furthermore, the chief executive officer of the newspaper *Mast*—a publication that often criticizes the government—said, "Media institutions are working under fear of the government, with the help of the Chinese." Such open criticism of the government can be met with serious punishment in Zambia. Social media posts that criticize Zambian President Edgar Lungu have landed several people in prison for defamation charges.[59] In Zambia's capital, Lusaka, ZTE is installing cameras in public places. This is part of a $210 million "Safe City" initiative, which aims to enhance policing capabilities. (Never mind that Lusaka is already known as one of southern Africa's safest cities.) Though Zambian officials deny this project will have any political applications, in China, as I've described in previous chapters, surveillance systems regularly use facial recognition to track dissenters.[60] Zambia's government supports this arrangement, but it is costing the people their freedom. Gregory Chifire, the director of an organization focused on anti-corruption efforts who fled Zambia, said, "We have sold ourselves to the Chinese." He noted that "[p]eople's freedom to express themselves—their freedom of thought, their freedom of speech—is shrinking by the day.... What is remaining about democracy in Zambia is the name."[61]

There is real potential that in addition to its goods and services, China is exporting digital tyranny. Research Director for Technology and Democracy Adrian Shahbaz said that China is "passing on their norms for how technology should govern society."[62] Permitting China to dictate the digital global order seriously jeopardizes individual freedoms. China is a totalitarian society that heavily restricts internet usage and content. It also uses technology to surveil, monitor, and control its people. Imagine if these practices were adopted worldwide.

China's leadership and shaping of this modern, digital world are a priority for the government. Chen Zhaoxiong, the vice minister of industry and information technology for China, said that the Digital Silk Road will work to "construct a community of common destiny in cyberspace." Sound familiar? According to the USCC, this language of a "community of common destiny" directly reflects the "language China uses to describe its preferred vision for global order aligned to Beijing's liking." It's similar to Xi's idea for a "community with a shared future for humanity" that I described earlier.[63]

As China's various Belt and Road projects expand, there is real danger that it could erode the sovereignty and undermine governance in host countries. Chinese Communist Party leaders have often dismissed the notion that the Belt and Road Initiative is aimed at advancing China's geopolitical ambitions. Yet, it is squeezing out competition for projects, using projects as pipelines to export Chinese goods and technology standards, acquiring control of critical infrastructure, and receiving bailout money from international institutions.

Additionally, as the Chinese Communist Party's influence grows, there is potential for China to expand its military presence using the Belt and Road Initiative. Many analysts say China will probably construct a naval base in Pakistan. China denies such intentions.[64] (Remember, China also denied it would militarize the South China Sea.) In fact, China outlined in its 2015 defense white paper that a core task for the Chinese military is "to safeguard the security of China's overseas interests."[65] Not only is China likely to expand its overseas military presence with the Belt and Road Initiative, it is likely to spread its authoritarian model to other countries or encourage its repressive practice in its disciple countries. As the USCC reported, the initiative "may enable China to export its model of authoritarian governance and encourages and validates authoritarian actors abroad."[66]

THE GREAT REBRANDING

China has been attempting to rebrand and rehabilitate its Belt and Road Initiative amid the widespread criticism it has been receiving. Some of these efforts have been successful. As I mentioned earlier, the Malaysian prime minister who won an election after criticizing Chinese investments is now fully supportive of the initiative—and made a deal with China to resume a previous project at a lower cost. He had initially terminated the project in January 2019. Moreover, in March 2019, Italy signed up to be a part of China's Belt and Road Initiative, becoming the first Group of Seven country to do so.[67]

At the Second Belt and Road Forum for International Cooperation in April 2019, Xi outlined tweaks to the initiative to prevent further backlash. Xi said that, moving forward, initiative participants must "adopt widely accepted rules and standards"; "follow general international rules and standards in project development, operation, procurement, and tendering and bidding"; and "ensure the commercial and fiscal sustainability of all projects."[68] Xi also emphasized "zero tolerance for corruption."[69] The Chinese government has also published a framework to analyze debt sustainability, while the Governor of the People's Bank of China announced that the central bank would "build an open, market-oriented financing and investment system."[70] As a result, according to Xi, during the forum $64 billion worth of deals were signed.[71] Even developed countries such as Singapore, Switzerland, and Austria also signed on to be a part of third-party market cooperation efforts to aid with building infrastructure for developing countries. Countries including Japan, France, Canada, Spain, the Netherlands, Belgium, Italy, and Australia were already signatories to this agreement.[72]

Regardless of what this new rebranding rhetoric claims, the US and countries across the world must keep in mind the risks associated with signing on to the Chinese Communist Party's Belt and Road Initiative. We must deeply consider what the initiative aims to accomplish. Aside from the physical developments, the Belt and Road Initiative is a leading aspect of China's global foreign policy strategy that aims to replace the US-led world order.[73] In response, the US and other major powers have developed their own alternatives to the Belt and Road Initiative to deter countries from signing up to be the next potential victims of an authoritarian debt-trap model.

True, developing countries throughout the world are in desperate need of infrastructure. Specifically in developing countries in Asia, the Philippines-based Asian Development Bank estimates that buildout will cost $26 trillion in investments from 2016 through 2030.[74] The Trump administration has realized the importance of promoting a free, fair, and transparent American model to counteract China's efforts. According to the 2017 US National Security Strategy:

> "The United States will encourage regional cooperation to maintain free and open seaways, transparent infrastructure financing practices, unimpeded commerce, and the peaceful resolution of disputes. We will pursue bilateral trade agreements on a fair and reciprocal basis. We will seek equal and reliable access for American exports. We will work with partners to build a network of states dedicated to free markets and protected from forces that would subvert their sovereignty. We will strengthen cooperation with allies on high-quality infrastructure."[75]

The United States needs to construct and implement a strategy for building alliances and for developing financial and other economic ties with third world countries. The Chinese Communist Party's model has been to reach out and seek friendly ties and contracts everywhere—often using economic incentives in forms and on a scale that the United States currently cannot match. China's communist government uses a whole range of tools that the United States does not have. It also has an affinity for authoritarian regimes where the Chinese Communist Party's repressive systems and policing systems are attractive options. We need a new synthesis of all of our society's assets to maximize our ability to cultivate friends, serve markets, and build alliances and relationships across the planet using the strengths of our American system and values.

The Trump administration has already taken essential first steps to put this into action. In July 2018, Secretary of State Mike Pompeo announced new American initiatives valued at $113 million to support and enhance the "foundational areas of the future: digital economy, energy, and infrastructure."[76] In August 2018, Secretary Pompeo announced an additional $300 million to be put toward regional security assistance. These funds were allocated to heighten maritime security, develop capabilities for humanitarian and peacekeeping initiatives, and improve programs aimed at counteracting transnational threats.[77] Additionally, the bipartisan Better Utilization of Investments Leading to Development, or BUILD Act, was signed into law in October 2018. The passage of the BUILD Act is an important milestone for Congress and the Trump administration. The law improves and strengthens the United States' international development financing capabilities.[78] Such reform has been a priority of the Trump administration. According to the National Security Strategy:

> "The United States will modernize its development finance tools so that U.S. companies have incentives to capitalize on opportunities in developing countries. With these changes, the United States will not be left behind as other states use investment and project finance to extend their influence."[79]

Moreover, according to the Overseas Private Investment Corporation (OPIC), a US government agency that gives American businesses the assistance and tools they need to invest in emerging markets, the United States' development finance tools were last significantly updated in 1971—the year of OPIC's inception.[80] With China's efforts under the Belt and Road Initiative, the US recognized that a new alternative was needed to tackle global development challenges while protecting the foreign policy and national security interests of the United States. Fortunately, the BUILD Act addresses these priorities. The BUILD Act establishes a new agency, the US International Development Finance Corporation which, according to OPIC, "will be a modern, consolidated agency that brings together the capabilities of OPIC and USAID's Development Credit Authority, while introducing new and innovative financial products to better bring private capital to the developing world." This new agency will give the United States the ability to drive economic growth. Overall, OPIC wrote that the US International Development Finance Corporation will strengthen America and protect developing countries from predatory lending schemes.[81]

These are exactly the type of initiatives the United States needs to fend off the Chinese Communist Party's Belt and Road Initiative entrapment. The US cannot successfully persuade developing countries against joining the Belt and Road without providing a viable alternative. However, this is not strictly a foreign affairs problem. Already, according to the 2018 USCC Report, American companies such as Honeywell, General Electric, Citigroup, and Goldman Sachs are participating in the Belt and Road Initiative.[82] Just as we need to encourage other options for developing countries, we need to also encourage alternative investment opportunities for these American companies. The United States must recognize the Chinese Communist Party's economic and strategic goals and challenges associated with the Belt and Road Initiative and act accordingly to protect US interests.

CHAPTER FOURTEEN

THE NEW HIGH GROUND

> As you know, other nations are moving aggressively to weaponize space with new technologies that can disrupt vital communications and blind satellites that are critical to our battlefield operations.
>
> It is a time for America to reclaim the ultimate high ground and prepare our young warriors of today for victory on the battlefield tomorrow.
>
> —President Donald Trump, May 2019[1]

> Developing the space program and turning the country into a space power is the space dream that we have continuously pursued.
>
> —General Secretary Xi Jinping, June 2013[2]

The competition for leadership in space is the single most important challenge we face. The nation that aggressively travels to, harnesses, and inhabits space and other planets will be the nation that writes the rules for the future of humanity. China fully understands this and has been working energetically to advance its space capabilities. It is true that China is presently behind the United States in technology, experience, and achievement. But it is not terribly far behind—and the gap is closing quickly.

Further, China's goal is not to catch up to the United States and share in our discoveries. China wants to surpass the United States and be the world's preeminent spacefaring nation. General Secretary Xi Jinping understands that the country that dominates in space will dominate the future. Space dominance is a major part of his plan to make China a "fully developed, rich, and powerful nation" by 2049—the 100th anniversary of the founding of the People's Republic of China. The easiest mistake for Westerners to make about China's space program is to assume that it is organized like NASA, the European Space Agency, or some other civilian science- or exploration-focused model. In fact, China has arranged its space efforts within a model of civil-military fusion.

China's space bureaucracy is a confusing alphabet soup of various government agencies, state-owned corporations, and appointed councils (with all paths leading toward fulfilling the objectives of the Chinese Communist Party, of course). The public face of China's official actions in space is the China National Space Administration; however, the military (through its Equipment Development Department) ultimately controls the bureaucracy by researching, developing, and procuring the country's spacecraft, satellites, space-based weaponry, and major engineering projects.[3] In this way, virtually every aspect of China's space sector is guided by the Communist Party's People's Liberation Army (PLA). The US-China Economic and Security Review Commission (USCC) reported on April 11, 2019, that:

> "The [Chinese] military plays a role in planning space policy, as well. For example, in 2004 the State Council and the Central Military Commission, China's highest-ranking military body, formed a joint leading small

> group for the lunar probe project which convened at least 14 times from 2004 to 2015. . . . Military entities are even heavily involved in China's ostensibly nonmilitary space projects."[4]

This heavy military involvement in the space program was all by design. (Keep in mind that Xi is also Chairman of the Central Military Commission.) Shortly after he took power in 2012, Xi began to reorganize the PLA so it could easily integrate into China's then-behind-the-times space sector—and vice versa. The first step was to blend all of the Chinese government's space programs and departments with the military. By 2014, the USCC reports the Chinese government opened the space industry to non-state actors (integrating them into the hybrid, civil-military Chinese space model). In 2015, China announced the creation of the PLA's Strategic Support Force (SSF), which is a service branch of the Chinese military that focuses specifically on warfare in the space, cyber, and electronic domains. As the Defense Intelligence Agency reported in its 2019 *Challenges to Security in Space* report, "The SSF forms the core of China's information warfare force, supports the entire PLA, and reports directly to the Central Military Commission."[5]

Today, virtually every major Chinese space project or program is led or advised by a PLA operative.[6] Dr. Namrata Goswami, who studies and writes on China's activity in space, laid some of this out as part of a testimony before the USCC on April 25, 2019. According to Dr. Goswami:

- Major General Liu Shangfu leads the Chinese military's critical Equipment Development Department (EED). His résumé also includes deputy commander and chief of staff of the military's SSF, commander of the Xichang Satellite Launch Center, deputy commander of the human spaceflight program, chief of staff for the now defunct General Armament Division (GAD, which was replaced by the EED in the reorganization), and deputy commander of the China Lunar Exploration Program.

- General Zhang Yulin is assistant director for the EED and working with the SSF. He was previously with the GAD and deputy head of China's space program.
- Xie Gengxin is the deputy head of the Chongqing Collaborative Innovation Research Institute for Civil-Military Integration, oversees China's space-based solar power project, and designed one of the experiments carried on the Chang'e-4 spacecraft.
- Yang Shizhong is a professor at Chongqing Institute and the Chinese Academy of Engineering. He is also a consultant for the Military Science and Technology Research Commission at the PLA Headquarters of the General Staff.[7]

So, when we talk about China's activities in space—whether it's hatching silkworms on the Moon, creating a lunar relay satellite system, or creating a Chinese version of the International Space Station—it is important to understand that there is a potential military application for everything China is doing. This dual-use space activity exists because Xi views dominance in space as central to China's dominance on Earth. The Chinese state-run media has reported Xi's clear intentions to make China a "space power."[8] After the June 11, 2013, launch of the Shenzhou-10 mission, Xi told those working the mission that "developing the space program and turning the country into a space power is the space dream that we have continuously pursued." In a June 24, 2013, video call to Chinese astronauts aboard its Tiangong temporary space laboratory, Xi told them, "The space dream is part of the dream to make China stronger. With the development of space programs, the Chinese people will take bigger strides to explore further into space." This language is mirrored in the Chinese government's own 2016 white paper on space activities. The memo describes China's vision:

> "To build China into a space power in all respects, with the capabilities to make innovations independently, to make scientific discovery and research at the cutting edge, to promote strong and sustained economic and social development, to effectively and reliably guarantee national security, to exercise sound and efficient governance, and to carry out mutually beneficial international exchanges and cooperation; to have an advanced and open space science and technology industry, stable and reliable space infrastructure, pioneering and innovative professionals, and a rich and profound space spirit; to provide strong support for the realization of the [China] Dream of the renewal of the Chinese nation, and make positive contributions to human civilization and progress."[9]

While this vision statement seems fairly innocuous, remember it is a part of the Chinese Communist Party's overall strategy to say what the world wants to hear—and keep doing whatever advances its interest. China joined the World Trade Organization in good faith and almost immediately began breaking all of its promises.[10] China committed to the Obama administration that it would not militarize the South China Sea and then began building militarized islands. As the Defense Intelligence Agency reported, "China officially advocates for peaceful use of space, and it is pursuing agreements at the United Nations on the nonweaponization of space. Nonetheless, China continues to improve its counterspace weapons capabilities and has enacted military reforms to better integrate cyberspace, space, and [electronic warfare] into joint military operations."[11]

The April 11, 2019, USCC report on China's quest for dominance in space points out that China is remedying its historic technological and experiential shortfalls in space activity at an astonishing pace. In fact, China is moving twice as fast as the United States did when we were building our own space program. In 1961, the US sent our first manned mission to outer space. In 1973, we launched Skylab (a temporary space station). Finally, by 1998, we were operating a long-term module on the International Space Station. As the USCC report points out, only eight years passed between China's first crewed mission in 2003 and the launch of its Tiangong-1 temporary space station. According to the report, "If plans hold to launch its first long-term space station module, Tianhe-1, in 2020, it will have matched NASA's nearly 40-year progression from first human spaceflight to first space station module in less than 20 years."

There is no indication that China will be slowing down. The Chinese have met or exceeded almost every one of their major project deadlines for three decades, according to Dr. Goswami's April 25, 2019, testimony to the USCC. It's much more likely that Xi and the Chinese Communist Party will continue increasing the pace of China's advances in space. As of March 31, 2019, China has the second highest number of satellites in orbit, with 299, according to the Union of Concerned Scientists' Satellite Database. The US has 901 in orbit.[12] Further, Todd Harrison with the Center for Strategic and International Studies (CSIS) told the USCC at the hearing on April 25 that China is already outpacing the United States (and the rest of the planet) on orbital launches. Harrison is director of the CSIS Aerospace Security Project and its Defense Budget Analysis. According to his testimony, China had 38 successful orbital space launches in 2018. The US had only 34, and Russia had 19.[13]

Harrison added that China's space-based ambitions show no signs of waning. In addition to its Tianhe-1 space station plans, China is building a space telescope that boasts a field of view 300 times larger than Hubble Space Telescope, which launched in 1990. Meanwhile, our own Hubble replacement, the James Webb Telescope, was supposed to launch in 2007 with a price tag of $1 billion. Due to a series of delays and cost increases (which are typical for today's old guard US space industry and NASA bureaucracy), the launch date is now

2021—and the deep space telescope is currently expected to cost $10 billion. On top of all this, China is expected to spend $11 billion a year on space-related programs (both civil and military). As Harrison puts it, that is "a sum that is second only to the United States." NASA's budget averages just over $20 billion per year. President Trump's latest 2020 budget also calls to spend $14.1 billion on military space programs.[14] Yes, the US is spending much more, but Chinese manufacturing costs and the Chinese bureaucracy are both significantly less expensive than their American counterparts.

One of the most recent—and clearest—signals that China intends to lead the world in space was its successful, historic landing on the farside of the moon. In January 2019, the Chang'e-4 lander touched down on the far lunar surface and released the Yutu-2 rover.[15] This was a first for humankind. No nation had previously landed a spacecraft on the farside of the Moon—much less deploy a lander. It was the fourth step of a multipart Chang'e series of missions to survey the Moon and establish a permanent presence there. It is worth noting that the project's namesake is a mythical Chinese goddess who made her home on the Moon.[16]

Perhaps the most critical—and underappreciated—step of this landmark mission, however, wasn't the landing. It was China's preliminary move to launch the Queqiao relay communications satellite into a halo orbit at the second Earth-Moon Lagrange point. In basic terms, Lagrange points are areas between planetary bodies where gravitational forces cancel themselves out. Spacecraft in Lagrange points don't have to spend a lot of energy to stay in orbit, because they aren't being pulled too much in any direction. So, Lagrange points are like the parking lots of space—and they potentially represent incredibly valuable real estate. It is clear that China intends to establish a long-term presence on the surface of the Moon—and in cislunar space (the space between Earth and the Moon).

CISLUNAR SPACE—THE NEW HIGH GROUND

China's placement of a relay satellite at Earth-Moon-2 could be a first step in building out a larger cislunar commercial-military infrastructure. Already, the satellite used for Chang'e-4 is also transmitting information for another space project China is doing with the Netherlands. Make no mistake: If China builds out the infrastructure and architecture of cislunar space, China will reap the rewards, because more and more countries will look to partner with them rather than the United States.

China's public explanation for what it plans to do with the Chang'e missions include analyzing and collecting minerals, attempting to hatch silkworms, attempting to grow cotton, and other primarily science-based projects. However, many experts are trying to determine the potential unstated dual-use of the Chang'e missions. According to *The Washington Times*, top US Air Force officials are concerned that China would be able to conceal anti-satellite and other space-based weapons on the farside of the Moon.[17] Indeed, military leaders in the US and China have described cislunar space as the new high ground in war fighting. Retired US Marine Corps General James Cartwright told the USCC on April 25, 2019, that cislunar space "is the gateway" to the Moon and space and "the high ground from which you can observe all of earth's orbits."

This means that the country that controls this high ground will have the potential ability to deny other nations or companies access to space—or to attack other nations from space (both their space-based and terrestrial assets). Cartwright warned that "not knowing what's going on there. Not having a good command and control architecture at [cislunar space] will tremendously disadvantage us as we go to the future.... It is very important to understand the advantage you have from that high ground. That is critical from a national security standpoint—from a military standpoint." Similarly, the Chinese Military Strategy of 2015 plainly stated, "outer space and cyber space have become new commanding heights in strategic competition among all parties."[18] If this isn't a clear enough message, Ye Peijian, the chief commander and chief designer of China's lunar exploration program, said:

> "The universe is an ocean, the moon is the Diaoyu Islands, Mars is Huangyan Island. If we don't get there now even though we're capable of doing so, then we will be blamed by our descendants. If others go there, then they will take over, and you won't be able to go even if you want to. This is reason enough."[19]

This language does not reflect a view of space as a global common from the military perspective. Inherent in China's space program is the notion that cislunar space is territory to claim. Further, China's actions show that it intends to defend its new territory. The country has been creating and testing space-based weapons (in space and terrestrially) for years.

William Roper, the assistant secretary of the US Air Force for acquisition, technology, and logistics, told the USCC on April 25, 2019, that China and other nations have "already demonstrated their intention to escalate hostilities into space."[20] In addition to a 2007 Chinese anti-satellite weapon test that created a swarm of dangerous space debris (as well as international uproar), Roper said that China is currently developing directed energy weapons for taking out space assets. "Directed energy weapon" is a catch-all term that includes lasers, high-powered microwaves, and weaponized radio frequencies. These weapons could be complemented by cyberattacks, signal jamming, chemical spray attacks, and other malicious actions on important satellite constellations. This is not science fiction. The Defense Intelligence Agency reported that "China likely will field a ground-based laser weapon that can counter low-orbit space-based [optical] sensors by 2020, and by the mid-to-late 2020s, it may field higher power systems that extend the threat to the structures of non-optical satellites."

Presently, the US has no meaningful system of deterrence against these types of activities in cislunar space. The 1967 Outer Space Treaty prohibits weapons of mass destruction—but not smaller targeted weapons or general military activity. Despite this lack of legal or practical methods of deterring violence in space, the US has expensive, vital, and mission-critical assets in orbit.

China's conventional military has almost no chance of defeating the United States in a conventional war. Generally, we have far more terrestrial power. China's conventional military is useful as a regional power, but not yet as a global one. However, the US has integrated our satellite constellations into nearly every level of our war fighting—from guided missile systems to directing ground troops. China watched and learned as we capitalized on this exquisite integration during the two Gulf Wars. As Roper pointed out to the USCC, "Why would you want to fight the joint strike fighter, if you can fight the satellites that support it getting to where it needs to be? Why would you want to fight a carrier strike group, if you can take out satellites that help it navigate?"

Indeed, the Defense Intelligence Agency also reported that "PLA analysis of U.S. and allied military operations states that 'destroying or capturing satellites and other sensors' would make it difficult to use precision guided weapons. Moreover, PLA writings suggest that reconnaissance, communications, navigation, and early warning satellites could be among the targets of attacks designed to 'blind and deafen the enemy.'" The US military is beginning to replace some of its larger—high value target—satellites with disaggregated constellations of satellites. This makes disabling our satellite systems more difficult and costly by creating more targets for enemies to hit. It also decreases the amount of time it takes to replace satellites that are potentially knocked out. A constellation of 100 smaller satellites is far more resilient to attack than a single, large satellite. However, we are years behind in replacing all of our systems.

Furthermore, many in the defense field agree that China is creating space-based weapon systems faster than we are creating ways to counter them.

The commercial sector is more disaggregated, but it is still vulnerable in some ways. In this vein, according to the Defense Intelligence Agency report, we should not underestimate how much commercial and civil satellite systems impact our daily lives. This includes position, navigation, and timing systems (such as GPS); communications satellites; and remote sensing satellites. As the Defense Intelligence Agency explained in its 2019 report:

> "[Position, navigation, and timing] signals, especially precise timing, also provide critical support to modern infrastructure. Without precise timing, financial institutions would be unable to create timestamps for transactions, impacting the public's ability to use ATMs and credit cards, and utility companies would be unable to efficiently transmit power.
>
> "Communications satellites—which comprise the majority of satellites on orbit—support global communications and complement terrestrial communications networks. Losing these satellites can have wide-ranging impacts, which was illustrated in 1998 when a U.S. communications satellite suffered a computer failure—people were unable to pay for gas, hospitals were unable to contact physicians who relied on pagers, and television stations were unable to deliver programming. For militaries, satellite communications improve situational awareness and allow forces greater mobility by eliminating the need for ground-based infrastructure.
>
> "Without remote sensing satellites—which provide data on the Earth's land, sea, and atmosphere—society would be unable to benefit from weather forecasting, including preparing for weather emergencies. These

> satellites provide data about the terrain and environment, which range from assisting businesses in determining areas with mineral resources to assisting farmers in identifying potential agricultural disasters."[21]

The prospect of space-based weapons and warfare also creates a serious geopolitical challenge for the United States. What is the appropriate, proportionate response if a nation attacks a US satellite—government or commercial? Certainly, destroying a satellite we use to detect ballistic missile launches is threatening. It would have high potential consequences, but such an attack would be unlikely to cause direct danger to Americans. Similarly, what if a country were to disable or destroy commercial satellites we use for banking or communication?

This question of proportionate response gets even more difficult if the satellites involved are taken out with a cyberattack or a laser that is difficult to track and causes no dangerous space debris. What should be the consequences for the destruction of property in outer space? This represents a profound challenge in our ability to deal with China and other nations—in space and on Earth.

ECONOMIC COMPETITION

As it does in every domain, China is also challenging our access to space economically. Lorand Laskai, a researcher with Georgetown Center for Security and Emerging Technology, told the USCC on April 25, 2019, that once China opened its space sector to private companies in 2014 and made commercial space a national priority, the industry immediately began to grow.

Again, the idea of a private company in China is nothing like the American model. Most Chinese companies are required to incorporate cells of the Chinese Communist Party with substantial authority into their corporate structure. Further, commercial sectors that have been declared national priorities or serve dual purposes for the government—such as the space sector—are heavily subsidized with state funding. This subsidization serves to get the industries off the ground, but China has mastered the art of weaponizing it. It is routine for China to identify a market, heavily subsidize it so Chinese companies (private and state-owned) can offer rock-bottom prices that bankrupt industries in other nations, and then become the dominant global producer. We have seen this in industries including steel, aluminum, solar panels, telecommunications, and many others. We are now seeing these same tactics in the space sector. Laskai pointed out in his testimony that this is exactly the playbook supposedly private Chinese launch company OneSpace is using:

> "Revealingly, in an interview last year, OneSpace founder and CEO Shu Chang said his goal was not to be 'China's SpaceX,' but to be the 'Huawei of the space industry.' The goal is not so much to push the bounds of commercial space technology as to commercialize existing technology and sell it at a lower cost."[22]

Laskai added that "some launch companies have offered small satellite companies free launch services as a way to gain market share."

Mike Gold, vice president of regulatory policy at Maxar Technologies, echoed Laskai's comments at the April 25, 2019, hearing. Maxar is a major California-based US space company. According to Gold's testimony, a little more than a decade ago, China had only two satellites in geosynchronous orbit (this means an orbit that mirrors Earth's orbit and therefore appears to stay in the same place in the sky). One of China's failed in 2006 and the other failed in 2008. "Today, China has become a global leader in satellite manufacturing, producing 40 satellites in a two-year period, a rate that rivals the productivity of the U.S. and Europe," Gold said. Gold told the USCC that China has achieved this largely through its Belt and Road Initiative and its China Great Wall Industry Corporation (CGWIC)—the premier state-owned contractor for China's official space program. The Chinese communist government is granting loans to CGWIC, so it can then garner cheap satellite contracts from countries targeted in the Belt and Road Initiative. Gold said it is unclear if CGWIC is even turning a profit—or if the Chinese Communist Party is happy to take the economic hit in exchange for choking out international competition and gaining influence in the Belt and Road Initiative countries.

One tactic the state-owned company is using is to offer artificially competitive financing options to customers. These financial incentives are almost impossible for competitors to match. When Gold's company was bidding to build a satellite for a joint venture of two Indonesian companies in 2016 he testified that "we discovered that CGWIC was offering 70 percent financing... which would be immediately available at contract signing," he said. Normally, financing isn't released for six months to a year, he said. Naturally, China got the contract. This is a strategy China is also using with its version of GPS (BeiDou), and many other aspects of the satellite industry. In its report, the Defense Intelligence Agency warned, "China has embarked on several ambitious plans to propel itself to the forefront of the global satellite communications (SATCOM) industry. China is testing multiple next-generation capabilities, such as quantum-enabled communications, which could supply the means to field highly secure communications systems."

In addition to creating an unfair playing field in the commercial space industry, the subsidization schemes China is employing are helping Chinese companies skirt US import/export laws and other regulations—and steal trade secrets from American companies. In his testimony, Laskai pointed to an instance in December 2018. *The Wall Street Journal* uncovered that a Chinese start-up (which was financially propped up by a government-owned investment firm) had ordered a satellite system from Boeing. US export controls essentially make it illegal to sell satellites to the Chinese government. But the start-up appeared commercial in nature. However, in this case, Laskai said the satellites also included sensitive technology that has additional export prohibitions. Nevertheless, due to the murky paper trial, Boeing was able to obtain an export license for the sale. It was the news story—not any watchdog or regulator—that caused Boeing to cancel the sale and prevent China from obtaining the restricted satellite system.

Similarly, on April 23, 2019, *The Wall Street Journal* discovered another plot in which Hong Kong–based company AsiaSat (which is partially owned by the Chinese communist government) had acquired a fleet of nine US-made satellites from Boeing and SSL, a branch of Maxar Technologies.[23] Under export controls, companies from the semi-independent Hong Kong can buy US satellites. On paper, AsiaSat uses the communication satellites to broadcast sports and television programming. However, the newspaper reported that various parts of the fleet had been used to broadcast propaganda for the Chinese Communist Party, been used by Chinese police forces for rapid response, and some had been used to quell anti-government protests in Tibet and Xinjiang—where the Communist Party has persecuted or imprisoned millions of Uyghurs and other Muslim and ethnic minorities. Additionally, the Chinese government-owned Citic Group, which markets for AsiaSat, listed the Chinese Ministry of State Security (China's chief spy agency) and the Communist Party's People's Liberation Army as its customers.

A RACE FOR THE SUN

In January 2019, China officially moved forward on a program to pioneer space-based solar power. The project involves putting an enormous satellite in geosynchronous orbit. The satellite would capture solar rays (undiluted by Earth's atmosphere), convert the solar energy into radio waves, and then beam it to a base plant on Earth, where it would be converted to electricity.

According to Dr. Goswami, the plant is set to be generating 24 megawatts of electricity by 2040.

Now, this sounds wild, but space-based solar power would revolutionize the space economy and humankind as we know it. Solar power on Earth is hit or miss. If the sun isn't shining, you don't get power. In fact, most of the advancements over the last few decades in terrestrial solar power have been related to battery improvements to make up for this cloudy day–nighttime problem. Outside Earth's atmosphere, this is no longer an issue. A satellite can be positioned so that it catches uninterrupted sunlight. Beaming the energy back to Earth in radio waves is settled science. So, the ultimate implication of this technology is 100 percent carbon-free baseload energy. The nation (or company) who fully develops this technology will be able to deliver electricity anywhere on the globe—or anywhere in outer space. Consider how dramatically this could help China's Belt and Road Initiative, its lunar mission, or its ability to influence impoverished third world countries. As Wang Xiji, the chief engineer for China's main rocket program, said:

> "The world will panic when the fossil fuels can no longer sustain human development. We must acquire space solar power technology before then.... Whoever obtains the technology first could occupy the future energy market. So it's of great strategic significance."[24]

Space-based solar power generation would drive the economy in space (power generation is big business) and pay for future space missions. One of the biggest hurdles for mining water from the Moon and minerals from asteroids—and in-space robotic manufacturing—is figuring out how to power all of the assets you need to make these systems work. The ability to beam energy-filled radio waves to robotic moon miners or a lunar habitat would significantly speed the time line for establishing permanent habitats outside of Earth.

Sadly, no US government space program meets the utility or practicality of China's space-based solar power program. However, there is a US company seeking to beat China to this milestone of human achievement. I have met several times with a company called Solaren, which has its own system for generating power from space.[25] Solaren's system is one-tenth the weight of the Chinese design. If the company can secure funding, it is ready to launch a prototype system in 2020. Its full 250-megawatt system could be up by as early as 2023. That would be 10 times more productive than China's facility and implemented 17 years sooner (this mirrors the Trump Wollman Rink model that I wrote about in *Understanding Trump*). Although Solaren's design has already been reviewed and verified by scientists at Lockheed Martin, the California-based company is currently working with the US Naval Research Laboratory for additional testing and verifications. The company is searching for private investors, but it is also in talks with the US Department of Energy for possible initial funding options.

Achieving space-based solar power will be a major tipping point. If an American company like Solaren has the first viable system in orbit, it will be able to start selling power anywhere on the planet. It could contract with the military to supply uninterruptible power to remote bases. It could beam power to allied foreign cities and nations that are not connected to major electrical infrastructure—or are currently dependent on energy from hostile nations such as Russia or Iran. If China masters this technology first, it will be able to do these things—and its influence in space and on Earth will grow significantly. It is imperative that the United States (both government and private) wins this race for the future.

THE TRUMP-PENCE SOLUTION

Meeting and outmatching the China challenge in space is critical.

In summary, China is developing three parallel challenges

to American space superiority. First, in a repeat of the Huawei model, the Communist Chinese government is beginning to build a strategy of undercutting the American private sector launch companies and buying up American technological breakthroughs. Second, China has a determined effort to establish a claim on the Moon faster than the NASA bureaucracy can get there. Third, China is developing a variety of war fighting approaches to space which will require a much more aggressive development by the American Space Force. All three of these challenges must be met if America is to retain leadership in space.

The good news is the Trump administration has taken tremendous steps to reinvigorate the US space sector. Despite China's recent rise, we do have a window of opportunity to ensure that the United States remains the global leader in space. This is not simply important for economics. We must ensure that freedom, fairness, and the rule of law guide humankind's expansion into the future. If China's Communist Party leads, the ruling regime in space (and eventually Earth) will be one of tyranny and oppression. President Donald Trump's vision for the future in space—executed by Vice President Mike Pence and the National Space Council—is exactly what America needs to ensure this doesn't happen.

One of the most powerful steps the president took, early in his term, was reconstituting the National Space Council and placing the vice president at its head. Because the council is made up of cabinet secretaries who have to report their progress—publicly—to the vice president at every meeting, there is tremendous pressure to move the bureaucratic system. This step has been critical in reorganizing and empowering the Department of Commerce to engage with and encourage growth in the commercial space sector. It has also moved the Department of Transportation to develop advanced traffic control systems for launch and spaceflight. It will also be integral in seeing the establishment of the US Space Force—whether as an independent branch or a corps within the US Air Force.

Most recently, on March 26, 2019, in Huntsville, Alabama, Vice President Pence made a remarkably bold and historic challenge to NASA, the US bureaucracy, and the old guard US space companies—many of which have milked government funds for decades without making meaningful progress in human spaceflight. The vice president announced that the United States would return Americans to the Moon by 2024—and that at least one of these astronauts would be the first woman to walk on the lunar surface. Failure, according to Vice President Pence, "is not an option." This was a vitally important directive to the space community because it came on the heels of a recent NASA announcement that had actually pushed the US Moon mission back to 2028. Vice President Pence sent a decisive message that missed deadlines, cost overruns, and inactivity would simply not be tolerated. The traditional space bureaucracy (both government and private) could no longer slow-walk America's destiny in space to pad their pockets or protect their pet programs. As the vice president said:

> "We're not committed to any one contractor. If our current contractors can't meet this objective, then we'll find ones that will. If American industry can provide critical commercial services without government development, then we'll buy them. And if commercial rockets are the only way to get American astronauts to the Moon in the next five years, then commercial rockets it will be."

In the best-case scenario, NASA will get the message and begin to behave like its Apollo era counterparts—rather than point to past accomplishments. NASA will become open to accepting risk, begin to measure itself on real progress rather than procedure, and achieve the vice president's directive. With

NASA Administrator Jim Bridenstine at the helm, I have strong faith these things will happen.

Similarly, the large, legacy space companies will reassess, wake up, and realize that the old way of doing business (with cost-plus contracts, multiyear delays, and multibillion-dollar overruns) is over. As more and more lean, efficient, and effective space start-ups emerge, the dinosaurs of the past will have to change or will become extinct. In the perfect outcome, new American innovators will continue to bring down the cost of access to space. The hardware we use for launch and spaceflight will become increasingly reusable, reliable, and cheaper to manufacture. And every American in middle school today will be able to have a career in an incredibly successful American space industry if they so choose.

Finally, everyone in the entire space community will, as Vice President Pence said, learn "to think bigger, fail smarter, and work harder than ever before." The vice president was exactly right in Huntsville, when he said:

> "The United States must remain first in space, in this century as in the last, not just to propel our economy and secure our nation, but above all because the rules and values of space, like every great frontier, will be written by those who have the courage to get there first and the commitment to stay.
>
> "And as Americans, and as heirs of this great nation dedicated to life, to liberty, and the pursuit of happiness, it's nothing less than our duty to ensure that our most cherished values are the foundation of mankind's future in space."[26]

As I said in the beginning of this chapter, this is the most important competition we face in this century. It is one we must win.

CHAPTER FIFTEEN

WAR FIGHTING VS. WAR POSTURING

We are guided by outcomes, not ideology. We have a policy of principled realism, rooted in shared goals, interests, and values. That realism forces us to confront a question facing every leader and nation in this room. It is a question we cannot escape or avoid. We will slide down the path of complacency, numb to the challenges, threats, and even wars that we face. Or do we have enough strength and pride to confront those dangers today, so that our citizens can enjoy peace and prosperity tomorrow?

—President Donald Trump, September 2017[1]

An ancient Chinese said: "If decrees are not obeyed, government affairs will be mismanaged." The Party exercises overall leadership over all areas of endeavor in every part of the country. The theories, guidelines and policies defined by the CPC [Chinese Communist Party] Central Committee are the foundation to ensure all Party members and people of all ethnic groups in China are united in mindset, determination and action. Only with authority can the CPC Central Committee pool the strength of all Party members and unite

> the whole Party and the whole nation, bringing into being an invincible force of the same aspiration.
>
> —General Secretary Xi Jinping, February 2017[2]

As the United States begins to focus on the emergence of communist-ruled China as a competitor on a global scale, there is a serious lack of understanding about how hard this challenge is going to be—and how much thoughtful change it is going to require on our part. Make no mistake, over the next two decades, responding to the challenge that communist-controlled China poses to the US (and avoiding defeat) will be as big of a project as preparing to fight World War II or creating new institutions for the Cold War. (Think: NATO, Strategic Air Command, Central Intelligence Agency, unified Department of Defense, and extensive anti-Soviet spying activities by the FBI.)

This scale of study, analysis, and change will have to involve the executive branch, the Congress, the news media, the private sector, and ultimately the American people. This is what it took to win World War II and beat the Soviets, and this is what it will take to win the competition with communist-ruled China. A key part of this process must be a ruthlessly honest analysis of who the Chinese Communist Party is and who we are. We must live out Sun Tzu's injunction to know the enemy and know yourself as a precondition for winning a hundred battles.

In undertaking this rigorous examination of communist-ruled China as a national security threat, we must remember Vice President Mike Pence's warning regarding the new space race. He said, "What we need now is urgency.... But it's not just competition against our adversaries; we're also racing against our worst enemy: complacency."[3] There is a grave danger that in peacetime, our national security bureaucracies will fall prey to war posturing rather than war fighting. War posturing is a favorite behavior of bureaucracies, because it allows them to avoid change. With war posturing, the bureaucracies can look good in peacetime and minimize the necessary changes, while reassuring themselves and others that everything is fine.

In the late 1930s, there was a joint planning board to coordinate the US Army and Navy. In theory, the board was supposed to develop a coordinated, unified plan for both services. In practice, the navy developed a plan that fit its capabilities, and the army developed a plan that fit its capabilities. In order to impress the Japanese and hopefully convince them that we were too powerful to attack, we engaged in war posturing in the Philippines. We sent a completely unbalanced air force that had too many B-17s, not enough fighter aircraft, not enough ammunition, and a totally inadequate warning system. It was largely destroyed on the first day of the war by a Japanese military, which had been practicing actual war fighting in China for four years and knew what had to be done.

With the combined failures of the surprise at Pearl Harbor on December 7, 1941, and the elimination of American air power in the Philippines on December 8, the absurdity of the war posturing model became clear. It was a complete disaster. The army had a plan to hold on in the Philippines for three months until it could be rescued by the navy. The Navy's plan was to mobilize and fight its way to the Philippines in three years. The absurdity of this mismatch of schedules was appalling and led to much greater efforts to insist on serious coordination in planning.

A similar example of a war posturing failure occurred in the army during the preparation for World War II. David E. Johnson explained in his excellent study, *Fast Tanks and Heavy Bombers: Innovation in the U.S. Army, 1917–1945*, that after watching German armor make decisive gains in Poland and France, Army Chief of Staff George Marshall called in the Army's Chief of Cavalry and asked what the American cavalry was doing to rethink plans for dealing with German innovations. The cavalry chief reassured Marshall that the cavalry had been studying the Germans carefully. The cavalry chief concluded he needed trucks to take the horses closer to the edge of the battlefield, so they would be fresh when they went into battle against German tanks. Marshall listened in disbelief and thanked him for his report. After the cavalry chief left, Marshall told his secretary to retire the chief as of noon and abolish the post of chief of cavalry. It obviously could not meet the challenge of the modern world. I mention this story often, because I believe it perfectly captures the way bureaucracies can become self-sustaining, resistant to change, practice self-deception, and eventually discover through disaster that they are obsolete.

Additionally, one of the most famous examples of war posturing leading to decisive defeat is the three French disasters in the Middle Ages at Crecy, Poitiers, and Agincourt. The French nobility in their heavy armor and heavily armored horses were the key striking force of the French army. Their role as expensive mounted knights was central to their posturing—but also their self-esteem and social status. As individuals in tournaments, the skills these knights spent years acquiring were powerful and thrilling. However, as an instrument of war, they met disaster three times. The English had developed the use of the longbow as an offensive weapon. This was a remarkable national investment. It took years to acquire the strength and skill to be effective as an archer against mounted heavily armored knights and horses. They fired so many arrows that an entire industry emerged in Britain gathering up goose feathers, cutting the right wood, and making the arrows. There was a further investment in a logistics system capable of gathering the arrows from village fletchers, packing them in specialized cases, and moving them to the army in France.

The English longbow was a national strategy implemented in an all-of-society effort to acquire dominance over the French. The French hated the archers, because they were a mortal threat to the entire structure of the French aristocracy. Whenever they captured archers, the French would cut off their fingers so they could no longer draw the string on their bows. So, three times in a century, the French postured at war, while the English fought a war. Three times the French were annihilated with enormous losses. They simply could not adapt to the new technology and new organization.

There is a grave danger that all of our vast expenditures and massive professional bureaucracies will find it easier to engage in war posturing, while retaining the habits, doctrines, and organizational structures that make them comfortable and that they are used to living with.

CHINA CAN PLAN, DECEIVE, AND FIGHT

With the emphasis on the Chinese approach to winning bloodless victories, long-term plans, and go-like focus on incrementally gaining territory and advantages rather than destroying opponents, it is easy to forget that there are times when deception, patience, and maneuver result in direct combat. The Communist Party's military (which is loyal to the party, not the state) has a tradition of hard-fought campaigns. First, there were two decades of civil war with the Kuomintang, in which many were killed. At the same time, there was an eight-year war with the Japanese, in which there were bitter, hard-fought battles and campaigns.

Just a year after Mao Zedong declared the establishment of the People's Republic of China on October 1, 1949, the Communists found themselves drawn into a much more ferocious war than they had imagined. On June 25, 1950, the North Korean Communists (with approval and implied commitment of support from Stalin) attacked South Korea. The unprepared American ally was rapidly overrun. As the Communists poured south, the Americans hastily sent in under-trained and under-equipped peacetime forces. They gradually stabilized a front down near the port of Pusan at the very southeastern end of Korea. In a brilliant maneuver, General Douglas MacArthur launched an amphibious landing at Inchon, near Seoul, and far behind the North Korean army's lines. Faced with being cut off, the North Koreans withdrew toward the north—losing men and equipment. They were beginning to fall apart under the punishment of American airpower and the renewed combat power of mobilized US Army and Marine units.

MacArthur suffered from what the Japanese called "victory disease" (which had ruined their efforts in 1942 when they became overextended). He thought it was impossible for the year-old Chinese communist government to successfully intervene—and he even said so. He promised that the war would be over by year's end and that US troops would be home for Christmas. Meanwhile, Mao's new government publicly warned that it would not accept an American presence on the Chinese border. As the Americans moved into North Korea, the Chinese began to mobilize.

Some American units actually reached the Yalu River, the border between Korea and China. Filled with overconfidence and with instructions from MacArthur's headquarters in Tokyo to ignore reports of Chinese troops infiltrating along the ridgelines and mountains, the American forces were stretched far too thin. They were wholly unprepared to defend against a major attack. The Chinese achievement in moving as many as 300,000 troops into Korea without being detected is one of the greatest stories of operational mismatches in military history. America had total air superiority. Its aircraft flew all over Korea looking for signs of Chinese forces. However, Americans assumed the enemy would have vehicles. They looked for movement along roads and visible detectible signs of Chinese presence and the presence of their logistical support.

In what has to be considered one of the great feats of deception, concealment, and surprise in all of military history, the Chinese Communists moved at night, stayed quietly in the forests during the day, and surrounded the American forces in North Korea with virtually no detection. The few instances where Chinese soldiers were captured or otherwise detected were simply rejected by MacArthur's headquarters in Tokyo.

When the assault came, the results were astounding. In the west, the Second Division of the US Army virtually disintegrated while running a gauntlet of Chinese forces. In the east, the Marines found themselves surrounded and, as Marine Major General Oliver Smith said, "Retreat, Hell! We're just attacking in a different direction!" There is no saga in Marine Corps history more amazing than the fight to the sea against overwhelming numbers of Chinese forces. The fact that all of this was occurring in bitter winter weather made the defeat all the more disastrous. Anyone who believes that the Chinese cannot fight, cannot run a massive deception operation, and cannot to continue parallelism persevere against a much stronger opponent needs to study carefully the 1950 campaign. It is true that eventually our massive advantages in firepower and airpower stabilized the front and ultimately drove the Chinese back with heavy casualties. Today, we would not have the massive technological advantages we had over the Chinese forces in 1950. In some ways we are still stronger, but in some ways we have begun to fall behind.

There are two important lessons from the 1950 experience. First, the Chinese communists will fight and, if necessary, the leadership will accept casualties at a level we would consider horrifying (recall the Great Leap Forward in the late 1950s). Second, their potential for methodical planning and deception is great—almost beyond our imagining. We need to build into all of our analysis and planning the possibility that the Chinese Communist Party will deceive us tactically, operationally, or strategically (or in the worst case all three).

CHINESE PLANNING, PATIENCE, AND DECEPTION TODAY

You don't have to have clearance for secrets or get highly classified briefings to know that the Chinese Communist Party has been methodically preparing to dominate its immediate neighborhood—and is beginning to develop the capacity to compete with the United States in the rest of the world.

Their first efforts to close out the United States involved Taiwan. It is hard for Americans to appreciate how sensitive the Chinese Communist Party is about Taiwan. For them, Taiwan is an integral part of China and while it is outside of the Chinese government, it feels almost like an amputated limb. For the Chinese communist leadership, China will never be complete until Taiwan rejoins the country. The Communists in Beijing also have a practical, survival reason for wanting Taiwan back in the fold. As long as Taiwan is independent with nearly 24 million hardworking, free citizens (the majority of whom are Han Chinese), it is a reminder to their 1.4 billion subjects that freedom "with Chinese characteristics" exists.

For 70 years, the Chinese Communist Party has worked to delegitimize Taiwan and force it back under the control of Beijing. One part of this campaign has been to diplomatically isolate Taiwan so that it has no official existence in other capitals. Chinese communist leaders have been increasingly successful, and now, only a handful of countries recognize Taiwan as a separate country.

A second strategy has been to militarize the Taiwan Strait so that the correlation of forces will ultimately make it impossible for the United States to intervene. To this end, the areas across from Taiwan have an enormous number of both antiaircraft and surface-to-surface missiles. China has also invested in a submarine force that could make it very dangerous to sail near Taiwan.

Barring a major diplomatic mistake (e.g., Taiwan declaring itself independent) there will probably be no aggressive Chinese military action in the near future. There is no sign today that the Chinese Communist Party will use its military superiority to occupy Taiwan. However, there is every evidence that with each passing year, its ability to isolate and, if necessary, occupy, Taiwan grows. China in fact has warned that it wouldn't rule out the use of force against Taiwan.[4] Moreover, a July 2019 defense white paper criticized forces advocating for Taiwan's indepence by claiming it threatens stability and national security. Echoing previous statements from General Secretary Xi, the paper declared that China "must and will be reunited." The paper warned, "We make no promise to renounce the use of force, and reserve the option of taking all necessary measures.... The [People's Liberation Army] will resolutely defeat anyone attempting to separate Taiwan from China and safeguard national unity at all costs."[5] There is no plausible American investment that would successfully defend Taiwan short of a general war with China. At the end of that hypothetical war, Taiwan would be wrecked.

In addition, the brilliant, methodical South China Sea campaign gives China increasing control of a key region every year. It is already too late to force the Chinese Communist Party out of its island-building military campaign. Sending an American ship by a Chinese artificial island is a good example of war posturing, but it does nothing to challenge or change Chinese military domination of this vital ocean at a practical level. Beyond China's immediate oceanic neighborhood, the Chinese Communist Party has begun to develop a global power projection and war fighting capability with three major strategies: asymmetric capabilities, develop highest-end global technologies, and the military value of the Belt and Road Initiative. Let's consider each one.

ASYMMETRIC CAPABILITIES

A number of Chinese military writers have proposed that instead of trying to defeat the United States by matching our conventional forces that they instead develop a system of asymmetric capabilities, doctrines, and systems. These asymmetric measures would enable China to defeat America in a conflict despite having a conventional force disadvantage.

The American investment in traditional war fighting capability is so massive that matching it and then defeating it would be prohibitively expensive. China can build a few aircraft carriers, and this might be useful in impressing smaller countries. However, it would take several generations to build an aircraft carrier fleet capable of competing with the massive American investment in carriers (which have been dominant globally since June 1942). China might eventually build an antiaircraft system capable of defeating the B-2 stealth bomber. But as the Russians learned in the Cold War, nationwide antiaircraft systems are extraordinarily expensive and can be made obsolete with much less expensive changes in the penetrating vehicles. (The stealth bomber rendered a $250 billion Soviet investment in antiaircraft defenses useless.)

Some asymmetric responses are militarily based. For example, a hypersonic missile is much cheaper to build and maintain than an aircraft carrier. If produced in sufficient quantities, hypersonic weapons might make it too dangerous to bring a carrier in a range close enough to be effective.

Other asymmetric responses are nonmilitary. To give just one example, suppose the United States collides with China in the South China Sea or off of Taiwan. Instead of trying to sink an American warship, the Chinese Communist Party could use a cyberattack to close down all of the ATMs in America. This possible first response might be a devastating strategic weapon. It would be a nonviolent act in which no one died and that much of the American media would interpret as a moderate, even conciliatory act. How many days could an American government sustain a campaign if no American could get cash from an ATM or use a debit card? Because asymmetric systems do not fit either the culture or the organizational interests of our national system, we do not explore them deeply enough or try to develop both offensive and defensive asymmetric systems to overmatch the Chinese Communist Party in this area. Yet, it could be a war-winning domain. (To repeat an earlier example, an invasion from China did not fit General MacArthur's system, so the possibility was ignored and denied. We saw how that turned out.)

As a result, the United States must allocate much more resourcing toward assessments of asymmetric warfare approaches. Asymmetric warfare reflects much of the indirect thinking of Sun Tzu and other classic Chinese students of warfare. The United States still focuses far too much on traditional battlefields and kinetic capabilities. This zone of unknown and in some ways unknowable innovation in asymmetric warfare captures one of the great challenges that we will face in trying to cope with the communist, totalitarian Chinese system over the next half century.

DEVELOP HIGHEST-END GLOBAL TECHNOLOGIES

The Chinese communist leadership learned a lot from the military developments of the last half century. The United States made the entire Soviet investment in World War II-style military capabilities obsolete in the 1970s and 1980s. The Soviets had focused on building a bigger and better version of the World War II military. Their thinking was that sheer weight of armor and artillery would overwhelm their opponents by mass. The Soviet style of large, but traditional, forces was exported to Egypt and Syria, where they were decisively defeated in 1973 by an Israeli military—which was modeled along American lines. Israel focused on smart weapons, rapid communications, flexibility, and agility—which turned into effectiveness through intensive, realistic training.

The Soviet military experts consoled themselves by thinking Russian troops would perform better than their Arab allies. A catastrophic defeat forced them to confront how rapidly the Western systems were evolving. In 1982, after more than a month of fighting, the Israelis shot down an estimated 87 Syrian aircraft while Israel lost two jets.[6] This sort of one-sided exchange rate made winning by massed forces impossible. When carefully examined, it turned out that the Israelis were developing an American-style, theater-wide communication system that could shift information at the speed of light. They knew what the Syrians were doing as quickly as they started doing it. The result was a massacre of Syrian aircraft.

Meanwhile, the Soviet dictatorship (which considered a Xerox machine a state secret) could never share information quickly enough to keep pace with modern information age warfare. The Chinese watched the Soviet Union fall behind militarily and then collapse. They also watched the American military in Iraq and Afghanistan. It was clear that the Americans were moving beyond their earlier capabilities and were combining space-based assets, drones, and traditional weapons systems into a devastating symphony of military capability.

In response, the Chinese began revamping their large, but incapable, forces and investing in modern systems. The Chinese Communist Party knew its investments in technology could make them regionally competitive with American forces, but it would take a generation or more to be able to project conventional forces against the Americans globally. Given the realities of the time, the United States would remain a global hegemon even if it lost some ground to China regionally. China had to find new strategies if it was going to break out and become genuinely competitive.

The Chinese Communist Party began investing in space, cyber capabilities, artificial intelligence, quantum computing, and electromagnetic pulse (EMP) technologies. Combined with its interest in asymmetric warfare, China's new approach is designed to give it an advantage over the traditional American conventional investment in military technology. If the Chinese military can dominate space, it can sweep the seas of the American Navy and make American air bases untenable. If it can dominate the cyber domain, it can take control of the American economy, dominate the American command and control systems, block the effectiveness of American advanced weapons, and make it virtually impossible for Americans to oppose China. If the Chinese Communist Party can achieve breakthroughs in artificial intelligence and quantum computing, it could have unimaginable advantages—because no one has yet broken through in these fields.

Finally, an EMP attack against a still-vulnerable American

economy would lead to a catastrophic collapse of our civilization, as Bill Forstchen outlined so vividly in his amazing book, *One Second After.* We should not underestimate the intensity, seriousness, and scale of resources with which the Chinese Communist Party is trying to dominate in advanced technologies. These could give China dominance over the battlefield no matter how many traditional weapons the United States has.

THE MILITARY VALUE OF THE BELT AND ROAD INITIATIVE

Finally, the Chinese Communist Party's Belt and Road Initiative is a framework for a global effort to make American dominance unsustainable. The massive Chinese Communist Party investment worldwide is a great example of grand strategy and thinking like a go player instead of a chess player. The Belt and Road Initiative in many ways parallels the way in which Europe steadily spread across the world after 1450. There were trading posts, naval ports, small enclaves, and growing colonies. In some cases, the Europeans governed through alliances with local leaders. In other cases, the Europeans replaced the local leaders and simply ran the region directly with a colonial administrator.

In a remarkably short time, China has begun to emulate the trajectory of the European expansion. When looking at the speed and breadth of the emergence of the Belt and Road Initiative, it is an astonishing project. A mere 40 years ago, China was just emerging from the chaos of the Great Leap Forward and the Cultural Revolution. Mao had only recently died. Deng Xiaoping was just beginning to move China toward a productive, growth-oriented economy. Deng was calling on a worldwide network of successful Chinese businessmen and women to invest in China and help the country grow. Now, in one generation, China has the second largest economy in the world (which the US played a big role in building up) and has launched a breathtakingly bold idea for building an investment and trading system that could presently dwarf American activities around the world.

Consider the current developments in Africa as an example. Arthur Herman of the American Enterprise Institute wrote in the *National Review* on December 26, 2018:

> "Africa in the 21st century is going to be the next frontier of globalization. It contains more than 30 percent of world's hydrocarbon reserves and minerals, including rare earths essential for defense needs, and is experiencing the world's biggest population explosion."[7]

Herman also noted that sub-Saharan Africa is the second fastest-growing area economically in the world. Africa also possesses huge amounts of oil and natural gas and an amazing number of minerals—including some of the rarest needed for advanced technologies. Herman wrote that in 2015, China had close to $300 billion a year in trade with Africa. Now it is more than $500 billion a year. By contrast, the United States does about $5 billion a year in trade with Africa—and this has been declining. The Chinese have extended more than $60 billion in commercial loans and as of December 2018, have more than 3,000 infrastructure projects underway across the continent.[8] According to the John Hopkins School of Advanced International Studies, in 2017, there were approximately 200,000 Chinese working in Africa.[9]

In the sixteenth to nineteenth centuries, this kind of activity by a European power would have been seen as a clear sign of imperial growth. American leaders are only now waking up to the gap between American and Chinese activities on the continent. The boldness and scale of the Belt and Road Initiative remarkable. However, in the context of this chapter, this must be seen as a powerful effort to shape the future contest with America. There will be millions of experienced Chinese nationals pre-positioned in every part of the world. Almost all of this work for the initiative will be done in the commercial world without showing up as part of the military budget.

SHIFTING AMERICAN NATIONAL SECURITY PLANNING FOR CHINA

With all of these activities by communist-ruled China there has been a significant shift in how our military and national security systems have thought about the world. China has been, by far, the largest reason for that shift. China is rapidly becoming a peer competitor in Asia and is beginning to develop worldwide capabilities much faster than we expected. At the same time, there has been a healthy realization that we have spent the last 18 years overly focused on the global war on terror and on specialized tactical operations in Iraq, Afghanistan, and a number of third-world countries. As a result, our ability to think strategically and to develop forces that can operate at the strategic and operational level has atrophied.

The United States, under the Trump administration, is beginning to take the challenge of communist totalitarian China seriously. We are starting to develop professional efforts to analyze China's strategies, find ways to counter them, and, if necessary, defeat them. Despite the seriousness and good intentions, it is not clear that the American effort to shift focus and strategy is proceeding rapidly enough.

A LACK OF IN-DEPTH STUDY

When it became clear the United States and its allies were threatened by the Soviet Union, the United States launched a substantial intellectual effort to study and understand the nature of the Soviet regime and its military, diplomatic, economic, and political doctrines. Scholars were organized. Student fellowships for military and diplomatic personnel became commonplace. Internally, professional military and diplomatic training became much more focused on the Soviet threat. Institutions like the RAND Corporation were established to study both the Soviet threat and the nature of the emerging field of nuclear war. Some scholars, such as Henry Kissinger and Herman Kahn, became famous as provocative and insightful thinkers about survival in the nuclear age. Entire careers were spent studying the Soviet Union and trying to understand how to influence it and ultimately how to defeat it.

Seeking more accurate knowledge about the Soviet system led to the development of the U-2 spy plane (and later, the SR-71) and rapidly evolving capabilities in spy satellites flying over Russia. The scale of investment in new espionage technology would have been unthinkable before World War II. Military doctrine development focused on stopping the Soviets in Western Europe. The United States committed itself to building a vast peacetime military-industrial complex to contain and, if necessary, defeat the Soviet Union.

The Marshall Plan of economic aid for Western Europe (about $100 billion in 2018 dollars) was designed to stop communism.[10] The United States spent heavily through covert operations to stop communists in France and Italy. Intellectual left-wing alternatives to communism were subsidized secretly. American radio activities that beamed actively into the Soviet Empire grew dramatically. The list goes on and on. Nothing like this scale of intellectual and bureaucratic effort exists with regard to communist-ruled China.

Another key difference was that the public debate about the Soviet threat and the news coverage of Soviet behavior led the vast majority of Americans to conclude that there was no alternative but to contain the Soviet Union. The Soviets took over countries in Eastern Europe (often with selective violence and police state methods of dictatorships reporting to Moscow). There were specific aggressive Soviet actions, such as the Berlin Blockade, which were met by a British-American airlift of heroic proportions. The American people by a wide majority in both political parties concluded that communism was a worldwide threat and the United States had to do whatever was necessary to protect its allies and defend freedom. This bipartisan consensus survived the traumas of the Korean and Vietnam wars. Even the least anti-Soviet president (Jimmy Carter) maintained and indeed increased American military strength to contain the Soviet Union.

This national debate about whether communism was a threat—and whether in its specific Soviet form it had to be contained and ultimately defeated—was initially launched by George Kennan. While stationed at the US Embassy in Moscow in 1946, he was asked to summarize the nature of the Soviet system. He answered with what became known as the "Long Telegram" because it was 8,000 words long. That telegram was the basis for a July 1947 article in *Foreign Affairs* magazine titled "The Sources of Soviet Conduct."[11] Kennan had created the intellectual framework for most Americans—who had little firsthand experience with communism at that time—to agree that the Soviet Union was a relentless opponent seeking global domination for deeply ideological reasons and would have to be contained until it gave up its ambitions.

The national security establishment is increasingly worried about the Chinese Communist Party's actions. The news media is beginning to recognize the wide variety of China's activities. The American people are instinctively moving toward a greater fear of the Chinese communist dictatorship. However, we do not yet have the clarity Kennan provided. We have not had the national debate we need to build a sustainable, long-term, military-diplomatic-economic-political strategy. Matching China's military developments will require a sense of urgency and a commitment of willpower and resources that cannot occur until the American people, the news media, and our representatives in the Congress have had a thorough national debate about the nature, scale, and frightening implications of China's buildup.

THE LACK OF RIGOR

The American military system has been dominant for three quarters of a century. For the last quarter century, it has been unchallengeable except for guerrilla tactics, terrorism, and small skirmishes. Within the largest and most expensive military in the world, there is an enormous inertia in favor of continuing to implement what has worked in the past. Chinese communist leaders have methodically studied American military and diplomatic capabilities. They analyzed the first and second Iraqi campaigns. They study our military's testimonies to Congress, budgets, professional publications, and so on. They read the advertisements and statements of all of our military contractors; it is amazing how much you can learn in a free society from open-source material.

As a result, the Chinese Communist Party is building a strategic, operational, and tactical system designed to overmatch the United States in ways that we are very uncomfortable analyzing and competing against. Taking the Chinese communist system seriously would require deep and profound changes in both our general national security system (which extends across defense, intelligence, state, commerce, treasury, and includes all of the major White House operations) and our military systems. The challenge is so big that intelligent, serious people simply flinch from the effort.

There was once a *New Yorker* magazine cartoon that showed a desk with three trays—marked: in, out, and too hard. So far, taking China seriously and thinking through a response that would overmatch the Chinese Communist Party's efforts has been put in the "too hard" tray. We don't play society-on-society competition war games. If we had, we would have seen the competition with Huawei coming in 2010 and been forced to build a society-on-society response. We don't play global diplomatic-economic competition war games, or we would have a vastly bolder program underway in Africa. We don't take seriously the rapid evolution of new technological programs, or we would have a crash program hardening our systems against an EMP attack.

Vice President Pence's comments about competing against complacency were about NASA and President Trump's goal of putting Americans back on the Moon (to stay). However, those very words could be used to describe the challenge to us in war gaming and thinking through the communist totalitarian China challenge. When we lose a war game, we must rethink the institutions and systems that failed. We must not replace the war game with a more forgiving and less stressful model.

EXTRAORDINARY INERTIA AND RESISTANCE OF THE BUREAUCRACIES

No one should be surprised at how hard it is going to be to recognize the scale and sophistication of the Chinese communist totalitarian threat and develop responses on the level of scale and sophistication needed. There will be a lot of rhetorical acknowledgments of the emerging China challenge. But converting words into real strategic, institutional, and cultural changes will be immensely hard.

Thinking through and responding to the threat of the Chinese Communist Party will prove more difficult than dealing with the Cold War—and even the developing that took place from 1945 to 1950. There are several reasons this will be much more challenging.

First, there are many more American billionaires and businesses who have made, are making, or expecting to make money in China than ever invested in the Soviet Union. Second, the news media is much more intimidated by pressure from the Chinese Communist Party than they are by public pressure. Moreover, there is a larger group of academics misexplaining China than there were ever apologists for the Soviet Union. (Compare the avoidance of condemning concentration camps for Uyghurs with the positive response to Solzhenitsyn's *One Day in the Life of Ivan Denisovich*.)

Further, the national security bureaucracies in the mid-1940s were much smaller and more adaptable than they are today. The Congress after serving in World War I, watching aggressive dictators emerge in the 1930s, and fighting in World War II also took national security much more seriously than the current Congress. The key leaders had served in World War I, had led in World War II, and were used to making big decisions and enforcing big changes. There were dramatically fewer lawyers and regulations, so the system could evolve and adapt at a fast pace compared to the current political-bureaucratic-legal mess. The news media had covered two wars and dealt with foreign and national security with a seriousness and sophistication impossible to achieve in the current shallow, overly partisan, inflammatory, gossip, and rumor-ridden system.

For all of these reasons, developing an effective response to communist-ruled China will be much harder than the 1945–1955 effort to develop a specific strategy for the Soviet Union.

Nevertheless, it must be done.

As a basic step, we must develop a modern, society-level war gaming center focused on understanding and anticipating China's strategies and developing our own countervailing strategies. This might be located at the National Defense University and must be well resourced. There must be satellite centers around the country where the best minds on a variety of topics could work and focus on their specialties. As a totalitarian dictatorship, the Chinese Communist Party can use a range of tools totally beyond the responsibilities of national security systems as we have historically known them.

Furthermore, given the Chinese tradition of indirect and psychological warfare, many of China's strategies simply don't register in our kinetically focused model of war and our narrow definition of national security. Sun Tzu expressed this point in *The Art of War* when he wrote, "Hence to fight and conquer in all your battles is not supreme excellence; supreme excellence consists in breaking the enemy's resistance without fighting."

Finally, our complex system of federal, state, and local government, and our division of authority and power in the federal government between the executive, legislative, and judicial branches present major hurdles for addressing the challenge.

Though the separation of powers is a fundamental cornerstone of our national system, the bottom line is it makes it extraordinarily difficult for America to develop a consistent, coherent strategy for dealing with a centralized totalitarian adversary prepared to use every aspect of its society. The war gaming center must have responsibilities for studying China's systems and identifying the Chinese Communist Party's strategies—at every level, from all-of-society projects to tactics—and developing American responses.

Then, that center needs to coordinate with many different war gaming systems in the military, intelligence, diplomatic, and economic spheres, in both government and the private sector. This is the scale of change we need if we are really going to compete successfully with China.

Our responses must include the necessary reforms to enable us to match (or exceed) the speed and intensity of the Chinese communist system. Because of the central role of Congress in funding and in reforming the executive branch, the war gaming center should have a congressional advisory board and a substantial capacity for educating both members and staffs. The goal of this center is to develop a proactive American-centered strategy that emphasizes our strengths and draws on the best of our innovative, entrepreneurial, and productive traditions. This must be a strategy center focused on constructing the whole-of-society strategy needed to overmatch the communist totalitarian dictatorship. It cannot be allowed to degenerate into either a tactical center focused on small things, or a reactive center trying to play whack-a-mole with China's initiatives. We must define the world we want to achieve, and build the systems, structures, cultures, and projects to achieve them.

CHAPTER SIXTEEN

NOT CHINA'S FAULT

> I don't blame China for taking advantage of us—I blame our leaders and representatives for allowing this travesty to happen.
>
> —President Donald Trump, February 2019[1]

It is clear that the communist totalitarian system of China and the free society system of America are engaged in a long competition. China's communist totalitarian system is based on thousands of years of authoritarianism and is combined with the Leninist principles of centralized control. The free, American model is based on the rule of law and inalienable rights endowed by God.

The Chinese communist dictatorship has a rational, long-term strategy to establish itself as the world's dominant power. The Chinese Communist Party aims to establish its superiority economically, politically, and militarily. As a result, it hopes to supplant the position of global leadership that the United States has long held. China has a coherent, integrated grand strategy for achieving this goal (though it is not immune to internal party power disputes nor the evolving external environment). The strategy is rooted in global outreach—combining dominance in new technologies such as 5G, so-called aid packages that create debt traps for nations receiving such aid, and a sophisticated concept known as the "Three Warfares" that combines media, psychological, and legal system operations. For too long, the United States has ignored the strategic implications of what success under a Chinese Communist Party–controlled China means for our own stability, security, and prosperity.

It is possible that at some point in the distant future, China will repudiate its dictatorship and establish a freer system compatible with the values of Western civilization. But there is a grave danger that the United States and Western civilization will simply be overwhelmed and dominated by China's communist totalitarian system long before that country ceases to be a dictatorship. There is no reason to believe that China will evolve away from authoritarianism in the near future. Surrounding Deng Xiaoping's economic reforms beginning in the late 1970s—and especially after his Southern Tour in 1992—there was substantial American optimism that this evolution would take place. The reality is that Deng was ultimately seeking economic growth to strengthen the Chinese Communist Party's dictatorship and make it acceptable to the Chinese people.

China will most likely maintain the authoritarian nature of its state in the future. Americans respect the notion of individuality. China's Communist Party media and propaganda support the state's aim to maintain centralized rule through collective identity and strong nationalism. These concepts undergird China's guiding aim to achieve the party's most important and urgent goal: self-preservation. For those who would change things, there is a 90-million-member Chinese Communist Party with ties into every part of the country. Beyond the Communist Party, there is a massive security apparatus that suppresses dissent and protects the current dictatorial system. Thus, there is a great contest that is currently transpiring between the Western tradition of freedom under the law (dating back at least 3,000 years with roots in Athens, Rome, and Jerusalem) and the Chinese tradition of order imposed by a centralized system (a pattern that goes back at least approximately 3,500 years). It is not clear today which system—freedom or dictatorship—will win.

The contest could go on for centuries until the Chinese communist leadership gradually (or with cataclysmic speed if the system collapsed) moves toward freedom. Alternatively, the contest could end in the next generation if the West remains confused, divided, and incapable of coherent modernization. In this case the world will be defined as a "civilization with Chinese communist characteristics."

There are a number of things that the United States and its allies can do to contain and ultimately help transition China from dictatorship to freedom. However, there are a lot of steps America must take that are a reflection of American failures. Some of the greatest failures and weaknesses in America can't be blamed on China. Rather, we have to look at ourselves and our own mistakes and failures. The burden on us to modernize and reform our own system is enormous.

Consider this list as a starting point for American renewal:

- *It is not China's fault* that in 2017, 89 percent of Baltimore eighth graders couldn't pass their math exam and the decay of American primary and secondary education threatens the economic and citizenship capabilities of America.[2]
- *It is not China's fault* that too few Americans in K–12 and in college study math and science to fill the graduate schools with future American scientists.
- *It is not China's fault* that, faced with a dramatic increase in Chinese graduate students in science, the American government has not been able to revive programs like the 1958 National Defense Education Act, which responded to the challenge of Sputnik by educating a generation of American postsecondary students. Let us be objective in assessing fault for this failure: It falls upon both political parties and the leadership of both political parties.

- *It is not China's fault* that in many states, funding actually favors recruiting foreign students over in-state students, because the foreign students pay more in tuition and are therefore more desirable to the college or university administration.
- *It is not China's fault* that the Department of Defense bureaucracy is cumbersome and convoluted. The slow pace blocks small entrepreneurs from competing. It guarantees that most major procurement will take so long that it will be a decade or more behind the available technology by the time it is adopted. (This also raises the cost of new equipment unnecessarily.) Our current system favors old systems and old habits over the needed breakthroughs to new technologies and new strategies.
- *It is not China's fault* that the way our defense bureaucracy functions serves to create exactly the "military-industrial" complex that President Dwight Eisenhower warned against. It is worse than bad bureaucracy. It is a federal Frankenstein that chokes off innovation and fosters a corporate welfare state that benefits large defense contractors. It keeps those charged with ensuring our national security from tapping into the expertise and experience of some of our best and most talented individuals. The system rewards bloated funding for obsolete but familiar systems favored by military brass over funding that would develop the weapons and systems needed to dominate the battlefield of the future. It curbs our military preparedness—and the weapons, training, and resources required to meet the new threat environment that has emerged, and will evolve, over the next two decades.
- *It is not China's fault* that NASA has been so bureaucratic, and its funding so erratic, that despite the US vastly outspending China in space, there is every reason to believe that China is catching up rapidly and may outpace us. This is because of *us* not because of *them*.

- *It is not China's fault* that the US Air Force has clung to an obsolete model of space. It is focused on supporting Earth-bound operations while China is preparing for warfare in space that could give it decisive dominance.
- *It is not China's fault* that the American military continues to be organized around theater-level combatant commands, when the real threat is a global campaign moving at the speed of cyber and space.
- *It is not China's fault* that the United States produces too many lawyers and not enough scientists and engineers.
- *It is not China's fault* that the cost of our litigation system is a major hindrance to our ability to compete in the world.
- *It is not China's fault* that we have tolerated an opioid-fentanyl crisis that has contributed to killing more Americans each year than died in action in the entire Vietnam War.[3,4]
- *It is not China's fault* that the old, bureaucratic entrenched American telecommunications companies failed to develop a global strategy for 5G over the 11 years that the Chinese company Huawei has been working to become the world leader. This is an American failure that was doubly tragic, because America dominated 4G and, with leadership, could have moved faster than the Chinese company.
- *It is not China's fault* that the American news media is so infantile and childish that gossip, trivia, leaks, and political infighting dominate coverage while great changes in the world are mostly ignored or only poorly covered.
- *It is not China's fault* that because of overregulation and hostile bureaucracy America is 100 percent dependent on imports for 18 minerals—14 of which are considered critical by departments of interior or defense.[5]
- *It is not China's fault* that the combination of absurdly inefficient regulations and equally absurd union work

rules makes rebuilding American infrastructure far more expensive and time-consuming than in other countries.

- *It is not China's fault* that the union work rules and the red tape have made it impossible to build high-speed trains—even on the Boston-Washington corridor where it would make economic sense. At the end of 2018 China had more than 18,000 miles of high-speed rail and it is adding to that total every year.[6]
- *It is not China's fault* that a number of states have pension programs that are almost guaranteed to go broke.
- *It is not China's fault* that the politicians in both parties can't find some solution to trillion-dollar deficits and runaway entitlement costs.
- *It is not China's fault* that the United States has the most expensive health care system in the world by an enormous margin.[7]
- *It is not China's fault* that political partisanship is now so deep and bitter that people react to new ideas based upon *who* raises them, rather than their content. The American discourse has put identity politics that fosters divisive tribalism ahead of national unity. It personalizes and demonizes individuals who have different viewpoints. In the name of equality and redress of some grievance, we actively punish and choke off debate on college and university campuses. We treat political opponents as enemies, rather than decent Americans espousing divergent viewpoints. America has a serious problem with the integrity of intellectual discussion and debate.
- *It is not China's fault* that the United States has tolerated China's massive intellectual property theft and hacking—or that the United States accepts lies from the Chinese communist government—while the People's Liberation Army runs entire units, which the FBI estimated in 2016, are filled with more than 30,000 military cyberspies, and 150,000 private-sector computer experts dedicated

to hacking into and stealing American military and technological secrets.[8]

- *It is not China's fault* that in trying to stop intellectual property theft, the United States has failed to avail itself of proper remedies by taking China to the World Trade Organization (WTO) under the TRIPS (Trade Related Aspects of Intellectual Property Rights) Agreement. We have failed to expose China's communist government as a pirate state and eviscerate its efforts to seize and maintain the moral high ground on this issue. We have failed to obtain a legal ruling under the rules of the WTO that would empower our nation to impose significant compensatory sanctions against China to help deter theft. This strategy needs to be implemented in tandem with other victim states, whose intellectual property China has also pilfered.
- *It is not China's fault* that too many large, transnational global corporations—including American companies—have put short-term profits ahead of long-term shareholder value by capitulating to the Chinese Communist Party's demands that they turn over their companies' confidential and proprietary information. Putting it another way, too many American companies are putting short-term financial greed ahead of the security interests of the United States and its working families.
- *It is not China's fault* that in meeting all of the challenges described, both political parties and the White House have devoted their time and energy to political partisanship and finger-pointing. We instead should be working cooperatively to forge a coherent, effective grand strategy, as well as doctrines, topical strategies, operations, and tactics to counter communist-ruled China. We must ensure that the United States retains its position as the planet's champion of freedom, dignity, the rule of law, religious tolerance, democratic pluralism, good health, clean air and water, and innovation in science and manufacturing.

CONCLUSION

WHERE WE ARE AND WHAT WE MUST DO

I wrote this book in part because I believe that a communist totalitarian Chinese system is a global threat capable of submerging the United States over the next generation. As I said earlier in this book, this represents the fifth great challenge to America's survival. We must recognize this challenge and develop a response powerful enough and comprehensive enough to protect freedom and the rule of law until the totalitarian system collapses or is transformed. Steady persistence and consistent progress are critical, as success will be realized as a result of a long-term effort and could be a matter of centuries, not decades.

Today, most Americans, and indeed most government officials, do not realize how devastating failure could be to the values and way of life that we hold dear and have fought to protect. The scale of the challenge the United States faces with China is so great that we have to focus on a large, system-wide response. There are many small steps that need to be taken, but without planning and coordination, all of our energy and time could be absorbed into a mound of activities that yield no strategic impact.

Let's start by outlining three requirements that must be included in an American strategy.

1. We must educate the public and have a national dialogue about the challenges we face with China. It should involve every American citizen. This must continue until at least 70 percent of the country agrees that success in meeting the challenge of the Communist Chinese dictatorship is the key to our national survival.
2. We must develop an American-based national strategy for this era of society-on-society competition that capitalizes on our strengths as a country. This strategy must include a framework for implementation fully as large as the challenge that we are trying to meet. We must ensure that every action needed for success is being done effectively, diligently, and efficiently. As an overwhelmingly nongovernmental country, the vast majority of the response must be done outside of the government and implemented by private enterprises and nonprofit institutions.
3. We must define metrics for success in order to keep our rhetoric and planning in touch with reality. Words without action are a fantasy. For example, the growth in understanding of the threat of the Soviet Union in 1945–1950 led to the United States:
   - Establishing the Point Four Program to help developing countries;
   - Implementing the Marshall Plan to help rebuild Europe;
   - Reorganizing our national defense systems into a unified Department of Defense;
   - Providing covert aid to anti-communist forces in France, Italy, Greece, and elsewhere;
   - Developing the Voice of America, Radio Free Europe, academic exchanges, and so on;
   - Using an aggressive effort by the FBI to track down Communist agents in the United States;

- Executing the Berlin Airlift to overcome Stalin's Berlin Blockade without war;
- Deciding to build the hydrogen bomb;
- Deciding to build intercontinental bombers to deliver nuclear and hydrogen weapons;
- Creating the Strategic Air Command to wage global war;
- Developing the RAND Corporation as a think tank by the Air Force;
- Instituting the North Atlantic Treaty Organization to defend Western Europe;
- Defining the containment strategy in National Security Council (NSC) 68;
- Establishing the Central Intelligence Agency; and
- Deciding to defend South Korea when the North attacked.

In each of these examples, the US used the ingenuity, intelligence, and skill of our officials, military, and citizens to act strategically against the Soviet threat. We now must decide what a comparable scale of invention and innovation for our generation will be and how we can put it into action.

Now, we face the fifth great challenge to our survival as a free country (following the American Revolution, the Civil War, World War II, and the rise of the Soviet Union). To paraphrase William Faulkner's 1950 Nobel Prize speech, can we, the American people, think through the totalitarian, communist Chinese threat and understand its many patterns and strategies? Can we effectively design, implement, and sustain the strategies needed for freedom to survive and then prevail?

We must start thinking and planning with the understanding of the same potential for failure and defeat that existed in the previous four challenges to America's survival. A totalitarian, communist Chinese system could dominate a generation from now. This is not an exaggeration. It is a practical reality based on the patterns that exist today. What we do, how we respond, the level of our commitment to preserving American values and freedom will decide the outcome of this new challenge.

What is fascinating about these critical moments of decision making and active implementation is that they all follow the same pattern:

1. **Recognition:** There is a recognition that there is a problem threatening the survival of our nation.
2. **Debate:** Public debate follows about how big and how real the danger is, which is paralleled by some bureaucratic moves toward containing the problem.
3. **Consensus:** A general consensus is formed (that is almost never unanimous) that the problem is real and must be solved.
4. **Mobilization:** Mobilization toward a solution begins that includes new strategies, new structures, and new systems that incorporate new language and intellectual formulas.
5. **Implementation:** There is persistent implementation of the strategies, structures, and systems that include learning from failures and constantly modifying activities and ideas until they work. This process occurs with a remarkable focus on the main effort despite the ebb and flow of politics, events, and attitudes.
6. **Success:** Success is won, leading to new challenges.

Let's apply these six stages to the five challenges to the survival of the United States.

RECOGNITION

First, it took almost a decade for the militant minority of American colonists to conclude that they had no choice but to seek independence from Britain. Beginning in 1765 with the Stamp Act Congress, there was continuous tension and irritation until the Declaration of Independence was signed in 1776. This was an intense period of internal dialogue and political propagandizing influenced by Thomas Paine's *Common Sense* as the bestselling and most powerful argument for freedom.

In the case of the Civil War, the tensions between slave-owning states and free states began to grow around 1820. As the North's population and wealth grew faster, the slave owners felt more and more threatened in their way of life. The publication of Harriet Beecher Stowe's *Uncle Tom's Cabin* in 1852 popularized antislavery sentiment in the North but increased slave-owner paranoia in the South. The book sold 300,000 copies within three months.[1] Additionally, the Whig Party collapsed because it could not find a formula to bring together pro- and antislavery forces. It was replaced by a Republican Party that was much more committed to freedom and to stopping the expansion of slavery.

Before the United States entered World War II, there was a deep fight in the 1930s about whether or not we should get involved in overseas wars. The frustration from the failure of the first World War to "end wars" and the failure to create a truly democratic peace—as President Wilson had advocated—led to the passage of the Neutrality Acts. These laws were designed to limit the involvement of the United States in foreign wars. The Irish, German, and Italian populations in America opposed our getting into another war. There was a powerful and popular America First group that was championed by the heroic aviator Charles Lindbergh and created real counterpressure against helping Great Britain or France. (See Lynne Olson's *Those Angry Days: Roosevelt, Lindbergh and America's Fight over World War II, 1939–1941.*) There was vastly greater opposition to getting involved against Germany, Japan, and Italy than many people are aware of today.

As a result of World War II, Americans had a positive view of the Russians and often thought of the "good" Russians helping us beat the "bad" Germans and the "bad" Japanese. Stalin was portrayed fondly as "Uncle Joe," and as late as 1944, movies (about 20 films in all) were made that were clearly pro-Soviet. Furthermore, there were a substantial number of Soviet agents in the American government, including Alger Hiss (the number three person in the State Department). Some estimates suggest that there were 500 Soviet agents of influence in the US government. It took a series of aggressive Soviet actions in Eastern Europe and Iran to convince President Truman that we had to undertake a major effort in response. In February 1946, George Kennan sent the "Long Telegram" from the American embassy in Moscow. As I previously mentioned, this document captured the essence of the Soviet threat and began to focus American elites on the danger that the Soviet system had a goal of worldwide domination.

Today, Americans are just now beginning to recognize that our view of China was romantic and inaccurate. Americans who have accepted this realization are beginning to reach three big conclusions as a result:

1. China is a communist totalitarian state—and neither Tiananmen Square in 1989 nor the persecution of the Uyghurs, Tibetans, and other ethnic and religious groups is abnormal. In fact, repression is the norm for everyone in the totalitarian state.
2. China is following an expansionist policy in the South China Sea and in the Belt and Road Initiative. China is modernizing its military to project power worldwide that includes building up space, cyber, artificial intelligence, and other advanced technologies.
3. Cheating on trade and innovation efforts is at the very heart of the Chinese Communist Party's operating system. The Communist Party implements a wide range of aggressive strategies including stealing intellectual property, cheating on agreements, rigging the rules in China on ownership of companies, forcing technology transfer, and using predatory financing and pricing to destroy foreign competitors and drive them out of the market.

These conclusions are not universally held and there is no systematic strategy or change in policy and structures that would logically result from such conclusions. The news media continues to cover the trade negotiations as if they are the sole focus of the challenge the United States is facing with China's communist leadership, when in reality they are a symptom of a much larger threat. Many China "scholars" may say these conclusions are too strong and unsophisticated. The American military and defense system is split between those who see China as a threat to our survival as a free country that will require real change and those who believe that with a little more equipment and training, the United States will be able to contain China for another generation.

While the rhetoric about China is growing harsher, there is still an underlying assumption that a "reasonable" deal can be made and China will alter its behavior and abide by the terms. There are isolated efforts to address specific problems, including targeted legislation, but as of yet, there is no coherent American vision of success or strategy for decisively competing with China or its communist system.

We are clearly still in this initial recognition phase.

DEBATE

In each of the four earlier challenges, there was a period where events began to force a public debate. The US government began to take steps during this time to meet the present challenges—even before a coherent strategy was formed.

In the 1770s, a government had to be organized, an army had to be raised and organized, and money had to be found to pay for the war. Diplomats also had to be sent out to key countries, and allies had to be sought. All of these efforts needed to continue while convincing the American people that, despite a series of military defeats, freedom was worth the high cost. Thomas Paine's second great pamphlet, *The Crisis*, probably did as much as any single effort to convince the patriots to persevere and hang on to hope despite "the times that try men's souls."

In the period from 1860–1862, both the Union and the Confederacy were in a race to attract adherents; to raise, organize, equip, and train armies and navies; to convince other countries to side with them; and to invent methods of financing a huge war. People had to be convinced over and over to stay committed despite numerous defeats and frustrations.

From 1937–1941, as the world increasingly found itself at war, there was an enormous faction of Americans opposed to the United States getting into a war again. As late as the weekend before the 1940 election, President Franklin Roosevelt felt that reelection required him to pledge that no Americans would fight in a European war. While the government kept moving incrementally to rearm and to provide limited aid to Great Britain, the debate was only ended by the Japanese surprise attack at Pearl Harbor.

In the Cold War period, Stalin's aggressive actions convinced a majority of Americans to support strong government actions. However, throughout the entire 46-year period of the Cold War, there was always a significant minority opposed to American military and intelligence activities that were undertaken during this time.

Today, we have only barely begun to enter this period of public debate. Americans are becoming increasingly aware of the rise of the Chinese communist totalitarian system. More conversations are beginning to take place, but we have not achieved broad national awareness, and we are a long way from forming a consensus about what to do.

CONSENSUS

By the summer of 1775, the Continental Congress realized the New England rebellion against British tyranny had to become a national cause. It sent a Virginian, George Washington, to command at Boston to communicate the national nature of the struggle. One year later it adopted the Declaration of Independence and protest had turned into revolution. Still, many of the colonists probably remained loyal to the British Crown throughout the eight years of war.

In 1860, Americans were deeply divided and they remained deeply divided. Southerners were largely convinced they had been forced into a war of survival for slavery but even in the South many mountain counties opposed secession. In the North there was probably never more than 65 percent willing to wage war to keep the Union alive. President Lincoln's astonishing management of public opinion to keep his faction in charge despite a series of defeats is one of the greatest examples of leadership in American history.

In 1941, the Japanese surprise attack at Pearl Harbor on a Sunday morning made American determination to win World War II as close to unanimous as we have ever been. The result was an amazing four years of mobilization and victory.

The impressive thing about the Cold War consensus was how long it held together. With the exception of deep opposition to the Vietnam War there was never a serious challenge to the consensus that we had to be militarily, technologically, economically, and diplomatically strong to contain the Soviet Empire. Every time there was a weakening in the consensus, the Soviets would do something (the bloody repression of the Hungarian freedom fighters in 1956 was an example) that would rebuild the consensus.

Today, we are years away from the kind of decisive consensus that would sustain a bold program to overmatch the Chinese Chinese communist totalitarian system. It will take a lot of articles, books, speeches, and continued aggressiveness by the Chinese dictatorship to convince Americans we face a genuine threat that requires response.

MOBILIZATION

Overall, America's mobilization skills have been pretty good—with the exception of the Revolutionary War where the structure of the Continental Congress and the weakness of the Articles of Confederation made it almost impossible to do anything quickly or effectively. Despite those weaknesses, George Washington held the American Revolution together by force of personality for eight years in an heroic effort that truly made him the father of the country.

The other three mobilization efforts were much more powerful and effective. As weak as the federal government was in 1861, the Constitution—which had been written by Washington and his allies precisely to strengthen the government's effectiveness—gave President Lincoln the authority he needed to mobilize the Union effort with remarkable speed both militarily and financially.

The generation in charge in 1941 had fought in World War I and spent 20 years thinking about the lessons of that war. They brought enormous professional competence and decisiveness to establishing and implementing strategies.

Shortly after, the same generation that had fought in World War I and led the effort in World War II proved to be more than prepared to design and implement the containment policy at the heart of the American approach to the Cold War. They thought and acted on a global scale based on more than 30 years of experience. No generation has been better prepared to develop a global campaign.

Now, if we can build a consensus about dealing with the Chinese communist totalitarian dictatorship, we will discover that we have more internal challenges than any mobilization effort since the Revolutionary War.

Our current problem is the exact opposite of the Founding Fathers' mobilization problem. We have the largest entrenched bureaucratic structure in American history. The massiveness of our rules and regulations, the growth of lawyers as the dominant definer of acceptable government behavior, and the defense of entrenched public and private interests, all will be vastly more difficult to navigate and coordinate with than in 1860, 1939, or 1946. Our own systems, habits, interest groups, and bureaucracies may be a bigger problem than the threat from China's communist system.

IMPLEMENTATION

One of the key lessons from American history is the necessity of constant focus on implementation. As Senator Connie Mack once taught me: "You get what you inspect not what you expect." We developed the concept of "cheerful persistence" for precisely this reality. Anyone who is serious about surviving the Chinese communist totalitarian challenge must confront the reality that each decision will have to be followed by constant pragmatic leadership and implementation. Nothing will happen automatically or easily.

SUCCESS

It is important to remember that even if America succeeds in developing and implementing a strategy to deal with the Chinese communist totalitarian threat, it will not be the end of the game.

There was a brief period following the collapse of the Soviet Union in 1991 when hubris affected a number of Western leaders and thinkers. People spoke of a new world order and an end of history.

History came off of vacation with a vengeance by September 11, 2001. The new world order collapsed under the combination of Islamic extremism, the revival of Russia under Putin, and the steady growth in power and capability of communist-ruled China. Coping with the reality of the world—rather than the fantasized ideal—is a permanent condition of safety and security in a dangerous world. That should remind us that what we are doing in this immediate challenge is necessary and unavoidable. There will be no holiday from responsibility even if everything goes well with China.

WHAT TO TAKE AWAY FROM THIS BOOK

This book covers a lot of ground and has a lot of specifics. But the key lessons can be summarized as five big principles:

1. The Chinese Communist Party's totalitarian system is big, getting bigger, getting richer, and becoming

more sophisticated. It is the greatest competitor that America has faced in our history.
2. General Secretary Xi Jinping and the 90 million members of the Chinese Communist Party are dedicated to the maintenance of their Leninist system of control. The party measures policy options with that goal in mind as the top value.
3. The Chinese system is investing in dramatic technological advances and in buying markets and partners. Its influence and its capabilities are expanding much faster than Americans realize.
4. Any gradual, incremental American response will simply fail. The Chinese Communist Party's system is so big and has so much momentum that only a dramatic, deep resetting of American policy and the development of new American institutions will enable us to turn back the totalitarian challenge. America needs new energy, resources, rules, and decisiveness to make technological investments and achievements, acquire new markets, and build new broader alliances.
5. *You* are the key to American survival. Change on this scale must be citizen-based and must have a broad range of grassroots support. *Your* voice with family, friends, neighbors, and coworkers can make a difference. *Your* voice on social media, on talk radio, on blogs, at town hall meetings, and at presidential campaign rallies can make a difference.

Together, *we* must once again help our country survive a great challenge to American survival.

Acknowledgments

Trump vs. China is the most important and one of the most challenging books that I have written. It would not have been possible without the generous advice and counsel of the people who contributed their expertise and knowledge to this project.

Thank you to the experts and team at the Air University who organized and provided exceptional briefings. I am grateful for their efforts toward this project and their selfless dedication to our country. In particular I want to thank Lieutenant General Steve Kwast, who has shown remarkable courage in fighting for an effective American response to China in space.

I would like to thank the numerous scholars at the Heritage Foundation, the Hudson Institute, the Wilson Center, and the American Enterprise Institute for providing such helpful analyses.

Thank you to the US-China Economic and Security Review Commission for publishing some of the best open-source reports and hosting such informative hearings on China. You will find their reports and hearings often cited throughout this book. Leslie Reagan was very helpful in providing helpful resources to further my research efforts.

As I mentioned earlier in this book, expert Go players and teachers from the National Go Center came to teach our Gingrich 360 Team how to play one of the most difficult games in existence. Thank you to their team for sharing their talents, for a fun evening spent with our two teams, and for their patient teaching.

Herman Pirchner and his team at the American Foreign Policy Council (AFPC) have been invaluable in this effort. I am grateful for all of the work that the AFPC has done to contribute to this project and for creating opportunities for dialogues between leaders in the United States and across the world. The work that Herman and the AFPC do is essential for facilitating understanding and cooperation between countries and their leaders across the globe.

The team at the National TRUST Center has been helpful in providing insight into the cyber and espionage challenges that the United States and American people face with the Chinese Communist Party. Their continued efforts to educate the public on the totality of this threat is important for the future protection of private citizens, institutions, and businesses alike.

There are many experts who provided helpful information for this project. Thank you to Diana Liu and the Gallup team, who shared useful data and analyses. Also, I would like to thank Karl Rove, who was an essential partner in developing the 5G strategy. Thank you also to Declan Ganley and Steve Conlon for offering their expertise in the 5G and telecommunications industry. Finally, Brett Haan lent his remarkable expertise on telecommunications. I am grateful for their contributions.

Dimon Liu and Bob Suettinger have been invaluable resources and advisers. Their wealth of knowledge is remarkably vast. I am thankful for their counsel. Thank you to Michael Sobolick, who has also been a remarkable contributor to this project. He has done great work to shed light on the challenge from communist-ruled China and how to protect the United States against further aggression.

Dr. Henry Kissinger has been a remarkable friend and mentor for over 30 years. His book *On China*, which you will find often referenced throughout this book, provided invaluable insight to the United States' historical relationship with China.

Michael Pillsbury has done incredible work exposing the challenge that the United States faces with the Chinese Communist Party. His ideas and his book *The Hundred-Year Marathon* greatly influenced my thinking.

Thank you to those who provided expert strategic analyses. I had the honor of visiting the late Andy Marshall to ask him about his thoughts on the current situation with China. Andy was an American national treasure and his legacy will forever be remembered. Our country is better because of him and his work. His associate, Andrew May, has been a great asset in this effort as well. I am grateful for his work. Thank you to James Farwell for sharing his very insightful feedback and improving this project. Thank you to Alex Gray, who provided great recommendations and analyses that helped augment my thinking.

Roger Robinson and the team at RWR Advisory Group have been irreplaceable partners. Their careful, diligent study of China's worldwide efforts and its impact on the United States will help to carry us through this challenging era.

Brigadier General Rob Spalding is a true expert whose insight into the US-China challenge was incredibly helpful. Thank you also to Bob Zoellick, who is a remarkably smart individual and shared his expertise. Peter Navarro's work has been very influential in my thinking and I am grateful for his contributions.

Thank you to Joe Gaylord, who has long been my adviser, for providing his feedback on this project. Joe is a remarkably intelligent strategist who knows how to effectively communicate big and important messages to the American people.

My longtime colleague and partner, Bob Walker and his team at MoonWalker Associates were essential for developing the chapter on space. Bob's knowledge from years of experience greatly helped formulate the ideas for one of the next great arenas of US competition with China. Thank you also to Sean Kennedy, who greatly contributed to the chapter on intellectual property theft. I am grateful for his sharing of such a deep level of knowledge.

Thank you to General Jim Jones and his team at the Jones Group International. Jim is remarkably knowledgeable, and I am thankful for his contributions to this project. The experts at the Asia Research Services were indispensable resources in helping to shape my thinking on the issue of Taiwan. I am grateful for their efforts and contributions to this project.

My longtime advisers and colleagues Vince Haley, Ross Worthington, and Randy Evans gave me the idea for a book on China. Vince and Ross pointed out that the challenge with China was coming to fruition, while Randy came up with the title and direction. The book you are holding containing these important messages for the American people would not have been possible without all of their foresight. I am grateful for their invaluable counsel.

We are fortunate to have an incredible team at Gingrich 360 who make everything possible.

Thank you to my coauthor on this project, Claire Christensen, who helped write, influence, and shape the thinking of this book. Thank you to Louie Brogdon and Rachel Peterson, who were indispensable in our researching, drafting, and editing efforts.

Thank you to our president, Debbie Myers, who does a remarkable job of leading the company toward new ventures and new possibilities. Joe DeSantis is an exceptional strategist and adviser. Audrey Bird masterfully markets and sells all of our products. Woody Hales is our expert director of operations who masterfully organizes my schedule and keeps me focused. Taylor Swindle is our brilliant CFO who keeps all of our finances in check. Christina Maruna has been essential in growing and engaging with our social media following. Garnsey Sloan has been great in helping produce episodes on China for my new podcast, *Newt's World*. Michael Dutton has done a great job in growing our business endeavors. Grace Davis does an excellent job keeping up operations as our office manager. And Riley Carlson, Brendan Dodd, Courtney Rau, and Jenna Ruffoni are a great group of hardworking interns.

Thank you also to Bess Kelly, who keeps everything running for us. Thank you to my daughter Kathy Lubbers, who has been an exceptional book agent and did a remarkable job representing us in negotiations. Thank you to my second daughter, Jackie Cushman, an accomplished writer who just published her own book, who always provides helpful feedback.

And thank you to my wife, Callista, who both served America as our ambassador to the Holy See and supported me in this effort to outline the scale of the Chinese challenge—she makes it all work and she makes it all worthwhile.

Appendix

Remarks by President Trump at Business Event with President Xi of China

November 9, 2017
Great Hall of the People
Beijing, China
11:21 A.M. CST

PRESIDENT TRUMP: Thank you very much. Thank you. And thank you, Minister Zhong Shan, for that introduction. And especially thank you to President Xi and Madam Peng for serving as such warm and gracious hosts to Melania and me during our time here in your very, very beautiful country.

To both the American delegation and to the Chinese business representatives here, your discussions greatly strengthen our partnership and provides a critical bridge between our business community and yours. And thank you for that.

During my time in Beijing, President Xi and I have had several conversations about our common goals and interests. Beyond that, we talk often. There's a very good chemistry between the two of, believe me.

My administration is committed to improving our trade and business relationships with China. And this relationship is something which we are working very hard to make a fair and reciprocal one. Trade between China and the United States has not been, over the last many, many years, a very fair one for us.

As we all know, America has a huge annual trade deficit with China—a number beyond anything what anybody would understand. This number is, shockingly, hundreds of billions of dollars each year. Estimates are as high as $500 billion a year. We must immediately address the unfair trade practices that drive this deficit, along with barriers to market success. We really have to look at access, forced technology transfer, and the theft of intellectual property, which just, by and of itself, is costing the United States and its companies at least $300 billion a year.

Both the United States and China will have a more prosperous future if we can achieve a level economic playing field. Right now, unfortunately, it is a very one-sided and unfair one. But—but I don't blame China. After all, who can blame a country for being able to take advantage of another country for the benefit of its citizens? I give China great credit.

But, in actuality, I do blame past administrations for allowing this out-of-control trade deficit to take place and to grow. We have to fix this because it just doesn't work for our great American companies, and it doesn't work for our great American workers. It is just not sustainable. I look forward to working toward that goal and to pursuing fair and lasting engagement.

At home, my administration is supporting American workers and American businesses by eliminating burdensome regulations and lifting restrictions on American energy and all other businesses. Restrictions are being seriously lifted.

Our work is already taking hold. The stock market in the United States is at an all-time high, adding already $5.5 trillion in new wealth since the very, very well-known and now very important November 8th election.

Unemployment is at a 17-year low, and so many other great things are happening to the United States, economically and otherwise. Frankly, too many to mention.

Abroad, we're committed to a free and open Indo-Pacific based [on] respect for the rule of law, private enterprise, and trade reciprocity.

In order to achieve prosperity, we must also have security. Security cooperation is critical to addressing a range of emerging threats throughout the Indo-Pacific region and around the world, and I have been very encouraged by my conversations, both over the last number of weeks and, in particular, last night and this morning with President Xi. We're very, very much on the same plane when it comes to security. We both want it for our countries, and we both want it for the world.

Chief among these threats is the North Korean nuclear menace. As I stated in my address to the National Assembly in Seoul yesterday, the United States is committed to the complete and permanent denuclearization of North Korea. So important. China can fix this problem easily and quickly, and I am calling on China and your great President to hopefully work on it very hard. I know one thing about your President: If he works on it hard, it will happen. There's no doubt about it.

We call on all nations to implement U.N. Security Council sanctions and resolutions and to cease doing business with the North Korean regime. All nations must come together to ensure that this rogue regime cannot threaten the world with its nuclear weapons.

I thank President Xi for his recent efforts to restrict trade with North Korea and to cut off all banking ties. Mr. President, thank you, and thank you to all of the Chinese business leaders here today for standing with the United States and our coalition of responsible nations. But time is quickly running out. We must act fast, and hopefully China will act faster and more effectively on this problem than anyone. I'm also calling on Russia to help rein in this potentially very tragic situation.

The contributions of the business community represented here today are vital to our efforts to ensure peace and prosperity for our two nations. Together, we can unlock a future of opportunity, wealth, and dignity far beyond anybody's wildest dreams.

In your discussions today, I hope you will learn from each other and identify new ways to advance our economic cooperation. I am depending on all of you to work together to find opportunities of mutual agreement and shared prosperity. The hardworking people of America and the hardworking people of China deserve the very best solutions to achieve prosperity, happiness, and peace.

Thank you very much. Thank you.[1]

Remarks by President Trump at APEC CEO Summit

November 10, 2017
Ariyana Da Nang Exhibition Center
Da Nang, Vietnam
1:19 P.M. ICT

PRESIDENT TRUMP: What an honor it is to be here in Vietnam—in the very heart of the Indo-Pacific—to address the people and business leaders of this region.

This has already been a remarkable week for the United States in this wonderful part of the world. Starting from Hawaii, Melania and I traveled to Japan, South Korea, and China, and now to Vietnam, to be here with all of you today.

Before we begin, I want to address all those affected by Typhoon Damrey. Americans are praying for you and for your recovery in the months ahead. Our hearts are united with the Vietnamese people suffering in the aftermath of this terrible storm.

This trip comes at an exciting time for America. A new optimism has swept all across our country. Economic growth has reached 3.2 percent, and going higher. Unemployment is at its lowest level in 17 years. The stock market is at an all-time high. And the whole world is lifted by America's renewal.

Everywhere I've traveled on this journey, I've had the pleasure of sharing the good news from America. But even more, I've had the honor of sharing our vision for a free and open Indo-Pacific—a place where sovereign and independent nations, with diverse cultures and many different dreams, can all prosper side-by-side, and thrive in freedom and in peace.

I am so thrilled to be here today at APEC, because this organization was founded to help achieve that very purpose. America stands as a proud member of the community of nations who make a home on the Pacific. We have been an active partner in this region since we first won independence ourselves.

In 1784, the first American ship sailed to China from the newly independent United States. It went loaded with goods to sell in Asia, and it came back full of porcelain and tea. Our first president, George Washington himself, owned a set of tableware from that ship.

In 1804, Thomas Jefferson sent the explorers, Lewis and Clark, on an expedition to our Pacific Coast. They were the first of the millions of Americans who ventured west to live out America's manifest destiny across our vast continent.

In 1817, our Congress approved the first full-time Pacific development [deployment] of an American warship. That initial naval presence soon grew into a squadron, and then a fleet, to guarantee freedom of navigation for the growing number of ships, braving the high seas to reach markets in the Philippines, Singapore, and in India.

In 1818, we began our relationship with the Kingdom of Thailand, and 15 years later our two countries signed a treaty of friendship and commerce—our first with an Asian nation.

In the next century, when imperialist powers threatened this region, the United States pushed back at great cost to ourselves. We understood that security and prosperity depended on it.

We have been friends, partners, and allies in the Indo-Pacific for a long, long time, and we will be friends, partners, and allies for a long time to come.

As old friends in the region, no one has been more delighted than America to witness, to help, and to share in the extraordinary progress you have made over the last half-century.

What the countries and economies represented here today have built in this part of the world is nothing short of miraculous. The story of this region in recent decades is the story of what is possible when people take ownership of their future.

Few would have imagined just a generation ago that leaders of these nations would come together here in Da Nang to deepen our friendships, expand our partnerships, and celebrate the amazing achievements of our people.

This city was once home to an American military base, in a country where many Americans and Vietnamese lost their lives in a very bloody war.

Today, we are no longer enemies; we are friends. And this port city is bustling with ships from around the world. Engineering marvels, like the Dragon Bridge, welcome the millions who come to visit Da Nang's stunning beaches, shining lights, and ancient charms.

In the early 1990s, nearly half of Vietnam survived on just a few dollars a day, and one in four did not have any electricity. Today, an opening Vietnamese economy is one of the fastest-growing economies on Earth. It has already increased more than 30 times over, and the Vietnamese students rank among the best students in the world. And that is very impressive.

This is the same story of incredible transformation that we have seen across the region. Indonesians for decades have been building domestic and democratic institutions to govern their vast chain of more than 13,000 islands. Since the 1990s, Indonesia's people have lifted themselves from poverty to become one of the fastest-growing nations of the G20. Today, it is the third-largest democracy on Earth.

The Philippines has emerged as a proud nation of strong and devout families. For 11 consecutive years, the World Economic Forum has ranked the Philippines first among Asian countries in closing the gender gap and embracing women leaders in business and in politics.

Kingdom of Thailand has become an upper middle-income country in less than a generation. Its majestic capital of Bangkok is now the most visited city on Earth. And that is very impressive. Not too many people here are from Thailand.

Malaysia has rapidly developed through recent decades, and it is now ranked as one of the best places in the world to do business.

In Singapore, citizens born to parents who survived on $500 dollars a day [year] are now among the highest earners in the world—a transformation made possible by the vision of Lee Kwan Yew's vision of honest governance and the rule of law. And his great son is now doing an amazing job.

As I recently observed in South Korea, the people of that Republic took a poor country ravaged by war, and in just a few decades turned it into one of the wealthiest democracies on Earth. Today, South Koreans enjoy higher incomes than the citizens of many European Union countries. It was great spending time with President Moon.

Everyone knows of China's impressive achievements over the past several decades. During this period—and it was a period of great market reforms—large parts of China experienced rapid economic growth, jobs boomed, and more than 800 million citizens rose out of poverty. I just left China this morning and had a really productive meeting and a wonderful time with our gracious host, President Xi.

And, as I saw on my first stop of this trip, in Japan we see a dynamic democracy in a land of industrial, technological, and cultural wonders. In fewer than 60 years, that island nation has produced 24 Nobel Prize winners for achievements in physics, chemistry, medicine, literature, and the promotion of peace. President Abe and I agree on so much.

In the broader region, countries outside of APEC are also making great strides in this new chapter for the Indo-Pacific.

India is celebrating the 70th anniversary of its independence. It is a sovereign democracy, as well as—think of this—over 1 billion people. It's the largest democracy in the world. Since India opened its economy, it has achieved astounding growth and a new world of opportunity for its expanding middle class. And Prime Minister Modi has been working to bring that vast country, and all of its people, together as one. And he is working at it very, very successfully, indeed.

As we can see, in more and more places throughout this region, citizens of sovereign and independent nations have taken greater control of their destinies and unlocked the potential of their people.

They've pursued visions of justice and accountability, promoted private property and the rule of law, and embraced systems that value hard work and individual enterprise.

They built businesses, they built cities, they built entire countries from the ground up. Many of you in this room have taken part in these great, uplifting national projects of building. They have been your projects from inception to completion, from dreams to reality.

With your help, this entire region has emerged—and it is still emerging—as a beautiful constellation of nations, each its own bright star, satellites to none—and each one, a people, a culture, a way of life, and a home.

Those of you who have lived through these transformations understand better than anyone the value of what you have achieved. You also understand that your home is your legacy, and you must always protect it.

In the process of your economic development, you've sought commerce and trade with other nations, and forged partnerships based on mutual respect and directed toward mutual gain.

Today, I am here to offer a renewed partnership with America to work together to strengthen the bonds of friendship and commerce between all of the nations of the Indo-Pacific, and together, to promote our prosperity and security.

At the core of this partnership, we seek robust trade relationships rooted in the principles of fairness and reciprocity. When the United

States enters into a trading relationship with other countries or other peoples, we will, from now on, expect that our partners will faithfully follow the rules just like we do. We expect that markets will be open to an equal degree on both sides, and that private industry, not government planners, will direct investment.

Unfortunately, for too long and in too many places, the opposite has happened. For many years, the United States systematically opened our economy with few conditions. We lowered or ended tariffs, reduced trade barriers, and allowed foreign goods to flow freely into our country.

But while we lowered market barriers, other countries didn't open their markets to us....

Countries were embraced by the World Trade Organization, even if they did not abide by its stated principles. Simply put, we have not been treated fairly by the World Trade Organization. Organizations like the WTO can only function properly when all members follow the rules and respect the sovereign rights of every member. We cannot achieve open markets if we do not ensure fair market access. In the end, unfair trade undermines us all.

The United States promoted private enterprise, innovation, and industry. Other countries used government-run industrial planning and state-owned enterprises.

We adhered to WTO principles on protecting intellectual property and ensuring fair and equal market access. They engaged in product dumping, subsidized goods, currency manipulation, and predatory industrial policies.

They ignored the rules to gain advantage over those who followed the rules, causing enormous distortions in commerce and threatening the foundations of international trade itself.

Such practices, along with our collective failure to respond to them, hurt many people in our country and also in other countries. Jobs, factories, and industries were stripped out of the United States and out of many countries in addition. And many opportunities for mutually beneficial investments were lost because people could not trust the system.

We can no longer tolerate these chronic trade abuses, and we will not tolerate them. Despite years of broken promises, we were told that someday soon everyone would behave fairly and responsibly. People in America and throughout the Indo-Pacific region have waited for that day to come. But it never has, and that is why I am here today—to speak frankly about our challenges and work toward a brighter future for all of us.

I recently had an excellent trip to China, where I spoke openly and directly with President Xi about China's unfair trade practices and the enormous trade deficits they have produced with the United States. I expressed our strong desire to work with China to achieve a trading relationship that is conducted on a truly fair and equal basis.

The current trade imbalance is not acceptable. I do not blame China or any other country, of which there are many, for taking advantage of the United States on trade. If their representatives are able to get away with it, they are just doing their jobs. I wish previous administrations in my country saw what was happening and did something about it. They did not, but I will.

From this day forward, we will compete on a fair and equal basis. We are not going to let the United States be taken advantage of anymore. I am always going to put America first the same way that I expect all of you in this room to put your countries first.

The United States is prepared to work with each of the leaders in this room today to achieve mutually beneficial commerce that is in the interest of both your countries and mine. That is the message I am here to deliver.

I will make bilateral trade agreements with any Indo-Pacific nation that wants to be our partner and that will abide by the principles of fair and reciprocal trade. What we will no longer do is enter into large agreements that tie our hands, surrender our sovereignty, and make meaningful enforcement practically impossible.

Instead, we will deal on a basis of mutual respect and mutual benefit. We will respect your independence and your sovereignty. We want you to be strong, prosperous, and self-reliant, rooted in your history, and branching out toward the future. That is how we will thrive and grow together, in partnerships of real and lasting value.

But for this—and I call it the Indo-Pacific dream—if it's going to be realized, we must ensure that all play by the rules, which they do not right now. Those who do will be our closest economic partners. Those who do not can be certain that the United States will no longer turn a blind eye to violations, cheating, or economic aggression. Those days are over.

We will no longer tolerate the audacious theft of intellectual property. We will confront the destructive practices of forcing businesses to surrender their technology to the state, and forcing them into joint ventures in exchange for market access.

We will address the massive subsidizing of industries through colossal state-owned enterprises that put private competitors out of business—happening all the time.

We will not remain silent as American companies are targeted by state-affiliated actors for economic gain, whether through cyber-attacks, corporate espionage, or other anti-competitive practices. We will encourage all nations to speak out loudly when the principles of fairness and reciprocity are violated.

We know it is in America's interests to have partners throughout this region that are thriving, prosperous, and dependent on no one. We will not make decisions for the purpose of power or patronage. We will never ask our partners to surrender their sovereignty, privacy, and intellectual property, or to limit contracts to state-owned suppliers.

We will find opportunities for our private sector to work with yours and to create jobs and wealth for us all. We seek strong partners, not weak partners. We seek strong neighbors, not weak neighbors. Above all, we seek friendship, and we don't dream of domination.

For this reason, we are also refocusing our existing development efforts. We are calling on the World Bank and the Asian Development Bank to direct their efforts toward high-quality infrastructure investment that promotes economic growth.

The United States will also do its part. We are also committed to reforming our development finance institutions so that they better incentivize private sector investment in your economies, and provide strong alternatives to state-directed initiatives that come with many strings attached.

The United States has been reminded time and time again in recent years that economic security is not merely related to national security. Economic security is national security. It is vital to our national strength.

We also know that we will not have lasting prosperity if we do not confront grave threats to security, sovereignty, and stability facing our world today.

Earlier this week, I addressed the National Assembly in Seoul, South Korea and urged every responsible nation to stand united in declaring that every single step the North Korean regime takes toward more weapons is a step it takes into greater and greater danger. The future of this region and its beautiful people must not be held hostage to a dictator's twisted fantasies of violent conquest and nuclear blackmail.

In addition, we must uphold principles that have benefitted all of us, like respect for the rule of law, individual rights, and freedom of navigation and overflight, including open shipping lanes. Three principles and these principles—create stability and build trust, security, and prosperity among like-minded nations.

We must also deal decisively with other threats to our security and the future of our children, such as criminal cartels, human smuggling, drugs, corruption, cybercrime, and territorial expansion. As I have said many times before: All civilized people must come together to drive out terrorists and extremists from our societies, stripping them of funding, territory, and ideological support. We must stop radical Islamic terrorism.

So let us work together for a peaceful, prosperous, and free Indo-Pacific. I am confident that, together, every problem we have spoken about today can be solved and every challenge we face can be overcome.

If we succeed in this effort, if we seize the opportunities before us and ground our partnerships firmly in the interests of our own people, then together we will achieve everything we dream for our nations and for our children.

We will be blessed with a world of strong, sovereign, and independent nations, thriving in peace and commerce with others. They will be places where we can build our homes and where families, businesses, and people can flourish and grow.

If we do this, will we look at the globe half a century from now, and we will marvel at the beautiful constellation of nations—each different, each unique, and each shining brightly and proudly throughout this region of the world. And just as when we look at the stars in the night sky, the distance of time will make most of the challenges we have and that we spoke of today seem very, very small.

What will not seem small—what is not small—will be the big choices that all of our nations will have to make to keep their stars glowing very, very brightly.

In America, like every nation that has won and defended its sovereignty, we understand that we have nothing so precious as our birthright, our treasured independence, and our freedom.

That knowledge has guided us throughout American history. It has inspired us to sacrifice and innovate. And it is why today, hundreds of years after our victory in the American Revolution, we still remember the words of an American founder and our second

President of the United States, John Adams. As an old man, just before his death, this great patriot was asked to offer his thoughts on the 50th anniversary of glorious American freedom. He replied with the words: independence forever.

It's a sentiment that burns in the heart of every patriot and every nation. Our hosts here in Vietnam have known this sentiment not just for 200 years, but for nearly 2,000 years. It was around 40 AD when two Vietnamese sisters, the Trung Sisters, first awakened the spirit of the people of this land. It was then that, for the first time, the people of Vietnam stood for your independence and your pride.

Today, the patriots and heroes of our histories hold the answers to the great questions of our future and our time. They remind us of who we are and what we are called to do.

Together, we have it in our power to lift our people and our world to new heights—heights that have never been attained,

So let us choose a future of patriotism, prosperity, and pride. Let us choose wealth and freedom over poverty and servitude. Let us choose a free and open Indo-Pacific.

Finally, let us never forget the world has many places—many dreams, and many roads. But in all of the world, there is no place like home.

And so, for family, for country, for freedom, for history, and for the glory of God, protect your home, defend your home, and love your home today and for all time.

Thank you. God Bless You. God Bless the Pacific region. And God Bless the United States of America. Thank you very much. Thank you.[2]

Seizing the Opportunity of a Global Economy in Transition and Accelerating Development of the Asia-Pacific

Keynote Address by H. E. Xi Jinping
APEC CEO Summit
Da Nang, November 10, 2017

Chairman Vu Tien Loc,

Leaders of the APEC Business Community,

Ladies and Gentlemen,

Dear Friends,

Good afternoon! I am glad to come to Da Nang and meet all of you again.

Our region, the Asia-Pacific, has the biggest share of the global economy; and it is a major engine driving global growth. The business community is a primary contributor to growth, as it keeps exploring new ways of development. That's why during the APEC Economic Leaders' Meeting over the last several years, I have always taken time to meet business leaders and discuss with you approaches and measures to address the challenges we face.

It has been 10 years since the international financial crisis broke out. Over the last decade, the international community have worked in concert to steer the global economy back to the track of recovery. Thanks to our efforts, the global economy is improving. Despite risks and uncertainties, global trade and investment are picking up, people are more optimistic about the outlook of financial markets, and confidence is growing in all sectors.

Development is a journey with no end, but with one new departure point after another. An ancient Chinese philosopher once observed, "We should focus our mind on the future, not the past." We live in a fast changing world, and the global economy is undergoing more profound changes. We must therefore closely follow the trend of the global economy, identify its underlying dynamics, keep to the right direction, and, on that basis, take bold action.

—We are seeing a profound change in growth drivers. Countries are turning to reform and innovation to meet challenges and achieve growth. The potential of structural reforms is being unlocked and its positive impact of boosting growth of various countries has become more evident. A new round of technological and industrial revolutions is gaining momentum. Digital economy and sharing economy have registered rapid growth. New industries as well as new forms and models of business are flourishing. As a result, new growth drivers are being created.

—We are seeing a profound change in the model of global growth. As time advances, development has taken on profoundly richer implications. The vision of innovative, coordinated, green and open development for all is gaining increasing public support. To achieve more comprehensive, higher quality and more sustainable development has become the shared goal of the international community. To implement the 2030 Agenda for Sustainable Development and adapt to climate change and other challenges of a global nature has become an important international consensus.

—We are seeing a profound change in economic globalization. Over the last few decades, economic globalization has contributed greatly to global growth. Indeed, it has become an irreversible historical trend. Against the backdrop of evolving global developments, economic globalization faces new adjustments in both form and substance. In pursuing economic globalization, we should make it more open and inclusive, more balanced, more equitable and beneficial to all.

—We are seeing a profound change in the system of global economic governance. The evolving global economic environment demands more from the system of global economic governance. We should uphold multilateralism, pursue shared growth through consultation and collaboration, forge closer partnerships, and build a community with a shared future for mankind. This, I believe, is what we should do in conducting global economic governance in a new era.

Ladies and Gentlemen,

Dear Friends,

Faced with the profound changes in the global economy, should we, the Asia-Pacific economies, lead reform and innovation, or just hesitate and proceed haltingly? Should we steer economic globalization, or dither and stall in the face of challenge? Should we jointly advance regional cooperation, or go our separate ways?

This is my answer: We must advance with the trend of times, live up to our responsibility and work together to deliver a bright future of development and prosperity for the Asia-Pacific.

First, we should continue to foster an open economy that benefits all. Openness brings progress, while self-seclusion leaves one behind. We the Asia-Pacific economies know this too well from our own development experience. We should put in place a regional cooperation framework that ensures consultation among equals, wide participation and shared benefits, build an open Asia-Pacific economy and promote trade and investment liberalization and facilitation. We should make economic globalization more open, inclusive and balanced so that it benefits different countries and people of different social groups. We should proactively adapt to the evolving international division of labor and actively reshape the global value chain so as to upgrade our economies and build up new strengths. We should support the multilateral trading regime and practice open regionalism to make developing members benefit more from international trade and investment.

The building of a free trade area of the Asia-Pacific (FTAAP) is the long-cherished dream of the business community in our region. It was in response to the call of the business community that APEC leaders, for the first time, initiated the FTAAP vision in Hanoi in 2006. In 2014, the FTAAP process was launched in Beijing. We should get into action, fully implement the Beijing Roadmap, move toward the FTAAP and provide an institutional underpinning for growing an open economy in the Asia-Pacific.

Second, we should continue to pursue innovation-driven development and create new drivers of growth. The current global economic recovery is, to a large extent, the result of cyclical factors, while the lack of self-generating driving forces remains a nagging problem. To avoid the risk of the global economy entering a "new mediocre," we must sustain growth through innovation.

The new round of technological and industrial revolutions is unfolding before us. Digital economy and sharing economy are surging worldwide, and breakthroughs have been made in new technologies such as artificial intelligence and quantum science. We in the Asia-Pacific cannot afford to be just onlookers. What we should do is to seize the opportunity, increase input in innovation, change the model of development and nurture new growth areas. We should promote structural reform, remove all institutional and systemic barriers to innovation and energize the market. We should implement the APEC Accord on Innovative Development, Economic Reform and Growth adopted in Beijing, deepen cooperation on the internet and digital economy and strive to be a global leader of innovative growth.

Third, we should continue to enhance connectivity and achieve interconnected development. Interconnected development is the best way to achieve mutual benefit and win-win outcome. We the Asia-Pacific economies are closely connected, and our interests are interlocked. Such an interconnected development will both open up new horizon for our own development, and create driving force for us all to achieve common development as partners. In 2014, the APEC Connectivity Blueprint was formulated. This Blueprint should guide our efforts to build a comprehensive, all-round and multi-tiered Asia-Pacific connectivity network. We should boost the real economy through the building of connectivity, break bottlenecks to development and unlock potentials. With these efforts, we can achieve coordinated and interconnected development.

In May this year, the Belt and Road Forum for International Cooperation was successfully held in Beijing. The Belt and Road Initiative calls for joint contribution and it has a clear focus, which is to promote infrastructure construction and connectivity, strengthen coordination on economic policies, enhance complementarity of development strategies and boost interconnected development to achieve common prosperity. This initiative is from China, but it belongs to the world. It is rooted in history, but it is oriented toward the future. It focuses on the Asian, European and African continents, but it is open to all partners. I am confident that the launch of the Belt and Road Initiative will create a broader and more dynamic platform for Asia-Pacific cooperation.

Fourth, we should continue to make economic development more inclusive and deliver its benefits to our people. The current headwinds confronting economic globalization is mostly generated by the lack of inclusiveness in development. Hard work is still needed if we are to bring the benefits of development to countries across the globe and people across our society, and thus turn our vision into reality.

Over the past few years, we have actively explored ways to promote inclusive development and have built strong consensus about it. We should deepen regional economic integration, develop an open and inclusive market and strengthen the bond of shared interests. We should make inclusiveness and sharing a part of our development strategies, improve systems and institutions to uphold efficiency and fairness, and safeguard social equity and justice. We should invest more in education, medical care, employment and other areas that are important to people's livelihood, and address poverty and the widening gap between the rich and the poor. We should reach out to disadvantaged groups, improve business environment for micro, small and medium-sized enterprises, and enable the workforce to better adapt to industrial transformation, so that everyone will have his fair share of opportunity and benefits.

Ladies and Gentlemen,

Friends,

As an old Chinese saying goes, a commitment, once made, should be delivered. Boosting development in the Asia-Pacific requires real actions by all of us members. As the world's second largest economy, China knows fully well its responsibility. Over the past five years, we have taken proactive steps to adapt to, manage and steer the new normal of China's economy and deepened supply-side structural reform. As a result, China's economy has maintained steady performance, and we are pursuing better-quality, more efficient, fairer and more sustainable development. Over the past four years, China's economy has grown by 7.2% on the average annually, contributing over 30% of global growth. China is now a main driver powering global growth.

We have worked hard to remove systematical institutional barriers that impede development through comprehensive reform. As many as 360 major reform initiatives and more than 1,500 reform measures have been taken. Breakthroughs have been made in key areas, and general frameworks for reform have been put in place in major sectors. We have sped up efforts to build new institutions of the open economy and transform models of foreign trade and outbound investment to continue the shift from quantitative to qualitative improvement in trade.

We have advanced theoretical, practical, institutional, cultural and other explorations to unleash new impetus for growth. China has become a huge platform where all factors and players of innovation converge to make a real difference. From infrastructure to various economic sectors, from business models to ways of consumption, innovation is leading the way.

We have pursued a people-centered philosophy of development to make our development more inclusive and beneficial to all. Individual income has registered sustained growth, outpacing GDP growth for many years. Income gaps between urban and rural areas and between different regions have been narrowing, middle-income group expanding, and Gini coefficient dropping. More than 13 million new urban jobs have been created every year for four consecutive years. Significant advances have been made in pursuing green development, resulting in considerable reduction in the intensity of energy and resource consumption and marked improvement in the ecological environment.

To lift all the remaining poor people out of poverty is a solemn commitment made by the Chinese government to the people. It is uppermost in my mind, and I have spent more energy on poverty alleviation than anything else. Over the past five years, I have been to many poor areas in China to pin down the causes of poverty and address them in a targeted way. As a result, decisive progress has been made in the fight against poverty. Over the past five years, we have lifted more than 60 million people out of poverty. The poverty headcount ratio has declined, and per capita rural income in poor areas has maintained double-digit growth. This has not come easily, and we are proud of what we have achieved in poverty alleviation.

Ladies and Gentlemen,

Friends,

China's development is an evolving historical process. Last month, the 19th National Congress of the Communist Party of China was successfully convened in Beijing. Responding to our people's desire for a better life, the Congress formulated a guide to action and a development blueprint for China in the new era. It is envisaged that by 2020, China will turn itself into a moderately prosperous society in all respects, and by 2035, China will basically realize socialist modernization. By the middle of this century, China will become a great modern socialist country that is prosperous, strong, democratic, culturally-advanced, harmonious and beautiful. Under the leadership of the Communist Party of China, the Chinese people will embark on a new journey.

First, this is a new journey of deepening reform across the board and unleashing dynamism for development. To resolve difficulties and problems on the way forward, we must deepen all-round reform. We will focus more on solving problems, get rid of all outdated thinking and ideas and all institutional ailments and break through the blockades of vested interests to inspire creativity and vitality throughout society. We will develop a set of institutions that are well conceived, fully built, procedure based, and efficiently functioning and achieve modernization of China's system and capacity for governance. Next year, we will celebrate the 40th anniversary of China's launching of the reform and opening-up initiative. China's reform will cover more areas; and more and stronger steps will be taken in pursuing this endeavor.

Second, this is a new journey of moving with the times and exploring new model of development. China's economy is in a transition from a phase of rapid growth to a stage of high-quality development. We will be guided by a new development philosophy, put quality first, give priority to performance and develop a modernized economy. We will pursue supply-side structural reform as our main task, work hard to achieve better quality and higher efficiency performance, and create more robust growth through reform. We will raise total factor productivity and accelerate the building of an industrial system that promotes coordinated development of the real economy with technological innovation, modern finance, and a talent pool. We will endeavor to develop an economy with more effective market mechanisms, dynamic micro-entities, and sound macro-regulation. All these efforts will make China's economy more innovative and competitive. We will promote further integration of the internet, big data, and artificial intelligence with the real economy, and cultivate new drivers of growth in digital economy, sharing economy, clean energy and other areas. We will continue to explore new mechanisms and pathways for achieving coordinated development among regions, promote coordinated development of the Beijing-Tianjin-Hebei region, Yangtze Economic Belt, Xiongan New Area, and Guangdong-Hong Kong-Macao Greater Bay Area, build world-class city clusters and foster new source of growth.

As China works hard to pursue innovation and higher quality of growth, new forms of business will keep emerging, more innovations will be used, and development of various regions in China will become more balanced. All this will create a more powerful and extensive impact, present more opportunities of cooperation and enable more countries to board the express train of China's development.

Third, this is a new journey toward greater integration with the world and an open economy of higher standards. China will not slow its steps in opening up itself. We will work together with other countries to create new drivers of common development through the launching of the Belt and Road Initiative. We will adopt policies to promote high-standard liberalization and facilitation of trade and investment. We will implement the system of pre-establishment national treatment plus a negative list across the board, significantly ease market access, further open the service sector, and protect the legitimate rights and interests of foreign investors. All businesses registered in China will be treated as equals. We will grant more powers to pilot free trade zones to conduct reform, and explore the opening of free trade ports. We will speed up negotiations with partner countries on the concluding of free trade agreements and investment treaties, advance the building of FTAAP, work for the speedy conclusion of RCEP negotiations, and endeavor to establish a global network of free trade areas.

In the next 15 years, China will have an even larger market and more comprehensive development. It is estimated that China will import US$24 trillion worth of goods, attract US$2 trillion inbound direct investment and make US$2 trillion of outbound investment. In November next year, China will hold the first China International Import Expo in Shanghai, which will provide a new platform for expanding cooperation in China's market among all parties.

Fourth, this is a new journey toward a better life for the people. To secure a better life for our people is what we aim to achieve in everything we do. We will ensure and improve living standards through development and meet people's ever-growing needs for a better life. We will continue to promote social fairness and justice to see that our people will always have a strong sense of gains, happiness, and security. We will continue to implement targeted poverty reduction and alleviation measures and ensure that by the year 2020, all rural residents living below the current poverty line are lifted out of poverty. Each and every one of the over 1.3 billion Chinese people should lead decent lives. No one will be left behind!

We will speed up institutional reform for ecological conservation, pursue green, low-carbon and sustainable development, and implement the strictest possible system for environmental protection. By 2035, there will be a fundamental improvement in the environment; the goal of building a Beautiful China will be basically attained. We will actively tackle climate change, and protect our common home for the sake of human survival. China's carbon dioxide emission is expected to peak around 2030, and we will make every effort for such emissions to reach the peak ahead of time. We will increase the share of non-fossil fuels in primary energy consumption to around 20% by 2030. Once we set a target, we will not stop our efforts until it is met!

Fifth, this is a new journey toward a new type of international relations and a community with a shared future for mankind. The dream of us Chinese is closely connected with the dreams of people of other countries. Our world is full of challenges and the road ahead will not be smooth. But we will not give up on our dream. We will double our efforts and work with all others to build an open, inclusive, clean, and beautiful world that enjoys durable peace, universal security, and common prosperity.

We Chinese believe that peace is most precious and that there should be harmony among all nations. We are committed to peaceful development and we will remain an anchor for peace and stability in the Asia-Pacific region and beyond. China will, guided by the principle of upholding justice while pursuing shared interests, actively develop global partnerships, expand the convergence of interests with other countries, and work to foster a new type of international relations featuring mutual respect, fairness, justice, and win-win cooperation. Acting on the principle of achieving shared growth through consultation and collaboration, we will get actively involved in reforming and developing the global governance system to make the international political and economic order more just and equitable.

Ladies and Gentlemen,

Dear Friends,

All of our people in the Asia-Pacific deserve peace, stability and prosperity; and all of us in the region should jointly deliver a bright future for the Asia-Pacific. Partnerships based on mutual trust, inclusiveness, cooperation and mutual benefit: This is what keeps our big Asia-Pacific family together and ensures the success of Asia-Pacific cooperation. Let us take solid steps to promote cooperation and usher in an even brighter future for the Asia-Pacific.

Thank you.[3]

Several Issues on Adhering to and Developing Socialism with Chinese Characteristics

Speech Excerpts by General Secretary Xi Jinping Given to Members and Alternate Members of the Newly-Appointed Central Committee at a Seminar on Learning and Implementing the Spirit of the 18th National Congress of the Communist Party of China
January 5, 2013

First, socialism with Chinese characteristics is socialism rather than any other socialism. The basic principles of scientific socialism cannot be lost, and if lost, it will not be socialism. Our party has always stressed that socialism with Chinese characteristics not only adheres to the basic principles of scientific socialism, but also endows it with distinct Chinese characteristics according to the conditions of the times. That is to say, socialism with Chinese characteristics is socialism and nothing else. What kind of nationalism a country implements depends on whether it can solve the historic problems that the country faces. During the period when the Chinese nation was poor, weak and oppressed, all kinds of doctrines and ideological trends had been tried. The capitalist road did not go through. Reformism, liberalism, social Darwinism, anarchism, pragmatism, populism, and unionism were all "you sing and I come on stage," but none of them could solve the problems of China's future and destiny. It was Marxism-Leninism and Mao Zedong Thought that led the Chinese people out of the long night and established New China. It was socialism with Chinese characteristics that made China develop rapidly. Not to mention the earlier period, since the beginning of reform and opening up, especially after the disintegration of the Soviet Union and the drastic changes in Eastern Europe, the international public opinion denouncing China has never stopped, and all kinds of "China Collapse Theory" have never stopped. However, instead of collapsing, China's overall national strength is increasing day by day, and the people's living standard is continuously improving, "the scenery here is unique." Both history and reality tell us that only socialism can save China and only socialism with Chinese characteristics can develop China. This is the conclusion of history and the choice of the people.

In recent years, some public opinions at home and abroad have raised the question of whether what China is doing is still socialism. Some people say it is "capitalist socialism," while others simply say it is "state capitalism" and "new bureaucratic capitalism." These are all completely wrong. We say that socialism with Chinese characteristics is socialism, that is, no matter how we reform and open up, we must always adhere to the road of socialism with Chinese characteristics, the theoretical system of socialism with Chinese characteristics, the socialist system with Chinese characteristics, and the basic requirements for winning new victories of socialism with Chinese characteristics set forth at the 18th National Congress of the Communist Party of China. This includes, under the leadership of the Chinese Communist Party, basing itself on the basic national conditions, centering on economic construction, adhering to the four cardinal principles, adhering to reform and opening up, liberating and developing social productive forces, building a socialist market economy, socialist democratic politics, advanced socialist culture, socialist harmonious society and socialist ecological civilization, promoting the all-round development of human beings, gradually realizing the common prosperity of all the people, and building a prosperous, prosperous, democratic, civilized and harmonious socialist modern country. Including adhering to the fundamental political system of the people's congress system, the multi-party cooperation and political consultation system under the leadership of the communist party of China, the system of regional ethnic autonomy and the system of grassroots self-government, the socialist legal system with Chinese characteristics, the basic economic system with public ownership as the main body and the common development of various ownership economies. These are the contents that embody the basic principles of scientific socialism under the new historical conditions. If these are lost, it will not be socialism.

Comrade Deng Xiaoping once pointed out profoundly and summarily: "Our modernization must proceed from China's reality. No matter whether it is revolution or construction, we should pay attention to learning from foreign experiences. However, copying other countries' experiences and models has never been successful. We have learned many lessons in this regard." In the past, it was not possible to carry out an all-out Soviet modernization, and now it is not possible to carry out an all-out westernization or anything else. After the end of the Cold War, many developing countries were forced to adopt the Western model. As a result, party disputes, social unrest and people's displacement have all been difficult to stabilize up to now. "Chuang Tzu colchicine" wrote: "and the son alone did not hear of fu shou ling Yu zi's study in Handan and? If you don't win the national power, you'll lose it and go straight to your ears." We must never "learn to walk in Handan and lose our way." We are just sinicizing Marxism and building socialism with Chinese characteristics. In recent years, with China's overall national strength and international status rising, there have been more discussions and researches on "Beijing Consensus," "China Model" and "China Road" in the world, among which there are many praisers. Some foreign scholars believe that China's rapid development has led to some western theories being questioned, and a new version of Marxist theory is subverting western traditional theories. We have always believed that the development path of each country should be chosen by its people. The so-called "China model" is the socialist road with Chinese characteristics created by the Chinese people in their own struggle and practice. We firmly believe that with the continuous development of socialism with Chinese characteristics, our system will be more and more mature, the superiority of our socialist system will be further revealed, our road will be wider and wider, and our development road will have more and more influence on the world. We just need to have such road confidence, theoretical confidence and institutional confidence so as to truly achieve the goal of "making the most of the difficulties and difficulties and letting the east, west, north and south prevail."

Second, the socialist construction carried out by our party's leaders and people has two historical periods before and after the reform and opening up. These are two interrelated and significantly different periods, but in essence they are all the practical explorations of socialist construction carried out by our party's leaders and people. Socialism with Chinese characteristics was initiated in the new historical period of reform and opening-up, but it was also initiated on the basis that the basic socialist system has been established in New China and has been built for more than 20 years. To correctly understand this problem, we must grasp three aspects. First, without our party's decisive decision to carry out reform and opening up in 1978, and unswervingly pushing forward the reform and opening up, and unswervingly grasping the correct direction of reform and opening up, socialist China would not have had such a good situation as it is today, would have faced a serious crisis, and would have faced a crisis of losing the party and subjugating the country like the Soviet Union and Eastern European countries. At the same time, without the establishment of new China in 1949 and the socialist revolution and construction, we have accumulated important ideological, material and institutional conditions and accumulated positive and negative experience, and the reform and opening-up will be difficult to advance smoothly.

Second, although there are great differences in the ideological guidelines, principles and policies and practical work of socialist construction between the two historical periods, the two are by no means separated from each other, let alone fundamentally opposed. Our party put forward many correct ideas in the practice of socialist construction, but they were not really implemented at that time. After the reform and opening up, they were really implemented and will continue to be adhered to and developed in the future. Marx has long said: "People create their own history, but they do not create it at will, not under the conditions they choose, but under the conditions they meet directly, set and inherited from the past." Third, the historical period before the reform and opening up should be correctly evaluated. The historical period after the reform and opening up cannot be used to negate the historical period before the reform and opening up, nor can the historical period before the reform and opening up be used to negate the historical period after the reform and opening up. The socialist practice exploration before the reform and opening up has accumulated the conditions for the socialist practice exploration after the reform and opening up. The socialist practice exploration after the reform and opening up is the persistence, reform and development of the previous period. To explore the socialist practice before the reform and opening up, we must adhere to the ideological line of seeking truth from facts, distinguish between mainstream and tributary, adhere to the truth, correct mistakes, carry forward the experience and draw lessons, and on this basis continue to push forward the cause of the party and the people.

The reason why I emphasize this issue is that if this major political issue is not handled properly, it will have serious political consequences. The ancients said: "To destroy a country, one must first go to its history." Hostile forces at home and abroad often use the history of the Chinese revolution and the history of New China to make an issue of it and do their best to attack, defame and slander it. Their fundamental purpose is to confuse the people and incite the overthrow of the leadership of the Communist Party of China and the socialist system in our country. Why did the Soviet Union disintegrate? Why did the Soviet Communist Party fall? An important reason is that the struggle in the ideological field is very fierce. It totally negates the history of the Soviet Union, the history of the Soviet Communist Party, Lenin and Stalin. It engages in historical nihilism and confuses thoughts. Party organizations at all levels have almost no effect and the army is no longer under the leadership of the Party. In the end, the Soviet Communist Party's large party fell apart and the Soviet Union's large socialist country fell apart. This is a warning! Comrade Deng Xiaoping pointed out: "Mao Zedong Thought is a banner that cannot be lost. Losing this banner actually negates the glorious history of our party. On the whole, our party's history is still glorious. Although our Party has made some big mistakes in history, including the 30 years since the founding of the People's Republic of China, and even made such big mistakes as the "Cultural Revolution," our Party has succeeded in the revolution after all. China's position in the world was greatly improved after the founding of the People's Republic of China. Only with the establishment of the People's Republic of China will we, a large country with a population accounting for nearly a quarter of the world's total population, stand up and stand still in the world." He also stressed: "The evaluation of Comrade Mao Zedong and the exposition of Mao Zedong Thought are not only related to Comrade Mao Zedong's personal problems, which are inseparable from the entire history of our Party and our country. To see this overall situation." "This is not only a theoretical issue, especially a political issue, but also a major political issue at home and abroad." This is the vision and mind of a great Marxist politician. Just imagine, if Comrade Mao Zedong was totally rejected at that time, could our party still stand up? Can the socialist system in our country still stand up? If you can't stand it, there will be chaos. Therefore, correctly handling the relationship between socialist practice and exploration before and after the reform and opening up is not only a historical issue, but also a political issue. It is suggested that everyone find out the "Resolution on Several Historical Issues of the Party Since the Founding of the People's Republic of China" and look at it again.

Third, Marxism must develop continuously with the development of the times, practice and science. It cannot remain unchanged.

Socialism has always been advancing in development. Adherence to and development of socialism with Chinese characteristics is a great article for which Comrade Deng Xiaoping has defined the basic ideas and principles. The third generation of central collective leadership with Comrade Jiang Zemin at the core and the Party Central Committee with Comrade Hu Jintao as General Secretary have all written wonderful chapters. Now, the task of our generation of Communists is to continue to write this great article. Over the past 30 years, socialism with Chinese characteristics has made great achievements, which, together with the foundation laid after the founding of New China, is an important foundation for it to stand up and go far. Our understanding of socialism and our grasp of the laws of socialism with Chinese characteristics have reached an unprecedented new height, which is beyond doubt. At the same time, we should also see that socialism in our country is still in its primary stage, and we still face many unclear problems and unsolved problems. The understanding and handling of many major issues are still in the process of deepening, which is beyond doubt. The understanding of things needs a process, while the understanding and grasp of socialism, which we have only been engaged in for decades, are still very limited and need to be deepened and developed in practice.

Adhering to Marxism and socialism requires a viewpoint of development. We must focus on the practical problems of China's reform, opening up and modernization drive, take what we are doing as the center, focus on the application of Marxist theory, focus on theoretical thinking on practical problems, and focus on new practices and new developments. As we have said, there is no universally applicable development path and mode in the world, nor is there a fixed development path and mode. The practical and theoretical achievements we have made in the past can help us better face and solve problems in our progress, but they cannot be grounds for complacency or a burden for us to continue our progress. The more our cause advances and develops, the more new situations and problems we will face, the more risks and challenges we will face, and the more unpredictable things we will face. We must strengthen the sense of hardship and prepare for danger in times of peace. Emancipating the mind, seeking truth from facts and keeping pace with the times are the living soul of Marxism and the fundamental ideological weapon for us to adapt to the new situation, understand new things and complete new tasks. All Party members and leading cadres at all levels must first adhere to the

Marxist viewpoint of development, adhere to the fact that practice is the only criterion for testing truth, give full play to historical initiative and creativity, clearly understand the changes and invariability of the world, national conditions and the Party's situation, and always have the spirit of opening up the mountain and bridging the river, forge ahead with determination, boldly explore, dare and be good at analyzing and answering the urgent problems in real life and people's thoughts, continuously deepen reform and opening up, continuously discover, create and advance, and continuously promote theoretical innovation, practical innovation and system innovation.

Fourth, our party has always adhered to the lofty ideals of communism. Communists, especially leading cadres, should be staunch believers and faithful practitioners of the lofty ideals of communism and the common ideals of socialism with Chinese characteristics. The belief in Marxism, socialism and communism is the political soul of the communists and the spiritual prop of the communists to withstand any test. The party constitution clearly stipulates that the highest ideal and ultimate goal of the party is to realize communism. At the same time, the party constitution clearly stipulates that the communist ideal pursued by the Chinese communists can only be realized on the basis of the full development and highly developed socialist society. It is unrealistic to expect to enter communism in one or two strokes. Comrade Deng Xiaoping said that the consolidation and development of the socialist system still needs a very long historical period and requires our generations, more than a dozen generations and even dozens of generations to make unremitting efforts. Dozens of generations, how long it is! From Kong Old Master Q to now, there are only 70 generations. This way of looking at the problem fully demonstrates our Chinese communists' political soberness. We must realize that our current efforts and the sustained efforts of many generations in the future are all moving towards the ultimate goal of communism. At the same time, we must realize that the realization of communism is a very long historical process, and we must base our efforts on the Party's objective at this stage and push forward our cause on the ground. If we lose the lofty goals of our communists, we will lose our direction and become utilitarianism and pragmatism. Socialism with Chinese characteristics is the unity of the Party's highest and basic programs. The basic program of socialism with Chinese characteristics, in a word, is to build a prosperous, democratic, civilized and harmonious socialist modern country. This is not only based on China's basic national conditions, which are in the primary stage of socialism for a long time to come, but also does not depart from the Party's highest ideal. We must not only firmly believe in taking the road of socialism with Chinese characteristics, but also embrace the lofty ideals of communism, and unswervingly implement the Party's basic line and program in the primary stage of socialism and do a good job in every work at present.

Revolutionary ideal is higher than heaven. Without lofty ideals, they are not qualified communists. Leaving real work to talk about lofty ideals is not a qualified communist. In the more than 90 years of our party's history, generations of communists have sacrificed their lives to pursue national independence and people's liberation, relying on a belief and an ideal. Although they also know that the ideals they pursue will not be realized in their own hands, they firmly believe that as long as generations continue to work for them and generations make sacrifices for them, the lofty ideals will certainly be realized. The so-called "beheading does not matter, as long as socialism is true." Today, there is an objective standard for judging whether a communist party member or a leading cadre has lofty communist ideals. It depends on whether he can adhere to the fundamental purpose of serving the people wholeheartedly, whether he can endure hardship before and enjoy the rest, whether he can work hard and be honest in performing his duties, whether he can go all out to fight for his ideals, struggle and give all his energy and even his life. All perplexed and hesitant views, all thoughts of having fun in a timely manner, all acts of coveting personal gain, and all styles of doing nothing are totally incompatible with this. Some people think that communism is out of reach, even that it is out of sight, out of sight and illusory. This involves the question of whether the world outlook is materialistic or idealistic. The reason why some of our comrades have dim ideals and wavered in their beliefs is that the viewpoint of historical materialism is not firm. We should educate and guide the majority of Party members and cadres to unite the fulfillment of the common ideal of socialism with Chinese characteristics with the determination of the lofty ideal of communism, so as to be devout and persistent, faithful and profound. With firm ideals and beliefs, one can stand tall, broaden one's horizons and broaden one's mind, so that one can adhere to the correct political direction, not be arrogant or impatient in victory and prosperity, not be depressed or wavered in difficulties and adversities, stand up to various risks and difficulties, consciously resist the erosion of various decadent ideas, and maintain the true political qualities of communists.

Facts have repeatedly told us that Marx and Engels' analysis of the basic contradictions in capitalist society is not out of date, nor is their historical materialism view that capitalism must die out and socialism must win. This is an irreversible general trend in social and historical development, but the road is tortuous. The final demise of capitalism and the final victory of socialism will certainly be a long historical process. We should have a deep understanding of the self-regulation ability of capitalist society, fully estimate the objective reality of the long-term dominance of western developed countries in economic, scientific, technological and military aspects, and earnestly prepare for the long-term cooperation and struggle between the two social systems. In a long period of time, socialism in the primary stage must also have long-term cooperation and struggle with capitalism with more developed productive forces. It must also earnestly learn from and draw lessons from the beneficial civilization achievements created by capitalism. It must even face the reality that people use the advantages of western developed countries to compare and criticize the shortcomings in China's socialist development. We must have strong strategic determination, resolutely resist all kinds of erroneous ideas of abandoning socialism, and consciously correct erroneous ideas beyond the stage. The most important thing is to concentrate on running our own affairs well, continuously strengthen our comprehensive national strength, continuously improve the life of our people, continuously build socialism with superiority over capitalism, and continuously lay a more solid foundation for us to win initiative, advantage and future.

Through the above analysis, we can realize more deeply that the road problem is the first issue that concerns the success or failure of the party's cause, and the road is the life of the party. Comrade Mao Zedong pointed out: "The revolutionary party is the guide of the masses. No revolutionary party led the wrong way in the revolution and the revolution did not fail." In all historical periods of revolution, construction and reform, our party has persisted in proceeding from China's national conditions and has explored and formed a new democratic revolutionary road, a socialist transformation and socialist construction road, and a socialist road with Chinese characteristics that are in line with China's actual conditions. This spirit of independent exploration and this firm determination to stick to its own path are the essence of our party's continuous awakening from setbacks and its continuous progress from victory to victory. Lu Xun has a famous saying: in fact, there is no road on the ground, when there are too many people walking, it becomes a road. Socialism with Chinese characteristics is the dialectical unity of the theoretical logic of scientific socialism and the historical logic of China's social development. It is scientific socialism rooted in China, reflects the wishes of the Chinese people, and meets the requirements of China and the development and progress of the times. It is the only way to build a well-off society in an all-round way, accelerate the socialist modernization and realize the great rejuvenation of the Chinese nation. As long as we persist in taking our own road independently and unswervingly adhere to and develop socialism with Chinese characteristics, we will surely be able to build a well-off society in an all-round way in the 100 years since the founding of the Communist Party of China and a prosperous, democratic, civilized and harmonious socialist modern country in the 100 years since the founding of New China.[4]

Remarks by Vice President Mike Pence on the Administration's Policy toward China

Hudson Institute
October 4, 2018

Thank you, Ken, for that kind introduction. To the Members of the Board of Trustees, to Dr. Michael Pillsbury, to our distinguished guests, and to all of you who, true to your mission, "think about the future in unconventional ways"—it's an honor to be back at the Hudson Institute.

For more than half a century, this Institute has dedicated itself to "advancing global security, prosperity, and freedom." And while Hudson's hometowns have changed over the years, one thing has held constant: You have always advanced that vital truth, that American leadership lights the way.

And today, I bring greetings from a champion of American leadership, at home and abroad—the 45th President of the United States of America, President Donald Trump.

From early in this administration, President Trump has made our relationship with China and President Xi a priority. On April 6th of last year, President Trump welcomed President Xi to Mar-a-Lago. On November 8th of last year, President Trump traveled to Beijing, where China's leader welcomed him warmly.

Over the course of the past two years, our President has forged a strong personal relationship with the president of the People's Republic of China, and they've worked closely on issues of common interest, most importantly the denuclearization of the Korean Peninsula.

But I come before you today because the American people deserve to know...as we speak, Beijing is employing a whole-of-government approach, using political, economic, and military tools, as well as propaganda, to advance its influence and benefit its interests in the United States.

China is also applying this power in more proactive ways than ever before, to exert influence and interfere in the domestic policy and politics of our country.

Under our administration, we've taken decisive action to respond to China with American leadership, applying the principles, and the policies, long advocated in these halls.

In the "National Security Strategy" that President Trump released last December, he described a new era of "great power competition." Foreign nations have begun to "reassert their influence regionally and globally," and they are "contesting [America's] geopolitical advantages and trying to change the international order in their favor."

In this strategy, President Trump made clear that the United States of America has adopted a new approach to China. We seek a relationship grounded in fairness, reciprocity, and respect for sovereignty, and we have taken strong and swift action to achieve that goal.

As the President said last year on his visit to China, "we have an opportunity to strengthen the relationship between our two countries and improve the lives of our citizens." Our vision of the future is built on the best parts of our past, when America and China reached out to one another in a spirit of openness and friendship.

When our young nation went searching in the wake of the Revolutionary War for new markets for our exports, the Chinese people welcomed American traders laden with ginseng and fur.

When China suffered through indignities and exploitation during her so-called "Century of Humiliation," America refused to join in, and advocated the "Open Door" policy, so that we could have freer trade with China, and preserve their sovereignty.

When American missionaries brought the good news to China's shores, they were moved by the rich culture of an ancient but vibrant people, and not only did they spread faith; they also founded some of China's first and finest universities.

When the Second World War arose, we stood together as allies in the fight against imperialism. And in that war's aftermath, America ensured that China became a charter member of the United Nations, and a great shaper of the post-war world.

But soon after it took power in 1949, the Chinese Communist Party began to pursue authoritarian expansionism. Only five years after our nations had fought together, we fought each other, on the mountains and in the valleys of the Korean Peninsula. My own father saw combat on those frontlines of freedom.

Not even the brutal Korean War could diminish our mutual desire to restore the ties that for so long bound us together. China's estrangement from the United States ended in 1972, and soon after, we re-established diplomatic relations, began to open our economies to one another, and American universities began training a new generation of Chinese engineers, business leaders, scholars, and officials.

After the fall of the Soviet Union, we assumed that a free China was inevitable. Heady with optimism, at the turn of the 21st Century, America agreed to give Beijing open access to our economy, and bring China into the World Trade Organization.

Previous administrations made this choice in the hope that freedom in China would expand in all forms—not just economically, but politically, with a newfound respect for classical liberal principles, private property, religious freedom, and the entire family of human rights. But that hope has gone unfulfilled.

The dream of freedom remains distant for the Chinese people. And while Beijing still pays lip service to "reform and opening," Deng Xiaoping's famous policy now rings hollow.

Over the past 17 years, China's GDP has grown nine-fold; it has become the second-largest economy in the world. Much of this success was driven by American investment in China. And the Chinese Communist Party has also used an arsenal of policies inconsistent with free and fair trade, including tariffs, quotas, currency manipulation, forced technology transfer, intellectual property theft, and industrial subsidies doled out like candy, to name a few. These policies have built Beijing's manufacturing base, at the expense of its competitors—especially America.

China's actions have contributed to a trade deficit with the United States that last year ran to $375 billion—nearly half of our global trade deficit. As President Trump said just this week, "we rebuilt China" over the last 25 years.

Now, through the "Made in China 2025" plan, the Communist Party has set its sights on controlling 90 percent of the world's most advanced industries, including robotics, biotechnology, and artificial intelligence. To win the commanding heights of the 21st century economy, Beijing has directed its bureaucrats and businesses to obtain American intellectual property—the foundation of our economic leadership—by any means necessary.

Beijing now requires many American businesses to hand over their trade secrets as the cost of doing business in China. It also coordinates and sponsors the acquisition of American firms to gain ownership of their creations. Worst of all, Chinese security agencies have masterminded the wholesale theft of American technology—including cutting-edge military blueprints. And using that stolen technology, the Chinese Communist Party is turning plowshares into swords on a massive scale.

China now spends as much on its military as the rest of Asia combined, and Beijing has prioritized capabilities to erode America's military advantages—on land, at sea, in the air, and in space. China wants nothing less than to push the United States of America from the Western Pacific and attempt to prevent us from coming to the aid of our allies.

Beijing is also using its power like never before. Chinese ships routinely patrol around the Senkaku Islands, which are administered by Japan. And while China's leader stood in the Rose Garden of the White House in 2015 and said that his country had "no intention to militarize the South China Sea," today, Beijing has deployed advanced anti-ship and anti-air missiles atop an archipelago of military bases constructed on artificial islands.

China's aggression was on display this week, when a Chinese naval vessel came within 45 yards of the USS Decatur as it conducted freedom-of-navigation operations in the South China Sea, forcing our ship to quickly maneuver to avoid collision. Despite such reckless harassment, the United States Navy will continue to fly, sail, and operate wherever international law allows and our national interests demand. We will not be intimidated; we will not stand down.

America had hoped that economic liberalization would bring China into greater partnership with us and with the world. Instead, China has chosen economic aggression, which has in turn emboldened its growing military.

Nor, as we hoped, has Beijing moved toward greater freedom for its people. For a time, Beijing inched toward greater liberty and respect for human rights, but in recent years, it has taken a sharp U-turn toward control and oppression.

Today, China has built an unparalleled surveillance state, and it's growing more expansive and intrusive—often with the help of U.S. technology. The "Great Firewall of China" likewise grows higher, drastically restricting the free flow of information to the Chinese people. And by 2020, China's rulers aim to implement an Orwellian system premised on controlling virtually every facet of human life—the so-called "social credit score." In the words of that program's official blueprint, it will "allow the trustworthy to roam everywhere under heaven, while making it hard for the discredited to take a single step."

And when it comes to religious freedom, a new wave of persecution is crashing down on Chinese Christians, Buddhists, and Muslims.

Last month, Beijing shut down one of China's largest underground churches. Across the country, authorities are tearing down crosses, burning bibles, and imprisoning believers. And Beijing has now reached a deal with the Vatican that gives the avowedly atheist Communist Party a direct role in appointing Catholic bishops. For China's Christians, these are desperate times.

Beijing is also cracking down on Buddhism. Over the past decade, more than 150 Tibetan Buddhist monks have lit themselves on fire to protest China's repression of their beliefs and culture. And in Xinjiang, the Communist Party has imprisoned as many as one million Muslim Uyghurs in government camps where they endure around-the-clock brainwashing. Survivors of the camps have described their experiences as a deliberate attempt by Beijing to strangle Uyghur culture and stamp out the Muslim faith.

But as history attests, a country that oppresses its own people rarely stops there. Beijing also aims to extend its reach across the wider world. As Hudson's own Dr. Michael Pillsbury has said, "China has opposed the actions and goals of the U.S. government. Indeed, China is building its own relationships with America's allies and enemies that contradict any peaceful or productive intentions of Beijing."

China uses so-called "debt diplomacy" to expand its influence. Today, that country is offering hundreds of billions of dollars in infrastructure loans to governments from Asia to Africa to Europe to even Latin America. Yet the terms of those loans are opaque at best, and the benefits flow overwhelmingly to Beijing.

Just ask Sri Lanka, which took on massive debt to let Chinese state companies build a port with questionable commercial value. Two years ago, that country could no longer afford its payments—so Beijing pressured Sri Lanka to deliver the new port directly into Chinese hands. It may soon become a forward military base for China's growing blue-water navy.

Within our own hemisphere, Beijing has extended a lifeline to the corrupt and incompetent Maduro regime in Venezuela, pledging $5 billion in questionable loans that can be repaid with oil. China is also that country's single largest creditor, saddling the Venezuelan people with more than $50 billion in debt. Beijing is also corrupting some nations' politics by providing direct support to parties and candidates who promise to accommodate China's strategic objectives.

And since last year, the Chinese Communist Party has convinced three Latin American nations to sever ties with Taipei and recognize Beijing. These actions threaten the stability of the Taiwan Strait—and the United States of America condemns these actions. And while our administration will continue to respect our One China Policy, as reflected in the three joint communiqués and the Taiwan Relations Act, America will always believe Taiwan's embrace of democracy shows a better path for all the Chinese people.

These are only a few of the ways that China has sought to advance its strategic interests across the world, with growing intensity and sophistication. Yet previous administrations all but ignored China's actions—and in many cases, they abetted them. But those days are over.

Under President Trump's leadership, the United States of America has been defending our interests with renewed American strength.

We've been making the strongest military in the history of the world stronger still. Earlier this year, the President signed into law the largest increase in our national defense since the days of Ronald Reagan—$716 billion to extend our military dominance in every domain.

We're modernizing our nuclear arsenal, we're fielding and developing new cutting-edge fighters and bombers, we're building a new generation of aircraft carriers and warships, and we're investing as never before in our armed forces. This includes initiating the process to establish the United States Space Force to ensure our continued dominance in space, and authorizing increased capability in the cyber world to build deterrence against our adversaries.

And at President Trump's direction, we're also implementing tariffs on $250 billion in Chinese goods, with the highest tariffs specifically targeting the advanced industries that Beijing is trying to capture and control. And the President has also made clear that we'll levy even more tariffs, with the possibility of substantially more than doubling that number, unless a fair and reciprocal deal is made.

Our actions have had a major impact. China's largest stock exchange fell by 25 percent in the first nine months of this year, in large part because our administration has stood up to Beijing's trade practices.

As President Trump has made clear, we don't want China's markets to suffer. In fact, we want them to thrive. But the United

States wants Beijing to pursue trade policies that are free, fair, and reciprocal.

Sadly, China's rulers have refused to take that path—so far. The American people deserve to know that, in response to the strong stand that President Trump has taken, Beijing is pursuing a comprehensive and coordinated campaign to undermine support for the President, our agenda, and our nation's most cherished ideals.

I want to tell you today what we know about China's actions—some of which we've gleaned from intelligence assessments, some of which are publicly available. But all of which is fact.

As I said before, Beijing is employing a whole-of-government approach to advance its influence and benefit its interests. It's employing this power in more proactive and coercive ways to interfere in the domestic policies and politics of the United States.

The Chinese Communist Party is rewarding or coercing American businesses, movie studios, universities, think tanks, scholars, journalists, and local, state, and federal officials.

Worst of all, China has initiated an unprecedented effort to influence American public opinion, the 2018 elections, and the environment leading into the 2020 presidential elections.

To put it bluntly, President Trump's leadership is working; and China wants a different American President.

China is meddling in America's democracy. As President Trump said just last week, we have "found that China has been attempting to interfere in our upcoming 2018 [midterm] election[s]."

Our intelligence community says that "China is targeting U.S. state and local governments and officials to exploit any divisions between federal and local levels on policy. It's using wedge issues, like trade tariffs, to advance Beijing's political influence."

In June, Beijing circulated a sensitive document, entitled "Propaganda and Censorship Notice," that laid out its strategy. It states that China must "strike accurately and carefully, splitting apart different domestic groups" in the United States.

To that end, Beijing has mobilized covert actors, front groups, and propaganda outlets to shift Americans' perception of Chinese policies. As a senior career member of our intelligence community recently told me, what the Russians are doing pales in comparison to what China is doing across this country.

Senior Chinese officials have also tried to influence business leaders to condemn our trade actions, leveraging their desire to maintain their operations in China. In one recent example, they threatened to deny a business license for a major U.S. corporation if it refused to speak out against our administration's policies.

And when it comes to influencing the midterms, you need only look at Beijing's tariffs in response to ours. They specifically targeted industries and states that would play an important role in the 2018 election. By one estimate, more than 80 percent of U.S. counties targeted by China voted for President Trump in 2016; now China wants to turn these voters against our administration.

And China is also directly appealing to the American voter. Last week, the Chinese government paid to have a multipage supplement inserted into the Des Moines Register—the paper of record in the home state of our Ambassador to China, and a pivotal state in 2018. The supplement, designed to look like news articles, cast our trade policies as reckless and harmful to Iowans.

Fortunately, Americans aren't buying it. For example: American farmers are standing with this President and are seeing real results from the strong stands that he's taken, including this week's U.S.-Mexico-Canada Agreement, where we've substantially opened North American markets to U.S. products—a great win for American farmers and manufacturers.

But China's actions aren't focused solely on influencing our policies and politics. Beijing is also taking steps to exploit its economic leverage, and the allure of China's large domestic market, to advance its influence over American corporations.

Beijing now requires American joint ventures that operate in China to establish "party organizations" within their company, giving the Communist Party a voice—and perhaps a veto—in hiring and investment decisions.

Chinese authorities have also threatened U.S. companies that depict Taiwan as a distinct geographic entity, or that stray from Chinese policy on Tibet. Beijing compelled Delta Airlines to publicly apologize for not calling Taiwan a "province of China" on its website. It also pressured Marriott to fire a U.S. employee who liked a tweet about Tibet.

Beijing routinely demands that Hollywood portray China in a strictly positive light, and it punishes studios and producers that don't. Beijing's censors are quick to edit or outlaw movies that criticize China, even in minor ways. "World War Z" had to cut the script's mention of a virus originating in China. "Red Dawn" was digitally edited to make the villains North Korean, not Chinese.

Beyond business, the Chinese Communist Party is spending billions of dollars on propaganda outlets in the United States, as well as other countries.

China Radio International now broadcasts Beijing-friendly programming on over 30 U.S. outlets, many in major American cities. The China Global Television Network reaches more than 75 million Americans—and it gets its marching orders directly from its Communist Party masters. As China's top leader put it during a visit to the network's headquarters, "The media run by the Party and the government are propaganda fronts and must have the Party as their surname."

That's why, last month, the Department of Justice ordered that network to register as a foreign agent.

The Communist Party has also threatened and detained the Chinese family members of American journalists who pry too deep. And it has blocked the websites of U.S. media organizations and made it harder for our journalists to get visas. This happened after the New York Times published investigative reports about the wealth of some of China's leaders.

But the media isn't the only place where the Chinese Communist Party seeks to foster a culture of censorship. The same is true of academia.

Look no further than the Chinese Students and Scholars Associations, of which there are more than 150 branches across American campuses. These groups help organize social events for some of the more than 430,000 Chinese nationals studying in the United States; they also alert Chinese consulates and embassies when Chinese students, and American schools, stray from the Communist Party line.

At the University of Maryland, a Chinese student recently spoke at her graduation ceremony of what she called the "fresh air of free speech" in America. The Communist Party's official newspaper swiftly chastised her, she became the victim of a firestorm of criticism on China's tightly-controlled social media, and her family back home was harassed. As for the university itself, its exchange program with China—one of the nation's most extensive—suddenly turned from a flood to a trickle.

China exerts academic pressure in other ways, too. Beijing provides generous funding to universities, think tanks, and scholars, with the understanding that they will avoid ideas that the Communist Party finds dangerous or offensive. China experts in particular know that their visas will be delayed or denied if their research contradicts Beijing's talking points.

And even scholars and groups who avoid Chinese funding are targeted by that country, as the Hudson Institute found out firsthand. After you offered to host a speaker Beijing didn't like, your website suffered a major cyberattack, originating from Shanghai. You know better than most that the Chinese Communist Party is trying to undermine academic freedom and the freedom of speech in America today.

These and other actions, taken as a whole, constitute an intensifying effort to shift American public opinion and public policy away from the America First leadership of President Donald Trump. But our message to China's rulers is this: This President will not back down—and the American people will not be swayed. We will continue to stand strong for our security and our economy, even as we hope for improved relations with Beijing.

Our administration will continue to act decisively to protect American interests, American jobs, and American security.

As we rebuild our military, we will continue to assert American interests across the Indo-Pacific.

As we respond to China's trade practices, we will continue to demand an economic relationship with China that is free and fair and reciprocal, demanding that Beijing break down its trade barriers, fulfill its trade obligations, and fully open its economy, just as we have opened ours.

We will continue to take action until Beijing ends the theft of American intellectual property, and stops the predatory practice of forced technology transfer....

And to advance our vision of a free and open Indo-Pacific, we're building new and stronger bonds with nations that share our values, across the region—from India to Samoa. Our relationships will flow from a spirit of respect, built on partnership, not domination.

We're forging new trade deals, on a bilateral basis, just as last week, President Trump signed an improved trade deal with South Korea, and we will soon begin negotiating a historic bilateral free-trade deal with Japan.

And we're streamlining international development and finance programs, giving foreign nations a just and transparent alternative to China's debt-trap diplomacy. To that end, President Trump will sign the BUILD Act into law in the days ahead.

And next month, it will be my privilege to represent the United States in Singapore and Papua New Guinea, at ASEAN and APEC. There, we will unveil new measures and programs to support a free and open Indo-Pacific—and on behalf of the President, I will deliver the message that America's commitment to the Indo-Pacific has never been stronger.

To protect our interests here at home, we've strengthened CFIUS—the Committee on Foreign Investment in the United States—heightening our scrutiny of Chinese investment in America, to protect our national security from Beijing's predatory actions.

And when it comes to Beijing's malign influence and interference in American politics and policy, we will continue to expose it, no matter the form it takes. And we will work with leaders at every level of society to defend our national interests and most cherished ideals. The American people will play the decisive role—and in fact, they already are.

As we gather here, a new consensus is rising across America. More business leaders are thinking beyond the next quarter, and thinking twice before diving into the Chinese market if it means turning over their intellectual property or abetting Beijing's oppression. But more must follow suit. For example, Google should immediately end development of the "Dragonfly" app that will strengthen Communist Party censorship and compromise the privacy of Chinese customers.

More journalists are reporting the truth without fear or favor, and digging deep to find where China is interfering in our society, and why—and we hope that more American, and global, news organizations will join in this effort.

More scholars are speaking out forcefully and defending academic freedom, and more universities and think tanks are mustering the courage to turn away Beijing's easy money, recognizing that every dollar comes with a corresponding demand. We're confident that more will join their ranks.

And across the nation, the American people are growing in vigilance, with a newfound appreciation for our administration's actions to reset America's economic and strategic relationship with China, to finally put America First.

And under President Trump's leadership, America will stay the course. China should know that the American people and their elected representatives in both parties are resolved.

As our National Security Strategy states: "Competition does not always mean hostility." As President Trump has made clear, we want a constructive relationship with Beijing, where our prosperity and security grow together, not apart. While Beijing has been moving further away from this vision, China's rulers can still change course, and return to the spirit of "reform and opening" and greater freedom. The American people want nothing more; the Chinese people deserve nothing less.

The great Chinese storyteller Lu Xun often lamented that his country "has either looked down at foreigners as brutes, or up to them as saints, but never as equals." Today, America is reaching out our hand to China; we hope that Beijing will soon reach back—with deeds, not words, and with renewed respect for America. But we will not relent until our relationship with China is grounded in fairness, reciprocity, and respect for sovereignty.

There is an ancient Chinese proverb that tells us that "men see only the present, but heaven sees the future." As we go forward, let us pursue a future of peace and prosperity with resolve and faith. Faith in President Trump's leadership, and the relationship that he has forged with China's president. Faith in the enduring friendship between the American people and the Chinese people. Faith that heaven sees the future—and by God's grace, America and China will meet that future together.

Thank you. God bless you. And God bless the United States of America.[5]

Notes

Chapter One: America's Greatest Challenge

1. https://www.whitehouse.gov/briefings-statements/remarks-president-trump-72nd-session-united-nations-general-assembly/
2. https://www.whitehouse.gov/briefings-statements/the-inaugural-address/
3. Xi Jinping, *The Governance of China* Volume II "Complete a Moderately Prosperous Society and Realize the Chinese Dream"
4. http://time.com/4912055/donald-trump-phoenix-arizona-transcript/
5. Xi Jinping *The Governance of China* Volume II "Today We Must Succeed in a New 'Long March'"
6. Mühlhahn *Making China Modern*
7. https://www.cnn.com/2017/08/01/asia/xi-jinping-military/index.html
8. https://www.census.gov/foreign-trade/balance/c5700.html#2015
9. https://www.reuters.com/article/us-johnson-china/everything-you-need-to-know-about-the-south-china-sea-conflict-in-under-five-minutes-idUSKBN0OQ03620150610
10. https://sites.tufts.edu/lawofthesea/chapter-ten/
11. https://obamawhitehouse.archives.gov/the-press-office/2015/09/25/remarks-president-obama-and-president-xi-peoples-republic-china-joint

Chapter Two: The Real Modern China

1. https://www.whitehouse.gov/briefings-statements/remarks-president-trump-people-poland/
2. http://translate.sogoucdn.com/pcvtsnapshot?from=auto&to=zh-CHS&tfr=translatepc&url=http%3A%2F%2Fwww.qstheory.cn%2Fdukan%2Fqs%2F2019-03%2F31%2Fc_1124302776.htm&domainType=sogou
3. https://www.newyorker.com/news/daily-comment/the-cost-of-the-cultural-revolution-fifty-years-later
4. https://www.history.com/news/what-was-the-cultural-revolution
5. https://www.pbs.org/wgbh/commandingheights/shared/minitext/prof_dengxiaoping.html
6. https://www.nytimes.com/2017/10/25/world/asia/china-xi-jinping-titles-chairman.html
7. http://translate.sogoucdn.com/pcvtsnapshot?from=auto&to=zh-CHS&tfr=translatepc&url=http%253A%252F%252Fwww.qstheory.cn%252Fdukan%252Fqs%252F2019-03%252F31%252Fc_1124302776.htm&domainType=sogou
8. http://www.xinhuanet.com/english/2017-10/17/c_136686770.htm
9. http://www.xinhuanet.com/english/2017-10/17/c_136686770.htm

10. https://www.nytimes.com/2013/06/05/opinion/global/xi-jinpings-chinese-dream.html
11. Economy, Elizabeth *The Third Revolution*
12. http://www.chinadaily.com.cn/china/19thcpcnationalcongress/2017-11/04/content_34115212.htm

Chapter Three: Trade & Theft

1. https://www.whitehouse.gov/briefings-statements/president-donald-j-trumps-state-union-address-2/
2. Xi Jinping *The Governance of China* Volume II "Build China into a World Leader in Science and Technology"
3. https://www.forbes.com/sites/jacknasher/2019/05/27/trumps-gamble-how-hardball-negotiation-tactics-can-win-the-us-china-trade-war/#6454f69d340d
4. https://www.whitehouse.gov/wp-content/uploads/2018/06/FINAL-China-Technology-Report-6.18.18-PDF.pdf
5. https://asia.nikkei.com/Economy/Trade-war/China-is-trying-to-steal-our-future-Navarro
6. https://abcnews.go.com/Politics/10-times-trump-attacked-china-trade-relations-us/story?id=46572567
7. http://www.ipcommission.org/report/IP_Commission_Report_Update_2017.pdf
8. https://www.bea.gov/data/gdp/gdp-state
9. https://www.whitehouse.gov/wp-content/uploads/2017/12/NSS-Final-12-18-2017-0905.pdf
10. https://hbr.org/2016/12/why-leaders-are-still-so-hesitant-to-invest-in-new-business-models
11. https://www.cnbc.com/2019/02/28/1-in-5-companies-say-china-stole-their-ip-within-the-last-year-cnbc.html
12. https://www.wsj.com/articles/how-china-systematically-pries-technology-from-u-s-companies-1537972066
13. https://www.justice.gov/opa/pr/prc-state-owned-company-taiwan-company-and-three-individuals-charged-economic-espionage
14. https://www.wsj.com/articles/how-china-systematically-pries-technology-from-u-s-companies-1537972066
15. https://www.wsj.com/articles/how-china-systematically-pries-technology-from-u-s-companies-1537972066
16. https://www.bloomberg.com/features/2016-stealing-dupont-white/
17. https://www.usatoday.com/story/news/nation/2014/05/19/us-accuses-china-of-cyber-espionage/9273019/
18. https://www.worldsteel.org/internet-2017/steel-by-topic/statistics/steel-data-viewer/P1_crude_steel_total/CHN/USA
19. https://www.bloomberg.com/news/articles/2019-02-28/from-bounty-payments-to-espionage-u-s-alleges-chinese-ip-theft
20. https://money.cnn.com/2018/01/25/technology/china-us-sinovel-theft-conviction/index.html

21. https://www.axios.com/doj-indictment-reveals-threat-of-chinese-ip-theft-to-us-energy-innovation-b2ca3e28-bf2f-484e-b3e7-a874b1652f33.html
22. https://www.wsj.com/articles/how-china-systematically-pries-technology-from-u-s-companies-1537972066
23. https://www.whitehouse.gov/wp-content/uploads/2018/06/FINAL-China-Technology-Report-6.18.18-PDF.pdf
24. https://www.wsj.com/articles/how-china-systematically-pries-technology-from-u-s-companies-1537972066
25. https://www.whitehouse.gov/wp-content/uploads/2018/06/FINAL-China-Technology-Report-6.18.18-PDF.pdf
26. https://www.npr.org/2019/04/12/711779130/as-china-hacked-u-s-businesses-turned-a-blind-eye
27. https://www.scmp.com/magazines/post-magazine/long-reads/article/2170132/how-chinas-rampant-intellectual-property-theft
28. https://www.theatlantic.com/ideas/archive/2018/06/normalizing-trade-relations-with-china-was-a-mistake/562403/
29. http://www2.itif.org/2015-false-promises-china.pdf
30. https://www.justice.gov/archive/opa/pr/2006/September/06_opa_657.html
31. https://www.reuters.com/article/us-usa-china-obama-idUSKBN0JP20120141211
32. https://2009-2017.state.gov/r/pa/prs/ps/2013/07/211861.htm
33. https://obamawhitehouse.archives.gov/the-press-office/2015/09/25/remarks-president-obama-and-president-xi-peoples-republic-china-joint
34. https://webcache.googleusercontent.com/search?q=cache:R7lbLbqc4CwJ:https://www.bloomberg.com/news/articles/2015-11-18/no-sign-china-has-stopped-hacking-u-s-companies-official-says+&cd=1&hl=en&ct=clnk&gl=us
35. https://www.armed-services.senate.gov/imo/media/doc/Rogers_04-05-16.pdf
36. https://www.latimes.com/politics/la-na-pol-china-economic-espionage-20181116-story.html
37. https://piie.com/blogs/trade-investment-policy-watch/us-china-trade-disputes-wto-usually-sides-united-states
38. https://piie.com/blogs/trade-investment-policy-watch/us-china-trade-disputes-wto-usually-sides-united-states
39. http://www2.itif.org/2015-false-promises-china.pdf
40. https://ustr.gov/sites/default/files/2018-USTR-Report-to-Congress-on-China%27s-WTO-Compliance.pdf
41. https://ustr.gov/sites/default/files/2019_Special_301_Report.pdf
42. https://www.bloomberg.com/news/articles/2018-09-07/trump-advisers-said-to-weigh-hacking-sanctions-on-china-in-trade
43. https://www.wsj.com/articles/u-s-deploys-new-tactics-to-curb-chinas-intellectual-property-theft-1542027624
44. https://www.treasury.gov/press-center/press-releases/Pages/jl23331.aspx
45. http://www.usatoday.com/story/news/politics/2016/05/11/obama-signs-trade-secrets-bill-allowing-companies-sue/84244258/

46. http://www.aei.org/press/an-american-strategy-for-cyberspace-advancing-freedom-security-and-prosperity/
47. https://www.whitehouse.gov/wp-content/uploads/2018/06/FINAL-China-Technology-Report-6.18.18-PDF.pdf
48. https://www.theglobalipcenter.com/why-is-ip-important/
49. http://dev.theglobalipcenter.com/wp-content/uploads/reports/documents/IP_Jobs_Study_Exec_Summary.pdf

Chapter Four: Big Data, AI, & E-Tyranny

1. https://www.whitehouse.gov/briefings-statements/president-trump-protects-americas-cyber-infrastructure/
2. Xi Jinping *The Governance of China* Volume II "Social Governance under Socialism with Chinese Characteristics"
3. https://www.technologyreview.com/s/611815/who-needs-democracy-when-you-have-data/
4. https://www.apnews.com/4a749a4211904784826b45e812cff4ca
5. https://www.cbc.ca/news/world/china-data-for-sale-privacy-1.3927137
6. https://www.cbc.ca/news/world/china-data-for-sale-privacy-1.3927137
7. https://www.abacusnews.com/digital-life/chinese-apps-are-collecting-way-too-much-data/article/3000377
8. https://www.cnn.com/2019/05/20/politics/dhs-chinese-drone-warning/index.html
9. https://www.ft.com/content/b4193d5e-7b2b-11e9-81d2-f785092ab560
10. https://www.bloomberg.com/news/features/2019-04-18/tiktok-brings-chinese-style-censorship-to-america-s-tweens?cmpid=socialflow-twitter-business
11. https://www.theverge.com/2019/3/14/18265230/china-is-about-to-overtake-america-in-ai-research
12. https://www.forbes.com/sites/bernardmarr/2019/05/24/the-amazing-ways-chinese-face-recognition-company-megvii-face-uses-ai-and-machine-vision/#187c4d9012c3
13. https://www.statista.com/chart/17896/quantum-computing-developments/
14. https://www.npr.org/2018/10/31/662436265/china-tests-a-social-credit-score
15. https://www.businessinsider.com/china-social-credit-system-punishments-and-rewards-explained-2018-4
16. https://www.nytimes.com/interactive/2019/04/04/world/asia/xinjiang-china-surveillance-prison.html?emc=edit_NN_p_20190404&nl=morning-briefing&nlid=83316484ion%25253DlongRead§ion=longRead&te=1&auth=login-smartlock
17. https://www.forbes.com/sites/kateoflahertyuk/2019/02/18/china-facial-recognition-database-leak-sparks-fears-over-mass-data-collection/#5e1aa5ffb408
18. https://uk.reuters.com/article/uk-china-rights-xinjiang/big-data-predictions-spur-detentions-in-chinas-xinjiang-human-rights-watch-idUKKCN1GB0CZ

19. https://uk.reuters.com/article/uk-china-rights-xinjiang/big-data-predictions-spur-detentions-in-chinas-xinjiang-human-rights-watch-idUKKCN1GB0CZ

Chapter Five: Crushing Dissent

1. https://www.whitehouse.gov/briefings-statements/remarks-president-trump-people-poland/
2. Xi Jinping *The Governance of China* Volume II "Improve the Work of the United Front"
3. https://www.justice.gov/eoir/page/file/1022971/download
4. https://www.nytimes.com/2019/07/30/world/asia/china-xinjiang.html
5. Freedom House Special Report: *The Battle for China's Spirit*
6. https://www.cfr.org/backgrounder/christianity-china
7. http://tech.mit.edu/V114/N27/china.27w.html
8. http://tech.mit.edu/V114/N27/china.27w.html
9. https://www.reuters.com/article/us-china-xinjiang-insight/china-says-pace-of-xinjiang-education-will-slow-but-defends-camps-idUSKCN1P007W
10. https://www.theguardian.com/world/2019/jan/13/china-christians-religious-persecution-translation-bible
11. https://www.cnn.com/2018/12/26/asia/china-christian-crackdown-christmas-intl/index.html
12. https://www.nytimes.com/2019/05/22/opinion/china-religion-human-rights.html
13. https://www.cnn.com/2018/12/26/asia/china-christian-crackdown-christmas-intl/index.html
14. http://www.xinhuanet.com/english/2018-04/03/c_137084970.htm
15. https://www.cfr.org/backgrounder/christianity-china
16. https://www.cfr.org/backgrounder/religion-china
17. https://www.cfr.org/backgrounder/religion-china
18. http://www.xinhuanet.com/english/2018-04/03/c_137084970.htm
19. https://www.nytimes.com/2018/12/25/world/asia/china-christmas-church-crackdown.html
20. https://www.cnn.com/2018/12/26/asia/china-christian-crackdown-christmas-intl/index.html
21. https://www.theguardian.com/world/2019/jan/13/china-christians-religious-persecution-translation-bible
22. https://www.theguardian.com/world/2019/jan/13/china-christians-religious-persecution-translation-bible
23. https://www.nytimes.com/2018/09/22/world/asia/china-vatican-bishops.html
24. https://www.theguardian.com/world/2019/jan/13/china-christians-religious-persecution-translation-bible
25. https://www.theguardian.com/world/2019/jan/13/china-christians-religious-persecution-translation-bible
26. https://www.lawfareblog.com/chinas-human-rights-abuses-against-uighurs-xinjiang

27. https://www.wsj.com/articles/chinas-hard-edge-the-leader-of-beijings-muslim-crackdown-gains-influence-11554655886
28. https://www.bloomberg.com/news/articles/2018-09-27/the-architect-of-china-s-muslim-camps-is-a-rising-star-under-xi
29. https://www.lawfareblog.com/chinas-human-rights-abuses-against-uighurs-xinjiang
30. https://www.lawfareblog.com/chinas-human-rights-abuses-against-uighurs-xinjiang
31. https://www.washingtonpost.com/opinions/chinas-attack-on-uighurs-isnt-counterterrorism-its-ugly-repression/2019/05/22/7bfb1d60-7ccb-11e9-a5b3-34f3edf1351e_story.html?utm_term=.bf83a1814426
32. https://www.nchrd.org/2018/07/criminal-arrests-in-xinjiang-account-for-21-of-chinas-total-in-2017/
33. https://www.theguardian.com/world/2018/jul/25/china-one-in-five-arrests-take-place-in-police-state-xinjiang
34. https://www.hrw.org/report/2018/09/09/eradicating-ideological-viruses/chinas-campaign-repression-against-xinjiangs
35. https://www.hrw.org/report/2018/09/09/eradicating-ideological-viruses/chinas-campaign-repression-against-xinjiangs
36. https://www.hrw.org/report/2018/09/09/eradicating-ideological-viruses/chinas-campaign-repression-against-xinjiangs
37. https://www.nchrd.org/2018/08/china-massive-numbers-of-uyghurs-other-ethnic-minorities-forced-into-re-education-programs/
38. https://www.foreign.senate.gov/imo/media/doc/120418_Busby_Testimony.pdf
39. http://www.xinhuanet.com/english/2019-07/13/c_138222183.htm
40. https://www.nytimes.com/2019/07/30/world/asia/china-xinjiang.html
41. Bishop, Bill *Sinocism* newsletter 4/1/2019
42. Ibid.
43. Ibid.
44. https://www.hrw.org/tag/liu-xiaobo#
45. https://www.cecc.gov/sites/chinacommission.house.gov/files/Annual%20Report%202018.pdf
46. https://www.usatoday.com/story/news/world/2018/07/10/liu-xia-wife-liu-xiaobo-late-nobel-peace-prize-winner-leaves-china/770490002/
47. https://www.cecc.gov/sites/chinacommission.house.gov/files/Annual%20Report%202018.pdf
48. https://www.nytimes.com/2018/04/09/opinion/china-oppression.html?rref=collection%252Fsectioncollection%252Fopinion
49. https://www.nytimes.com/2018/04/09/opinion/china-oppression.html?rref=collection%2Fsectioncollection%2Fopinion
50. https://www.cnn.com/2017/11/23/asia/china-lawyers-disappeared/index.html
51. https://www.washingtonpost.com/opinions/chinas-vicious-campaign-to-silence-human-rights-lawyers-deserves-us-condemnation/2017/05/10/4c39fc12-2e8b-11e7-9dec-764dc781686f_story.html?utm_term=.4a3d41bdda99

52. http://chrlawyers.hk/en/content/1100-14-july-2015-146-lawyers-law-firm-staffhuman-right-activists-have-been-detainedarrested
53. https://www.cnn.com/2017/11/23/asia/china-lawyers-disappeared/index.html
54. https://www.cnn.com/2017/11/23/asia/china-lawyers-disappeared/index.html
55. https://thediplomat.com/2018/01/michael-caster-on-chinas-forced-disappearances/
56. https://www.cnn.com/2017/11/23/asia/china-lawyers-disappeared/index.html
57. https://www.bbc.com/news/world-asia-china-47024825
58. https://www.reuters.com/article/us-china-rights/china-jailing-of-rights-lawyer-a-mockery-of-law-says-rights-group-idUSKCN1PM04C
59. https://www.bbc.com/news/world-asia-china-47024825
60. https://www.bbc.com/news/world-asia-china-47024825
61. https://www.state.gov/sentencing-of-wang-quanzhang/
62. https://www.washingtonpost.com/world/asia_pacific/us-diplomats-help-chinese-lawyers-family-stage-dramatic-escape/2017/05/08/33e64f40-33fd-11e7-ab03-aa29f656f13e_story.html?utm_term=.b39dcecaaeee
63. https://www.washingtonpost.com/opinions/chinas-vicious-campaign-to-silence-human-rights-lawyers-deserves-us-condemnation/2017/05/10/4c39fc12-2e8b-11e7-9dec-764dc781686f_story.html?utm_term=.fc187c11947d
64. https://www.washingtonpost.com/business/2019/05/22/trump-administration-considers-banning-another-major-chinese-firm/?utm_term=.0d0c3ff3462f
65. https://theintercept.com/2019/04/09/hikvision-cameras-uk-parliament/
66. https://www.nytimes.com/2019/05/21/us/politics/hikvision-trump.html
67. https://www.reuters.com/article/us-hikvision-usa/u-s-could-blacklist-chinese-surveillance-tech-firm-hikvision-nyt-idUSKCN1SS04D
68. https://www.bloomberg.com/news/articles/2019-05-22/trump-weighs-blacklisting-two-chinese-surveillance-companies
69. https://www.washingtonpost.com/opinions/global-opinions/think-twice-about-your-investment-portfolio-it-likely-undermines-human-rights-in-china/2019/04/17/a981b85a-6125-11e9-bfad-36a7eb36cb60_story.html?utm_term=.b4aed7ed88ba
70. Ibid.
71. Ibid.
72. https://www.nystrs.org/NYSTRS/media/PDF/About%20Us/equity_international.pdf
73. https://www.calstrs.com/investment-table/international-equities#C
74. https://www.washingtonpost.com/opinions/global-opinions/think-twice-about-your-investment-portfolio-it-likely-undermines-human-rights-in-china/2019/04/17/a981b85a-6125-11e9-bfad-36a7eb36cb60_story.html?utm_term=.b4aed7ed88ba
75. https://www.ft.com/content/36b4cb42-50f3-11e9-b401-8d9ef1626294
76. Ibid.

77. https://www.forbes.com/sites/jeanbaptiste/2019/07/19/confirmed-google-terminated-project-dragonfly-its-censored-chinese-search-engine/#2c2698207e84

Chapter Six: The Art of Persuasion

1. https://abcnews.go.com/Politics/read-president-trumps-full-remarks-united-nations-general/story?id=49949302
2. Xi Jinping *The Governance of China* Volume I "Cultivate and Disseminate the Core Socialist Values"
3. https://www.marxists.org/reference/archive/mao/works/1937/guerrilla-warfare/ch06.htm
4. https://www.cia.gov/library/readingroom/docs/CIA-RDP78-00915R000600210003-9.pdf
5. https://www.bbc.com/news/magazine-34932800
6. http://chinamediaproject.org/2016/03/03/39672/
7. https://www.bloomberg.com/quicktake/great-firewall-of-china
8. James Griffiths, The Great Firewall of China: How to Build and Control an Alternative Version of the Internet
9. https://chinadigitaltimes.net/2015/01/youth-league-propaganda-work-universities/
10. https://chinadigitaltimes.net/2015/01/youth-league-propaganda-work-universities/
11. https://www.uscc.gov/sites/default/files/annual_reports/2009-Report-to-Congress.pdf
12. https://www.uscc.gov/sites/default/files/annual_reports/2009-Report-to-Congress.pdf
13. https://www.uscc.gov/sites/default/files/annual_reports/2009-Report-to-Congress.pdf
14. https://www.scmp.com/news/china-insider/article/1299795/china-orders-nations-journalists-take-marxism-classes
15. http://chinamediaproject.org/2016/03/03/39672/
16. http://chinamediaproject.org/2016/03/03/39672/
17. https://www.theepochtimes.com/chinas-growing-influence-on-hollywood_2690693.html
18. https://www.scmp.com/news/china/diplomacy/article/2169837/china-quietly-opens-door-more-foreign-films
19. https://www.nytimes.com/interactive/2018/11/18/world/asia/china-movies.html
20. https://journals.sagepub.com/doi/abs/10.1177/2059436416681576
21. https://variety.com/2017/film/asia/china-box-office-expands-by-2-billion-in-2017-1202650515/
22. https://www.statista.com/statistics/252730/leading-film-markets-worldwide--gross-box-office-revenue/
23. https://www.businessinsider.com/hollywood-movies-in-china-2016-10
24. https://www.businessinsider.com/doctor-strange-popular-in-china-2016-11

25. https://www.cinemablend.com/new/Blunt-Yet-Difficult-Reason-Doctor-Strange-Ancient-One-Isn-t-Asian-126937.html
26. https://www.thewrap.com/fearing-chinese-censors-paramount-changes-world-war-z-exclusive-83316/
27. https://www.theepochtimes.com/chinas-growing-influence-on-hollywood_2690693.html
28. https://www.latimes.com/entertainment/la-et-china-red-dawn-20110316-story.html
29. https://www.businessinsider.com/zara-marriott-qantas-apologized-to-china-listing-taiwan-as-country-2018-1
30. http://www.xinhuanet.com/english/2018-01/11/c_136888952.htm
31. https://www.reuters.com/article/us-china-delta/china-cracks-down-on-foreign-companies-calling-taiwan-other-regions-countries-idUSKBN1F10RC?il=0
32. https://www.uscc.gov/sites/default/files/Research/China%2527s%2520Overseas%2520United%2520Front%2520Work%2520-%2520Background%2520and%2520Implications%2520for%2520US_final_0.pdf
33. http://ciml.250x.com/archive/lenin/english/lenin_1920_left_wing_communism-an_infantile_disorder-1940-.pdf
34. https://www.wilsoncenter.org/sites/default/files/magic_weapons.pdf
35. https://www.uscc.gov/sites/default/files/Research/China%2527s%2520Overseas%2520United%2520Front%2520Work%2520-%2520Background%2520and%2520Implications%2520for%2520US_final_0.pdf
36. https://www.wilsoncenter.org/sites/default/files/magic_weapons.pdf
37. https://www.wilsoncenter.org/sites/default/files/magic_weapons.pdf
38. http://www.chinadaily.com.cn/china/19thcpcnationalcongress/2017-11/04/content_34115212.htm
39. http://www.chinadaily.com.cn/china/19thcpcnationalcongress/2017-11/04/content_34115212.htm
40. https://www.uscc.gov/sites/default/files/Research/China%27s%20Overseas%20United%20Front%20Work%20-%20Background%20and%20Implications%20for%20US_final_0.pdf
41. https://www.nas.org/blogs/dicta/how_many_confucius_institutes_are_in_the_united_states
42. https://nas.org/storage/app/media/images/documents/NAS_outsourcedToChinaMediaPacket.pdf
43. https://www.gao.gov/products/GAO-19-278
44. https://www.ciru.rutgers.edu/academics/chinese-studies/170-credit-courses
45. https://www.economist.com/special-report/2009/10/22/a-message-from-confucius
46. https://foreignpolicy.com/2017/05/09/american-universities-are-welcoming-chinas-trojan-horse-confucius-institutes/
47. https://www.hsgac.senate.gov/imo/media/doc/PSI%20Report%20China%27s%20Impact%20on%20the%20US%20Education%20System.pdf
48. https://nas.org/storage/app/media/images/documents/NAS_outsourcedToChinaMediaPacket.pdf

49. https://www.gao.gov/products/GAO-19-278
50. https://www.gao.gov/products/GAO-19-278
51. https://www.hsgac.senate.gov/imo/media/doc/PSI%20Report%20China%27s%20Impact%20on%20the%20US%20Education%20System.pdf
52. https://www.congress.gov/115/crpt/hrpt874/CRPT-115hrpt874.pdf
53. https://www.universityworldnews.com/post.php?story=20190301140432282
54. https://researchfunding.duke.edu/new-american-cultural-centers-and-cultural-programming-people's-republic-china
55. https://www.hsgac.senate.gov/imo/media/doc/PSI%20Report%20China%27s%20Impact%20on%20the%20US%20Education%20System.pdf
56. https://researchfunding.duke.edu/new-american-cultural-centers-and-cultural-programming-people's-republic-china
57. https://www.nytimes.com/2018/12/30/world/asia/china-american-centers-culture.html
58. https://www.uscc.gov/sites/default/files/annual_reports/2009-Report-to-Congress.pdf
59. https://freebeacon.com/national-security/cia-warns-extensive-chinese-operation-infiltrate-american-institutions/
60. https://www.uscc.gov/sites/default/files/4.30.09Terrill_0.pdf
61. https://www.uscc.gov/sites/default/files/annual_reports/2009-Report-to-Congress.pd
62. http://en.cfau.edu.cn/col/col2563/index.html
63. https://www.cruz.senate.gov/?p=press_release&id=4517

Chapter Seven: The 5G Challenge

1. https://www.whitehouse.gov/briefings-statements/remarks-president-trump-united-states-5g-deployment/
2. Xi Jinping *The Governance of China* Volume II "Build China into a World Leader in Science and Technology"
3. http://nymag.com/intelligencer/2019/02/5g-is-going-to-transform-smartphones-eventually.html
4. https://www.cio.com/article/3235971/5g-connection-density-massive-iot-and-so-much-more.html
5. https://www.bloomberg.com/news/features/2019-04-18/tiktok-brings-chinese-style-censorship-to-america-s-tweens?cmpid=socialflow-twitter-business
6. https://www.rwradvisory.com/services/inteltrak/
7. https://www.presidency.ucsb.edu/documents/second-annual-message-9
8. https://www.telegraph.co.uk/politics/2019/04/28/huawei-legally-obliged-co-operate-chinese-intelligence-services/
9. https://www.reuters.com/article/us-huawei-tech-usa-pompeo/pompeo-says-huawei-ceo-lying-over-ties-to-china-government-cnbc-idUSKCN1ST1EF
10. https://www.atlanticcouncil.org/images/acevents/BrentScowcroftCenter/Strategic_Insights_Memo_vF_2.11.pdf

11. https://republicans-foreignaffairs.house.gov/blog/icymi-mccaul-talks-iran-china-and-news-of-the-day-on-fox-news-and-bloomberg/
12. https://www.cnbc.com/2019/02/23/fred-kempe-battle-over-5g-huawei-is-the-biggest-test-yet-for-trumps-approach-for-china.html
13. https://www.wsj.com/articles/huawei-long-seen-as-spy-threat-rolled-over-u-s-road-bumps-1515453829?mod=article_inline
14. https://www.realcleardefense.com/articles/2019/05/02/national_security_and_winning_the_race_to_5g_114386.html
15. https://www.atlanticcouncil.org/images/acevents/BrentScowcroftCenter/Strategic_Insights_Memo_vF_2.11.pdf
16. https://arstechnica.com/information-technology/2019/03/atts-5g-e-is-actually-slower-than-verizon-and-t-mobile-4g-study-finds/
17. https://www.washingtonpost.com/opinions/global-opinions/on-5g-the-united-states-is-building-betamax-while-china-builds-vhs/2019/04/18/1b9cd096-620c-11e9-bfad-36a7eb36cb60_story.html?utm_term=.2294d607d86b
18. https://arstechnica.com/information-technology/2019/04/millimeter-wave-5g-will-never-scale-beyond-dense-urban-areas-t-mobile-says/
19. https://arstechnica.com/information-technology/2019/04/millimeter-wave-5g-isnt-for-widespread-coverage-verizon-admits/
20. https://www.whitehouse.gov/briefings-statements/remarks-president-trump-united-states-5g-deployment/
21. https://media.defense.gov/2019/Apr/04/2002109654/-1/-1/0/DIB_5G_STUDY_04.04.19.PDF
22. https://www.washingtonpost.com/opinions/global-opinions/on-5g-the-united-states-is-building-betamax-while-china-builds-vhs/2019/04/18/1b9cd096-620c-11e9-bfad-36a7eb36cb60_story.html?utm_term=.2294d607d86b
23. https://media.defense.gov/2019/Apr/04/2002109654/-1/-1/0/DIB_5G_STUDY_04.04.19.PDF
24. Ibid.
25. https://www.wsj.com/articles/the-u-s-wants-to-ban-huawei-at-t-mexico-relies-on-it-11555407001
26. https://www.ft.com/content/a7f5eba4-5d02-11e9-9dde-7aedca0a081a
27. https://www.reuters.com/article/us-poland-huawei/poland-to-hold-off-blanket-ban-on-huawei-5g-gear-due-to-cost-concerns-idUSKCN1RS0QI
28. https://www.bloomberg.com/news/articles/2019-04-16/poles-and-u-s-said-to-close-in-on-deal-to-build-fort-trump
29. https://www.wsj.com/articles/huaweis-video-surveillance-business-hits-snag-in-philippines-11550683135
30. http://cheatsheet.com/entertainment/what-ever-happened-to-the-olsen-twins-their-lives-now-are-weirder-than-you-thought.html/
31. http://cheatsheet.com/entertainment/what-ever-happened-to-the-olsen-twins-their-lives-now-are-weirder-than-you-thought.html/
32. https://2o9ub0417chl2lg6m43em6psi2i-wpengine.netdna-ssl.com/wp-content/uploads/2018/04/RSTREETSHORT50-1.pdf

33. https://www.energymanagertoday.com/compete-study-consumers-better-off-retail-choice-electricity-0113715/
34. https://www.nrel.gov/docs/fy17osti/67106.pdf

Chapter Eight: Gathering Sand

1. https://www.realclearpolitics.com/video/2019/04/03/full_speech_trump_tells_republicans_to_be_more_paranoid_about_vote_counts_at_nrcc_dinner.html
2. http://www.chinadaily.com.cn/china/19thcpcnationalcongress/2017-11/04/content_34115212.htm
3. Sun Tzu, The Art of War
4. https://www.cov.com/~/media/files/corporate/publications/2015/06/china_passes_new_national_security_law.pdf
5. https://www.cov.com/~/media/files/corporate/publications/2015/06/china_passes_new_national_security_law.pdf
6. https://www.cov.com/~/media/files/corporate/publications/2015/06/china_passes_new_national_security_law.pdf
7. https://www.lawfareblog.com/beijings-new-national-intelligence-law-defense-offense
8. https://www.lawfareblog.com/beijings-new-national-intelligence-law-defense-offense
9. https://www.wsj.com/articles/chinas-tech-giants-have-a-second-job-helping-the-government-see-everything-1512056284
10. https://www.wsj.com/articles/chinas-tech-giants-have-a-second-job-helping-the-government-see-everything-1512056284
11. https://www.uscc.gov/sites/default/files/Michelle%20Van%20Cleave_Written%20Testimony060916.pdf
12. https://www.weeklystandard.com/ethan-epstein/the-spy-who-drove-her-dianne-feinstein-and-chinese-espionage
13. https://www.sfchronicle.com/bayarea/matier-ross/article/Sen-Feinstein-had-a-Chinese-connection-she-13121441.php
14. https://www.foxnews.com/politics/feinstein-was-mortified-by-fbi-allegation-that-staffer-was-spy-for-china-report
15. https://www.uscc.gov/sites/default/files/Poindexter%20Testimony.pdf
16. https://www.washingtonpost.com/news/federal-eye/wp/2015/07/09/hack-of-security-clearance-system-affected-21-5-million-people-federal-authorities-say/?utm_term=.1885fcd33843
17. https://www.cnbc.com/2015/09/25/us-china-agree-to-not-conduct-cybertheft-of-intellectual-property-white-house.html
18. https://freebeacon.com/national-security/bolton-hits-chinese-hack-opm-records/
19. https://www.washingtonpost.com/news/powerpost/paloma/the-cybersecurity-202/2019/05/10/the-cybersecurity-202-trump-administration-raises-pressure-on-china-with-more-hacking-indictments/5cd4d373a7a0a43760915963/?utm_term=.e54f49d0b31b

20. https://thehill.com/policy/cybersecurity/427511-fbi-director-china-is-most-complex-and-concerning-counterintelligence
21. https://theintercept.com/2019/04/09/hikvision-cameras-uk-parliament/
22. https://www.uscc.gov/sites/default/files/Michelle%20Van%20Cleave_Written%20Testimony060916.pdf
23. https://www.uscc.gov/sites/default/files/Michelle%20Van%20Cleave_Written%20Testimony060916.pdf
24. https://www.uscc.gov/sites/default/files/Michelle%20Van%20Cleave_Written%20Testimony060916.pdf
25. https://www.fdd.org/analysis/2018/09/05/understanding-the-chinese-communist-partys-approach-to-cyber-enabled-economic-warfare/
26. https://www.cyberscoop.com/linkedin-china-spies-kevin-mallory-ron-hansen/
27. https://www.nytimes.com/2018/06/08/us/politics/cia-officer-kevin-mallory-convicted-spying.html
28. https://www.nytimes.com/2018/06/08/us/politics/cia-officer-kevin-mallory-convicted-spying.html
29. https://www.nytimes.com/2018/06/08/us/politics/cia-officer-kevin-mallory-convicted-spying.html
30. https://www.nytimes.com/2018/06/08/us/politics/cia-officer-kevin-mallory-convicted-spying.html
31. http://www.lefigaro.fr/actualite-france/2018/10/22/01016-20181022ARTFIG00246-les-revelations-du-figaro-sur-le-programme-d-espionnage-chinois-qui-vise-la-france.php
32. https://www.heritage.org/asia/report/sources-and-methods-foreign-nationals-engaged-economic-and-military-espionage
33. https://www.heritage.org/asia/report/sources-and-methods-foreign-nationals-engaged-economic-and-military-espionage
34. https://www.heritage.org/asia/report/sources-and-methods-foreign-nationals-engaged-economic-and-military-espionage
35. https://www.heritage.org/asia/report/sources-and-methods-foreign-nationals-engaged-economic-and-military-espionage
36. https://www.heritage.org/asia/report/sources-and-methods-foreign-nationals-engaged-economic-and-military-espionage
37. https://www.uscc.gov/sites/default/files/Michelle%20Van%20Cleave_Written%20Testimony060916.pdf
38. https://www.dni.gov/files/NCSC/documents/news/20180724-economic-espionage-pub.pdf
39. https://thehill.com/policy/cybersecurity/427511-fbi-director-china-is-most-complex-and-concerning-counterintelligence
40. https://www.cnas.org/publications/congressional-testimony/chinas-non-traditional-espionage-against-the-united-states-the-threat-and-potential-policy-responses
41. https://www.aspi.org.au/report/picking-flowers-making-honey
42. https://www.aspi.org.au/report/picking-flowers-making-honey
43. https://www.justice.gov/opa/pr/michigan-man-sentenced-48-months-attempting-spy-people-s-republic-china

44. https://www.fbi.gov/news/stories/advice-for-us-college-students-abroad
45. https://www.youtube.com/watch?v=Fw8ZorTB7_o
46. https://www.youtube.com/watch?v=Fw8ZorTB7_o

Chapter Nine: The Return of the Middle Kingdom

1. https://www.whitehouse.gov/briefings-statements/remarks-president-trump-people-poland/
2. Xi Jinping *The Governance of China* Volume II "CPC Leadership is Essential to Chinese Socialism"
3. http://np.china-embassy.org/eng/ChinaABC/ls/t167458.htm
4. http://afe.easia.columbia.edu/mongols/pop/menu/class_timeline.htm
5. Kissinger, Henry *On China*
6. https://thediplomat.com/2016/04/the-three-kingdoms-three-paths-for-chinas-future/
7. http://afe.easia.columbia.edu/timelines/china_timeline.htm
8. https://www.ancient.eu/Warring_States_Period/
9. https://www.history.com/topics/ancient-china/qin-dynasty
10. https://www.history.com/topics/ancient-china/qin-dynasty
11. https://www.nationalgeographic.com/archaeology-and-history/archaeology/emperor-qin/
12. https://news.nationalgeographic.com/2016/10/china-first-emperor-terra-cotta-warriors-tomb/
13. Kissinger, Henry *On China*
14. https://www.oxfordbibliographies.com/view/document/obo-9780199920082/obo-9780199920082-0069.xml
15. https://www.encyclopedia.com/history/news-wires-white-papers-and-books/tribute-system
16. http://afe.easia.columbia.edu/special/china_1750_macartney.htm
17. https://china.usc.edu/emperor-qianlong-letter-george-iii-1793
18. https://china.usc.edu/sites/default/files/forums/Chinese%20Inventions.pdf
19. http://www.ggdc.net/maddison/oriindex.htm
20. Kissinger, Henry *On China*
21. Kissinger, Henry *On China*
22. Kissinger, Henry *On China*
23. Kissinger, Henry *On China*
24. https://www.history.com/news/john-jacob-astor-opium-fortune-millionaire
25. https://asiapacificcurriculum.ca/learning-module/opium-wars-china
26. https://history.state.gov/milestones/1830-1860/china-1
27. Kissinger, Henry *On China*
28. Kissinger, Henry *On China*
29. https://www.history.com/topics/china/boxer-rebellion
30. https://www.archives.gov/publications/prologue/1999/winter/boxer-rebellion-1.html
31. https://www.history.com/topics/china/boxer-rebellion
32. https://www.history.com/topics/china/boxer-rebellion
33. https://www.youtube.com/watch?v=AcwbMmUWHGw

34. http://acienciala.faculty.ku.edu/communistnationssince1917/ch9.html
35. https://link.springer.com/chapter/10.1057/9781403919755_6
36. http://acienciala.faculty.ku.edu/communistnationssince1917/ch9.html
37. http://acienciala.faculty.ku.edu/communistnationssince1917/ch9.html
38. https://china.usc.edu/Mao-declares-founding-of-peoples-republic-of-china-chinese-people-have-stood-up
39. https://www.washingtonpost.com/news/volokh-conspiracy/wp/2016/08/03/giving-historys-greatest-mass-murderer-his-due/?utm_term=.1534ae528793
40. https://www.nytimes.com/2016/05/15/world/asia/china-cultural-revolution-explainer.html

Chapter Ten: Ally, Enemy, Strategic Partner

1. https://www.realclearpolitics.com/video/2019/04/03/full_speech_trump_tells_republicans_to_be_more_paranoid_about_vote_counts_at_nrcc_dinner.html
2. Xi Jinping *The Governance of China* Volume II "There Are a Thousand Reasons to Make the China-US Relationship a Success"
3. http://www.thesandpebbles.com/mckenna/richard_mckenna.html
4. https://www.history.com/this-day-in-history/the-battle-of-tsushima-strait
5. https://www.smithsonianmag.com/history/surprisingly-important-role-china-played-world-war-i-180964532/
6. https://www.trumanlibrary.gov/education/presidential-inquiries/invasion-manchuria
7. https://www.english.upenn.edu/Projects/Buck/biography.html
8. https://www.airspacemag.com/history-of-flight/once-more-over-the-hump-180964763/
9. https://www.airspacemag.com/history-of-flight/once-more-over-the-hump-180964763/
10. https://www.nytimes.com/1995/04/02/books/times-man-in-china.html
11. https://www.cbsnews.com/news/the-korean-war-timeline/
12. https://www.va.gov/opa/publications/factsheets/fs_americas_wars.pdf
13. http://www.bbc.co.uk/history/worldwars/coldwar/korea_hickey_01.shtml
14. https://www.history.com/topics/korea/korean-war#section_5
15. https://www.cia.gov/library/readingroom/docs/CIA-RDP79R00967A000800010012-0.pdf
16. Kissinger, Henry *On China* p. 202
17. Kissinger, Henry *On China*
18. Kissinger, Henry *On China*
19. Kissinger, Henry *On China* p. 229
20. Kissinger, Henry *On China*
21. http://www.cnn.com/2008/WORLD/asiapcf/02/25/pingpong.diplomacy/index.html
22. https://www.history.com/news/ping-pong-diplomacy
23. https://www.history.com/news/ping-pong-diplomacy
24. Kissinger, Henry *On China*

25. Kissinger, Henry *On China*
26. Kissinger, Henry *On China*
27. Pillsbury, Michael *The Hundred-Year Marathon*
28. Pillsbury, Michael *The Hundred-Year Marathon*
29. Pillsbury, Michael *The Hundred-Year Marathon*
30. Pillsbury, Michael *The Hundred-Year Marathon*
31. Pillsbury, Michael *The Hundred-Year Marathon*
32. Pillsbury, Michael *The Hundred-Year Marathon*
33. Pillsbury, Michael *The Hundred-Year Marathon*
34. http://www.chinadaily.com.cn/business/2008-10/30/content_7169055.htm
35. Pillsbury, Michael *The Hundred-Year Marathon*
36. Pillsbury, Michael *The Hundred-Year Marathon*
37. Pillsbury, Michael *The Hundred-Year Marathon*
38. Pillsbury, Michael *The Hundred-Year Marathon*
39. Pillsbury, Michael *The Hundred-Year Marathon*
40. Pillsbury, Michael *The Hundred-Year Marathon*
41. Pillsbury, Michael *The Hundred-Year Marathon*

Chapter Eleven: Sobered Realism

1. https://www.whitehouse.gov/briefings-statements/remarks-president-trump-apec-ceo-summit-da-nang-vietnam/
2. Xi Jinping *The Governance of China* Volume II "A Deeper Understanding of the New Development Concepts"
3. https://www.abc.net.au/news/2018-12-01/40-years-of-reform-that-transformed-china-into-a-superpower/10573468
4. Mühlhahn, Professor Klaus *Making China Modern* Chapter 11
5. https://www.brookings.edu/testimonies/u-s-china-economic-relations-implications-for-u-s-policy/
6. Mühlhahn, Professor Klaus *Making China Modern* Chapter 11
7. Kissinger, Henry *On China*
8. https://www.cnn.com/2013/09/15/world/asia/tiananmen-square-fast-facts/index.html
9. http://www.tsquare.tv/chronology/Deng.html
10. http://www.tsquare.tv/chronology/Deng.html
11. "Reform or Die!" *Week in China* Jan 27, 2012
12. "Reform or Die!" *Week in China* Jan 27, 2012
13. http://edition.cnn.com/2001/WORLD/asiapcf/east/09/18/china.wto.timeline/
14. https://data.worldbank.org/indicator/NY.GDP.MKTP.CD?locations=CN
15. https://data.worldbank.org/indicator/NY.GDP.MKTP.CD?locations=US
16. https://data.worldbank.org/indicator/SP.POP.TOTL?locations=CN
17. http://movies2.nytimes.com/library/world/asia/030900clinton-china-text.html
18. https://books.google.com/books?id=B5RWAAAAYAAJ&q=%22 *Congressional Quarterly* Volume 58
19. https://www.nytimes.com/2000/05/18/world/in-bush-s-words-join-together-in-making-china-a-normal-trading-partner.html

20. Pillsbury, Michael *The Hundred-Year Marathon*
21. http://www.china.org.cn/english/features/Archaeology/131298.htm
22. https://fas.org/man/eprint/lai.pdf
23. http://www.china.org.cn/english/features/Archaeology/131298.htm
24. https://archive.org/stream/Learning-from-the-Stones-A-Go-Approach-to-Mastering-Chinas-Strategic-Concept-Shi-2004/Learning%20from%20the%20Stones%20-%20A%20Go%20Approach%20to%20Mastering%20China%27s%20Strategic%20Concept%2C%20Shi%20%282004%29_djvu.txt
25. https://fas.org/man/eprint/lai.pdf
26. https://fas.org/man/eprint/lai.pdf
27. https://fas.org/man/eprint/lai.pdf

Chapter Twelve: Stealing the Sea

1. https://www.whitehouse.gov/briefings-statements/remarks-president-trump-apec-ceo-summit-da-nang-vietnam/
2. https://www.reuters.com/article/us-china-defence/president-xi-says-china-loves-peace-but-wont-compromise-on-sovereignty-idUSKBN1AH2YE
3. http://isdp.eu/publication/understanding-chinas-position-south-china-sea-disputes/
4. "Indonesia does not view itself as a South China Sea claimant as it does not claim sovereignty over any contested outposts, although its exclusive economic zone (EEZ) overlaps with China's nine-dash line." US DOD 2018 https://media.defense.gov/2018/Aug/16/2001955282/-1/-1/1/2018-CHINA-MILITARY-POWER-REPORT.PDF
5. Ward, Jonathan *China's Vision of Victory*
6. https://www.nytimes.com/interactive/2015/07/30/world/asia/what-china-has-been-building-in-the-south-china-sea.html
7. https://www.armed-services.senate.gov/imo/media/doc/Davidson_APQs_04-17-18.pdf
8. https://www.nytimes.com/interactive/2015/07/30/world/asia/what-china-has-been-building-in-the-south-china-sea.html
9. https://www.newsweek.com/china-south-china-sea-islands-build-military-territory-expand-575161
10. https://obamawhitehouse.archives.gov/the-press-office/2015/09/25/remarks-president-obama-and-president-xi-peoples-republic-china-joint
11. https://www.armed-services.senate.gov/imo/media/doc/Davidson_APQs_04-17-18.pdf
12. https://www.pacom.mil/Media/Speeches-Testimony/Article/1693325/halifax-international-security-forum-2018-introduction-to-indo-pacific-security/
13. https://amti.csis.org/island-tracker/china/
14. https://www.armed-services.senate.gov/imo/media/doc/Davidson_APQs_04-17-18.pdf
15. https://amti.csis.org/paracels-beijings-other-buildup/

16. https://www.scmp.com/news/china/diplomacy/article/3002229/beijing-plans-strategic-service-and-logistics-base-woody?MCUID=4672f7018e&MCCampaignID=d5603dfe35&MCAccountID=3775521f5f542047246d9c827&tc=3
17. https://www.armed-services.senate.gov/imo/media/doc/Davidson_APQs_04-17-18.pdf
18. https://news.usni.org/2019/02/12/41070
19. https://fas.org/sgp/crs/row/R42784.pdf
20. https://fas.org/sgp/crs/row/R42784.pdf
21. https://www.cfr.org/interactive/global-conflict-tracker/conflict/tensions-east-china-sea
22. https://fas.org/sgp/crs/row/R42784.pdf
23. https://fas.org/sgp/crs/row/R42784.pdf
24. https://www.washingtonpost.com/politics/2019/03/19/us-quietly-made-big-splash-about-south-china-sea/?utm_term=.5073dc3be04e
25. https://fas.org/sgp/crs/row/R42784.pdf
26. https://fas.org/sgp/crs/row/R42784.pdf
27. https://ocean.csis.org/spotlights/illuminating-the-south-china-seas-dark-fishing-fleets/
28. https://www.cfr.org/interactive/global-conflict-tracker/conflict/territorial-disputes-south-china-sea
29. https://www.eia.gov/todayinenergy/detail.php?id=33592
30. https://www.eia.gov/todayinenergy/detail.php?id=36952
31. https://chinapower.csis.org/much-trade-transits-south-china-sea/
32. http://time.com/4412191/nine-dash-line-9-south-china-sea/
33. https://www.forbes.com/sites/ralphjennings/2017/10/31/china-claims-most-of-a-contested-asian-sea-without-a-demarcation-line/#f7cd75a2e074
34. https://www.reuters.com/article/us-johnson-china/everything-you-need-to-know-about-the-south-china-sea-conflict-in-under-five-minutes-idUSKBN0OQ03620150610
35. http://time.com/4412191/nine-dash-line-9-south-china-sea/
36. http://time.com/4412191/nine-dash-line-9-south-china-sea/
37. https://www.uscc.gov/sites/default/files/Research/Issue%20Brief_South%20China%20Sea%20Arbitration%20Ruling%20What%20Happened%20and%20What%27s%20Next071216.pdf
38. https://www.nytimes.com/2016/07/13/world/asia/south-china-sea-hague-ruling-philippines.html
39. http://www.xinhuanet.com/english/2018-06/28/c_137285165.htm
40. https://policy.defense.gov/Portals/11/FY17%20DOD%20FON%20Report.pdf?ver=2018-01-19-163418-053
41. https://www.un.org/depts/los/convention_agreements/texts/unclos/part5.htm
42. https://sites.tufts.edu/lawofthesea/chapter-two/
43. https://fas.org/sgp/crs/row/R42784.pdf
44. https://sites.tufts.edu/lawofthesea/chapter-two/
45. https://fas.org/sgp/crs/row/R42784.pdf
46. https://fas.org/sgp/crs/row/R42784.pdf

47. https://www.nytimes.com/2018/11/08/world/asia/south-china-sea-risks.html
48. https://dod.defense.gov/Portals/1/Documents/pubs/NDAA%20A-P_Maritime_SecuritY_Strategy-08142015-1300-FINALFORMAT.PDF
49. https://fas.org/sgp/crs/row/R42784.pdf
50. https://www.foxnews.com/world/chinese-warship-warned-uss-decatur-it-would-suffer-consequences-for-passing-through-south-china-sea
51. https://www.cnn.com/2018/10/02/politics/us-china-destroyers-confrontation-south-china-sea-intl/index.html?no-st=1555469541
52. https://news.usni.org/2019/02/12/41070
53. https://news.usni.org/2018/05/23/china-disinvited-participating-2018-rimpac-exercise
54. https://fas.org/sgp/crs/row/R42784.pdf
55. https://fas.org/sgp/crs/row/R42784.pdf
56. https://www.cfr.org/backgrounder/south-china-sea-tensions
57. https://www.iwp.edu/events/detail/the-rise-of-chinese-seapower-fear-honor-and-interest
58. https://www.dia.mil/Portals/27/Documents/News/Military%20Power%20Publications/China_Military_Power_FINAL_5MB_20190103.pdf
59. Ward, Jonathan *China's Vision of Victory*
60. https://news.usni.org/2015/05/26/document-chinas-military-strategy
61. Xi Jinping *The Governance of China* Volume II "Continue to Strengthen our Military"
62. https://www.uscc.gov/sites/default/files/annual_reports/Executive%20Summary%202018%20Annual%20Report%20to%20Congress.pdf
63. https://www.dni.gov/files/ODNI/documents/2019-ATA-SFR---SSCI.pdf
64. https://www.dia.mil/Portals/27/Documents/News/Military%20Power%20Publications/China_Military_Power_FINAL_5MB_20190103.pdf
65. https://www.uscc.gov/sites/default/files/annual_reports/Executive%20Summary%202018%20Annual%20Report%20to%20Congress.pdf
66. https://www.uscc.gov/sites/default/files/annual_reports/Executive%20Summary%202018%20Annual%20Report%20to%20Congress.pdf
67. https://fas.org/sgp/crs/row/R42784.pdf
68. https://ocean.csis.org/spotlights/illuminating-the-south-china-seas-dark-fishing-fleets/
69. https://ocean.csis.org/spotlights/illuminating-the-south-china-seas-dark-fishing-fleets/
70. China Military Power DIA 2019 p 79 https://www.dia.mil/Portals/27/Documents/News/Military%20Power%20Publications/China_Military_Power_FINAL_5MB_20190103.pdf
71. https://fas.org/sgp/crs/row/R42784.pdf

Chapter Thirteen: Belt & Road to Everywhere

1. https://www.whitehouse.gov/briefings-statements/remarks-president-trump-apec-ceo-summit-da-nang-vietnam/
2. Xi Jinping *The Governance of China* Volume II "Promote the Belt and Road Initiative, Extend Reform and Development"

3. Axios AM Newsletter April 23, 2019
4. https://thediplomat.com/2019/04/second-belt-and-road-forum-top-level-attendees/
5. Axios AM Newsletter April 23, 2019
6. https://www.cfr.org/backgrounder/chinas-massive-belt-and-road-initiative
7. USCC 2018 Report to Congress
8. USCC
9. https://eng.yidaiyilu.gov.cn/info/iList.jsp?cat_id=10076
10. USCC 2018 Report to Congress
11. USCC 2018 Report to Congress
12. https://www.rfa.org/english/commentaries/bri-obstacles-01152019155613.html
13. https://www.history.com/topics/ancient-middle-east/silk-road
14. USCC 2018 Report to Congress
15. USCC 2018 Report to Congress
16. USCC 2018 Report to Congress
17. USCC 2018 Report to Congress
18. USCC 2018 Report to Congress
19. USCC 2018 Report to Congress
20. USCC 2018 Report to Congress
21. USCC 2018 Report to Congress
22. https://www.bloomberg.com/news/articles/2018-12-10/how-asia-fell-out-of-love-with-china-s-belt-and-road-initiative
23. USCC 2018 Report to Congress
24. https://www.cnbc.com/2019/01/18/countries-are-reducing-belt-and-road-investments-over-financing-fears.html
25. https://www.theepochtimes.com/sri-lankans-protest-against-its-governments-leasing-of-a-major-port-to-china_2657586.html
26. USCC 2018 Report to Congress
27. http://cpec.gov.pk/brain/public/uploads/documents/CPEC-LTP.pdf
28. http://cpec.gov.pk/brain/public/uploads/documents/CPEC-LTP.pdf
29. https://www.wsj.com/articles/chinas-belt-and-road-initiative-puts-a-squeeze-on-pakistan-11554289201
30. USCC 2018 Report to Congress
31. USCC 2018 Report to Congress
32. https://www.cgdev.org/sites/default/files/examining-debt-implications-belt-and-road-initiative-policy-perspective.pdf
33. USCC 2018 Report to Congress
34. USCC 2018 Report to Congress
35. USCC 2018 Report to Congress
36. https://www.wsj.com/articles/chinas-belt-and-road-initiative-puts-a-squeeze-on-pakistan-11554289201
37. USCC 2018 Report to Congress
38. https://www.csis.org/analysis/game-loans-how-china-bought-hambantota
39. https://www.nytimes.com/2018/06/25/world/asia/china-sri-lanka-port.html
40. https://www.france24.com/en/20190324-sri-lanka-new-chinese-silk-road-disappointment-economy-debt-italy-france-investment
41. https://www.nytimes.com/2018/06/25/world/asia/china-sri-lanka-port.html

42. https://csis-prod.s3.amazonaws.com/s3fs-public/publication/180717_Hillman_GameofLoans.pdf?bjj0dzdfO5jaedmhoC2Eq7pC6cknyvEz
43. https://rhg.com/research/new-data-on-the-debt-trap-question/
44. https://www.perdue.senate.gov/imo/media/doc/IMF%20China%20Belt%20and%20Road%20Initiative%20Letter.pdf
45. https://www.perdue.senate.gov/imo/media/doc/IMF%20China%20Belt%20and%20Road%20Initiative%20Letter.pdf
46. https://www.nytimes.com/2019/05/12/world/asia/pakistan-imf-bailout.html
47. https://www.wsj.com/articles/chinas-belt-and-road-initiative-puts-a-squeeze-on-pakistan-11554289201
48. https://www.cnbc.com/2018/08/09/pakistan-looks-to-imf-or-china-for-bailout.html
49. USCC 2018 Report to Congress
50. https://www.bloomberg.com/news/features/2019-01-10/china-s-digital-silk-road-is-looking-more-like-an-iron-curtain
51. https://www.bloomberg.com/news/features/2019-01-10/china-s-digital-silk-road-is-looking-more-like-an-iron-curtain
52. http://en.ndrc.gov.cn/newsrelease/201503/t20150330_669367.html
53. USCC 2018 Report to Congress
54. https://www.bloomberg.com/news/features/2019-01-10/china-s-digital-silk-road-is-looking-more-like-an-iron-curtain
55. https://www.whitehouse.gov/briefings-statements/remarks-national-security-advisor-ambassador-john-r-bolton-trump-administrations-new-africa-strategy/
56. https://www.whitehouse.gov/briefings-statements/remarks-national-security-advisor-ambassador-john-r-bolton-trump-administrations-new-africa-strategy/
57. https://www.bloomberg.com/news/features/2019-01-10/china-s-digital-silk-road-is-looking-more-like-an-iron-curtain
58. https://www.bloomberg.com/news/features/2019-01-10/china-s-digital-silk-road-is-looking-more-like-an-iron-curtain
59. https://www.bloomberg.com/news/features/2019-01-10/china-s-digital-silk-road-is-looking-more-like-an-iron-curtain
60. https://www.bloomberg.com/news/features/2019-01-10/china-s-digital-silk-road-is-looking-more-like-an-iron-curtain
61. https://www.bloomberg.com/news/features/2019-01-10/china-s-digital-silk-road-is-looking-more-like-an-iron-curtain
62. https://www.bloomberg.com/news/features/2019-01-10/china-s-digital-silk-road-is-looking-more-like-an-iron-curtain
63. USCC 2018 Report to Congress
64. USCC 2018 Report to Congress
65. USCC 2018 Report to Congress
66. USCC 2018 Report to Congress
67. https://www.bloomberg.com/news/articles/2019-04-28/xi-jinping-s-wins-and-losses-at-his-second-belt-and-road-forum
68. https://thehill.com/opinion/finance/442306-china-tweaks-its-belt-and-road-initiative-to-avoid-backlash

69. http://fi.china-embassy.org/eng/gdxw/t1659519.htm
70. https://www.bloomberg.com/news/articles/2019-04-28/xi-jinping-s-wins-and-losses-at-his-second-belt-and-road-forum
71. https://www.bloomberg.com/news/articles/2019-04-28/xi-jinping-s-wins-and-losses-at-his-second-belt-and-road-forum
72. https://www.bloomberg.com/news/articles/2019-04-28/xi-jinping-s-wins-and-losses-at-his-second-belt-and-road-forum
73. USCC 2018 Report to Congress
74. USCC 2018 Report to Congress
75. https://www.whitehouse.gov/wp-content/uploads/2017/12/NSS-Final-12-18-2017-0905.pdf
76. https://www.state.gov/remarks-on-americas-indo-pacific-economic-vision/
77. USCC 2018 Report to Congress
78. https://www.opic.gov/build-act/overview
79. https://www.whitehouse.gov/wp-content/uploads/2017/12/NSS-Final-12-18-2017-0905.pdf
80. https://www.opic.gov/build-act/faqs-build-act-implementation
81. https://www.opic.gov/build-act/overview
82. USCC 2018 Report to Congress

Chapter Fourteen: The New High Ground

1. https://www.whitehouse.gov/briefings-statements/remarks-president-trump-2019-united-states-air-force-academy-graduation-ceremony-colorado-springs-co/
2. http://english.cctv.com/2017/04/24/ARTIZBj8dd7ULWfpwuw8nJp5170424.shtml
3. https://www.uscc.gov/Research/china%E2%80%99s-pursuit-space-power-status-and-implications-united-states
4. https://www.uscc.gov/Research/china%E2%80%99s-pursuit-space-power-status-and-implications-united-states
5. https://media.defense.gov/2019/Feb/11/2002088710/-1/-1/1/SPACE-SECURITY-CHALLENGES.PDF
6. https://www.uscc.gov/sites/default/files/Namrata%20Goswami%20USCC%2025%20April.pdf
7. https://www.uscc.gov/sites/default/files/Namrata%20Goswami%20USCC%2025%20April.pdf
8. http://www.xinhuanet.com/english/2017-04/24/c_136232642.htm
9. http://english.gov.cn/archive/white_paper/2016/12/28/content_281475527159496.htm
10. https://itif.org/publications/2015/09/17/false-promises-yawning-gap-between-china%25E2%2580%2599s-wto-commitments-and-practices
11. https://media.defense.gov/2019/Feb/11/2002088710/-1/-1/1/SPACE-SECURITY-CHALLENGES.PDF
12. https://www.ucsusa.org/nuclear-weapons/space-weapons/satellite-database
13. https://www.uscc.gov/sites/default/files/Todd%20Harrison%20USCC%2025%20April.pdf

14. https://spacenews.com/militaryspace-gets-big-boost-in-pentagons-750-billio/
15. https://spacenews.com/change-4-spacecraft-enter-third-lunar-night-yutu-2-reaches-design-lifetime/
16. https://thediplomat.com/2019/05/china-has-a-head-start-in-the-new-space-race/
17. https://www.washingtontimes.com/news/2019/jan/9/trump-space-force-boosted-china-moon-landing/
18. http://english.gov.cn/archive/white_paper/2015/05/27/content_281475115610833.htm
19. https://www.maritime-executive.com/editorials/space-the-next-south-china-sea
20. https://www.uscc.gov/sites/default/files/William%20Roper%20USCC%2025%20April.pdf
21. https://media.defense.gov/2019/Feb/11/2002088710/-1/-1/1/SPACE-SECURITY-CHALLENGES.PDF
22. https://www.uscc.gov/sites/default/files/Lorand%20Laskai%20USCC%2025%20April.pdf
23. https://www.wsj.com/articles/china-exploits-fleet-of-u-s-satellites-to-strengthen-police-and-military-power-11556031771?mod=hp_lead_pos5
24. https://www.uscc.gov/sites/default/files/Namrata%20Goswami%20USCC%2025%20April.pdf
25. https://www.solarenspace.com/
26. https://www.whitehouse.gov/briefings-statements/remarks-vice-president-pence-fifth-meeting-national-space-council-huntsville-al/

Chapter Fifteen: War Fighting vs. War Posturing

1. https://abcnews.go.com/Politics/read-president-trumps-full-remarks-united-nations-general/story?id=49949302
2. Xi Jinping *The Governance of China* Volume II "CPC Leadership Is Essential to Chinese Socialism"
3. https://www.whitehouse.gov/briefings-statements/remarks-vice-president-pence-fifth-meeting-national-space-council-huntsville-al/
4. https://www.cnn.com/2019/07/24/asia/china-military-taiwan-white-paper-intl-hnk/index.html
5. http://www.xinhuanet.com/english/2019-07/24/c_138253389.htm
6. https://www.businessinsider.com/this-dogfight-between-more-than-200-israeli-and-syrian-jets-was-one-of-the-biggest-of-all-time-2015-11
7. https://www.nationalreview.com/2018/12/africa-china-united-states-foreign-policy-economic-development/
8. https://www.nationalreview.com/2018/12/africa-china-united-states-foreign-policy-economic-development/
9. http://www.sais-cari.org/data-chinese-workers-in-africa
10. https://tagtheflag.co/trivia/how-much-would-the-marshall-plan-cost-in-todays-dollars/
11. https://www.foreignaffairs.com/articles/russian-federation/1947-07-01/sources-soviet-conduct

Chapter Sixteen: Not China's Fault

1. https://www.whitehouse.gov/briefings-statements/president-donald-j-trumps-state-union-address-2/
2. https://www.baltimoresun.com/education/bs-md-nations-report-card-20180409-story.html
3. https://www.drugabuse.gov/related-topics/trends-statistics/overdose-death-rates
4. https://www.archives.gov/research/military/vietnam-war/casualty-statistics
5. https://www.realclearenergy.org/articles/2019/05/10/reliance_on_foreign_minerals_leaves_america_at_risk_110439.html
6. http://www.chinadaily.com.cn/a/201901/03/WS5c2d7755a310d9121 4053454.html
7. https://www.usatoday.com/story/money/2019/04/11/countries-that-spend-the-most-on-public-health/39307147/
8. https://www.uscc.gov/sites/default/files/Michelle%20Van%20Cleave_Written%20Testimony060916.pdf

Conclusion

1. https://www.history.com/this-day-in-history/uncle-toms-cabin-is-published

Appendix

1. https://www.whitehouse.gov/briefings-statements/remarks-president-trump-business-event-president-xi-china-beijing-china/
2. https://www.whitehouse.gov/briefings-statements/remarks-president-trump-apec-ceo-summit-da-nang-vietnam/
3. http://www.chinadaily.com.cn/world/2017-11/11/content_34393531.htm
4. http://translate.sogoucdn.com/pcvtsnapshot?from=auto&to=zh-CHS&tfr=translatepc&url=http%3A%2F%2Fwww.qstheory.cn%2Fdukan%2Fqs%2F2019-03%2F31%2Fc_1124302776.htm&domainType=sogou
5. https://www.whitehouse.gov/briefings-statements/remarks-vice-president-pence-administrations-policy-toward-china/

Index